KINDRED SPIRITS

KINDRED SPIRITS

CHINUA ACHEBE AND TONI MORRISON

Christopher N. Okonkwo

UNIVERSITY OF VIRGINIA PRESS

Charlottesville and London

University of Virginia Press
© 2022 by the Rector and Visitors of the University of Virginia
All rights reserved

First published 2022

9 8 7 6 5 4 3 2 1

Library of Congress Cataloging-in-Publication Data

Names: Okonkwo, Christopher N., author.
Title: Kindred spirits : Chinua Achebe and Toni Morrison / Christopher N.
    Okonkwo, University of Virginia Press.
Description: Charlottesville : University of Virginia Press, 2022. | Includes
    bibliographical references and index.
Identifiers: LCCN 2021030957 | ISBN 9780813947112 (hardcover ; acid-free
    paper) | ISBN 9780813947129 (paperback ; acid-free paper) |
    ISBN 9780813947136 (ebook)
Subjects: LCSH: Achebe, Chinua—Criticism and interpretation. | Morrison,
    Toni—Criticism and interpreation. | LCGFT: Literary criticism.
Classification: LCC PR9387.9.A3 Z8495 2022 | DDC 823/.914—dc23
LC record available at https://lccn.loc.gov/2021030957

Cover art: Toni Morrison portrait by Timothy Greenfield-Sanders (Toni
Morrison Papers, C1491, Manuscripts Division, Department of Special
Collections, Princeton University Library); Chinua Achebe portrait by
Michael Weisbrot (Bard College Archives and Special Collections)

In loving memory of my
brother Ernest Okonkwo (1973–2017)
and
mother, Agnes Okonkwo (1940–2018)

CONTENTS

ACKNOWLEDGMENTS

I am deeply indebted to several people and entities whose counsel, encouragement, and support, both direct and indirect, helped make this book possible. The University of Missouri (MU) Research Board granted my application for course release for the 2017–18 academic year. The time off from teaching helped me make more progress on the book. Thank you, Pat Okker and Alex Socarides, my dean and my chair, respectively, for your support and counsel.

Having the opportunity to share parts of the study with other scholars and with colleagues and students was tremendously valuable as I drafted the manuscript. I appreciate the invitation extended me in 2017 by Princeton University's African Studies Program to lecture on the work in progress. I want to thank the following people, especially, for the important roles they played in making my visit there a success: Carolyn Rouse, the Program's Director and Chair of Anthropology, for the official invite; Timothy P. Wald, Program Manager, for coordinating my trip's logistical details with aplomb; Chika Okeke-Agulu, for initially suggesting the talk to me, spearheading the endeavor, and for hospitality and lasting friendship; Simon Gikandi, for scholarly example, inspiration, advice, and warm reception; John W. Vincent and Delia Pitts, both Princeton community members, for a wonderful and eye-opening conversation after my presentation. Thank you also to these department colleagues: Emma Lipton, our Director of Graduate Studies, for inviting me to sketch the project as part of the 2019 Lighting Talk series on faculty and graduate research; Alex Socarides and Black Studies department chair April Langley, for, among many other things, inviting me to give a talk on Toni Morrison as part of a 2019 Black History Month event, "Reverencing Toni Morrison: Thinking, Writing, and Loving Morrison," on campus; Rachel Harper and Nancy West, for inviting me to lecture on Morrison's *Jazz* and Achebe's *Things Fall Apart* to the MU Honors College students and faculty. Thank you, Honors College faculty and students, for your welcome and our refreshing exchanges.

I must also acknowledge, with immense gratitude, the assistance I received from these offices and their staffs: MU Ellis Interlibrary Loan-Lending division, especially Tammy Green; Anne K. Barker, MU Research and Instructional Services librarian; Princeton University's African American Studies department staff and the archivists and other staff of Firestone Library's Special Collection, particularly Charles Doran; Omoy S. Lungange, of the Africa-America Institute; Conrad Lochner, of PEN, for access to the archive of Morrison reading Achebe's essay at PEN; Eric Kofi Acree, Director of John Henrik Clarke Africana Library and the Coordinator of Fine Arts and Music Libraries, Cornell University, for assistance with Toni Morrison's master's thesis; Leslie Morris, Curator of Modern Books and Manuscripts, Houghton Library, Harvard University, for important information on the acquisition and preservation of the Achebe papers at Harvard; Helen Tieger, of Bard College Special Collections, for attending to my inquiry regarding potential Achebe papers at Bard; Lisa Davis, Business Manager, University of Tennessee Press, for important marketing information on my last book; and Kassahun Checole, publisher, Africa World Press. Comments at the Africa America Institute Award, New York, NY, September 12th, 2000, reprinted in *The Source of Self-Regard,* © 2019 by Toni Morrison. I am deeply grateful to Sam Fox of ICM Partners for these permissions.

I also owe a world of thanks to these colleagues, mentors, and friends, here at MU and elsewhere, who took the time to critique and/or offer me incisive suggestions on early drafts and late revisions of this book's chapters and passages. You gave me much-needed boosts of confidence on the project as a whole: Stephanie Shonekan, Karen Piper, Devoney Looser, Maxine Lavon Montgomery, Chante Baker, and Warren Carson. I also extend my gratitude to the following: the MU Research Board's peer reviewers who evaluated my leave application that included an early iteration of the book proposal and the case for this study's scholarly and intellectual merits; the University of Virginia Press's internal scholars and outside proposal readers, whose enthusiastic endorsements and astute suggestions moved this project forward to the next phase; the press's manuscript readers, who subjected the completed manuscript to such rigorous, constructive, and affirming evaluation. This finished project owes lots to you. And lots more I owe to Eric Brandt, my Acquisitions Editor and the press's Editor in Chief, whose immediate and unequivocal interest and faith in the study, whose truly exemplary professionalism, expertise, guidance, and support, have made this a most wonderful publishing experience for me. Thank you, too, Helen Chandler, Acquisitions Assistant, for your encouragement and for skillfully helping me navigate the logistics of book production proper. And thanks to you, Morgan Myers, my project editor; Susan Murray, my copy editor; and the members of the design, production, and marketing teams—Ellen Satrom, Emma Donovan, Emily Grandstaff—for making the project read and look much better than it did when it showed up in your hands.

In the long, windy, arduous, and often solitary journey of scholarly book writing, and book writing in general, sometimes all that the writer craves is an inspiration, a listener, a word of encouragement, a rejuvenating chat, or a lay yet catalyzing curiosity. And so I want to thank these individuals, present or no longer with us, for contributing to this project, and to my career, in sometimes intangible but altogether positive ways they may not have realized: Vickie Thorp, Mary Moore, Stacey LaRocco, Herman Smith, Noor Azizan-Gardner, Elizabeth Chang, Noah Heringman, Mardy T. Eimers, Cyndi Frisby, Anand Prahlad, Michael Marlow, Sheri-Marie Harrison, David Dunkley, Mamadou Badiane, Joseph-Désiré Otabela Mewolo, Tola Pearce, the late Flore Zephir, the late Paula Fleming; Michael Ugarte, Rangila Béa Gallimore, Marvin Lewis, Jite Eferakorho, Ruth Simmons, Tunji Osinubi, Yogita Goyal; as well as friends and colleague-participants at African Literature Association and College Language Association conferences, for camaraderie and stimulating exchanges over the years. Thank you, Ernest Emenyonu (the prof's prof!), for your encouragement and intellectual example and Okey Ndibe, for friendship and insight.

Since joining MU, I have also benefited immeasurably from the sharp intellect, passion of, and enduring relationships with several of the undergraduate and graduate students in my African and African American literature classes, especially those in my "Major Authors" courses on Achebe and Morrison, respectively, and on my offering "Blues and Jazz Aesthetic." They and my official advisees, past and current, have heard me mention or hint that I was working on a book, a book on Morrison and Achebe. I only hope they think *Kindred Spirits* is worth the invocations. I sincerely regret that I am not able to mention all of you individually, but you know who you are. I want, however, to single out Shelli Homer, Constance Bailey, Jennifer Wilmot, Carlia Francis, Anja Boettcher, Aurélia Mouzet, Nadège Uwase, Dan Thater, Kate Harlin, Neriman Kuyucu, Kavita Pillai, Grace Gardiner, the late Naira Kuzmich, Tofunmi Omowunmi, Allison Wiltshire, Elorm Nutakor, Haley Anderson, and Kaylen Hayward.

And last, though not the least, my family. The public sees the finished book. But it is family and sometimes close friends who have the inside scoop on the circumstances, sometimes truly difficult circumstances, under which the book is completed. In the several years that it took for this study to take shape and come to fruition, and throughout the adversities that attempted to impede its way, I was heartened by my family members: my father, mother, brothers, sisters, cousins, nieces, and nephews, here in the United States and in Nigeria, and also by my in-laws. But most of all, I have been daily sustained by the love, prayers, patience, and understanding of my wife, Ijeoma, and our children: our sons, Ogochukwu and Chidindu, and our daughter, Chinonso. Especially Chinonso, who made this touching remark to me as I prepared the manuscript for transmission back to the press for copyediting: "Daddy, they better publish your book because you put your heart and soul in it." I tried. And it appears they will. In you, Ijay, Gogo, Didi, and Nonso, I am infinitely blessed.

KINDRED SPIRITS

Introduction

Toni Morrison, African Literature, Chinua Achebe

The new literature that erupted so dramatically and so abundantly [out of Africa] in the 1950s and 1960s . . . took almost everyone by surprise and elicited an impressive range of responses in different people and different places.
—CHINUA ACHEBE, "The Empire Fights Back"

White writers had always taken white centrality for granted. They inhabited their world in a central position and everything nonwhite was "other." These African writers took their blackness as central and the whites were the "other."
—TONI MORRISON, interview by Claudia Dreifus

In a conversation with his host, Mr. Isaac Okonkwo, the elder Ogbuefi Odogwu propounds his philosophy of greatness, an old concept which, he ruefully concedes, has inevitably undergone a cultural shift, especially with the younger generation, which has reframed and extended its domestic significations consistent with the new era's enchantment with colonial modernity. "Greatness has belonged to Iguedo from ancient times," he posits. "It is not made by man. You cannot plant greatness as you plant yams or maize. Whoever planted an iroko tree—the greatest tree in the forest? You may collect all the iroko seeds in the world, open the soil and put them there. It will be in vain. The great tree chooses where to grow and we will find it there, so it is with greatness in men [and women]." This exchange between the seeming incompatibles—the Christian convert Isaac and the non-Christian but syncretic Odogwu, whose goatskin bag *contains* as well as mediates "things that knocked against one another"—takes place during Umuofia's welcoming festivities for Isaac's son Obi. After his kin-sponsored education and his urban experience in England, Obi has returned home to his ancestral village.

But little does the storytelling Odogwu know perhaps that his local lore and logic would take flight. They would go viral, or is it global, as we say nowadays, thanks to text and other newer technologies of circulation, an increasingly interlinked world, and, most important, an eagerly awaited, modern African novel, *No Longer at Ease*, published in 1960.[1] That was the second book by its then-thirty-year-old author, Chinua Achebe (1930–2013). Begun by hand around 1955, his first novel—barely two hundred pages long and released tentatively by Heinemann in London on July 17, 1958—had already ripped apart, and let fall, the ignorant things enlightened Europe had long weaponized against his people. It said, among other things, that they were a different category of human; that they had no mind or wisdom deserving respect, and no histories or stories worth mentioning. Even if they had those, the ludicrousness went, whites always had greater pasts and better tales and would do a finer job of the telling, from the outside. At the time, little did Achebe know—in fact, "it was not intended," as James Baldwin reminded him years later—that he would ever cross paths, literarily and literally, with Toni Morrison (1931–2019), from whom he had also been separated for more than four hundred years. She was another star, assuredly ascending on the other side of the Atlantic. She had been impelled in part by the same imperial and postimperial fallacy to tell the untold, the distorted, and the vanishing stories of her people, *his* people. Odogwu's postulates may sound poetic and propositional. But they are also prescient, if not indeed teleological. For it would come to pass that they, Achebe and Morrison, would each reach and remain securely at the apogees of cultural and intellectual achievement. Two preeminent black novelists, two eagles on top of Odogwu's majestic iroko: he, from the Igbo town of Ogidi, east of the Niger River; and she, from the midwestern town of Lorain, Ohio, north of the Ohio River. They were agemates, born almost exactly three months apart. And their works are read perennially not just by academics and college students but by high school classes and literary enthusiasts across the world.

This book critically reconnects and celebrates two, now sadly late literary giants: the Nigerian novelist and Man Booker Prize–winner Chinua Achebe and the inimitable African American writer and Nobel laureate Toni Morrison. As indicated, Achebe saw his debut novel as an effort to rectify elisions and travesties in the then dominant and circulating narratives of empire, the colonial encounter, and modernity relative to his Igbo people, his young nation Nigeria, and Africa at large. Likewise, Morrison penned especially her first two novels because, she says, they were at the time untold and unpublished stories about black women, young black children, and African America that she yearned to read. In a similar vein, this project—the first book of any kind that I am aware of focused on Achebe and Morrison but hopefully merely the beginning of a rigorous and sustained Achebe-Morrison comparative scholarship—is a work I have long wished existed. As will be spelled out in the pages and chapters ahead, my overarching goal is twofold and interlocking. I aim, one, to direct attention to certain disciplinarily significant relations between both authors and, two, to synthesize a theoretical model with which I then attempt to elucidate the compelling intertextualities of their fiction. Of particular interest to me in that explication are the unstated historical, cultural, formal, and thematic convergences of the six critically acclaimed novels that collectively constitute their trilogies.

Before going further with the agenda delineation, however, it is important that I take a moment and lay bare at the outset what really is behind this study. What initially helped drive *Kindred Spirits* is a question, or rather a cluster of questions, my exegetical investments in which also make this book as a whole, in many respects, a counternarrative and restitutive act. That question, admittedly dangerous because of its implications, is, simply, this: Why the continued "African literature" and, particularly, "Chinua Achebe" gaps in Toni Morrison studies? Why has the seemingly limitless scholarship on her work carried on for years as though it is hardly cognizant of a certain "Chinua Achebe" and/ or Morrison's complimentary references to him? Judith Bryant Wittenberg reminds us that it is not often we find writers, especially, deliberately recognizing their predecessors (270) and, sometimes, even their coevals. To put it bluntly if convolutedly: How is it then that Morrison, bucking that orthodoxy of unrecognition, would since the mid-1980s write and talk about her gratitude to African literature in general and to Chinua Achebe more specifically, and those stated gestures, even with their critical economy, disciplinary valence, and black Atlantic imports, have yet to generate a monograph, until now? We keep intimating Achebe and Morrison's abiding friendship and mutual respect, the salutary affinities of their viewpoints on race, culture, art, and life. But how have both authors' vaunted connections also not qualified, to date, as the themes or even subthemes of professional meetings not tied to author birthdays and publication anniversaries? How have they not been suitable enough for a special issue of a major academic journal, perhaps, despite what anyone examining the matter closely would quickly realize are solid justifications and precedents for such colloquies?[2]

I say strong rationale because Achebe and Morrison have long pointed us in the directions of their multipoint comparability. And precedent, because were the critical lacunas in question the result of scholars' hesitation over Achebe and Morrison's nationalities, or because of both writers being commonly associated with disparate literatures and circuits of knowledge production, namely, African as well as the taut ecosystems called postcolonial studies and world literatures (for Achebe), and African American, American, and women's studies (for Morrison), those identifications should not dissuade or have dissuaded us. For numerous comparatists and a still-growing body of similar projects that *Kindred Spirits* is further energized by and now joins have not only usefully shown pathways to attenuate the writerly irresolution. They have also amassed tools to navigate the innately exacting terrains of comparative studies proper. Formulating new theories or recalibrating extant templates of authorial, contextual, and textual interconnectivity, they have read across geography and passport. They have demonstrated the possibilities of reading widely, wisely, and persuasively, despite the fissures of race and history, the politics of gender and religion, and the strictures of culture and literary canon.

Coming nonhierarchically and nonchronologically to mind are various landmark works. They include those by Edward Said, V. Y. Mudimbe, M. M. Bakhtin, Julia Kristeva, Henry Louis Gates, Paul Gilroy, Gay Wilentz, Filomina Chioma Steady, Toyin Falola, Isidore Okpewho and Nkiru Nzegwu, Michel Foucault, and John Gruesser, among others. Relatedly and more recently, Simon Gikandi's tracing of the entwining of dominion and colony and, particularly, of slavery's impact on the Enlightenment and on antebellum notions of "taste";[3] Wendy Belcher's idioms of "cultural contact" and "discursive possession";[4] Tsitsi Ella Jaji's "stereomodernism";[5] Ifeoma Kiddoe Nwankwo's black cosmopolitanism;[6] Yogita Goyal's runaway genres;[7] Shane Graham's notion of "cross-cultural entanglements,"[8] and, perhaps most important for our goals, Ernest A. Champion's *Mr. Baldwin, I Presume: James Baldwin–Chinua Achebe: A Meeting of the Minds* (1995)—all are works with which *Kindred Spirits* shares visions and purpose. Champion's monograph deserves immediate recognition in this study. An

Atlantic-straddling study that had been critically overlooked even before the fanfare that accompanied the recent revival of interest in Baldwin studies and Baldwin-Morrison connections,[9] the work holds a notable distinction. It is the first-ever comparative and to date the only other book-length study focused on Achebe *and* an African American or American writer. Its title is taken from Achebe's jocular greeting to Baldwin upon entering Baldwin's hotel room for their initial mutual introduction before their joint appearance at the 1980 African Literature Association (ALA) Conference in Gainesville, Florida, as Champion recalls. The fortieth anniversary of that historic meeting was marked by a two-day event captioned "Achebe I Baldwin @ 40" at the University of Florida, Gainesville, in October 2020. The Champion work is also, to date, the only such book-length comparative study I know on Achebe and *any* African-descended writer from the Western Hemisphere.

The possibilities of juxtaposing *Things Fall Apart* and F. Scott Fitzgerald's *The Great Gatsby* have been broached. And a couple of article and polemical comparisons of Achebe and some African American and American novelists including Morrison have been attempted.[10] *Mr. Baldwin, I Presume* remains, however, the only book project centered on Achebe and any writer whatsoever from that part of the world. Not only does Champion remind us, as does the present endeavor, of the various reasons African and African American literatures, in this case, should be institutionally taught and critically explored relationally, but what I find particularly refreshing, and also position as my methodological point of departure, is his avoidance of comparatists' object-captivation, or what I sometimes call the field's "objecentrism." Prudent, also, is his rejection of literary criticism's de facto and hierarchizing hesitancy to incorporate authorial self-diagnosis as hermeneutically appropriate. Favoring instead what could be deemed holistic exposition, he commingles firsthand anecdotes from his friendship and time with Achebe and Baldwin. He adds to those remembrances the two novelists' biographical information, interview reflections, and his textual analysis. The end result is a deeply illuminating discussion of not just Achebe and Baldwin's raced histories and distinguished works, but what Champion assesses as both men's brave and humanistic careers.

It is in a spirit of dialogue with the above forebears and allies that I explore the two conjoined propositions that guide but more especially dictate the earlier opening movement, as well as the contextualization, structure, theoretical framing, and scope of this study. I argue more specifically that, besides the sometimes expediently evoked analogies and realms—for instance, Achebe and Morrison's blackness and matching cultural prestige, their often-mentioned transmutations of the English language, and their redirection of authorial gaze on black humanity and on the inerasable Africanist presences in European and Anglo-American writings—both authors share other, much deeper and as yet critically uncorrelated attributes. Those profound parallels in their personal and professional histories, artistic visions, and works warrant imagining them as kindred spirits.[11] Furthermore, in a description that mirrors Achebe's denomination of his fiction, particularly his stories set in the (slavery, precolonial, and colonial) pasts, Morrison sketches her novels as "village literature." This qualification, I submit, identifies and links her work also with *African literature*, not just the low-hanging[12] and often indiscriminately plucked fruit, *African culture*. For more often than not, inquiries into that shrewd shape-shifter, that unstable signifier, "African culture," especially in pedagogy and literary criticism in the West, devolve to reflexive if not facile invocations of Yoruba cosmology and John Mbiti. I contend, then, indivisibly, that Achebe and Morrison are novelists of the village, without the trite pejoratives and dichotomies that the taxonomic "village," alongside its inescapable corollary the city, the urban, often elicits. As outlined in chapter 1, that multiprong and generative topos of "village," or what I coordinate as "villagism," for lack of a better word, a catchier "ism," is the study's main theoretical intervention and analytical terminology. I concisely define "villagism" here as a conceptual and aesthetic encapsulation of city- and modernity-inflecting rural sensibility or ruralist ethos of being, doing, seeing, and judging (in) the world. And in no interacting works of Achebe's and Morrison's respective canons, I claim, is some of the clear and inferred evidence of this constellar villagism and the other unities of their muses, stories, and crafts better illustrated than in their never-before-colligated trilogies. For Achebe: *Things Fall Apart* (1958), *No Longer at Ease* (1960), and *Arrow of God* (1964); and, for Morrison: *Beloved* (1987), *Jazz* (1992), and *Paradise* (1998).

Consider this: The two trilogies do not just have similar backstories. They also imbricate chronotopically. Spanning the same historical expanses, they engage identically with the major transgenerational events or themes that traverse, define, and couple those temporalities for Igbo-Nigerian-Africans and (African) Americans. The stories' underlying spirit is one of Achebean dialogue and balance of things as opposed to the assumed hierarchical discordance and cross-impenetrability of racial worlds and epistemologies, as Jago Morrison argues ("Tradition"). Both trilogies also have similarly remarkable evolutions. They were not originally drafted as trilogies. Achebe initially called his "the Okonkwo trilogy" ("Named" 33) and a "triptych." He also situates the inaugurating events around the 1850s and 1860s, with Kwame Anthony Appiah observing that the Igbo confrontation with the British at the heart of *Things Fall Apart* occurred in the 1870s, almost thirty years prior to de facto colonization (Foreword ix). "It must have been around 1875," writes Robert M. Wren, "that Okonkwo of *Things Fall Apart* threw Amalinze the Cat in a justly famous wrestling match" (*Achebe's World* 51). In a 1962 interview with the magazine *Afrique*, Achebe asserts this about his emerging canon: "I have only written two novels since 1958. In reality, they will eventually constitute only one, a kind of trilogy, when I have written the third. I wanted to write it, in fact, ever since I was young, since 1953. . . . I really wanted to write a long novel, the action of which would take place over a hundred years. I divided it into three parts. But when I got to the second panel of the triptych, I had to abandon it for the time being" (*Afrique* 7–8). Achebe also tells Lewis Nkosi in another 1962 interview: "What I've decided to do really is to oscillate between the past—the immediate past—and the present: *Things Fall Apart* is about a hundred years ago [putting its remotest action around the 1850s, 1860s]; *No Longer at Ease* is today; and I want to go back now to not quite the time of *Things Fall Apart*, but a little later" (Nkosi 4).

In a February 4, 2001, live interview with the then executive vice president of C-SPAN, Susan Swain, Morrison reflects on her works, among other things. Addressing Swain's question as to whether she approached *Beloved, Jazz,* and *Paradise* as a trilogy, given that emerging literary criticism was considering *Jazz* as the second installment of a series, Morrison, fascinatingly similarly, also talks imprecisely about the trilogy-ness, if you will, of her group of texts. In her response, slightly condensed below, she says that she (too) took some time getting to and through the middle story:

> No, I did originally. When I wrote *Beloved,* I had in mind three stories of the same theme, or variations of human love: love of a mother for children, romantic love, and spiritual love. And I call the whole thing "beloved" for all sorts of complicated reasons. . . . And then when I did the slavery part . . . I told my editor, I'm sorry, I just know I've exhausted all this time. I've only got a third of it. And he thought that I had written a book, and so therefore we would publish it. And I just decided to recast the ending. . . . And then the next story, which turned out to be *Jazz,* was also based on a sort of historical anecdote. . . . So it's a trilogy with quotes around it. (Swain)

Just as the three Achebe novels have been viewed as comprising an African trilogy, and his five novels "together represent a microscopic view of the making of modern Africa" (Wren, *Achebe's World* 51), so too have Morrison's focal narratives been designated relative to black American *and* American history and experience. "All three novels, taken together as Achebe's 'African Trilogy,' create a full and beautifully nuanced arc," Chimamanda Ngozi Adichie writes in her introduction to the compilation, "a human chronicle of the cultural and political changes that brought about what is now seen as the modern African state" (vii). As I will suggest in chapter 3, a part of those sociocultural and political changes—ones that lend additional weight to this study's bridging of Morrison and Achebe's texts—is the increased topical and active presence of things "America" and of African American and white American characters in Achebe's stories, in what I identify as the "America subplot" of his narratives. Nevertheless, as Justine Tally has also perceptively argued: "Taken as a whole, the [Morrison] trilogy encompasses a wide cross-section of African American life. All three books reach back to the 1870s for their historical grounding, though *Beloved* focuses on the 1870s, *Jazz* on the 1920s, and *Paradise* on the 1970s." The stories cover "one hundred years of the history of black people in the United States" (*Story of Jazz* 9).

In their fiction, Achebe and Morrison compatibly contemplate "generations." As others have also variously noted, both authors complicate the doxa and idiosyncratic pressures between the "village" ways *and* the putatively "modern." This modern, this purportedly radically "new" or "newer" dispensation, is gestalt significantly in "the city." With their stories not only swaying or zigzagging between earlier and present times and spaces but also anticipating black futures, both authors are ideationally preoccupied with "change," constancy, and continuities. They are principally concerned with the disruptions and progressions that their respective black "village" people and fictional characters have undergone, as they moved from slavery, abolition, and colonization (on the east side of the Atlantic), and from slavery, emancipation, and Jim Crow[13] (on its west), to the precariousness of freedom and the complexities of what Achille Mbembe, in *On the Postcolony*, affirms as "the African self." This African subject, and by extension this planetary black human being, is not only "reflexive" in that it is quite capable of "doing, seeing, hearing, tasting, feeling[,] . . . touching," and thinking. It and its "historicity" have also been intertwined with Europe at least since the fifteenth century (6, 9).

The Achebe-Morrison exchanges—their "international conversation[s]," to tweak Sam Durrant's apt phrase (2)—have material implications for pan-African history and solidarity. As indicated, their dialogues draw attention to the linkages of Africa, Europe, and the Americas. And perhaps more important, they also call for a thoughtful reconsideration of some of the most delicate, as yet unsettled, and possibly irresolvable kinship questions and tensions—the family quarrels, so to speak—between both groups: Africans and African Americans. Similarly monumental and haunting, the Achebe and Morrison trilogies, particularly their most famous and most widely taught novels *Things Fall Apart* and *Beloved*, together shed some of the most piercing literary lights on colonization and slavery. *Things Fall Apart*, whose slavery subthemes are continued in the trilogy's other volumes *No Longer at Ease* and *Arrow of God*, is imaginatively to the archaeology of colonization *and* slavery for Africans what *Beloved* is literarily to slavery for Africa's descendants in the New World. There are and have been many and even award-winning fictional, poetic, dramatic, musical, and cinematic renderings of those racism-inflicted, collective traumas that Mbembe categorizes as "forms of originary suffering" that also include the Holocaust and apartheid ("African Modes" 259). But in terms of enduring literary impact, many would valuate as quintessential *Things Fall Apart* and *Beloved*, the preludes of which Morrison explores in *A Mercy*, her "ninth and arguably most enigmatic novel," which functions "as a locus for discussion of her re-figuration of concerns central to her narrative project" (Montgomery 2).

In Achebe and Morrison's re-presentations, both racial catastrophes of slavery and colonization—their morphologies, transmogrifications, and continuations—lose much of their rudimentary typologies, as I hope to show particularly in the analytical chapters. With their temporal and locational distinctions evacuated, those two world-reshaping events transcribe as the grotesque evil cousins if not the evil twins in the scars they left on what Geneva Cobb Moore astutely calls "the black body-in-crisis" since slavery. The cicatrices of racial injuries, unflinchingly unbandaged and exposed by Morrison, who, as Moore adds, repeatedly "bodily mark[s] her characters" to suggest slavery's "*unnaturalness* and *abnormality*" (*Bodily* x–xi), those scars spur literal and metaphoric granulation tissue. They trigger complex, sometimes microscopic, but altogether rehumanizing ripostes from both novelists' African and African American characters. These regrowths are evidenced in *Things Fall Apart* and *Beloved*, *No Longer at Ease* and *Jazz*, and in *Arrow of God* and

Paradise. I submit that the epochal, thematic, and formal interfaces of these trilogic six stories are so astounding that we can view the novels, when paired, as "bookends," "companion stories," or "allied texts." I propose we recontextualize them as "a continuum"; indeed, as "complementary narratives" of what are substantially parallel stories of African-descended people in their ancestral "villages" and their new/modern urban settlements and settings.

It is those striking subtexts, as well as the power of mutual authorial admiration, that informed not only the now-historic and earlier-referenced meeting Ernest A. Champion arranged forty years ago between Achebe and Baldwin at the ALA Conference, which Achebe also recalls below. The affinities also inspirited the public dialogue between Achebe and Morrison in 2001. That turn-of-the-millennium exchange was later published as "Things Fall Together" by its convener, moderator, and the Bard College president Leon Botstein. Initially disclosed to Achebe by the anthropologist and his "friend from Biafra days" Stanley Diamond, Botstein's uplifting resolve to provide Achebe and his wife, Christie, a customized new house as well as conducive academic appointments at Bard College after his car accident is recounted by Phanuel Akubueze Egejuru in her Achebe biography (87–90). It was at that equally momentous Bard College dialogue that Achebe singled *Beloved* out as the one book he would take to the proverbial deserted island, as though buttressing the points I press shortly about Morrison's often unhailed impact on African literature.

Although Morrison did not divulge her choice of text at the Bard College event, Achebe did and defends his: He sees Morrison as "the only one who is probing what James Baldwin called the 'conundrum of color'—the question of what happened to us on the continent, and in the diaspora." Asserting that continental Africans have yet to adequately confront that question, and that Morrison has bravely waded into the water, Achebe delves into Sethe's child-murder. The issue, to him, is the repercussion of maternal responsorial infanticide: "The mother loves the child and wants to save her from the abomination of slavery." Paradoxically, "in doing so she commits another abomination. This is my reading," Achebe cautions, "and it may not be yours, but what the story says to me is that that's no solution." It is not an antidote, or even an elixir, he reasons, because "this daughter you killed will come back, and when she comes it is not going to be pleasant." Achebe then lays stark the intraracial conundrum for Africans: "A similar question will be asked on the continent: 'Is it true that you sold your own brothers?' Of course, it is not true that we sold our own brothers—something made us do it. There is some explanation, but still, it is never enough" (see Botstein). As I argue in chapter 2, the interesting thing about the Achebe pick of *Beloved* is not the choice itself. Rather, it is what, in the context of both writers' alliances, is concealed in his assessment of that novel relative to his own literary classic and classic village novel *Things Fall Apart.*[14]

Achebe's related response to a question Okey Ndibe poses to him in a 2008 interview could not be more relevant to this study's very existence, its governing goals, and the burden of the next section of this introduction. Ndibe asks if he could "speak to that tension between Europe's impression that you had no history and your insistence that you had a story and you were going to tell it?" In consensus with Morrison's statement that "Black people have a story, and that story has to be heard" (N. McKay), Achebe avers:

> Baldwin and I were invited to speak at an African literature conference somewhere in the South, and what Baldwin said in talking about me to the audience is that "This is a brother I had not seen for 400 years," and people laughed. And he said that it was not intended that he and I should ever meet. . . . Part of the center of the plan was that we should not know each other. So that's why our task is, in my view, so very important: that in spite of that intention to keep us apart, there will always be some people who would refuse and insist on knowing their brothers and sisters who had been sold away and lost. There were some people who knew that it was important to discover them, and I'm not talking in the past, because the problem remains. There are so many of us on both sides of the Atlantic who do not know the importance of that recognition, that this is my brother, this is my sister, that their story is the same as my story. Whatever variations, it is basically the same story. (Ndibe, "Learning" 82)

In his collection *The Education of a British-Protected Child,* published in 2009, Achebe reiterates almost verbatim that inseparability of self-narration, self-/group-knowledge, identity, and African and African American solidarities. "The first order of business for Africans and their relatives, African Americans," he enjoins "is to defeat the intention Baldwin speaks about. They must work together to uncover their story, whose truth has been buried so deeply in mischief and prejudice that a whole army of archaeologists will now be needed to unearth it. We must be that army on both sides of the Atlantic" (66). One of those racially and disciplinarily consequential but infrequently told and thus little-known stories definitely worth excavating and cohering at this outset is about Morrison's transatlantic association with modern and postindependence African literature. We will address it right after this intermissional project outline.

This study is organized as follows. After this introduction, chapter 1 is theoretical. Repurposing one of Morrison's most-cited essays, "Rootedness: The Ancestor as Foundation," I argue that "village," "the village," and not necessarily "the ancestor," is foundation, or rather *the* foundational entrance, into not only a study of the two authors' worlds and focal works but also the connections of, among other nodes, their respective inspirations of painting and music/jazz, for Morrison, and mbari and mask, the dancing mask, for Achebe. I engage with villagism's constitutive epistemic and aesthetic taxonomies of "village," "village literature," the "village novel." These prompt an interrogation of "the city" and also of the raced, cultural, and formal values of that category relative to the city novel and village-city narrative.

Chapters 2 through 4 are analytical. In chapter 2, I contend that the first installments of the respective trilogies, *Things Fall Apart* and *Beloved,* are linked in several ways. I explore them as "village novels," or narrations of "the village," as its differently located African descendants are dealt personal as well as racial traumas of slavery-colonization—or "pasts"—that still *spectrally* haunt them. These "pasts" also largely overdetermine the infanticides of the protagonists, Okonkwo and Sethe, and their love-implicated tragedies. Sethe's obsessive love (for Beloved, particularly) sheds light on Okonkwo's patriotism-as-love-act. I address, among other villagism-connected subjects, what I suspect Achebe left unsaid in his choice of *Beloved* as textual companion to the desert island, as well as, the stories' depictions of their white characters. In addition, what have been critically ignored are the many affinities of both novels' ironic closings.

In chapter 3, I argue that the second works of the trilogies, *No Longer at Ease* and *Jazz, continue* or "pass on" the stories of the village. They reframe and extend both authors' narrations of the tribe, as its focal and representative "New Nigerian/New African" and "New Negro" members—Obi Okonkwo and Clara Okeke, Joe Trace and Violet Trace—move from slavery and colonization to independence, and from slavery/Jim Crow colonization to freedom; migrating, as it were, from the village/the southeast/the South to the respective metropolises of Lagos and London, New York and Harlem. Unsettled by the stresses of "tradition" and "the modern"/"modernity," Obi and Joe dare to experiment with and break cultural proscriptions. Obi's deviant love for and intent to marry Clara (whose sociocultural caste, *osu,* is tied to slavery) parallel Joe's tragic infatuation with the much younger Dorcas. As with the *osu* situation, this Joe obsession could be viewed as reprehensible in "village" mores. Elongated in what I read as "Josephite betrayal" in both texts, this sense of (modern) freedom and transgression is captured in, in fact encouraged by, the historically interconnected and defining musical genres of the protagonists' eras: highlife and jazz, respectively.

In chapter 4, I maintain that the last novels of the trilogies are further about the village, as its differently situated African and African American members grapple with the implications of paradise, power, and "the past." *Arrow of God* and *Paradise* are, at their cores, stories about the continued significance of the black and village "pasts" for the tribe. Notice that the stories' respective geopolitical and amalgamated formations—*Arrow of God*'s "Umuaro" and *Paradise*'s "Haven" and "Ruby"—are seeming utopias impelled by black survival from and after slavery. What has been critically overlooked, relative to Umuaro-as-paradise, as *an idea*, an *ideal* fortress for the federated nine villages, however, is that "Umuaro," like "Haven" and "Ruby," is also a product of the transatlantic slave trade, territorial expansion, and land needs (Booker 33). Aside from the interrelated impacts of history and the white world on the communities, analogous other factors tear at them. Among those factors are the unjust and perplexing decisions by the village-communities' male leaders. Their actions of sacrificing their people contribute to the crises suffered by each of these religion-permeated, paradisiac black constructs/enclaves, hence the stories' tragic ends. After chapter 4, I offer some concluding thoughts, especially on my hopes for Achebe-Morrison comparative scholarship.

Forging Ahead (to)ward the Village Sphere but Pausing to Look Back

The story of Toni Morrison's decades-long connection to modern and postindependence African literature is not just fascinating in and of itself. It is also substructural to this study. That story, admittedly incompletely and imperfectly reconstituted here, is also one whose retrieval and Africa-diaspora and disciplinary implications cannot be adequately assessed without a retrospective on *another* story signaled earlier. In short, we cannot fully appreciate it without touching on a certain narrative circulated some time ago about Morrison and her works. As we are visually counseled by the forward-moving but backward-turned Sankofa bird and by a related, Achebe-deployed Igbo aphorism that, even in loose transcription, still speaks clearly to etiology and historicity: a person unsure where the rain began to beat him or her will be confused as to where it stopped, or stops. And as Morrison conveys in the Sethe–Amy Denver encounter in *Beloved*, "Anything dead coming back to life hurts" (35). It disturbs and delays. Yet the journey back has to be made, to phrasally echo Houston A. Baker Jr., especially because that recuperative look back, back to the restless and signifying dead, has everything to do not just with what Achebe saw as the need "Today" for a "Balance of Stories" between center and periphery (*Home* 73–105). It also bears on this study in its entirety.

Because of "the phenomenon of Toni Morrison," as Gurleen Grewal fittingly phrases it (2), there was what could be viewed as the academic and sometimes racialized version of the gold rush to locate the evidentiary Holy Grail of her imagination. Critics, especially white critics, were bent on cracking the code. They were determined to unravel what Nicholas Brown would call the "genetic connection[s]" of Morrison's authorial family tree, particularly as soon as the publication of *Song of Solomon* and *Beloved* trumpeted to the literary universe that it had a major talent on its hands. Not to be outdone, some well-known literary genealogists combatively linked her and her stories to all sorts of literary lineages. One cannot but wonder, then, if the immanent dialogism and cultural work of texts (Tompkins xv), the global citizenship and semantic unboundedness of stories, and the reader/audience license sufficiently explain what J. Brooks Bouson flagged as "the critical stampede" (1). This is an onslaught that has led to one writer, Morrison, drawing or being pulled into an unbelievable degree of colloquy. For Morrison has been discussed singly and in relation to a plethora of writers, traditions, tropes, theories, and philosophies, in two-, three-, and sometimes even four-author juxtapositions.[15]

Of the canonical white, or, for that matter, nonwhite, writers often credited with modeling and/or fostering Morrison's artistry or whose works are routinely paired with hers, the big three, so to speak—Virginia Woolf (Lisa Williams), William Faulkner, and James Joyce—have commanded the most posthumous recognition. The impulse to associate Morrison with Faulkner, most dominantly, has stemmed generally from a number of factors. That includes their standings as household names in American literature. They are also fellow Nobel laureates, as well as modernist and experimental novelists. Besides pointing to African American male writers Ernest Gaines, James Baldwin, and Ralph Ellison's affirmations of Faulkner's cultural significance and his influence on their works (Jackson 1–3), reviewers are quick to postulate that Morrison taught Faulkner's novels, particularly *Absalom, Absalom!* at

Princeton University. They also remind us that she used to marvel with her students at his brilliant but difficult technique of camouflaging racial cryptograms. Perhaps the most spotlighted of Morrison's ostensible relations with Faulkner, however, is her formal education, specifically her master's thesis at Cornell University.

Titled "Virginia Woolf's and William Faulkner's Treatment of the Alienated," this thesis submitted to Cornell University graduate school may well go down as one of the most prized and purportedly predictive humanities graduate treatises of the past half century in the United States. It is dated "September, 1955" and authored under the name "Chloe Ardellia Wofford." Her current name, "Morrison, Toni" [sic], is added as author in the appended Cornell University libraries' Standard Bibliographic Microfilm Target. The project is comprised of a one-paragraph, eight-line author biography, an introduction, analytical chapters 1 (on Woolf) and 2 (on Faulkner), a bibliography, and notes, all totaling forty-six pages.

Perhaps eager to present this thesis as material proof of Morrison's fascination with the legendary Faulkner and his supposed artistic and intellectual halo over her, many a critic have tended to disregard Morrison's attempt to explain the indirect if not indeed the accidental genesis of that project, particularly the point that what turned out to be the thesis's current focal authors and theme were not exactly the first- or even second-choice topic she initially proposed, or at least floated, to her thesis advisor. She therefore had seemed intent to deflate the evolutionary primacy continually attributed to the work. In addition to invoking Morrison's qualified comments at the 1985 Yoknapatawpha Conference at the University of Mississippi about her academic and, later, her readerly interest in Faulkner, reviewer after reviewer has conjured the thesis as the proverbial smoking gun. They have established it as the indisputable evidence of Morrison's captivation with and subsequent artistic *emulation* of Faulkner.

We are enjoined that Morrison read Faulkner "carefully" and *imitates* his "technique, one that withholds and delays information, forcing readers to question what it is they in fact know." From about 1989 to 2013, John N. Duvall further states in "Morrison and the (Faulknerian Dark) House of Fiction," almost "one hundred articles and book chapters" were published "on the Faulkner-Morrison relationship." So intense was the curiosity about Morrison's talent and so aggressive the effort to link her to white Western literary genes that, as many will recall, the late Harold Bloom, in his introduction to an edited collection on Morrison, ventures a bet. He proclaims confidently that Morrison "has few affinities with the masters of African-American fiction, her strongest influences being Faulkner and Woolf" ("Editor's Note" vii). Bloom goes so far as to call Faulkner and Woolf "the two dominant precursors who have shaped her narrative sensibility" (Introduction 2; see Christian, "Layered Rhythms"). They are, to him, "the father and mother of Morrison's art" (Introduction 4). That respected black literary theorists and critics have been complicit in this sustained critical practice and attributional travesty does not help matters (see Gates, Preface ix). One could see why Morrison, who "is *seven-eyed*" and thus "aware of all the traps" (C. Nwankwo 172), has not only had to be circumspect on the minefield discourse and questions of influence. She famously told Nellie McKay, in their much-quoted 1983 interview, how she is "not *like*" Joyce, Hardy, and Faulkner (N. McKay 152). Morrison has also been disinclined to encourage the unenlightening chatter about her master's thesis. One easily gleans this in her body language and response when Claudia Brodsky brings up the thesis again minutes into their 2013 chat posted on YouTube.[16]

Morrison's engagement with African literature becomes much more significant, then, if for nothing else but the fact that it initially occurred during two historical junctures. One is in the long 1960s decade and at the height of the second African American literary and cultural renaissance. Two, and notably, her interest began when that emergent body of post–World War II and modernist African cultural texts was lean and nascent. She admired it even as the simulacrum of Africa in colonialist and Western reason, in the Cold War chess game, and in African American historical dreamscape was still a problematic. A mere couple of decades prior, one of the New Negro Renaissance's most lyrical poets, Countee Cullen, had wondered, "What is Africa to me?" Morrison accepted the literature in spite of Cullen's dilemma. She read it with interest even when Afro-pessimist critics from Europe and the United States were either disparaging that literature as infantile, ethnographic, derivative, and documentary, or they were ambivalent toward its viability, respectability, and formal autonomy. And, in the same spirit as what Achebe recalls as Langston Hughes's "deus ex machina appearance at the critical moment in the intellectual and literary history of modern Africa" and Hughes's "unspoken message of support and solidarity after three hundred years of brutal expatriation" ("Spelling" 55), Morrison also became associated with the literature at a time it was undergoing transition, possibly unbeknownst to her.

For not only had white scholars been dominant, in the 1960s, over Africans and diasporic black Africanists in a major and influential platform such as the African Studies Association from which an independence-seeking African Literature Association would be founded in 1974 (Challenor). But also the leading African writers and artists themselves were at the time unsure and indefinite about other equally significant matters, as the agendas and proceedings of their historic, 1960s international conferences in Uganda, Senegal, and South Africa document. In their quest for what the art historian Chika Okeke-Agulu would describe fittingly as "the desire for postcolonial modernist authenticity" ("Drawing" 19), the writers were confronted with these and related matters: Who qualified as an *African* writer? Which part or parts of the continent must they come from? What did they, the writers, think about the "novel" in African literary expressivity? What name or names should they give their literary newborn? What should that newborn talk about and how? What are its cultural, ideological, and textual siblings? What role or roles should they and their literature play in the project of decolonization in their emerging nations, immediate societies, and political economies? What (indigenous African and/or colonial) language or languages should it speak? To whom should it speak, when, and how? Who has the right to publish it, to speak critically about and commercially promote their child? Was it compromising to be translated and read in foreign languages? What was the place not just of protest and the Negritude movement in Africa's quest for cultural and liberatory ideals but also of colonial curriculums in university instruction and assessment? among other fault lines.

It was *that* African-literature-in-transition that Morrison is thankful she encountered years ago. And it is that then-growing canon that she has helped promote in the United States. Although the maps of contemporary African literature generally elide Morrison's constructive involvement in its publication and institutional furtherance in the West, her direct and indirect marks on it to date are actually not negligible and thus must be duly recognized. In addition to her insights on African societies, cultures, authors, texts, and literary currents and on the Africa–African America relations—views discussed more fully in a moment—Morrison also notably published Chinweizu's still-influential *The West and the Rest of Us*. As an aside: the "Chinweizu" folder of the Morrison papers at Princeton University contains professional, personal, and in some cases handwritten exchanges between the two. They include, for instance, a card from Chinweizu in which he congratulates Morrison on what Chinweizu saw as the successful publication of *Song of Solomon*. He also offers Morrison, whom he calls "worldly wise," bits of financial and personal wisdom. There is also another 1977 note from Chinweizu seeking Morrison's blurb/quote for promotion of his work *Energy Crisis & Other Poems*. Chinweizu has recalled the difficulties he had placing *The West*. Just as another example: besides having read and absorbed Morrison's works, many African and African diaspora novelists, including Chris Abani, Okey Ndibe, Chimamanda Ngozi Adichie, Taiye Selasi, Tsitsi Dangaremgba, NoViolet Bulawayo, Dinaw Mengestu, Yaa Gyasi, Akwaeke Emezi, Chigozie Obioma, and Marlon James, among others, have also claimed Morrison as their inspiration. Morrison helped launch Selasi's career by indirectly pressuring her to complete her short fiction "The Sex Lives of African Girls," a story that became the kernel for Selasi's debut novel, *Ghana Must Go*. In his tribute to Morrison in the *Guardian* (August 7, 2019), Chigozie Obioma talks about how Morrison, whom he describes as his and many other writers' "literary mother," impacted him through *The Bluest Eye* and her reflective essays. She also "encouraged me," he says, "to write about African traditional religion, culture and philosophies without reserve, even if the rest of the world—and even Africans themselves—see it as backward and unpleasant."

We should note, however, that *that* charged debate that erupted at the June 1962 conference of African writers in English at Makerere University that Hughes attended was not and is not peculiar to African literature (see also Graham). It was an issue that has similarly confronted African American writers since about the 1890s, as Gene Andrew Jarrett argues in *Deans and Truants: Race and Realism in African American Literature*. Nevertheless, as Morrison stated, she had had the disappointment of reading, after World War II, "fiction set in Africa," works by European and white American storytellers and white American travelers (Introduction xi–xii; "The Foreigner's Home," 5–13). Then came not just this *other* upstart and confident cohort of English-language stories, nonfiction prose, poetry, and drama but also the young writer Chinua Achebe, who was its major flag-bearer. Although it was not intended, four centuries removed, that Morrison and Achebe should ever meet, as Baldwin knew, both authors' paths would once again cross, literally and literarily, most especially in 2000.

In that year, Achebe received the Africa-America Institute's "AAI Award for Excellence in Literature" at the organization's sixteenth annual awards gala held in New York City and captioned "Celebrate Africa in America." At the event, Morrison shared what she had for years considered a personal secret. But it was intended for the honoree Achebe, whose seventieth birthday that year set off academic and cultural celebrations in various parts of the world. Among the academics, artists, journalists, and political dignitaries in attendance to watch Morrison confer the prestige on Achebe and hear her express, or rather *reveal*, directly to him her long-confidential appreciation was Mora McLean, then AAI president. Also in attendance was Sheila Sisulu, the Republic of South Africa's first black ambassador to the United Nations, a Nelson Mandela appointee, and also the first woman to command that office in the country's history. In her conferment citation, Morrison delivered what I consider, and what many an Achebe or Morrison scholar would agree is, an apotheosis. It was her most emphatic testimonial to African literature's and particularly Achebe's transformative and lasting impact on her work.

To better appreciate the measure of Morrison's statement that evening, especially as it pertains to the preceding discussion and this study, however, I will later append the full text of her remarks, now published in Morrison's most recent volume *The Source of Self-Regard.* I purposely want to present the statement only after we have had a moment to survey the equally disciplinarily important observations she made relative to African literature and Achebe in the years prior to the AAI reception. I then reflect on those antecedent remarks and the AAI speech proper. There can be no doubt the AAI award was a capstone moment. But Morrison's personal, editorial, authorial, and scholarly attentiveness to modern and contemporary African literature predated the ceremony. It goes as far back as the mid- to late 1960s, as suggested.

Five or seven years after the fateful encounter with African literature in New York (depending on which of Morrison's recollections one adopts), and three or so years upon its conception, Morrison published the compilation *Contemporary African Literature* in 1972. Ambitious, 469 pages long, and richly illustrated with glossy pictures and paintings, the volume is subdivided into "Tales and Legends," "Short Stories," "Novel Excerpts," "Poetry," "Drama," and "Non-Fiction." Each section concludes with a page of refresher questions presumably for the high school teachers and students who seemingly were its target audience, as elaborated below. The anthology features excerpts as well as some complete works, especially folklore, poetry, scholarly criticism, and political essays by established and newer African writers, political leaders, and activists. For our purposes, it includes contiguously the entirety of *Things Fall Apart*'s chapters 5 and 6, albeit without chapter numbers. Also added is the whole of Achebe's piece "English and the African Writer," which had originally appeared in volume 18 of *Transition,* 1965. As Morrison recalls to an audience during her reading of this piece as part of PEN America's August 8, 2008, "Tribute to Chinua Achebe," commemorating *Things Fall Apart's* fiftieth publication anniversary, she had spared no expense to bring that anthology to life. As Random House's in-house project editor, however, she is not named on the title page. Although the cover credits the joint outside compilers she enlisted—University of Wisconsin–Madison emeritus professor Edris Makward and the African American writer Leslie [Alexander] Lacy, who cowrote the compilation's introduction—Morrison and the three-member design team are listed in the interior front matter, nonetheless.

Morrison's stated, main goal in publishing *Contemporary* was to close what she rightly saw as a noticeable gap in America's educational system. She was hoping to help diversify the very curriculum that had delimited her horizon years earlier. Morrison also desired, at the same time, to offer the various practitioners and purveyors of African literary culture an academic platform in the United States, consistent with Makward and Lacy's joint declaration that the anthology's controlling mission was "to give as complete an idea as possible of the variety of writings coming out of Africa today, without sacrificing quality for exhaustiveness" (3). As Morrison recalls at the PEN America event, literature classes in American public schools at the time customarily accentuated white, Western, and male novelists. In twelfth grade, she says, one was taught English literature, William Shakespeare, Geoffrey Chaucer, and the like. And in eleventh, one consumed American literature, with a good serving of Nathaniel Hawthorne, Herman Melville, Mark Twain, and others. In the tenth grade, she points out, one was introduced to the fringed and wieldy amalgam called "World Literature." To Morrison's surprise, however, *Contemporary* was not a commercial hit. It barely sold. She had thought it would be embraced as a "beautiful" world literature book, "an absolute gift . . . to the public school system of United States," but apparently not.[17]

In hindsight, one wonders if, in addition to bureaucratic or other interferences, design decisions and optics contributed to what Morrison suggested was the anthology's weak academic and commercial appeal. The anthology was discernibly initiated in the broader spirit of Pan-African consciousness. It was completed in an era of black cultural awakening. And, next to volumes such as Langston Hughes's early 1960s *An African Treasury* (1961) and *Poems from Black Africa* (1963), and Ulli Beier's *Introduction to African Literature: An Anthology of Critical Writing from Black Orpheus* (1967), it could be viewed as one of the postindependence attempts to showcase Africa's emergent creative and intellectual harvest. Given all that, it is curious a regional image that reinforces a continental/racial stereotype was chosen as an appropriate book cover. Reminiscent of the questionable, indeed problematic, choice of a black-and-white picture of a nude African boy/body for the front inside matter of James Currey's *Africa Writes Back, Contemporary's* cover art features, against a solid purple backdrop, a silhouetted headshot of a male Maasai. The figure has decorated, cigar-size ear log; multicolor, concentric, and beaded necklace; and a tribal garb, to boot. To repurpose world-class architect David Adjaye's keen observation regarding the persuasive or detractive power of frontages: "Façades are the narratives of architecture, in the end. Façades are the stories. The content is very important, but the façade is really what is marked in history" (207). In any case, it is this important publication activity that inaugurated Morrison's serious involvement with African literature and more especially Achebe, whose *Things Fall Apart* she believes she read for the first time ten or so years after its 1958 release. In 1975, three years after *Contemporary,* Morrison also published the earlier-mentioned *The West and the Rest of Us.* Chinweizu's two poems "The Crossroads" and "Kindness" and his essay "Towards a Liberated African Culture" are also anthologized in *Contemporary.*

Besides *Contemporary,* and publishing the anthology *Giant Talk* (1975) in which Acbebe's poem and short fiction appear, Morrison has also commented on African literature as a discipline and on Achebe in at least three interviews. As discussed below, the first remark dates back almost forty years. Morrison pens, in 2001, a prefatory close reading of Laye's *The Radiance of the King,* first published in French in 1954. She and her collaborators, Makward and Lacy, extract in *Contemporary* the second half of *The Radiance's* opening section "Adramé," with a half-page plot outline/critical abstract that anticipates the Morrison 2001 preamble. In that introduction to *Radiance,* Morrison reminisces: "In that racially charged context [of encountering the white fiction set in Africa post–World War II], being introduced in the early Sixties to the novels of Chinua Achebe, the work of Wole Soyinka, Ama Ata Aidoo, and Cyprian Ekwens[ ]i, to name a few, was more than a revelation—it was intellectually and aesthetically transforming. But coming upon Camara Laye's *Le Regard du roi,* in the English translation known as *The Radiance of the King* was shocking" (xiv).

Nevertheless, one of the interview questions Bessie W. Jones and Audrey Vinson pose to Morrison in 1981 deals with the writers who have had the "greatest influence" on her writing and how. "I can't think of one novelist that I could say that about," Morrison answers. "It doesn't mean that I haven't been overwhelmed by lots of writers. I suppose there is one writer, although I've never—it's not even the writing, but Camara Laye wrote a book called the *Radiance of the King* and that had an enormous effect on me. I cannot spot any of that in my writing because I don't know anybody who really writes the way I do and whose style I like that much to incorporate. It's the kind of job that only somebody else could do. I couldn't comment on those influences" (179).

And in her 1986 interview with Morrison, Christina Davis starts out noting that *that* year, 1986, "marks the 30th Anniversary of the First International Conference of Black Writers and Artists at the Sorbonne," a gathering focused on "the need for Africans to discover and explore the historical truth about Africa." To Davis's question of whether African American writers have engaged adequately with "the discovery and affirmation of the truth about the black experience in the United States," Morrison believes that issue has actually manifested as the dominant concern of African American literature. African American authors have, however, tackled it in different ways. The effort at the time, Morrison adds, is "to find whatever cultural connections there were between Afro-Americans and Africans, but it's always been interesting to me that Africans are not interested in it at all." Staying on the subject of intraracial kinship ostensibly in keeping with the spirit of the Sorbonne anniversary, Davis further wonders what Morrison sees as the tissues between African and African American literatures. Morrison reflects that she is newly realizing those linkages in her reading and scholarship. She cannot say which of the ties she is identifying are true. But one thing she is certain about, however, is "the impact that African authors have had on me as a reader, the doors that were opened for me by that contact through literature, because that's the only contact I had." Morrison infers one of those portals African writers opened is in the realm of language. The English language has historically been miswritten and misapplied to denigrate black speech in the United States, even though, as James Baldwin observes, black speech deeply inflects white mainstream accent. As Baldwin argues in "If Black English Isn't a Language, Then Tell Me, What Is?," "I do not know what white Americans would sound like if there had never been any black people in the United States, but they would not sound the way they sound" (650). This language, English, has to be overhauled. It must be divested of its racially charged symbolisms, Morrison maintains to Davis, before one can clearly articulate what the cultural bonds are. Adding to that, Morrison states that while writing, she used to depend heavily on her own memory and assessments of the intraracial and cultural unities. She also incorporated information she solicited from more knowledgeable Africans. Nonetheless, she views African Americans as indivisibly African *and* American, yet distinct, essentially "a brand new human being in this country" (Davis 225).

Another subject addressed at Sorbonne, Davis continues, is diaspora. Reflecting on this, Morrison notes that the perception of Africa in African American thought has altered over time. It has shifted, she reasons, from romantic to illusory and sometimes to monolithic. As to the question of variations she finds between African and African American literatures proper, Morrison identifies "skin color" and its "privileges" in America and Africa as one. Others are contrasting conceptions of "beauty" and "sexual license." Gender differences are immense also, she says, especially "the expectations of one gender of another." Then there is the considerable "impact of the white world" on African nations (Davis 228). And in response to Davis's next question about any African authors she particularly relates to or whose writings she has a special affinity with, Morrison says, "Well, neither akin nor close but certainly a real education for me. Chinua Achebe was a *real* education. And certainly the plays of Soyinka and *The Beautyful Ones Are Not Yet Born* of Ayi Kwei Armah—those things were at that time real, and they're the kinds of books that one can re-read with enormous discoveries subsequently." Not done with the Sorbonne spirit, Davis presses further, asking Morrison pointedly what she thinks the similarities and contrasts are between African American and African "*writers . . . as writers.*" One major commonality Morrison finds between both "is the clear identification of what the enemy forces" are (Davis 229). She also sees similarities in African American and African women writers' techniques. Mentioning Bessie Head and Gloria Naylor comparatively, Morrison observes: "There's a gaze that women writers seem to have that is quite fascinating to me." They are not overly concerned with conflicts with white men. Other things capture their attention more, and "their look, their gaze of the text is unblinking and wide and very steady." It is deeply interrogative, she says. It is undeterred. Nor is it petty or dispute-consumed. Morrison considers that amazing (Davis 230).

Years later, in another exchange, this time her 1994 interview with Claudia Dreifus, Morrison fields again a question on her literary influences. She also remarks once more on that all-important subject of authorial-cum-narrative viewpoint. To Dreifus wondering which writers inspired her early on, Morrison names James Baldwin. But then, she points to African authors, whose impact preceded her huge regard for Baldwin's linguistic dexterity. Baldwin "could say something in a phrase that clarified all sorts of conflicting feelings," Morrison states. "Before Baldwin, I got titillated by fiction through reading the African novelists, men and women—Chinua Achebe, Camara Laye. Also Bessie Head and the Negritude Movement, including Leopold Sedar Senghor, and Aime Cesaire." To Morrison, the African writers "did not explain their black world. Or clarify it. Or justify it. White writers had always taken white centrality for granted. They inhabited their world in a central position and everything non-white was 'other'. These African writers took their blackness as central and the whites were the 'other'" (Dreifus 101–2).

What is again clear is how significant but unsung a role African novelists and their texts, especially their perspectival orientation, played in Morrison's developing consciousness as a black and always-raced writer. Equally undeniable is the example of postcolonial African literature in general as she searched for the appropriate literary structures that would enable her to avoid, in her work, that artistic fallacy Abdul R. JanMohamed elucidates as Manichean aesthetics in a 1983 work by that title. To JanMohamed, this representational vantage presupposes, problematically, a diametrical opposition between the social and the literary.

Something else that those socially conscious *and* stylistically adept African literary artists understood is Chinua Achebe's paramount role in helping them optimize their craft. Of particular importance here is the project of prioritizing their humanity and stories. It is in view of that canonical impact and his decades-long championing of African and more broadly black peoples' causes through his influential art and bold pronouncements that the Africa-America Institute celebrated him in 2000, with Morrison asked to do the honors.

A Significant Moment in Achebe-Morrison Relations

I cite the Morrison speech at length below because, unlike the event's audience, for instance, many readers of this book may be unaware of the address. They may be grasping it for the first time here. Others may have become acquainted with it through Morrison's *The Source of Self-Regard*, in which the slightly edited version below is included or, earlier, by way of Nana Ayebia Clarke and James Currey's *Chinua Achebe: Tributes and Reflections* (2014), which contains the complete rendition. Whatever the source of the reader's present familiarity with the statement, I have included it in toto also for its value for Morrison and Achebe scholarship. Its import for the fields of African, American, and African diaspora literatures, more broadly, is equally undeniable.

I take great pleasure in having this opportunity to say some things in public which I have never said to the person who is the subject of these comments—Chinua Achebe. My debt to Mr. Achebe is the best kind. Large, minus repayment schedule and interest free. Let me describe it to you.

In 1965, I began reading African literature, devouring it actually. It was a literature previously unavailable to me, but then I discovered a New York bookstore called African House which offered among other things, back issues of *Transition, Black Orpheus* and works by a host of African writers from all over the continent. Amos Tutuola, Ayi Kwei Armah, Ezekiel Mphahlele, James Ngũgĩ, Bessie Head, Christina Ama Ata Aidoo, Mongo Beti, Leopold Senghor, Camara Laye, Ousmane Sembène, Wole Soyinka, John Pepper Clark: the jolt these writers gave me was explosive. The confirmations that African literature was not limited to Doris Lessing and Joseph Conrad was so stunning it led me to secure the aid of two academics who could help me anthologize this literature. At that time, African literature was not a subject to be taught in American schools. Even in so-called "World Literature" courses it had no reputation and no presence. But I was determined to funnel the delight, the significance and the power of that literature into my work as an editor. The publication of *Contemporary African Literature* in 1972 was the beginning of my love affair.

But the more profound and more personal consequence was the impact Chinua Achebe's novels had on my beginning as a writer. I had read his essay in *Transition,* on the struggle with definitions of African literature and knew its ramifications for African American writers. In that essay, Achebe quoted James Baldwin's comments on the subject of language choice and manipulation in defining national and cultural literatures and its resonance with marginalized writers. "My quarrel," said Baldwin, "with the English language has been that the language reflects none of my experience . . . Perhaps I had never attempted to use it, had only learned to imitate it. If this were so, then it might be made to bear the burden of my experience if I could find the stamina to challenge it, and me, to such a test." But then theorizing a definition is one thing. Executing a theory is another. Achebe's "answer," so to speak was in his work. He (along with Camara Laye, Bessie Head and others) constituted a complete education for me. Learning how to disassemble the gaze that I was wrestling with—the habitual but self-conscious writing toward a non-black reader that threatened and coated much African American literature; discovering how to eliminate, manipulate the Eurocentric eye in order to stretch and plumb my own imagination, I attribute these learned lessons to Chinua Achebe. In the pages of *Things Fall Apart* lay not the argument but the example; in the pages of *No Longer at Ease*, *Anthills of the Savannah* the assumption of the authenticity, the force, the valleys of beauty were abundant. Achebe's work liberated my artistic intelligence as nothing else had ever done. I became fit to re-enter and re-inhabit my own milieu without the services of a native guide.

So in fact that was not a debt in 1965. It was a gift. (285–86)

In Clarke and Currey's *Chinua Achebe: Tributes and Reflections,* the complete text of the speech includes Morrison's opening greeting "Good evening" and this concluding sentence of the last paragraph omitted above: "And I hope my presentation of this award to you Chinua will represent not only the African American Institute's regard and respect for you but also my personal gratitude as well" (26–27). In the original, typed draft of the address, dated September 22, 2000, and now archived with the rest of the Morrison papers at Princeton University, Morrison made a few edits in pen. Perhaps the most pertinent changes are in these constructions: The line ". . . was the beginning of my love affair" was originally phrased as "was the beginning of my love affair with the work of Chinua Achebe." And the initial phrasing, "I attribute to Achebe," now reads "I attribute these learned lessons to Chinua Achebe." The potentially wider breadth of those lessons can be further imagined when we consider three other points. One: *Things Fall Apart, No Longer at Ease,* and *Arrow of God*, the three and focal Achebe novels published and in circulation at the time Morrison encountered his writings, were viewed by literary and cultural historians as having invented an African narrative archetype: a blueprint, as it were, toward which many African novelists aspired for creative, critical, and commercial success. Two: as Bernth Lindfors writes relatedly in *Early Achebe,* at the time there were lots of Achebe imitators, especially in his native Nigeria. These were talented artists in their own right. They were not sheepish followers of what Lindfors calls the Achebe School, although some were not as successful as others (147–82). Three: as the first and arguably most important editor of Heinemann's influential African Writers Series, Achebe reviewed, published, and indirectly left his artistic mark on many—or conservatively, some—of the African novelists Morrison would have read into the early 1970s. And a great deal of what she may have appreciated about their recuperative stories of colonial encounter were quite likely adaptations and extensions of the Achebe standards, as Simon Gikandi notes (Booker vii–xv).

Should anyone need more corroboration, let these two moments suffice. One: even after prudently avoiding reference to specific works and writers when a caller asks her to rank her top five books, both classical and modern, besides her own works, during that February 2001 C-SPAN interview with Susan Swain, Morrison still mentions exemplarily a few authors whom she says she reads at various times and for different reasons. Among them are George Meredith, (Anton Pavlovich) Chekov, Camara Laye, and Achebe, whom she says she was recently rereading after so many years. Two: the original handwritten draft of her address, dated October 27, 2010, sent at the occasion of Achebe's Gish Prize award in 2010 and preserved with her papers at Princeton. In the short statement, Morrison writes, with her edits replicated here:

> Among the Gish prizes (for?) this one awarded to Chinua Achebe is among the most distinguished and most deserved. There are personal and professional reasons for my pleasure—the personal reasons have to do with our friendship secured by my admiration for a man of kindness, principle, integrity and courage. Professionally, his work—fiction and non-fiction has impressed and influenced me, limited as I was in the late sixties to literature which assumes the reader's default position was culturally de-raced, I learned otherwise from African writers-principal especially Chinua. As a beginning writer it was that plight that into from are in the reader-writer conversation that enabled me. acknowledge the debt and thank him for his gifts.

Perhaps two of the most inescapable challenges of influence and comparative studies, respectively, have to be content selection and interpretive restraint. I am consciously exercising both in this book, especially by not turning oneself into a David Cowart,[18] or African literature, Achebe, and his 1950s and 1960s contemporaries into James Joyce or Harold Bloom's Faulkner and Woolf (see Bloom, "Editor's Note" vii; and Introduction 2, 4). Having said that, there is no question the Morrison AAI address, particularly, appears as candid and critically generative today as it was unvarnished and catalyzing twenty years ago. However, in its tonal propriety and referential grace, it possibly intentionally creates for critics and the general reader a few rhetorical and analytical aporias. What with its arc of gratitude that appears at first glance to moderate the Achebe "lessons" and "gifts" through Morrison's seemingly equalizing invocations of other African authors at a special event organized in Achebe's honor. But even in prefixing the remarks as a long-held secret, Morrison still leaves no doubt whatsoever as to the extent of her debt to African literature. It is my belief that, at that AAI gala and by including the speech in what turned out to be her last published volume, *The Source of Self-Regard*, Morrison is engaged in an act of remediation as well. She does not seem to be merely embracing African literature and Achebe as close, cultural kin *and* artistic relative. She is also, I argue, directing our institutional, critical, and pedagogic attention to a significant disciplinary and scholarly gap. She appears to be prodding us to accord African literature and Achebe their rightful places in her literary history. Hinted in that is the recognition by Morrison that for so long comparatists, especially, with their interests focused or diverted elsewhere, have as a consequence denied readers a much richer understanding of her and Achebe's personal, professional, and artistic connections beyond, for instance, the dialogue she and Achebe had at Bard College to mark Achebe's seventieth birthday.

In all, and on a closer reflection, one senses something else on display—something confidently ancient, very village or village-inculcated—in Morrison's open modesty at the AAI event and elsewhere. In her affirmations of collectivity, in her acknowledgments of *group* assistance and example, direct and indirect, are instantiations of primal reciprocity. Laced in them are expressions of that timeless "Thank You" that parents and grandparents, ancestors and ancestral figures, in cities and villages, have taught children from time immemorial. It is that ethos of private and public gratitude that Mr. Isaac Okonkwo dramatizes when he invites his fellow Umuofians—many of whom he vehemently disagrees with but who nevertheless helped finance his son's education—to celebrate Obi's return from England to his village roots.

Let me also say a closing word or two more on that anthology *Contemporary African Literature* that Morrison possibly started conceiving in the late 1960s and very early 1970s. Although it was a venture for Random House, I see the compilation as an act of reciprocity on Morrison's part. I read it, village-style, as her indirect "pay back" or "Thank You," if you will, to modern African literature for its own invaluable "gift" to her. As an Igbo proverb edifies, right and left hands wash each other mutually beneficially. It is also my view that, besides their historicist reckoning with the African and (African) American worlds that respectively nurtured and steadied Achebe and Morrison's imaginations, scholars, critics, teachers, and students interested in both authors' canons and literary relationships would do well to linger on that little-known publication. Of importance here are Morrison's editorial decisions. They arguably anticipate her intimations in the AAI address that *Things Fall Apart* is at once a historic text and a craft-novel; a prototype of fresh, modernist storytelling. In short, in the fascinating guessing game of what it was *and* what it is *exactly* about one author that leaves a lasting impression on another writer, we could look to that anthology for a clue or two in the Achebe-Morrison case.

Could anything be gleaned from Morrison and her editors Makward and Lacy's choice of those specific portions of *Things Fall Apart* as well as his essay "English and the African Writer"? As Morrison asserts in the AAI speech, which is included in *The Source of Self-Regard*'s "Part II: God's Language": "In the pages of *Things Fall Apart* lay not the argument but the example." Not the *theorizing,* one infers Morrison as saying, but rather the practical, writerly tips. As Morrison and Achebe critics would agree, and as the uncountable Achebe protégés and imitators over the years could also attest, one simple answer to that question is that in *Things Fall Apart* are examples of how a black writer, or any writer for that matter, can mesh aesthetic innovation and political consciousness. The beginning novelist might discover in it pointers to, for instance, the art, act, and arc of dramatic dialogue in the (black) vernacular. In *Things Fall Apart* are lessons also on how to turn the narrative eye and employ a *new* English language, such that whites and the predilections of white racial audience and particularly *that* audience's dehumanizing spectatorship (a feature of many a white Western fiction set in Africa) are rendered peripheral. "For three thousand years," Jean-Paul Sartre writes, "the white man has enjoyed the privilege of seeing without being seen; he was only a look—the light from his eyes drew each thing out of the shadow of its birth" (115). And, George Yancy, who also invokes this same Sartre statement, writes, "Within the context of white racist America, whites inherited the privileged status of being the 'looker' and gazer, and with all the power that this entailed" (xviii). On *Things Fall Apart*'s pages, that white gaze that enslaves as it colonizes, and colonizes just as it enslaves, is decentered. Fearlessly repositioned by a skilled and in many ways

w gaze

immigrant artist Achebe who *creates dangerously,* to channel Edwidge Danticat's titular injunction, that historically weaponized white gaze and thought is subordinated to a restorative spotlight on African and black humanity and mind. Achebe's *new* English may have arrested Morrison. But it was probably *Things Fall Apart's* perspectival innovations, its abrupt and radical shifts in point of view, that so *jolted* the perspicacious Morrison—to use her own word—they seemingly reflect in those contiguous sections of *Things Fall Apart,* chapters 5 and 6, that she decides to include in *Contemporary.*

An editor and aspiring novelist at the time she encountered African literature in the mid-1960s, Morrison, through her outside editors, could not have picked better sections than those two plot sequences of *Things Fall Apart* she profiles in the anthology. For those two narrative movements—featuring collectively the Feast of the New Yam, Okonkwo's near-commission of homicide, the Ekwefi-Ezinma dynamic, the priestess Chielo substory, and the village wrestling match—show Achebe in his creative power and his vast grasp of Igbo culture and traditions. It should also not be lost on us that Morrison did not just excerpt sections of *Things Fall Apart* in which Achebe demonstrates how to interweave myth, folklore, magic, and history in modernist *and* postmodernist narrations; naturalize "evil," normalize the supernatural and superstition, and disrupt linear temporality, as in the Ezinma subplot and the *ogbanje* phenomenon. In her broad knowledge of African literature, Morrison was also familiar with Achebe's Nigerian and African precursor, Amos Tutuola of *The Palm-Wine Drinkard* and *My Life in the Bush of Ghosts* fame.

That last point should be of interest to Morrison scholars and especially to critics of *Beloved* and *Song of Solomon* who claim, with certainty, that Morrison's major aesthetic and cosmological inspirations in those two works are Gabriel García Márquez, whom Morrison admits admiring and rereading, *and* Latin American literature's so-called magical realism convention. Chidi Okonkwo has countered the notion of magical-realism's originary descent from Latin America in his study *Decolonization Agonistics in Postcolonial Fiction* (1999). And Morrison herself insists that her work not be labeled as such. Her foremost wellspring, she declares, is the rich and expansive constellation of African, African American, and other African diaspora cultures. Moreover, Morrison's anthologizing also of Soyinka's poem "Abiku"—the Yoruba corollary to the Igbo *ogbanje* idea—could be viewed as her being long intrigued by the philosophically and conceptually bounteous born-to-die myth. The cosmological and metaphoric dimensions of this belief are easily discerned in *Beloved.*

One could overindulge in the reading pleasure of Morrison's and Achebe's works. But, unfortunately, *Kindred Spirits* makes no pretensions whatsoever at exhaustiveness or perfection, hence the following caveats. It does not nurse any secret ambition to formulate a grand new theory for the cousin-canons of African and African diaspora literatures. Nor does it engage in what would amount to a validating and universalizing foregrounding of the idea, history, and conduct of village *in Europe,* and also, for instance, in Victorian and/or American pastoral literatures. Furthermore, some of this book's theoretical inferences in chapter 1 and elsewhere may raise more cultural, philosophical, and/or semiotic questions than they presently resolve. Whatever broader value the book's object of village/villagism and its analytical findings yield toward illuminating other (black) authors' works speak, however, to the heuristic elasticity of the decidedly local. In short, so much has been posited in the past sixty years about Achebe and Morrison and their oeuvres collectively that some of the issues argued and positions taken here may not be new or strange to Achebe and Morrison scholars and critics, or to the general student of African and African diaspora studies for that matter. It is also important to stipulate that a good number of the Achebe-Morrison associations identified in this study are not distinctive to their dyad, and that those affinities—authorial, contextual, and textual—are much stronger in some parts of the analysis than in others.

Which brings me to this important point: although I draw upon pertinent biographical material, particularly in this introduction and chapter 1, and also in the endnotes, *Kindred Spirits* is a work of literary criticism. Readers interested in Achebe and Morrison's biographies or literary biographies would be well-served by such works as Achebe's *There Was a Country* (2012), Egejuru's *Chinua Achebe* (2001), Ezenwa Ohaeto's *Chinua Achebe: A Biography* (1997), Barbara Kramer's *Toni Morrison* (2013), and Stephanie Li's *Toni Morrison* (2009).

Let me add a few more words on some of the "unconventional" decisions I made in this book. As earlier stated, I am aware of, but do not subscribe to, the tendency to devalue or utterly dismiss authorial introspection in literary criticism. In writing this book, I have had in mind not just college students nor merely the theoretically astute and discriminating academic. Given Achebe and Morrison's global, cross-disciplinary, and multilevel readerships, I was thinking also of, for example, the junior high or high school teacher of African, African American, American, or world literature, or English in general, who may acquire or recommend this book. To that teacher, such supposed, unverifiable biographic trivialities could be intriguing epiphanies that further heighten and hopefully help capture their young students' interests in both authors' worlds and works, and in literary studies in general. It is with that simple yet significant goal in mind that I have also included extra historical backdrops at the starts and sometimes in the course of the analytical chapters' close readings. My hope is that a majority of Kindred Spirits' readers will find those additional contexts helpful.

Nonetheless, to guard against the impulses of that Western Madman figure that "sees nothing but resemblances and signs of resemblances everywhere" when empirical differences also abound (Foucault 49–50),[19] we must recognize as well Achebe and Morrison's more remarkable divergences even as we pinpoint their irrefutable and implicit commonalities. As Claude Lévi-Strauss notes relatedly in his meditation on the kinship-rooting episteme of "the family": even anthropologists studying the subject descended into "bitter arguments." The disputes "resulted in a spectacular reversal of anthropological thought" due to the term's intricacy (39). And, "in affirming the comparability of its objects, textual or otherwise," Djelal Kadir similarly observes, "the comparative uncovers and ratifies the difference within and among phenomena and the contingencies of their existence, a sanctioning of difference that could mitigate solipsism and self-delusion" (644).

For instance, although deeply linked, colonization and slavery—subjects the experiences and afterlives of which preoccupy both writers' works—are not a single, undifferentiated entity. They are, rather, distinct ideas and historical occurrences; just as, as John Cullen Gruesser notes, African American and postcolonial studies should not be arbitrarily conflated (2). Also, aside from the two authors' deviating cultural sensibilities and their varied, intellectual interests and political projects, as should be expected, Morrison wrote operatic and theatrical pieces. To Achebe's five novels, she published eleven, with the twelfth, which she titled Justice, in the works before her death. But to Morrison's one major short fiction, "Recitatif," and one short, scarcely issued, and barely known poetry collection, Five Poems (2002), Achebe penned poetry and short-story volumes, although, to him, his "dozen pieces [of short fiction] in twenty years must be accounted a pretty lean harvest by any reckoning" (Girls at War 1). In "FIVE POEMS: The Gospel According to Toni Morrison," which is perhaps the most detailed publication history and intertextual examination of that evidently obscure work to date, Stephanie Li points out that a mere 425 copies were printed. Li notes that it was the Nobel laureate Wole Soyinka who, "on behalf of Rainmaker Editions," had initially asked Morrison "to submit an original unpublished manuscript." But in "numerous interviews Morrison has given since the publication of *Five Poems* she has never mentioned the book or discussed her approach to writing poetry," Li remarks (899). There is a bit more to those poems and that collection, though. Two of its five poems—chronologically: "Eve Remembering," "The Perfect Ease of Grain," "Someone Leans Near," "It Comes Unadorned," and "I Am Not Seaworthy"—were part of the four poems, "I Am Not Seaworthy," "The Lacemaker," "The Perfect Ease of Grain," and "The Town Is Lit," that Morrison sent to her then Princeton creative writing colleague Paul Muldoon for entry among other solicited and unsolicited titles in the journal *Ploughshares'* spring 2000 issue. Morrison may have or have not written more verses. Nevertheless, that she is a sage we already know. But that there is also a poet in her should be clear to anyone who contemplates not just the above pieces but the luminous passages from her fiction and nonfiction prose excerpted in *The Measure of Our Lives* (2019), to which Zadie Smith pens a foreword.

Furthermore, Achebe's fiction engages with gender in one way or another, with *Things Fall Apart, No Longer at Ease,* and *Anthills of the Savannah,* however, featuring arguably his most complexly rendered and consequential female characters, Ezinma, Clara, and Beatrice. This notwithstanding, Achebe's narrative commitment to women and their concerns has been variously and sometimes controversially parsed, as illustrated in the essays collected in Helen Chukwuma's volume *Achebe's Women: Imagism and Power* (2012), among other debates. As in Achebe's canon, black-male subjectivity and black male–black female relations in America interest Morrison greatly, with *Song of Solomon, Tar Baby, Beloved, Jazz, Love,* and *Home,* depicting—in inverse—her centered and most fully drawn male characters, Milkman, Son, Paul D, Joe Trace, Bill Cosey, and Frank Money, respectively. It is, however, African American women's experiences that predominate in and help unify her novels.

Morrison won the Nobel Prize in Literature; Achebe, the Man Booker Prize. Morrison sees her Nobel accolade as genuinely, personally affirming and racially dignifying in many ways as well. Achebe could not care less about winning the Nobel, for which, according to his biographer Egejuru, he was nominated five times, beginning "as far back as the nineteen seventies" (185–86). Like Chinweizu's pointed criticism of the Nobel committee's racial hegemony and cultural limitations which Bernth Lindfors recalls in "Africa and the Nobel" (222–24), Achebe once reputedly attacked the Swedish Academy's arrogance, especially the racial condescension of one of its most powerful board members.

Morrison, who said she completed graduate school in the era of New Criticism, has admitted to later favoring and adapting the aesthetic possibilities
enabled by deconstruction and postmodernism. Though he was not averse to
but instead adapted/Africanized the received semiotic conventions of literary
modernism, Achebe believed strongly that the project of modernity or modernization as a material fact and factor in people's real lives was unfinished,
particularly relative to Africa. Since his youth in Ogidi, Umuahia, and more
broadly in colonial Igboland, Ibadan, and Africa, and as his biographers have
variously indicated, Achebe was familiar with the ostensibly new logics of
being, thought, culture, and social articulation fancifully packaged and globally
propagated by deconstruction, postmodernism, and linguistics. That includes
irony, paradox, ambiguity, contingency, interconnectedness of utterance, texts,
and contexts; and relentless questioning—an abiding skepticism toward totalizing narratives. He was also unimpressed with what he viewed as the Western/
metropolitan origins, as well as the faddishness, the sloganeering, if you will, of
postmodernism (*Home* 81–82). Morrison pens an introduction to a later edition
of Camara Laye's *The Radiance of the King*. But Achebe is not thrilled by Laye's
privileging of white gaze in the work. "I admire *The Radiance of the King* quite
a lot," he acknowledges; "still, I do hope that the great African novel will not be
about a disreputable European" ("Thoughts" 99). Last though not the least: the
two writers are incisive social critics, as demonstrated, in Achebe's instance,
in such texts as his *A Man of the People, The Trouble with Nigeria, Anthills of the
Savannah, There Was a Country,* and in his essay volumes *The Education of a
British-Protected Child, Hopes and Impediments,* and *Morning Yet on Creation Day.*
In Morrison's case are her critiques in her novels and public pronouncements,
and in publications such as the essays assembled in *The Source of Self-Regard.*
Others are her Nobel Prize address, *The Dancing Mind; Playing in the Dark;
Race-ing Justice, En-gendering Power; Birth of a Nation'hood;* and notably the section "Politics and Society" in *What Moves at the Margin.* Yet, *Kindred Spirits* is
not about Achebe's and Morrison's political lives or leanings. When and where
warranted, however, I reference both authors' nonfocal fiction, as well as the
above-mentioned nonfictional works.

Also, the cultural and not biological term "kinship" (Sahlins) is used in reference to the Achebe-Morrison relations. But just as the study is not about the
theory of the novel, or of trilogy, it is also not about the anthropology or sociology of "kinship"—an epistemological category that is often naturalized without attention to its inherent semantic contestations. As I hope is clear in my

applications of it, the word "kinship" is employed here in nominal, pronominal, and adjectival environments. Therefore, no inordinate discursive space is carved out beyond this and subsequent usage clarifications to explicate "kinship." No matter Morrison's literary and cultural prominence, her works I focus on here are deepened through their dialogues, their kinship, with their Achebe counterparts. The same is true of Achebe's. As I hope to show further in chapter 1 and later in the analyses of the novels proper, the Achebe texts are defamiliarized by being explicated within new contextual and discursive floorplans and alongside Morrison's fecund imagination and intellect. I contend that, whatever Achebe and Morrison's authorial contrasts, their comparable ground(ing) in the village sphere, in villagism, is perhaps their strongest cultural, thematic, and aesthetic coefficient.

1

"Things Fall Together"

Or, Rootedness: The Village as Foundation

The owner was the village, and the village had a mind.
—CHINUA ACHEBE, *A Man of the People*

I write what I have recently begun to call village literature.
—TONI MORRISON, interview with Thomas LeClair

In her groundbreaking essay "Rootedness: The Ancestor as Foundation" (1984), a major premise of which she reprises three years later in her talk "The Site of Memory," Morrison ruminates on various subjects. They include the putative friction between the public and private spheres but with regard to narrative, the African American novel's roots in autobiography, and that mode's allowance of self-community interplays. She also reflects on the sociology, domesticity, and clarifying role of the novel form for especially the English peasant class at the novel's inception. And most important, at least for our purposes, she articulates what she deems the aesthetic blueprints of black art.[1] One of those distinctive tenets, Morrison proposes, is the presence of the ancestor or an ancestral figure. She would return to that postulation, and we will as well, in her piece "City Limits, Village Values: Concepts of the Neighborhood in Black Fiction." Morrison's critically riffed descriptions of the essentiality of these men and women in lived black experience and literary culture cannot but remind Achebe readers of, for instance, Ogbuefi Odogwu, whom we just encountered in the introduction. They recall also the prosperous farmer Nwakibie, who loans Okonkwo seed yams, the Priestess Chielo, Ogbuefi Ezeudu, Obierika, and Uncle Uchendu in *Things Fall Apart*. Her image of the saliency of such community members, who need not be related to one by blood although they can be, and whose racial forebears, literary cousins, and mythic archetypes we have also for decades witnessed in African folktales, proverbs, novels, dramas, children's storybooks, and lullabies, calls to mind these elders' shrewdness. But it also evokes, more importantly, their compulsive sense of duty. They exhibit this elder-obligation not just to the nine-village Umuofia clan at large but to Okonkwo, personally, from his youth to far into his adulthood.

I have tweaked the title of that paper, given by Morrison at the 1980 Conference on Literature and Urban Experience in New Jersey, as an apt entrance into this chapter. Unlike Morrison's completely logical centering of "the ancestor," however, I want to deviate somewhat and instead reposition "village" as foundation, *the* foundation, indeed the space that gestates the ancestor and his or her functions of possibility. Which is to say, as the originary locality and location of a system of values, and thus the context from whence the ancestor first came, and comes, the village precedes and yet is linked with the ancestor existentially, temporally, cosmologically, even philosophically. Content-heavy, "village" is, and can also serve as, a conceptual milieu and framework. As such, besides its emplacement here as cultural context, it is also deployed methodologically. In other words, I will distill and employ it also as a model, the main theoretical and critical register. Not the only analytical idea in use in the study, it must be stressed, but a major gateway into Achebe's and Morrison's worlds and works of art. It is considered here as a matrix from which emanates, and to which I will attempt later to connect, related and equally important nodal-subjects that will help us further comprehend the two authors' texts, contexts, and aesthetics. We can think of village here, then, as a portal to portals, the portal of portality.[2]

The question is, however, of Achebe and Morrison's numerous connectors, why focus on "village" as frame of reference? Why elect an archaic lexicon, a *backward* signifier, especially given the not-so-distant memories of white, Western critical linkages of African *and* African American literatures with the sociological? Or given the modernist and postmodernist complexity and deconstructionist predilections of Morrison's fiction, *village*'s seeming referential misalliance with some of the spatiotemporal settings of the trilogies; and those works' generic and modal diversity? Other than *Things Fall Apart* and *Arrow of God*, the driving events of which occur in the village settings of Umuofia and Mbanta *and* Umuaro, respectively, *No Longer at Ease* unfolds in a city-village-city (Lagos-Umuofia-Lagos) circularity. *Beloved*, for instance, is a neo–slave narrative with postmodernist texturing and is set in antebellum environments. *Jazz*, set mostly in Harlem/New York and a proto–city novel, is postmodernist in form. And *Paradise*, set mainly in Ruby and Haven and equally postmodernist in style, follows its characters close to 1980, while shifting backward in time.

An expedient answer to the above conglomerate would be village's temporal antecedence and geographic centrality to the ancestor and the ancestral figure, suggested above. The truest impetus is, however, the prominence Achebe and Morrison uniformly assign "the village"—as a meaning-full term—in their personal and historical experiences, cultural memory, and fictional universes. I know of no other African American novelists who have staked "the village" so cardinally to their canon as does Morrison to hers. This is why I believe the idea's lexical absence in important studies of African American literature is a notable oversight. Nonetheless, as the discussions that follow hopefully will elucidate, Achebe and Morrison both reject simplifications of the village in sociocultural and literary thought. They instead imbue it with scope and depth. They show that "village" does not contextually and conceptually misalign with, but can actually inform and enrich, many of the temporal fixations, the epistemological and philosophical concerns, and the representational practices and interventions of modernist and postmodernist black fiction. In short, to Achebe and Morrison, (seemingly) disparate things that may knock against one another can still concur in the conjunctional village, as Odogwu's *mediating* goatskin bag exemplifies.

Bound with *and* within the village as background and critical apparatus, then, are these equally important subject-nodes hinted above: namely, Achebe and Morrison's consonant concerns with "the ancestor," "the past," "generations," and "change"; their postures on "language," the English language; the composite question of "tragedy"/"the tragic mode" relative to their novels and their overarching goals as producers of literature and knowledge against a declining oral tradition that continues to defy erasure. And then, as I conclude the chapter, I engage interrelatedly with the two novelists' asserted cultural inspirations combined: painting/mimesis, music, mbari, and masquerade. I will expound on these village interlinkages, albeit not exactly chronologically, in order to help shed more light on the Achebe-Morrison connections. Put another way, and as others have variously noted with respect to Achebe: much of his and Morrison's attitudes to art and its ecosystem (its composition, concerns, forms, audiences, criticisms, practitioners, and social roles) is similarly and to a large extent shaped not just by those combined and village-implicated themes and artistic inspirations. It is also influenced experientially by their childhoods. Growing up, Achebe and Morrison imbibed a profound regard for the village as a semantically irreducible arena, encounter, and episteme.

Of Roots and Routes: Village as Foreground and Poetics

"Village" or "the village" is not a foreign and uncontested trope in African literature, particularly in subcontinental West Africa, West African literature, and especially in Nigerian literary history and criticism. Although often denied currency in modern parlance, "village" correspondingly undergirds Achebe and Morrison's perception and execution of art. It is worth restating that Achebe and Morrison grew up in the village, or, in Morrison's case, in the village-like environs of the "neighborhood" and black "community" of Lorain, Ohio (see Greenfield-Sanders). They came of age at the Achebean crossroad of cultures, in the "zones of interface," as Wendy Harding and Jacky Martin, though addressing another but interrelated context, would have characterized the interactivity of Morrison and Achebe's cultural moorings (10). Subscribers to the ethos of intermediacy, Achebe and Morrison compatibly conciliate the vanishing old and the emergent new, in-sight and out-sight, the African and the Western (see Kronenfeld). But as the trilogies illustrate, it is "village"/"the village" that helps root them in place. It grounds them as "village people," enabling them to branch outward in the modern world. And it helps them, as powerful cultural and moral voices, to put everything else—life, art, ideology, accolades—in a proper gaze. To Achebe and Morrison, in short, the village is the (artistic) point of departure and in many cases also the site of (philosophic) disembarkation. While the narrative and epistemic terrain of "community" has been duly ploughed in Achebe and Morrison studies and in African and African American literatures more broadly, the semantic integer "village" has yet to draw extended attention as a legitimate paradigm, an overarching lens, as it were, for a comparative study of both authors and their works.

In its multireferentiality, "village" is at once a geographic settlement and setting, a metaphysical entity, a social organization, an existential experience, a collective memory, a philosophical treatise, and fount of critical theory. My interest here is, however, not necessarily with the village's materiality: its topography, buildings, climates, vegetation, and the like. Rather, I am

concerned with its tropology. That is, its denotation and connotation of particular, complicated sociocultural arrangements and relationships, actions, and
attitudes to life and art. These propensities are manifest not just in the historical experiences of the trilogies' characters. They are evinced also aesthetically,
in terms of the apparent and subtle ways "village"—along with its offshoots:
Achebe and Morrison's artistic inspirations mentioned earlier—foregrounds
the two authors' ideological and narrative preoccupation with "the ancestor,"
"the past," "generations," generational "change," and "the tragic." These are not
extrinsic or tangential subjects but instead significant themes variously treated
in both novelists' trilogies, the articulatory vehicle of which is the raced and
inherited language, English.

In 1981, three years before "Rootedness" first appeared in Mari Evans's edited
volume *Black Women Writers, 1950–1980,* Morrison spoke with Thomas
LeClair. It was in this exchange that Morrison, in response to LeClair's question, first patently enunciates her village-centric aesthetic in the epigraph to
this chapter. "I write what I have recently begun to call village literature," Morrison announces, "fiction that is really for the village, for the tribe. Peasant literature for *my* people, which is necessary and legitimate but which also allows
me to get in touch with all sorts of people." She adds: "I think long and carefully about what novels ought to do. They should clarify the roles that have
become obscured; they ought to identify those things in the past that are useful
and those things that are not; and they ought to give nourishment" (LeClair
120–21). In "Rootedness," Morrison sharpens that authorial goal: "If anything
I do, in the way of writing novels (or whatever I write) isn't about the village or
the community or about you, then it is not about anything. I am not interested
in indulging myself in some private, closed exercise of my imagination that ful-
fills only the obligation of my personal dreams—which is to say, yes, the work
must be political" (64).

A couple of significant issues are prompted immediately by these mission and vision statements. One: implicit in the declarations is that Morrison
expects and *always already* sanctions findings of, among other things, villagism
even in narratives such as *Beloved, Jazz,* and *Paradise* in which that ideological embedding may be diffused and/or vague. Two: on hearing "village," "village literature," and "tribe," a person sold on racist stereotypes would neither
reflexively think, for instance, "medieval" "feudal," "preindustrial," "Victorian"

England, and/or "modern Europe." Nor would they automatically assume "the United States," "American countryside," "the South," and/or "the rural Deep South," where many whites lived and subsisted, as in villages, alongside enslaved Africans and their Africanisms.[3] Such a person probably will free-associate those key phrases with continental Africa, African literature, and African cultures. For the village-constituting "tribe," as Olakunle George writes, "suggests simple collectives as opposed to modern states that are seen as more advanced and governed by articulated rationality, not kinship" (6). And so it makes perfect sense, in this comparative context, to discuss those Morrison invocations and her later racial and literary reengagements with them relative to Achebe's thoughts on the composition and the character of the village, the illustrative Igbo village, in this case.

It must be stressed that this "archaeologic," or shall we say ethnologic, re-turn to Africa (and occasionally and especially to Igbo-Nigerian history, thought, and art) for cultural norms, generic modeling, and/or experiential alignments with black America's is not an unwarranted thread in tension with the study's historicist arguments. Nor is it an unprecedented practice in African diaspora literary theories and criticism. The approach is actually in lockstep with the direction taken by, for instance, Africanist Morrison scholars whose studies deploy similar recourses and gestures. They sometimes have had to reach to specific (West) African ethnicities or cosmologies for validations of Morrison's Africa-inspirited themes, allusions, and/or philosophy.[4] Also, it is my view that Morrison's assertion that she writes "village literature," one for "the tribe," is accurate yet sardonic. For it recalls, to me at least, the nominal causticity of *Things Fall Apart*'s "Umuofia" (or "People of the Bush," "People of the Forest," literally "Children of the Bush"); the ironic appellation "Sweet Home" in *Beloved*; and Henry Louis Gates Jr.'s titles *Signifying Monkey* and "Criticism in the Jungle," for instance. Morrison is not merely indirectly identifying herself and her work with Africa and *African literature*. She is also signifyin(g). Those phrases "village literature" and "tribe" are self-deprecating traps. Like "Umuofia" or the folkloric "tar baby" doll in Morrison's novel of the same title, those charged terms will ensnarl the racially prejudiced person, who, soon enough, realizes there is nothing backward in *her* and African literary canons. The village joke, then, the sociology joke, so to speak, is on *that* person. In addition, as implied earlier, Achebe is not the only African author or African artist-intellectual who has fictionalized *and* theorized the village. As such, I will be augmenting Achebe and Morrison's eruditions on "village" with

insight from other researchers and critics. The goal is to broaden our appre-
hension of the subjects and also to better demonstrate the parities of Achebe
and Morrison's constructions of the village as context and interpretive milieu.

Although Achebe has commented on the experience and theme of "village" at
different times, his 1980 and 1987 conversations with Jonathan Cott and Chris
Searle, respectively, offer important windows into his views on the question.
Drawing Achebe's attention to the ending of his 1966 and fourth novel, A Man
of the People, in which the narrator, Odili, introspects the above epigraph, "The
owner was the village, and the village had a mind" (149), Cott elicits his corroboration as to the centrality of the principle of "village" in his work. "My
world—the one that interests me more than any other—" Achebe agrees, "is
the world of the village" (77). As Achebe postulates, the Igbo and their stories
view the village as organic and evolving. This is in contradistinction to the
Manichean polarities that generally obtain in the Western world. In America and the mainstream American novel, for instance, the talk is generally of
"society," of "the bourgeois ethos of meritocratic individualism" and "central
characters [who] are pitted against society in a struggle between personal
desire and collective law," as Harding and Martin argue (87–88). Like other
African peoples, the Igbo fashion the village and the Igbo world as a complicated yet democratically spirited settlement permeated with mutually counterbalancing human life, life forms, and cosmic powers, as Victor Uchendu,
other scholars of Igbo world, and Achebe himself have noted (Cott 78–79). To
invoke a proverbial Achebe assertion about the Igbo outlook on the village's
extraordinary ontological, epistemological, and ethical diversity which Morrison would appreciate very much and which Arrow of God exemplifies, "In a
great [village, neighborhood, community] compound, there are wise people as
well as foolish ones, and nobody is scandalized by that" (Education 6).

Even when fictional narratives about the Igbo, in this regard, are set in urban
environments, Achebe further suggests, the village does not lose its explicit
geopolitical and implicit thematic sways, as demonstrated in No Longer at Ease,
for instance. Nor does it, for that matter, surrender its interwoven imprints
on plot. Although "disdained as the element of narrative that least sets off and
defines high art," as Peter Brooks argues, plot is still indispensable to the com-
prehensibility of any story, indeed "all written and oral narrative" (4–5). Villagism—the consciousness of the village, of modernity- and city-impacting rural

models of being, thinking, doing, and valuing the world and in the world—is not eclipsed. That is not to imply, however, an immutable and coherent pre-colonial and preindustrial Eden. As Achebe states, he fully embraces the new literary trend of younger Nigerian (and no doubt African) writers emphasizing urban histories, locales, characters, and economies, as well as the attendant crises of subjectivity and existential meaning confronting the emergent but still-small middle class. Achebe backs this literary turn because, to him, those upcoming artists and novelists need not duplicate the themes of traditional village life already realistically and naturalistically plowed by their literary forebears. Nor must African novels and novelists, as Evan Maina Mwangi concurs in *Africa Writes Back to Self,* continue the cultural-nationalist literature's preoccupation with "writing back" to the imperial center instead of, subversively, to themselves and to the gendered and sexual African self. Those younger writers should instead blaze their own trails, Achebe enjoins. That call is evidently already heeded. We find instances in the younger and newer writers' engagements with diasporic, transnational, Afropolitan, Afrofuturist, and queer African subjectivities, with gestures to postmodernist forms, Artificial Intelligence, and information technology.[5] To Achebe, then, the new authors and artists should contribute their talents, energies, and voices toward the larger project of completing the other uncharted quadrants of that same story. That is, Africa's experience within the perimeters of postcolonial and fast-paced modernities (Searle 156).

We are reminded here of Morrison making an analogous point of collectivist and multiperspectival authorship. Speaking with Gloria Naylor about African American women's works and, by extension, the larger body of African American history and literature, Morrison observes:

> You work with one facet of a prism, you know, just one side, or maybe this side, and it has millions of sides, and then you read a book and there is somebody who is a black woman who has this sensibility and this power and this talent and she's over here writing about that side of this huge sort of diamond thing that I see, and then you read another book and somebody has written about another side. And you know that eventually that whole thing will be lit—all of these planes and all of the facets. But it's all one diamond. (Naylor, "A Conversation" 214)

While prism and diamond are Morrison's material metaphors for the many-sided shapes and surfaces of that single and melding African American experience and particularly the African American woman's story, Achebe's image for the kaleidoscope that is the African story is the (Ijele) masquerade. It is stunning that Morrison and Achebe identify relatable symbols as their inspirations: a visual wonder (prism, which Morrison augments with crystal [see Silverblatt]); a precious, reflective stone (diamond), and an equally expensive and rare visual spectacle, the dancing Mask/(Ijele) masquerade. More will be said on this later in the chapter.

Suffice it to note for now that, although Achebe endorses the formal and thematic turns negotiated by the younger African writers, as indicated earlier, what he eschews is locational and experiential hierarchy. What he disapproves of, he says, "is sometimes the feeling that you come across that this concern for the urban . . . is the *real* story and the other, rural one, is not real." Emphasizing temporal and spatial conjunction, Achebe accedes to the rise of and expansion in city life and living. However, that development cannot be fully comprehended independent of the village. "These are village people living in the cities," he reminds us (Searle 158). The foregoing discourse on the interpenetrations of rural and urban spheres could very well have been about Morrison's *Jazz*. Achebe could have been talking about St. Louis, Chicago, Kansas City, Detroit, Philadelphia, New York, and the other big U.S. cities. During the long-twentieth-century's Great Black Migration, southern blacks flooded to these metropolises, bringing along their rural cultures and traditions.

In his study *Culture, Tradition and Society in the West African Novel* (1975), the late Emmanuel Obiechina concurs with Achebe. Reminiscent of what the earlier-cited Shane Graham might phrase as "cultural-entanglements" in reference to Langston Hughes's connections to African and Caribbean literatures, Obiechina's take on intersectionality and fluidity is appositely transatlantic and reinforcing. He opines that, unlike "the New Yorker or Londoner," the ordinary West African urbanite, with a few exceptions, but not excluding many in the intellectual and professional class, "is still a peasant at heart, with a thin layer of modernist sophistication concealing the deep centre of traditional beliefs and feelings" (36–37). Obiechina cautions, however, that the greater impact of "Culture-contact" on the villager than on the city resident should not be misinterpreted. It neither stipulates nor signifies contraposition between urban and rural. Rather, he contends, "there is traffic between them, with the village influence flowing into the town and the town influence flowing into the village" (36).

And with regard to the mostly Igbo characters that populate Achebe's village and village-city fiction, they are not unitary or tame. They are, instead, a restive, complicated, and adaptive group. This portrait reminds one of Morrison's fond memories of the older generations of African Americans she knew growing up whose phenotypic variegation and social idiosyncrasies never ceased to intrigue her. Echoing Simon Ottenberg's originary 1956 essay "Ibo Receptivity to Change," in which Ottenberg expounds on his thesis that "The Igbo are probably most receptive to culture change, and most willing to accept Western ways, of any large group in Nigeria" (130), Achebe postulates that the Igbo "have always lived in a world of continual struggle, motion and change—a feature conspicuous in the tautness, overreach and torso of their art," whether concerned with the village or the city. "Those who visit the Igbo in their home or run into them abroad or in literature are not always prepared for their tense and cocky temperament," Achebe adds. "The British called them argumentative" (*Home* 18).

The British may have deeply resented the Igbo truculence during the transatlantic slave trade, at which time, in the New World, the Igbo (mispronounced by many in the trading and planter class as Ebo or identified ethnically as Calabares) "did not take kindly to servitude, and were unpopular with planters for this reason." They developed a widely held reputation as unwise purchases for their intractability and agential self-murder (Isichei, *History* 44). The British imperialists equally disliked that pugnacity and belligerence. During colonization, they had to resort to pacificatory military expeditions and the sly tactics of Indirect Rule to administer the Igbo from afar. As Robert Wren writes, the evolutionist British, blind to the depth of Igbo society and cosmology and intent on wiping out "'savagery' with 'civilisation,'" saw the Igbo as "stateless," "anarchist," and "maddeningly difficult to deal with, proud, confident, self-satisfied, disinclined to proper humility, disdainful of any authority save their own, [and] apparently indifferent even to their own leaders" (*Achebe's World* 18). This perception notwithstanding, Igbo egalitarianism and village spirit survived the historic racial traumas that are the subtexts and subjects of Achebe's *Things Fall Apart*, *No Longer at Ease*, and *Arrow of God* in which, to borrow Charles Nnolim's apt phrase, Achebe's "theme of mutability looms large" ("Technique" 98). Furthermore, to Achebe, as Afam Ebeogu conveys, the home, the Igbo village home in this instance, can be considered "a semiautonomous unit within a communal system," one marked by the balancing act of individual-and-community (178).

If, for our purposes, the West African and particularly the Igbo Nigerian English-language village novel is proposed here as furnishing the framework for a nuanced understanding of that subgenre relative to Achebe and Morrison's

focal texts, then it makes sense to appreciate some of the supporting scholarship. I specify the narrative medium here simply to indicate the existence
and precedence of village-themed, pioneering works in indigenous Nigerian
languages such as those by D. O. Fagunwa, who, as Ernest Emenyonu points
out, started his writing career in 1938 and is "the father of the Yoruba novel,"
and by Pita Nwana, "the father of the Igbo novel" and author of "the first Igbo
novel, *Omenuko*," released in 1933 ("Chinua Achebe" 195). In his most recent
volume, *The Literary History of the Igbo Novel* (2020), Emenyonu brings both
breadth and depth to the subject. Among other things, he revisits formal and
aesthetic positions he took on the Igbo novel in his 1978 pioneering study *The
Rise of the Igbo Novel*; makes a persuasive case for literary history; discusses
Igbo literary beginnings and some illustrative authors, texts, and author interviews; and, perhaps, most important, includes an appendix of 127 Igbo language novels published, by decade, between 1933 and 2015, from *Omenuko* to
J. U. T. Nzeako's *Ewu Amuo N'Ogburi*.

Nevertheless, one such pertinent study on the Igbo English-language village
novel is George Nyamndi's *The West African Village Novel with Particular Reference to Elechi Amadi's "The Concubine"* (1982). In his discussion and periodizing
of the subgenre, Nyamndi argues that "In West Africa the birth of the village
novel is also that of the written literary tradition, so that to locate one is also to
locate the other" (15). He notes: "The village novel in West Africa belongs to
the mainstream of cultural awakening to which political independence gave rise.
Its genesis and development are therefore intimately bound with the historical
circumstances which went into the making of present-day Africa. These circumstances can be schematized into 1) the discovery of Africa by European explorers,
2) the myth of the Dark Continent, 3) the partitioning of Africa, 4) colonialism,
5) the struggle for independence, 6) independence, 7) post-independence" (2).

This mapping of the English-language West African village novel's twentieth-
century emergence is of historical and critical value. I would suggest, however,
a much longer timeline. I propose that we insert the periods and experiences
of domestic slaveries/the transatlantic slave trade as number 2 among those
sequential "historical circumstances" that ultimately gave rise to the genre. More
so, although slavery, a preeminent contributor to the rupturing of (West) African villages, is missing from the interacting forces enumerated above, Nyamndi
is not inattentive to its malevolence, incarnations, and reach. For later in the
discussion he rightly entwines colonialism and slavery: "The tone and texture
of the village novel tradition in West Africa derive their essence from the legacy

of these experiences" (16). He contends, nevertheless, that the village novel's "Aesthetic particularities" are vested in three attributes. Those fundamental features are delineable in Achebe and Morrison's focal texts. One of the principles, Nyamndi postulates, is Language, or the "desire to construct an idiom and a rhythm in which are reflected the African resources of diction" (17–18); two: Characterization, wherein characters bear out "the individual/society dichotomy in the traditional situation" (36); and three: Setting, which typically expresses the theme-locale dialectic. Or, as Nyamndi points out, "The village novel cannot be conceived of without a correlation between the subject-matter and the background against which it is developed" (42).

In addition to harnessing Nyamndi's conceptual lexicon, which I am also functionally extending by taking it on a perhaps unanticipated westward journey of transatlantic application to African American literature, this village novel theoretical framing-in-progress builds also upon the work of another important interlocutor, the literary sociologist Wendy Griswold. Griswold's discussion does more than reinforce Nyamndi's schematic of the subgenre. She takes the representations steps further. As with my cross-border elasticizing of Nyamndi's regionalization of the village-novel rubric, I am equally broadening Griswold's nation-centric parameters of the genre to continental North America. I want to assign the tenets not just new textual hosts. They are also given interpretive possibilities in Morrison's work.

In its context, scope, and depth of analysis, Griswold's *Bearing Witness* (2000) is a magisterial account of the Nigerian novel. In 1992, Griswold published "The Writing on the Mud Wall: Nigerian Novels and the Imaginary Village," an article that could very well be regarded as a ground-staking prequel to *Bearing Witness*. Invoking especially Benedict Anderson's *Imagined Communities*, which reminds us of, among other things, the inventedness of large social formations—nations, communities, etc.—Griswold lays out the study. She details its research, themes, texts, and conclusions, as well as what Griswold identifies as the sociohistorical, political, and Western institutional and market forces fueling the rise, growth, and persistence of the Nigerian village novel and its problematic promotion of "a particular image of 'the African community,'" of "the African village" (710–11). In *Bearing Witness* proper, sections of which are threaded by the interfaces of village and city in Nigerian literature, however, Griswold maintains but also supplements Achebe's foregoing deliberations. Her insight on the category of village finds correlation in Morrison's view of the village relative to her novels. Like Achebe, Griswold theorizes the village not reductively. She characterizes it as being "thick with human relationships, with rivalry, jealousy, support, sanctions, desire, bitterness, respect, contempt." To Griswold, the village is a place "where little goes unobserved, where what is observed is commented upon, and where 'transparency' is a virtue, secretiveness a sin—such a village would seem to exemplify the sociopolitical characteristics of community, and the virtues associated with community as well" (132).

The enduring remnants of village settings, scenarios, and values in African literature should not be misread. As earlier suggested, those residues do not imply temporal, spatial, and/or cultural fossilization. On the contrary, continual transformation, Griswold suggests, is the appropriate angle for apprehending the African village. Traditional African life was drastically altered, first by slavery, and then colonization and its associate forces. But the village has consolidated traditional activities, even if warped or vanishing. "Writers who depict lives as lived in the village see their role as one of preservation," Griswold states, significantly. Their work encodes "public memory, and their very concentration on 'preserving' a dynamic tradition tends to belie its dynamism" (133). In other words, and as the Achebe and Morrison trilogies under examination bear witness, a major conceptual attribute of the village novel is its attempt to "preserve the memory of a world that is passing," Griswold contends, augmenting Nyamndi's discussion. And the village novel's inextricable counterpart, the city narrative, she argues, characteristically strives "to capture the experience of moving between two worlds" (165). It explores the cultural, ethical, locational, and psychological hybridity of its inhabitants, whether that variegation is permanent or transient.

Griswold regards *Things Fall Apart* as the quintessential and most dominant African village novel. Furthermore, and significantly, she theorizes works in that subgenre as those that are not just set in conventional "rural communities." They also generally manifest what she draws as a "five-part mythic structure." That general tableau unveils as follows. There is "traditional stability," then some "disturbance from outside," followed by an "attempted restoration," a "climax," and completing on a note of "disintegration or reintegration" (136). In part because of its deceptive narrative fusion of anthropological material and its before-and-after sequence of events, with the earlier, precolonial era represented almost idyllically, *Things Fall Apart* may have created the erroneous impression that Igbo and more broadly Nigerian-African villages and their cultures were ahistorical. It may have given the sense that the villages were unchanging and "authentic," Griswold observes, or perhaps exotic. This is not the case, as Simon Gikandi argues. The reality is that those rural, culture-contact zones—for instance Umuofia, Mbanta, and those two villages' literal counterparts—were never fixed. They were hardly uncontaminated and uncontaminating, he opines in *Reading the African Novel* (28–31). The villages were instead chaotic, crisis-engulfed, and imperfect, as Obiechina suggested earlier, and as readers of *Things Fall Apart, No Longer at Ease,* and *Arrow of God* can attest. The same can be said of Morrison's *Beloved, Jazz,* and *Paradise.* The villages were/are "dynamic, churning, filled with new comers, with marginal members, traces of exiles, and other people profoundly not 'at home.' The village plots obscure this social dynamic," Griswold concludes (136). As fascinating a narrative and semiotic development, and as national as the literary and thematic turn to the city appears, it is not peculiar to Achebe's fellow Igbo writers, or to postcolonial Nigeria's literary history.

The pattern seems subcontinental, at the very least. For as Obiechina additionally contends, rural-urban interplay and contestation have tended to define West African fiction. "One can no more think of West African novels apart from traditional West African village environment and the new urban settlements," he writes, "than one could think of the Wessex countryside and the eighteenth-century England of country estates, inn-keepers and post-boys" (*Culture* 140). The preoccupation of many Nigerian novelists with locating their fictional stories in the city and related urban geographies potentially "got established because the Nigerian novel developed as the country was undergoing rapid, highly visible urbanization," Griswold remarks. But that was not quite the case in England and the United States. In those two places, she argues, the novel attained its cultural legitimacy and prominence way before the modern, business and manufacturing city assumed its real as well as its imagined reputation as an obstacle, if not indeed a setback (*Bearing* 154). If one thing is clear, it is that the village, the *modeling* Igbo, Nigerian, West African village, is a complicated and critically generative cultural formation.

Perhaps nothing makes that point more conclusively and lends the foregoing explication greater legitimacy than the case study of Umueke Agbaja, an actual Igbo village, in what is now Imo State. A composite map of M. M. Green's grounding descriptions of Umueke in her ethnographic study *Igbo Village Affairs* (1964) corroborates the above findings of the village's often-understated, inherent complexity. This dynamism is convertible in, and thus serviceable to, various fictional styles, as Achebe and Morrison demonstrate. Green summons such stock anthropological qualifiers of hinterlands as bush, poor, unenlightened, and supernatural. Yet, one cannot but register Green's admission to experiencing, from the Igbo-Umueke villagers, a remarkable level of hospitality she says she—a white woman and stranger among them—could not receive from most English villages. Green highlights the Umueke villagers' sense of and penchant for autonomy. Although "rivalries and disputes between inhabitants of a village" are pervasive among and habituated to the group, there is still a dominant aura of existential bonding. And, the "village is the framework within which the individual," including the ancestor and/or ancestral figure, identifies and "lives his daily life" (14, 15). In addition to recognizing, significantly, the village's predisposition to change, Green also stresses its intrinsic heterogeneity. She pinpoints its characteristic accommodation of difference, embodied in such marginalized persons as the *osu* (religious/cult slaves—a subject to which we will return in chapters 2 and 3). Others are the *ohu*, whom Green describes as "pawns": individuals "who have pledged themselves to someone in return for a sum of money but who can redeem themselves by repayment of the original debt" (23). There were, equally, strangers among them. Even with the existent alterity of some of its members, Green writes, or rather given village's stratification and ingrained ambivalence, it still allows for what could be best described as situation-transcendence. Village enables *and* affirms social and class mobility. "Alien elements in the population," she observes, can be "assimilated to the kindship" (24).

In the modern Nigerian and West African novels in which it is incorporated as location, theme, experience, and/or other element of form, "the village"—villagism's tropologic motherboard—is not existentially severed, even if it is geographically provincial. Rather, it is intimately entangled with the city and the city's demographic transplants—its cultural liminals, economic escapees, and death-defying other subalterns. To many of these in-betweens, the village had been both a material point of departure and a spiritual axis, which brings us, shortly, back to Morrison. One would think that Africa's increasing youth population, expansion of urban and industrial centers, intracontinental and international migration, and the residency of many younger African novelists in American and European cities would trigger a mass retirement or relegation of the village motif in late twentieth- and early twenty-first-century African fiction. That has not been the case. An old palimpsest, the trope has proven resilient. It has defied erasure and supersession by new narrative crafting and concerns.

Taiwo Adetunji Osinubi has noticed that persistence as well, as easily gleaned from his 2015 article "Slavery, Death, and the Village: Localizing Imperatives of Nigerian Writing." According to Osinubi, his piece is motivated mainly by Chelva Kanaganayakam's 2009 essay *"Things Fall Apart* from a Sri Lankan Perspective."* In addition to indirectly buttressing Griswold and categorizing Achebe's novels thusly—*Things Fall Apart* and *Arrow of God*: "village novels"; *No Longer at Ease* and *A Man of the People*: "coming of age novels"; and in *Anthills of the Savannah,* "the village disappears entirely"—Osinubi touches also on something else. He addresses that modal plasticity of the village novel *and* village life in post-2000 Nigerian/West African literature. To Osinubi, "the village and the formation of the village novel have been closely linked to African participation in the cultures of 'novelism.'" He credits that coinage to Clifford Siskin, who defines it as "the discursive site on which the naturalization of writing is negotiated." Referencing Chimamanda Ngozi Adichie's *Purple Hibiscus, Half of a Yellow Sun,* and *Americanah,* Helon Habila's *Measuring Time,* Okey Ndibe's *Foreign Gods, Inc.,* Chigozie Obioma's *The Fishermen,* and Traci Nwaubani's *I Do Not Come to You by Chance,* Osinubi recognizes that these post-2000 narratives conscript the compound tropes of village and villager. The notable difference, he points out, however, is in the overarching aim of the motifs' annexation in the newer stories. To him, these recent works are not exactly village novels in that their authors, he judges, are not principally "critiquing the genre's historical myth-making machinery or exploding utopian representations of the village." He finds ultimately that the above novels' and more broadly the contemporary fiction's "incorporation of the village or the villager" is driven largely by other considerations. It is motivated by "the necessity for aesthetic and thematic innovations in Nigerian fiction" (Osinubi, "Slavery" 134, 133). The quest for technical and ideological freshness may well be the paramount propellant behind the topical resilience of the village in the fiction. But another major and possibly more indisputable explanation is—as Achebe and Morrison would probably concur—the stubborn currency of "the old." It is the doggedness of "the past," the presumed "dead," in *and* to the village, as well as the city, in both Africa and (African) America.

Like Achebe, Morrison has pondered the village and the village-city topoi relative to her narrative canon and the African American experience. However, before engaging with her observations on the subject in her interview with Thomas LeClair and in "City Limits, Village Values" (1981), we should revisit her 1976 discussion with Robert Stepto. Morrison tells Stepto that by the time she got to her second and third novels, *Sula* and *Song of Solomon,* she had become more attuned to her memories of the potentials of the (Africa-transferred) village ground. She rekindled her fascination with its generative human and perspectival diversity. Unlike in *The Bluest Eye,* her debut work that relied on extracted autobiographical subjects, sources, and subtexts, however, she had started feeling "a very strong sense of place, not in terms of the country or the state," she says. She felt it relative to "the details, the feeling, the mood of the community, of the town" (10). Thus, with regard to *Sula,* for instance, her intention was to make "the town, the community, the neighborhood, as strong a character as I could" (Stepto 11).

When Morrison returned to the village sphere and the village-city theme and dynamic in conversations with LeClair, Judith Wilson, and Audrey T. McCluskey, and in "City Limits," as indicated, she reiterates but also extends the above retrospections. Morrison's sense of "the village" and village litera-ture aligns with Griswold and Achebe's depictions mentioned earlier. We recall Achebe reminding Searle that, although they may be city dwellers located at the disjunctions of traditional and modern systems of life, the African genera-tional characters in his and other African writers' urban-centered novels are, or once were, or have close kindship ties with, the village and villagers. Those urbanites' village or village-colored outlooks on life, society, (neighbor)hood, virtue, and vice tend to resist obliteration. As their novels *No Longer at Ease* and *Jazz* illustrate, a great many of the migrant, now-city folks (especially the first generation of them) are or were peasants, to use Morrison's description. Pointing to the foremost, clarifying task of the English novel for the inchoate British middle class at the outset of the Industrial Revolution, Morrison envi-sions her "village" stories (among which are *Beloved* and *Paradise,* as I argue in the next chapters) serving the dual but interwoven goals of commemoration and explication. She wants her fiction in general to testify, if you will; to render witness to change, to the receding pasts, the generational shifts and crossroads. She intends for it to re-present and—perhaps most critically significantly—to help preserve community's paradoxes and life affirmations, even in dysto-pia and tragedy. In doing so, her novels play a role compatible with that of their English precursors, to which we must add their African antecedents and contemporaries. But they will do that in the different backgrounds of African America's geographic location and racial history.

Morrison and Achebe consider it pressing to conserve the group-sustaining village and tribal memories, epistemologies, and (ritual) practices, which

Griswold theorizes usefully as a yardstick of the village novel. The preservation is so imperative that Morrison believes, as does Achebe, it is a thematic
inevitability. Village/clan/tribal beliefs and ideals find ways of thematically
intruding. They insist on their narrational representation and memorialization, even in African American fiction set in the city and focused on black
middle-class life. That remains true even under the brutal climates of slavery,
as *Beloved* illustrates. Morrison submits in "City Limits" that African American writers—female and male, past and contemporary—are also juggling those
obdurate interruptions of the vital black village pasts and mores. In a redux of
her much-cited interview with Stepto, Morrison hypothesizes that the ancestor or ancestral figure remains necessary in the lived, black urban spaces and
in black city-narratives. She contends that the differences in black and white
writers' reactions to the city and the village, as well as to the concreteness
and peculiar ambiences of those locations, are basically positional. They are a
function of each group's sociohistorical and material privileges, or lack thereof,
in America. Morrison insists, however, that so much hinges on the presence or
absence of *the village,* or of the village's backbone—that "wise Black ancestor"
("City Limits" 39)—in the urban-centered and/or urban-themed story, as well
as in actual city life. For that presence or absence impacts the black writer's
or the black urbanite's sense and level of well-being, engagement, and fulfill-
ment with the city. Or, conversely, it conditions and could exacerbate the literal
black urbanite's and the fictive black character's fears about, disillusion, and/or
disengagement with the city.

Naming, nonsequentially, but evidentially, canonical black authors from
Langston Hughes, James Baldwin, Toni Cade Bambara, Henry Dumas, Jean
Toomer, and James Alan McPherson, to Leon Forrest, Albert Murray, Paule
Marshal, R. Fischer, and Ralph Ellison, Morrison concludes: "Writer after
writer after writer concedes explicitly or implicitly that the ancestor is the
matrix of his yearning. The city is wholesome, loved when such an ancestor is
on the scene, when neighborhood links are secure," she asserts. "The country
is beautiful—healing, because more often than not, such an ancestor is there."
Harlem may best approximate a black metropolis in America, Morrison stipulates. And black music, particularly jazz, also may have given the impression
that African Americans are "urban types," she says, reminding us of Griswold's
point about *Things Fall Apart* and Umuofia's unwitting projection of the wrong
pictures of the Igbo-Nigerian-African village-community. To Morrison, however, the reality is that village values undergird all that ("City Limits"). If there

is one thing James Baldwin in "The Language of the Streets," Amiri Baraka in "Black Literature and the Afro-American Nation: The Urban Voice," Trudier Harris in *The Scary Mason-Dixon Line,* and the authors of the sixteen essays in *The City in African-American Literature* would agree with Morrison on, it is that "place" matters. The collection's editors, Yoshinobu Hakutani and Robert Butler, posit as follows: the city "has been—and continues to be—a live subject for black American writers." It has stirred "a rich diversity of literary visions of the city as it is captured by black writers from different times, places, backgrounds, and angles of perception" (12).

As the foregoing discussion shows, Achebe and Morrison affirm the legitimacy of the village-entangled and -inflected city as space, place, experience, sensibility, and leitmotif. They uniformly situate the village at the root of the socio-ethical verities interspersed in their fictional universes. Like Morrison, Achebe sees himself as reverential of the village's cornerstone, the ancestor. Also, the village is conceptually and creatively stimulating to both authors and to the analyses of their texts. Yet, it has to be underlined that the two novelists are not naïve and/or romantic about the village. As *Things Fall Apart* and *Beloved, No Longer at Ease* and *Jazz,* and *Arrow of God* and *Paradise* comparably demonstrate, neither the originating, traditional, antebellum "village" nor the sprawling, modern city or town is anything of a utopia, especially for their African and African American characters.

If in their respective modernist and postmodernist fictions Achebe and Morrison paint not facile but instead intricate pictures of village *and* city life, those unsentimental touches stem arguably from both writers' common interests in paradox. They are engendered, in this case, by the authors' shared appreciations of, but also their questioning attitudes toward, the "ancestor," "generations," "the past," and "change." I would like to address these intersecting factors, starting with "generation"/"generationality" and "the ancestor," and then working our way through the select rest, including "the past" and "change."

In the early 1960s, Achebe gave two important interviews that I would like to recall here. I want to engage with germane segments of those exchanges as important gateways into his thinking on generations and generational disjuncture. After that, I attend to Morrison's own views on that same temporal subject. The first Achebe interview in question was with the late, exiled South African novelist Lewis Nkosi in 1962. The second, occurring a year later in

1963, was a filmed and now YouTubed interview Achebe had with program-host Nkosi and (now Nobel laureate) Wole Soyinka together at the Nigerian Museum in Lagos. The interview was retranscribed by Bernth Lindfors and authorized for release by the English-language and Paris-based *Afrique Report* (or *Africa Report*). Achebe variably revisited the topic in subsequent years in his nonfiction prose writing or when reintroduced in an interview.

Prompted by Achebe's answer to his question that, yes, he, Achebe, was raised and attended school in the village in Eastern Nigeria, that his first actual encounter with a big city or town was Ibadan, and that change had been rapid although residues of the past remain, Nkosi wonders if Achebe sees all that as a dilemma. His response is poignant: basically, that, born into a pious Christian family, it took him until adulthood to appreciate the nature of the generational chasm and of those traditions he had all along assumed were invincible. In 1963, Nkosi, alongside questions he and Soyinka posed, returned again to that subject of generations, of the intersections and continuities of old and new relative to Achebe's writerly self and to Nigeria. Recognizing *that* disappearing present but equally highlighting the midway, Achebe did not see life in epochal frontiers as catastrophic. Rather, he viewed it as enlightening—a judgment Morrison shares. As Achebe tells Nkosi and Soyinka, he considers himself part of "a very fortunate generation," one that straddled intact old (village) ways and the upending new (Nkosi and Soyinka 13).

When Achebe reengages with those interwoven themes of the "middle ground," generational "crossroads," and "crossroads of cultures" in his 1973 autobiographical essay, in the lead piece of his 2009 retrospection *The Education of a British-Protected Child*, and in subsequent interviews, he brings greater nuance to the subjects. He reinforces their conceptual tapestry, broadening their relevance to art and creativity with an excursion into Igbo cosmology. In the whimsically titled "Named for Victoria, Queen of England," Achebe thinks of his generation as occupants of cultural "crossroads." He stresses the prospects as well as the perils of that rare but propitious historical emplace-ment ("Publishing" 90). To Achebe, "the crossroads" is precariously generative ("Named" 34). Perhaps in no other work by Achebe does he more lucidly lay out his view on generational and cultural interchanges than in his 1980 conver-sation with Jonathan Cott, aptly titled "Chinua Achebe: At the Crossroads." As though reminding Achebe of, or rather attesting to, his 1973 statement above, Cott suggests to him, in the course of their exchange, that he, Achebe, inhabits multiple "crossroads." To which Achebe then waxes:

I think this is the most important and fascinating thing about our life—
the crossroad. This is where the spirits meet the humans, the water
meets the land, the child meets the adult—these are the zones of power,
and I think this is really where stories are created. The middle of the
day is a very potent hour in our folklore—noon. This is the time when
morning merges into afternoon, and that is the moment when spirits
are abroad. When the adults go to the farm and leave the children at
home, then the spirits can come into the village. (Cott 80).

Just moments before the above erudition, another of Cott's assertions
about Achebe's generational bestriding of village values and those of a fast-
modernizing Nigeria obtained Achebe's amplification that residents of historical crossroads are indeed fortunate. But as exciting, lucky, and scarce as this
generational positioning is, Achebe broods, it engenders the twin burdens of
ambivalence and unbelonging (Cott 79). In the eponymous "The Education
of a British-Protected Child," Achebe extends these thoughts. Before its 2009
publication, the essay, in its initial iteration, was given as the Ashby Lecture at
Cambridge University on January 22, 1993. In it, he again invokes the enduring
authority of Igbo metaphysics. In an answer that sheds important light on why
he fictionalizes the village unblinkingly, he contends that his people prioritize "the *middle* ground." That stays true even though "That middle ground"
is unpopular and unpronounced. Regardless, the Igbo consider it fortuitous
and prudent. The reason is that, to them, it barricades totalizations and grand
narratives (5).

If Morrison readers can attest to one thing, it is her equally uncompromis-
ing preference of intricacy and intermediacy to binaries and extremes. On this
villagist philosophy of life lived and art created in the middle-ground, at the
crossroads, she and Achebe are consistent. Morrison similarly sees her artistic,
intellectual, and ideological postures on complexity and balance as generational. She regards them, together, as the village worldview of an equally, generationally transitional black person. They are the stances of a black woman and
author whose then-five-year-old maternal grandfather—living in an America
that was at "the crossroads between its slaveholding past and the possibility
of a truly inclusive, vibrant democracy" (C. Anderson 8)—not only witnessed
the dawn of Emancipation. He also came to maturation at the conjunctions of
early twentieth-century historical epochs. Thus, as Morrison acknowledges,
"The relationships of the generations have always been paramount to me in

all of my works" (Ruas 103), as illustrated in her focal novels, especially *Paradise*, which shares that theme with *Arrow of God*. Things are markedly not the same nowadays as they were when she was a child (Houston 249), Morrison has reflected. Sharing also Achebe's insistence that he would never adopt the position that "the Old must win or that the New must win" (Emenyonu and Emenyonu 41), Carolyn C. Denard maintains with Morrison that the challenge "is trying to balance those two environments" ("Blacks, Modernism" 181). The question is how to reconcile those contiguous temporalities and mind-sets. It is about how to mediate the cultural alienation they precipitated and could, even in one's village-community and most certainly in the city, as Achebe and Morrison's characters experience.

With her life journey begun in the village neighborhood, Morrison reached adulthood in the middle of the twentieth century with an abiding sense of change, as did Achebe. Looking back, she nursed a brooding awareness of how quickly moments were receding. She sensed things being "lost" from an inevitably vanishing present, to evoke the distinguished postcolonial theorist and feminist critic Gayatri Chakravorty Spivak. As Morrison once put it in a 1977 interview with Steve Cannon and Ntozake Shange: "I have this creepy sensation . . . of loss. Like something is either lost, never to be retrieved, or something is about to be lost and will never be retrieved" (qtd in Samuels and Hudson-Weems 139). Other than Morrison perceiving and deploring "the apparent loss of compound, of village, of community, of neighborhood," as Wilfred Samuels and Clenora Hudson-Weems aptly phrase *place* (140), however, there is another loss, another temporal change, she and Achebe uniformly highlight and regret. That "loss" is the prevailing trend of familial and sociocultural disinvestment in the village-inaugurated oral storytelling. Traditional storytelling, which hitherto entertained, enlivened, enlightened, and helped unify (village) families, has been displaced mostly by modern and technological alternatives.

Thus, it would not be unusual to find Morrison prefixing, elaborating, or concluding her village thoughts on generations and change with contrastive phrases of *loss*. She would say things like: "When I was growing up," "When I was a little girl," "it used to be," "as we used to," "as they used to," "now," "Today," "in those days," "These days," "this generation," "future generations," "I was born in a period where," "I was born at the time when," "when I was young," "I remember" my parents, grandparents, grandmother, and/or grandfather saying or doing such and such.[6] This Morrison-Achebe generational, philosophical, and affective overlap is so remarkable that Mustapha Marrouchi describes Morrison using exactly Achebe's terms and their Igbo cosmological underpinning mentioned earlier. In addition to qualifying Morrison's work as postcolonial, Marrouchi describes her as "the author at the 'crossroads'—noon—the most potent hour of African-American culture, when morning merges into afternoon. The crossroads itself is a site of creative imagination for her: 'This is where the spirits meet humans, the water meets the land, the child meets the adult—these are the zones of power, and I think this is where stories are created'" (256). It is inexplicable that Marrouchi fails to credit Achebe as the source of this riff and obvious misattribution in his book. Rather, and mystifyingly, he associates it with Morrison and Wilson Harris. Nevertheless, it is instructive that Marrouchi, through a Freudian slip of sorts, relativizes Igbo and African American cultural consciousness. But what the foregoing further evinces, however, is the extent of Morrison and Achebe's generational concordances. Also disclosed is how the temporal and geographic shifts and interconnections on both sides of the Atlantic filtered into their creativity and attitudes to life, especially their views on originary settlement, primogenitors, and anteriority.

As novelists of the village, Achebe and Morrison treasure the ancestor. They value the black ancestor's or ancestral figures' cultural, generational, and philosophical preeminence. But as coadherents of the interstitial—a positioning to which the postcolonial theorist Homi K. Bhabha equally subscribes (ix–27)—the two authors are not obsessed with affecting slogans. Nor are they enamored of exclusionary badges, and/or far-leaning logics. Rather, they are comparably pragmatists, especially on questions of racial pride and on the complicated serviceability of (racial) memory and the past. For as G. D. Killam has written of Achebe, he is not just "an interpreter of the cultural worth of his own society." He is also a "critic of the quality of that life" (10). So, too, is Morrison, relative to African America and America in general. To channel Denise Heinze, Morrison is "a mythbasher" in a nation where, for instance, "writers have been canonized for creating and perpetuating the myths that form the foundation of the American way of thinking" not only about itself and black people but also a host of other subjects (3). Maxine Lavon Montgomery agrees, noting that "much of the enduring appeal of her writing stems from her ability to challenge old ways of knowing, predictable ways of thinking, and established ways of seeing." In Morrison's stories, Montgomery adds, "there is no such thing as a singularly constituted past or a heritage that one can easily recover" (2, 3).

Consider this, then, in Achebe's case. In 1963, Achebe told Nkosi and Soyinka that he thought of himself as "an ancestor worshipper," not in the libational style of his grandfather, however, but rather in the manner of obligatory acknowledgment and commemoration (14). To Morrison, relatedly, ancestor annihilation can be culturally if not existentially catastrophic for a people (J. Wilson 131), she stipulates, reiterating her stances in "Rootedness" and "City Limits." In a 1962 interview with *Afrique,* Achebe addresses a purported Ezekiel Mphalele comment that his *No Longer at Ease* is overly pessimistic. He sees the matter differently. To him, it is not cynicism or melancholy per se. It is rather the bluntness that disallows the disguising of truth. That frankness eschews the unproductive camouflaging of national malaises "under a poetic veil or under a lyricism of the past." Old-school and old-villagist, Achebe is antislogan, as is Morrison. This is indicated in her mixed feelings about the 1960s insinuations of black peculiar soulfulness. She is thrilled neither with "reactionary myth-making" nor the slogan "Black Is Beautiful."[7] "I am against slogans," Achebe once declared. "I don't think, for example, that 'negritude' has any meaning whatsoever. Pan-Africanism? Perhaps. Negritude, no." Achebe acknowledges, as does Wole Soyinka in his piece "From a Common Backcloth" (8), that certain ideologies and their insignia served important purposes at particular historical junctures in Africa. However, Achebe could not fathom the hunger for the past among so many African writers, particularly the Francophone African authors. He could not comprehend the clamoring for "the golden age" most notable in the works of Leopold Senghor, Mongo Beti, and Camara Laye, whose *The Radiance of the King* he praised, though skeptical about its choice of white protagonist (*Afrique* 8–9).

Should one notice in modern African literature a recurring engagement with "the past" or what Achebe phrases as "the 'era of purity,' before the coming of Europe," that fixation is largely dialectical, a countertendency. It is in many ways African writers' and African intellectuals' contrapuntal response to the long-perpetuated and self-serving European delusions about the continent (Lindfors et al. 27). Achebe finds it preposterous that some people actually advocate disremembering the past because—as he insists in a point that mirrors Morrison's thesis in *Beloved*—the past conditions the present. Yet, he cautions, one should not "be mesmerized or immobilized" by it (Emenyonu and Emenyonu 38). He emphatically rejects returning and clinging to the past, even in matters as existentially consequential as religion (Ogbaa, "Interview" 69). The village and, concomitantly, the historical past may be *instructive*. Significantly, it may hold the light and the lessons. It may even encapsulate the delight of illumination as well as the necessity for caveats. But to Achebe, personally, the matter of "the past" was settled.

Morrison seems to agree, as she describes "fiddling around in my books with the past." In keeping with the Sankofa and village mandate, she has to gaze backward, retrieve, and address the earlier times, first, before proceeding to more recent concerns (Koenen 71). As does Achebe, Morrison finds the past—for which the village is synecdoche—prefatory, predictive, generative, even fascinating. Certainly, the novel should attempt to capture the past's grandeur and indicate the latter's purposiveness, Morrison has explained. Yet, she is equally restrained and realistic, even mediatory and far-sighted, about the past (Ruas 113). The inherent danger of novelistic obsession with the past is glamorization, she warns (LeClair 125). As she further explained in 1996, she does not wish "to reinvent the past as idyllic" or transform it into a menacing and enlightening weapon (Hackney 128–29).

In no other of his influential essays does Achebe, like Morrison in "Rootedness," more pointedly espouse the project of *instruction,* or elevation of consciousness as an authorial and aesthetic ideal, than in his frequently quoted 1965 piece "The Novelist as Teacher." Achebe wishes he could rephrase that essay's title in order to forestall the sometimes gross misreading of his associating of novelist and teacher. Like Morrison, he is well aware that the novelist, the creative artist, is literally not a classroom instructor. Nor is the storyteller an evangelist or political propagandist. However, as it is the village ancestral figure's obligation to enlighten, Achebe considers it his duty to help counteract the mental assault of colonization (and before that slavery). This is a psychological attack so deep and dispersed in foundational texts, fictional narratives, and in academic, visual, and material culture, and at times potently indeterminate, it almost afflicted Achebe's first child, Chinelo. In her white-run nursery school in Lagos in the early 1960s, Chinelo had started forming what Achebe and his wife, Christie, worried were "very strange notions about race and colour." This occurred after little Chinelo read a supposedly benign but actually racially damaging children's storybook that paints Africa/Africans as Europe's foil. In it, Africa is naked, primal, and superstitious, and Europe is modern, technologically superior, and divine.[8] It is that racial and psychological harm that is symptomized, in Morrison's debut novel, in the craving for bluest eyes by young Pecola Breedlove, whose story Morrison says she modeled after "a real little girl . . . a neighborhood friend" her age, when she was "seven or eight years," a "pitch black" girl who did not know how "beautiful" she was, but who was adamantly skeptical about God's existence because God never responded to her fervent prayers for blue eyes (Elkann 153–54). Besides God in heaven helping and protecting the black child besieged on earth, such as the now-grown but deeply scarred woman Frank's sister Cee, who was "Branded early as an unlovable, barely tolerated 'gutter child' by Lerone, the only one whose opinion mattered to her parents," Achebe—like the gifted "women with seen-it-all eyes" who heal Cee back to life and self-rescue in Morrison's *Home* (165–67)—deems it his earthly goal to beneficially deploy his skills and craft. He seeks to utilize what he unabashedly embraces as his "applied art" in reinforcing his people's slavery- and colonization-corroded sources of self-regard—to channel Morrison (Achebe, "Novelist as Teacher" 45). His stance on ethical art is firm because it is undergirded by a village and cosmological imperative. For the earth goddess Ani/Ana/Ala, that powerful and ubiquitous Igbo deity, "is also the goddess of art and morality" (see Cott 82).

Achebe and Morrison are therefore insistently opposed to narrative exhortation. That aversion holds, in Achebe's case, for instance, regardless of his belief that narrative, the story, whether concerned with the village or the city, should inspire antiphony with the reader. And the antipathy stands, irrespective of his championing of *applied* art, one that—like open-ended and inductive village folklore—delights just as it clarifies. It heightens awareness and thus *teaches* in the sense of "helping the pupil to discover . . . to explore" (Wilkinson 47). Achebe admits to being criticized by some for his disinclination to "prescribe," to "offer solutions." He would not dissuade other writers from proposing remedies, if they are so moved and sure of their visions and judgments. But, as he maintains, he himself has no desire to decree for the continent (T. Hall 24), a sentiment to which Morrison would nod in affirmation. Should a writer lack a fresh idea on the past or contemporaneous moment, Morrison has advised, then it perhaps should be rethought if not abandoned altogether (Jones and Vinson 183). Morrison's experience with her formative neighborhood's village heterogeneity, and her allowance of the ennobling as well as the bizarre, should be hint enough that she, like Achebe, is unwilling to mandate for others what to write. Nor has she any intention to dictate for them how to write it. Morrison's avid reading of detective stories, her viewing of soap operas, her indulgence in juicy gossip, and her tolerance of reality television speak additionally to her villagist accommodativeness. But were she to choose, she would be interested in fiction, in stories, that while sophisticatedly conceived and composed are neither overly pedantic nor lofty. For, to Morrison, outright and sententious didacticism would be "really a cardinal sin" for a black writer addressing black people, who, she said, "have never taken direction well" (Naylor, "A Conversation" 202). As such, Morrison declares, her "mode of writing is subliminally didactic" in the strict sense that she "can only warn by taking something away" (Koenen 74). In arguing that "Morrison constructs her role as [that of] artist-teacher" (151–52), Judylyn S. Ryan evokes Achebe's famous essay. She also additionally strengthens the two authors' philosophic and artistic ties. That Morrison's works are a beacon is a consensus shared by Juda Bennett, Winnifred Brown-Glaude, Cassandra Jackson, and Piper Kendrix Williams. In their recent collaborative project *The Toni Morrison Book Club* (2020), the group declares: "if you want to fully understand the evolving nature of America, Morrison's novels are the perfect guide and inspiration" (8).

Like the inspiring village storytellers, Morrison does not just curtail authorial explanation in narratives. She also accompanies and supports the reader in absorbing her often zigzagging and intense rendering of what she understates as her "very simple story about complicated people" (LeClair 121). Her aim is to "enlighten without pontification," she says. That helps explain her works' inclinations toward postmodernist ambiguities and irresolution. She shares those artistic tendencies with Achebe, who and whose work are not usually associated with literary postmodernism—a universalizing discourse and praxis that Madhu Dubey has questioned. Dubey challenges its "assuming a white Western subject as its normative center" when African American experience (to which one must add the situations of the Third World and other global subalterns), for instance, are central to its underlying assumptions (7). Like the village folktale that anteceded and in part informed it, Achebe's fiction is also often ambivalent. The reason, he says, is because he does not enervate subjects and inspirations in his novels (Fabre 50–51). Morrison suggests that conclusive denouements—the kinds that tidy every little loose end in character, theme, and/or form—can be negating. They sometimes abruptly terminate the active reader's participatory imagination and visceral judgment. As an author-protégé to traditional village storytellers, however, she counts on audience input in the realization of her novels' often unspecified and unexhausted agendas (Ruas 1). But whereas oral storytelling in familial settings of African villages was conventionally performed in the vernaculars, Achebe and

Morrison's textual trilogies, authored and printed in a novel form originally alien to Africa, also face the added challenge. They have to communicate in an equally inherited foreign tongue, especially for Achebe. Calling it a raced language, Morrison and Achebe routinely tweak English to be able to cast at the village and the city that blunt and unblinking look that both authors talk about.

We may recall George Nyamndi postulating earlier that one of the defining tendencies of village literature or the village novel, specifically, is linguistic consciousness and reform. The genre strives "to construct an idiom and a rhythm in which are reflected the African resources of diction" (17–18). Achebe and Morrison share that awareness. They were for years committed to that formal goal, as their literary corpuses demonstrate. The English language, or rather Achebe and Morrison's allied attitudes to it, have arguably been the most underscored of their connections. As previously suggested, those critical notations have somewhat followed Morrison's lead. She has, unwittingly, nudged commentators in that direction by way of her circumscription of the Achebean lessons on her work to language rectification and gaze reversal. It would not be an exaggeration to state, however, that since Achebe and Morrison's momentous emergences in the global literary scene, critics have expended enormous time and energy anatomizing their writerly approaches to the English language. As noted earlier, Morrison did not specify, even at the AAI address, what the Achebean linguistic influences are but instead acknowledged them in unspecific strokes. Thus, I hesitate to presume those particularities on her behalf. I would rather address my remarks to both writers' broad areas of ideological and practical consensus on language and language use.

It has been the bane of African, African American, African diaspora, and, as Barbara Hill Rigley appends, "African American feminine/feminist text[s]" (7), that they have had to remain deeply conscious of, if not always anxious about, their fraught relationship to the hegemonic English language. They have had to be superaware of their uneasy affinity to the other imposed and inherited European father-mother-tongues, for instance, French, Portuguese, and Spanish. Achebe and Morrison rank quite highly among African and African American writers who have more consistently and recognizably made overhauling the English language a mission in at least the past half century. And that opinion is proffered with due regard to Ngũgĩ wa Thiongo's well-publicized and ambitious counterpropensity in the late 1980s to write fiction in and have it translated from his native Gikuyu. As Simon Gikandi observes, however, Ngũgĩ promptly rethought and suddenly rescinded this linguistic divorce. He

was "defeated," Gikandi argues, "by the reality of exile and American professional life" ("Traveling" 194).

As Achebe recognizes in his 1964 essay "The Role of the Writer in a New
Nation," there are, unquestionably, significant drawbacks for an African writer
who elects English as narrative medium. One such difficulty, he suggests, is
the inadequacy of English to express certain African phenomena and/or logic
(12). As he construes the problematic in 1965, however, the actual contention
is not about Africans' proficiency in the language—if they can so master it to
the point of writing it with the left hand, as *Arrow of God* hypothesizes. Rather,
the core issue is one of prudence and loyalty, even ethics: "Is it right that a
man should abandon his mother-tongue for someone else's?," Achebe asks. "It
looks like a dreadful betrayal and produces a guilty feeling." But after invoking
James Baldwin's subversive stance on English—to which one must add Soyinka's reflection in his essay "Language" on the historical (mis)handling of
English by black diasporic and postcolonial writers, intellectuals, and activists
(88)—Achebe determines that, yes, the English language can convey his raced,
village-and-modern African self and existence. However, "it will have to be a
new English, still in full communion with its ancestral home but altered to suit
its new African surroundings" ("English" 30). For "the price a world language
must be prepared to pay," he insists, "is submission to many different kinds of
use" (29), one of them being the thematic and formal imperatives of the village
novel and village literature at large.

Morrison would agree with that assessment. As she asserts in "The Trouble with Paradise" (272–74) but more compellingly in the 1998 piece "Home"
in which she details her struggle for a different phrase for the one she originally penned as the most suitable summary to *Beloved*: "As an already- and
always raced writer, I knew from the very beginning that I could not, would
not, reproduce the master's voice and its assumptions of the all-knowing law of
the white father." She adds, significantly, that her enduring attempt to maneu-
ver American English was not narrowly a question of linguistic interchange, of
substituting standard English with black vernacular, for example. Her intents,
she declares, recalling Achebe above, were to peel off "the accretions of deceit,
blindness, ignorance, paralysis, and sheer malevolence embedded in raced language so that other kinds of perception were not only available but were inevitable" ("Home" 4, 7). "To dissect Morrison's language," Lucille P. Fultz correctly
observes, "is to be privy to a majestic mind at work" (9). Or, as Zadie Smith
puts it in her earlier-mentioned foreword to *The Measure of Our Lives*, "Just as

there is a Keatsian sentence and a Shakespearean one, so Morrison made a sentence distinctly hers, abundant in compulsive, self-generating metaphor, as full of sub-clauses as a piece of 19th century presidential oratory" (vi–vii).

To the critic, college student, or high school instructor new to Achebe and Morrison, or the general reader wondering where, besides their fiction, both authors have more elaborately voiced their uniform stances on the debate on English language, there are helpful illustrations.[9] Nonetheless, as earlier averred, Morrison—whom Yvette Christiansë calls "a writer who writes about writing" as much as she chronicles the undergirding African American experience (5)—is imprecise in her reference to Achebe's linguistic lesson. Yet, besides her verbal and written affirmations of his novels, I believe she also left clues in one particular location as to what she may have valued in his positions on the English-language issue. Just as I would point readers interested in the potential impact of Achebe's Conrad essay on Morrison's *Playing in the Dark* to Anne V. Adams's Baldwin-evoking tribute to Achebe, so too would I suggest that the hints lie in the 1965 Achebe essay "English and the African Writer." Morrison not only singled that piece out for praise and read it verbatim and almost in toto at PEN America; she also mentions it in the AAI speech. There are also philosophical consonances between Achebe's "Thoughts on the African Novel" and Morrison's meditations on language and on what she believes should be the distinctive topographies of black art.

And, finally, one area of narration into which Achebe and Morrison have consistently forayed beyond their villagist preoccupation with overhauling and tempering the racially thorny English language is the compound world of "tragedy," "the tragic," "the tragic mode." Achebe and Morrison seamlessly engraft their village-informed and unsentimental standpoints on existence in their common handling of this nodal mode. The two authors try to reach and *teach* particularly their black audiences, in the village and the city, through the tragic. To that end, they share an interest in the inner core of characters more than in the events around personae, as important and determinative as those circumstances often are or can be. It is interesting to note that both writers are also creatively and ideologically fascinated with character defeats and open-ended tragic closings more than in success and happy outcomes. As a result, their novels have been deemed pessimistic—an assessment they welcome.

Achebe's and Morrison's views on tragedy so cohere in phrasing and illustration they seem to have emanated from the same fount, or from "a common Backcloth," to lease Soyinka's phrase again. Take these, for example. Early in his career, as Achebe recalls in a 1973 chat with Michel Fabre, someone, possibly John Updike,[10] "suggested that there is a sense of failure in my novels. Why do my heroes fail, as Ezeulu does?" Achebe's direct answer to that self-query is simple yet sagacious and enlightening. He is thematically obsessed with failure, he says, because failure, particularly noble failure, is far more compelling than triumph, at least from the standpoint of narrative and affect. Death, he argues, compels more interest than the opposite. However, the critical question he believes ought to be asked about an individual is how well she or he manages. How does one "'perform in an extreme situation?' That, in itself, is a story." Achebe is convinced, then, that as a metaphysical and existential matter failure is often misapprehended. His take is that his stories' tragic heroes Okonkwo and Ezeulu actually live on, that they do not fail. Nor are they *failures,* given their transcendent narrative and earthly causes and our persistent postmortem remembrances of them. For those reasons, Achebe urges a rethinking of the idea, leitmotif, and sociocultural experience of failure (Fabre 45–51). Similarly, Morrison tells Nellie McKay, in 1983, that her fiction is replete with characters she intentionally subjects to considerable existential pressures, the objective being to ascertain their coping capacities and channels. Recalling Achebe's anecdote above about a reader who expressed shock and disappointment that he summarily deposed his larger-than-life hero Ezeulu in *Arrow of God,* Morrison talks about how "a woman once got angry with me because Pilate died. She was very incensed about it." Pilate's death at the hands of Guitar is purposeful, she says she clarified to the upset reader. It is consciously structured in the story as the hugely impactful murder of a high-profile and beloved community figure; an act, as it were, that helps unmask and paint a deeper picture of the nature, consequences, and occasional irrationality of violence. Morrison then muses, "Pilate is larger than life," anyway. She "never really dies in that sense." So, she concludes soundly, citing Pilate's absent navel and self-birth, the almost eschatological issues of "birth" and "death" are immaterial and perceptual.[11]

On the Sites, Sights, and Sounds of Achebe and Morrison's Village and Village-Connected Muses: Jazz, Painting, Mbari, Masquerade

In all, if Achebe and Morrison readers, whether dazzled or dazed, are wondering what *really* gives the two authors' texts their textures, their identifiably Achebean and Morrisonian touches of aesthetic intricacy and emotional intensity, the answer may lie in the equally kindred but, before now, critically unconnected muses that shape the two authors' shaping of their stories. It is not any white, Western author, text, or trope that Morrison encountered earlier or later in her life and career. Nor is it, for Achebe, Joseph Conrad's *Heart of Darkness* and Joyce Cary's *Mister Johnson* as generally presumed, and sometimes overly emphasized, given Achebe's well-known objections to both books and his avowed desire to revise and signify on them in his insider-narratives. Helping facilitate those Achebean and Morrisonian signatures of thematic and technical profundity, and concomitantly their complex renderings of black life and histories in villages and cities, are both authors' muses: painting and music for Morrison, and Igbo mbari art and the dancing Mask or masquerade, for Achebe.

That these are both authors' muses is remarkable, especially considering the prominence Houston A. Baker Jr., in *Modernism and the Harlem Renaissance*, also assigns the mask/masking in African American lived experience, intellectual history, and creative imagination (9–36). Achebe and Morrison have elected as their creative fires visual arrays and village-community-centered musical arrangements and performances that are arguably compatible as symbolizing categories. For, at least in the mimetic and semiotic relations I have in mind here and will broach in a moment, Morrison's representational fount of "painting" is, in essence and practice, apodictically parallel to (the architectural, sculptural, and painted modalities of) Achebe's mbari art. And, her model of "music" finds kinship in Achebe's dancing Mask or masquerade. These overlaps are fascinating and generative to me. As such, one should not be halted from even contemplating the four authorial inspirations together simply because, as the counterargument to the juxtaposition might go: art conception in "the West" is notoriously product-driven as opposed to process-oriented. It is not ritualistically produced or deitally commissioned. It is more often than not divested of communal celebratory and social utility through museum curation. Although she liked to dance and was good at it, although she has composed musicals and in college was a member of a drama group that toured the South, Morrison—the counter-reasoning might add—is actually not a musician. Nor did she ever participate in an Igbo and ethnic-specific mbari festival. So why view her work as *mbarist,* even if that usage in this study is clearly adjectival and relational? And, lastly, the jazz-mbari temporal concurrence, discussed below, is just coincidence and nothing more, the rebuttal continues. Thus, why not just leave it at that instead of indulging serendipity? That all these may be valid cautions and caveats to my transatlantic pairing of mbari and Morrison's muses, especially, makes the present intellectual labor, this cultural studies and comparative approach, even more warranted and worthwhile, as the following elucidation will hopefully show.

Although Morrison does not totally discount but rather, and often, qualifies the influence of other writers on her work, she does, however, unequivocally connect herself and her style with painters, painting, and music. "I always think I am much more influenced by painters in my writing than by novelists," she has said. "I can feel direct influence of painters. I can't feel them in novelists that I have read" (Jones and Vinson 175). Paintings and related architectural mnemonics help Morrison visualize her novels' plots and spatial settings, as well as the intricate patterns of human habitation, conduct, and relationships in the village as well as in the city communities of her stories. And instead of the incessant comparisons to white writers, especially Faulkner, Morrison regards herself and her work to be more in tune with "something that has probably only been fully expressed in music, or in some other culture-gen" perpetuated by community and tradition (N. McKay 153). To Morrison, jazz, that Africa-inspirited musical genre in question, is always her standard, the "mirror" that provides her aesthetic "clarity" and informs her deliberate effort to replicate the music's formal conventions in her texts (Rushdie 181). In writing *Jazz*, she has said, she did not just keep in mind the contrived angle of the writing exercise. She also imagined herself a jazz musician, one who has to rehearse extensively in a bid to innovate and make her art appear natural and elegant. Morrison describes jazz as highly involved, cosmopolitan, taxing, modern, potentially hedonistic, and unlawful. She would like her work to mimic jazz in terms of her art being, as she says, "demanding and sophisticated," yet affectively reachable to a wide reading and listening audience (Dreifus 106). While she strives for the story proper to be the engine that propels readers through a narrative's pages, she needs the aesthetic enchantment to come from "moving away from the story and coming back to it, looking around it, and through it, as though it were a prism, constantly turning" (Schappell 80). Achebe's narrative under-structures evoke this picture Morrison paints of the reader/audience/spectator turning and viewing the prism from multiple directions in order to apprehend that prism in its many-sidedness, its chromatic and refractive totality.

One of those understructures, for Achebe, is the village-/community-evolved mbari. Mbari lends his seminal fictional works, aesthetic formulations, and philosophical meditations their cosmological specificity, range, depth, credence, and panache. Achebe in his stories reminds us of griots, writes Omar Sougu in "Didactic Aesthetics: Achebe, the Griot and Mbari Artist" (2004). It is mbari, however, that inflects many of the (Igbo) views of existence and creativity that Achebe knits in his prose writings, lectures, interviews, and fiction, in this case *Things Fall Apart, No Longer at Ease,* and *Arrow of God.* "If we look only to the handful of occasions on which Achebe alluded to mbari in his biographical and essayistic output, we might be tempted to think that his engagement with mbari was cursory," but that is not the case, Terri Ochiagha points out, citing also Anthonia Kalu. Kalu has similarly commented on the aesthetic (re)generativity of mbari and other African cultural forms (Ochiagha, *Short History* 29–30).

So taken was Achebe with mbari, so visually splendid and theoretically enriching did he find it initially and afterward, he reflects on the tradition in many of his essays. They include "Africa and Her Writers," "The Writer and His Community," "The Igbo World and Its Art,"[12] and the essay volume *The Education of a British-Protected Child.* And so engraved in Achebe's artistic, ethical, and ideological consciousness have scholars adjudged mbari that one critic, Claudio Gorlier, adopts it as the metaphor for Achebe and his artistic vision in the essay "Mbari versus Conrad: Chinua Achebe's Aesthetics." According to Ezenwa-Ohaeto, whose earlier-mentioned literary biography of Achebe must be required reading for Achebe critics and/or students, it appears Achebe encountered mbari initially during his student days at Nekede, Owerri, in the 1930s and early 1940s. And it was he, Achebe, who suggested the word/tradition "Mbari" to Ulli Beier as the name for the literary association "Mbari Writers' and Artists' Club" that Beier, Soyinka, Achebe, Zeke Mphahlele, and others would found around 1961 (see also Currey, "Literary").

While Ezenwa-Ohaeto usefully sketches mbari as "the formal creation of art works as sacrifices to the gods" (19), Achebe calls it "a celebration, through art, of the world and of the life lived in it. It was performed by the community on command by its presiding deity, usually the earth goddess, Ala or Ana" (*Education* 110–11). Achebe points out that mbari was neither a presupposition of nor even a gesture to paradise. It was instead an affirmation of life, of the world, as it was concretely lived and conceptually relived by the celebrants (*Education* 110–11). Achebe's theorization of the grandeur and expressive platform of the village-/community-celebrated mbari tradition is quite incisive. Not only does it further validate Ernest Emenyonu's praise of Achebe's often unsung capacities at literary and aesthetic theorization. It also would be beneficial to readers curious about the mbari house's integrative but ephemeral materiality, guild construction, and disharmonious layout.

However, it is to Herbert M. Cole's authoritative study *Mbari: Art and Life among the Owerri Igbo*, upon which Achebe also draws, that I would like to turn for extra assistance in my limited attempt here to situate the tradition as a critically significant cultural and semiotic corollary to Morrison's aesthetic inspirations of painting and music/jazz. Cole depicts mbari in ways evocative of Morrison's many-sided prism and diamond. He pictures it as juxtapositional and combinatory; its directive is continual and seemingly effortless experimentation and transmutation. The mbari house incongruously blends "architecture, sculpture, and painting," Cole writes (155). It is matrix, mural, and mimesis (156). In an explanation that also brings to mind jazz's many-sidedness—its elemental ethos of syncopation, polyrhythm, solo improvisations, and instrumental riffs on changes—Cole posits that regardless of the degree to which mbari artists adhere to standards, to customary techniques and samples of portraiture, every substantial mbari exhibit strikingly discloses a combination of rearticulated and/or fresh objects, "variations on earlier themes" (157). As Cole states, a significant and signature feature of mbari "is the license, indeed the mandate, to update, change, and innovate. Both copying and inventing are sanctioned by the institution and the society in which artists operate" (158).

Following that injunction, then, mbari houses complicate their constitutive mediums and approximated figures. Achebe describes the exhibited or re-presented objects as "jostled together for space in that extraordinary convocation of the entire kingdom of human experience and imagination" (*Education* 109). To the conglomerate inventoried by Achebe, Cole adds consumer, domestic, imported, social, and technological products, among other displays. To Cole, mbari encapsulates the Igbo proclivity for "innovation and change" (167). And to Achebe, it reflects the Igbo view of art not as "product" but instead a "process," a reification of kinetic complementarity, in short, the intermediary between past and present, old and new, accepted conventionality and stupendous irregularity (Achebe, "Igbo World" 64, 65).

If one thing complements as well as upholds mbari's importance and its aesthetic labyrinthine in Igbo culture, thought, and creativity, it would be the village-connected mask, more specifically, the multigenre and multivalent spectacle that is the masquerade, with its accompanying music. Both are evident for readers in the mask discourses and *egwugwu* scenes in Achebe's works, especially *Things Fall Apart, No Longer at Ease, Arrow of God,* and *A Man of the People.* As Achebe has noted, were masquerading, especially the Ijele, not so male-dominated in Igboland, it would be regarded as the preeminent art. It does not just involve "dance." It also incorporates "sculpture, music, painting, drama, costumery, even architecture, for the Ijele masquerade is indeed a most fabulously extravagant construction" ("Igbo World" 65). The idea of the masquerade's male-centrism should be qualified, however. Chinyere G. Okafor argues persuasively throughout her study *Gender, Performance and Communication* that "the contribution of women as both persons and as conceptual ideas in mask performances" cannot be denied (138). This village-originated spectacle or "'wonder' popularly called the masquerade," Okafor writes, "has fascinated many indigenous African audiences as well as visitors and researchers in precolonial and postcolonial times. Global literature and folklore convey fascination of the masking concept through tales, rituals, dramatic and other expressions." The enchantment with mask, Okafor adds, "is played out in African traditional villages where it functions in entertainment, arbitration, communication, and social control" (6). Calling it "one of the most complex and secretive, yet profoundly important, phenomena in Africa," and concurring with Okafor that it serves "religious, political and social functions," Chika Okeke-Agulu contends, citing evidence offered by Phyllis Galembo's photographs, that despite all the "pressures" exerted on the "theatre" that is masking by "the forces of secularization, fundamentalist Christianity and radical Islam," the tradition perseveres in "vibrant form[s] in parts Africa and its diaspora" (Introduction 4–9).

It would be hard to overstate the implications of the above discussion and common denominators for Achebe-Morrison scholarship, inadequately described and substantiated though the confluences may be. As earlier inferred, both authors' stated influences (painting, music/jazz, mbari, masquerade,) correlate culturally and signally. For example: the Igbo village abhorrence of dichotomies and reductionism in favor of perspectival broadness and wholeness calls to attention Morrison's earlier equation of the thematic and stylistic spectrum of black women's and by extension African American writings to a multisided diamond. It also parallels her representation of the story—in this case her always complex, thought-provoking, and open-ended village texts—as a turning prism. As prism, or like a diamond, narrative refracts differently to each gaze/gazer (read: reading/reader/audience) based on observational/interpretive position, positioning, and methodology. The story, like the complexly outfitted (Ijele) masquerade, is something that one can appreciate fully only through close, sometimes detached, shifting, and/or circular viewing/

reading/critique. But perhaps the most fascinating of the correlations is the historical and generational congruencies of jazz[13] and modern mbari. Both date back to the 1920s and 1930s. For although extant photographs indicate the existence of mbari houses as far back as 1904, and although the tradition continued into the late 1960s, according to Cole, the modern forms of mbari evolved in the 1920s or early 1930s (167), contemporaneous with the Jazz Age.

The originary village-like context and/or atmosphere of jazz's beginnings could not be any more discernible than in the historic New Orleans Congo Square. In that (in)famous clearing, enslaved, overworked, and multiethnic Africans, through social interaction, commerce, song, and dance, found periodic and momentary release from—or was it rather a *masking* of—their private pains and collective suffering. As the poet Paul Laurence Dunbar suggests in his still-contemporaneous poem "We Wear the Mask" (Hill 615), the ethos of concealment and parody, of sometimes understated (black) intelligence and tactical rebellion, enacted particularly in white spaces and before white gaze and power, has often been a requisite for black people's success and survival, not only in America's midwestern and northern cities but also in its rural South and other parts of the world to this day. "In the face of white surveillance," Adam Lively writes, "blacks' principal weapon in this cultural war was humour, and the indirection allowed by disguise or mask." And jazz, he says, "is a music of disguises, of masks" (5, 8).

Furthermore, it should be stressed that the ingeniously subversive mbari art and artists, as well as Achebe and Morrison, *all* eschew essentialism. As such, and codifying an important element of both authors' art, mbari "did not idealize indigenous society" (Ochiagha, *Short History* 32). More specifically, it did not romanticize the village-community and its encounters and projected futures with (colonial) modernity. Also, mbari's inherent social consciousness, its politics, so to speak, does not compromise the craft itself. Nor does its tenet of continual experimentation and renewal, which Achebe assimilated, mean that mbari artists privileged form and artistic innovation over empirical concerns and critique. Balance seems to be the principle as well as the end goal. And lastly, mbari artists seem to be compulsively mindful of the village's contempt for pride. Consequently, even in their asceticism, technical sophistication, and institutional prestige, indeed even in their cosmological position and purposiveness in the village-community, they did not and would not dare confuse themselves with the Earth goddess Ala—the adjudicator of ethics and aesthetics—that commissioned and holds sway over them.

Coda

I want to close the chapter with a summative word or two on "village" and "villagism." As the foregoing discussion has attempted to tease out, these and of course other conceptual attributes or arguments should easily jump to mind when we think of the terminologies, especially as they pertain to the focal Achebe and Morrison texts: As epistemes and tropes, the terms, "village"/"villagism," singly or together, give expression to a rural or traditionalist orientation to being, seeing, doing, and valuing the world, and *in* the world. Not only does the village, foundationally, antedate the ancestor and the ancestral figure whose conditions and conducts of efficacy it engenders, sustains, and memorializes. It is also, significantly, complicated. It is organic, as well as existentially bound and mutually impactful with its corollary "the city," "the urban." It stresses kinship and allows for the coexistence of human lives and the interactivity of life forces and life ideas. Disrupted by local slavery, the Atlantic slave trade, and colonization, the African "village" is not static. It is rather continually evolving. It brims with tension and fosters knowledge-intimacy among its members. It privileges mutual support and well-being and embraces ontological and epistemological diversity—accommodating evil, welcoming strangers, accepting difference, empowering multiperspectives, and reverencing age, ancestors, and the past. However, it disdains excess. Most especially, it disapproves of inordinate pride, which must not be confused with either self-cognition or nobility. Its inclinations toward mythmaking and determinism are counterweighted by force of reality and an emphasis on individual agency. Villagism speaks, then, to inherent cultural contradictions and linguistic impurity. And although it is not strictly tied to geography—to specific land, location, and/or space, as demonstrated by the villagism of black city dwellers and the modernity of villagers in villages—it is still about place. It is concerned with actions and memories (of slavery, colonization, love, loyalty, migrations, generations, etc.) that land/location spurs, habituates, or sublimates. As fertile context and concept, village generates the seeds for and also nourishes the inventive imagination of the village novel and/or village-city novelist, and equally that of the author of modernist and postmodernist fiction.

Let me also touch on that primordial and borderless force—imagination—and how socioculturally vital and psychologically transformative Achebe and Morrison consider works that it (em)powers. Both authors decry modern culture's devaluation of traditional village oral storytelling. However, they justify the novel's significance not just in their particular countries and cultural groups, but also elsewhere. Take, for instance, Achebe's 1990 piece "The Judge and I Didn't Go to Namibia." In this essay, Achebe recalls how a chance-reading of "an African novel"—his *Things Fall Apart* specifically—upended a respected German judge's long-held narrow view of Africa. Encounter with the novel moved that judge to scrap his plan to emigrate and settle in racist Namibia upon his retirement (84–85). Speaking with Kalu Ogbaa in 1980, Achebe continues his case for literature in a speedily modernizing country and former colony such as Nigeria. That event was actually not the first time nor would it be the only occasion at which Achebe mounted a vigorous defense of art and creativity, especially narrative fiction. For, two years earlier, in 1978, for instance, in his Convocation Lecture at the University of Ife, Nigeria, and eight years afterward at his Nigerian National Merit Award Lecture delivered in Sokoto on August 23, 1986, he lent what is perhaps his most public and forceful support to the literary. Articulating that endorsement are the pieces "The Truth of Fiction" and "What Has Literature to Do with It?"

Coming from one of the world's most distinguished flag bearers for the arts and humanities, that robust Achebe validation cannot be any more pertinent and needed today, what with the STEM turn, the emphatic academic, cultural, and economic elevation of science, technology, engineering, math. In any case, like Morrison, Achebe hints at how epochal *and* structural reforms had helped undermine village and social institutions. Those institutions hitherto served as vectors for prized cultural practices. But then he asks: "How do you transmit a national culture to Nigerians if not through works of imagination? . . . So literature is not a luxury for us. It is a life and death affair because we are fashioning a new man. The Nigerian is a new man. How do we get to his mind? Is it by preaching to him once in a while—by the leaders? No, I think it is something solid and permanent that we must put into his consciousness" (Ogbaa, "Interview" 75).

This idea of the Nigerian as a new man is so significant I will revisit it in chapter 3. Nevertheless, like Achebe, Morrison has also contemplated the novel's implicit complicity in the relegation of village oral storytelling. She, however, also recognizes literature's necessity for and in the new, multicultural, technological, and sometimes deeply unsettling global/planetary age. Morrison sees the novel, hers at least, as contributing to African American life. Consistent with her goals for the anthology *Contemporary African Literature*, she hopes (her) narrative fiction would help close cultural gaps. These gaps were created not just by limiting education but social and generational change as well. As earlier indicated, Morrison intends her village-literature texts to pursue a mission not unlike the defining domestic purposes of their eighteenth-century antecedent and archetype for the then-emergent British middle class. As she points out: "My people, we 'peasants,' have come to the city, that is to say, we live with its values. There is a confrontation between old values of the tribe and new urban values. It's confusing. There has to be a mode to do what the music did for blacks, what we used to be able to do for each other in private and in that civilization that existed underneath the white civilization. . . . The music kept us alive, but it's not enough anymore" (LeClair 120–21).

It is not just the music that Morrison finds somewhat inadequate for the scope, complexity, and repercussions of the generational changes in question. It is the other, previously dependable village lifelines as well, perhaps including religion. Things have so fallen apart in the beloved community, are so no longer at ease these days, she seems to say, that god's normally steely and seething arrow is no longer strong and straight as it had been in paradise. It is now warped and brittle, if not improvised. In short, so upturned and beleaguered by winged viral "ideas from all parts of the world" are black families and neighborhoods today that "the old [village] stories" are no longer effective all by themselves. And neither is music, "that folk art that kept us alive," Morrison worries (Jones and Vinson 183). What could help, however, is imagination, she suggests in "The Source of Self-Regard," concurring with Achebe. Both authors urge that, with its myth-making power, with its epic capacities of space and time, and with what Simon Gikandi, in his study *Reading Chinua Achebe*, recognizes as the "archaeological" and "utopian impulse that underlies the novel as a genre" (4), narrative fiction particularly can uncover, sieve, and, if necessary, replot those social formations and transformations. Perhaps most significant, in bringing contexts, subtexts, and clarities to "change," the novel can also point readers, especially its black audience, toward possible ways of navigating "the past," their past, one that has been torn apart. It can assist the-village-within-the city, and vice versa, in negotiating crossroads at the mediations of noon.

But then, again, "crossroads"—a village normative—marks and illuminates planetary black geographies. It has defined forced, migratory, and creolized black bodies and black subjectivities. Think about crossroads' cosmographic interfaces with(in) the village and with noon. And, what with its concretization of Houston A. Baker's metonymic railroad X, along with that letter's local logic of locomotion and portals, but also, perhaps more important, of deletion or cancellation of stasis. "Crossroads" characterizes black life in motion, not just in the United States, as Philip Page also suggests in *Reclaiming Community in Contemporary African American Fiction* (1–35). It expresses the *matter* and mattering of black lives, before, now and always, in Africa and the African diaspora, but particularly in the village-communities and the metropolises of those localities. "Crossroads," or rather recurrent *complexity*, captures the spirits as well as the villagism of Achebe and Morrison's muses.

It should be borne in mind that, even as their muse-inspirited and critically acclaimed works thematically straddle the Atlantic and the "crossroads of cultures," Achebe and Morrison do not exalt and propagate modern print— historically a newer technology of "text-ing" and circulation. They do not, as earlier implied, promote it as a superior format to, or a permanent replacement for, the ancient but waning oral traditions and forms first rooted and (re) routed in the village. This is evident in the two authors' trilogies under close comparison in the next three chapters. Madhu Dubey notes, "As a commodity, the printed book cannot presuppose the immediately visible, face-to-face audiences of folk and oral forms of communication" (3). Achebe and Morrison indirectly concur with Anthonia Kalu's argument (50) for the indispensability of oral tradition for the African writer's creative process and product. Both novelists uniformly see narrative fiction only as oral tradition's companion and continuum, its complement and ally, as are Morrison's focal works to Achebe's and vice versa. The two authors envision fiction as a befitting supplement to the primordial village story's verbal, performative, and improvisational modalities of delivery. For, like oral storytelling, narrative, "far from being one code among many that a culture may utilize for endowing experience with meaning . . . is a meta code, a human universal on the basis of which transcultural messages about the nature of a shared reality can be transmitted" (White 1). Or as Achebe emphasizes in *Anthills of the Savannah* (113–14) and amplifies in other contexts, "The *story*," whether of the village, the city, or elsewheres, "is more important than the writer," even though both are connected. The story is indispensable, always complicated. "To convey this to the next generation is the only way we can keep going and keep alive" (see Searle 159).

2

ReMemorying the (Village) Pasts
Where the Rains Began to Beat Us

Things Fall Apart and *Beloved*

Colonialism and slavery are twins that have been separated since birth but
have lived parallel lives.
   —ERNEST A. CHAMPION, *Mr. Baldwin, I Presume?*

Universal racism did create, among early African and Afro-American writers,
similarities of style, theme and point of view.
   —EDRIS MAKWARD AND LESLIE LACY, *Contemporary African Literature*

The tragic and entangled legacies of colonization and slavery that Chinua
Achebe and Toni Morrison limn distinctively in their respective village novels
Things Fall Apart and *Beloved* had preoccupied their minds as kernels for fiction
years before they set out, pen, pencil, paper, and a winnowed English language
in hand, to flesh out and stylize those thematic seeds. In inscribing the foundational installments of their trilogies, Achebe and Morrison, like mbari artists,
were committed in their crafts and concerns. They were unsentimental in their
gazes and unseduced, apparently, by the allure of Eurocentric universalism
and the privileged logic of apolitical art. Yet, they "had no idea where it would
lead," as Achebe said of *Things Fall Apart*'s uncertain welcome at publication
(Moore and Heath 31). They were unsure how both experimental works would
be received by the changing regions and regimes of aesthetic taste. Nor could

they foretell that the two projects would turn out as such societally impactful and paradigm-turning fictionalizations of the watersheds of colonization and slavery. In this chapter, I attempt to substantiate the claim that, on close reading, and well beyond their standings as village literature, *Things Fall Apart* and *Beloved* reveal far more overlap than one would otherwise have imagined.

Africa, African America, and the Burdens of Transatlantic History and Memory

The intimated connections of *Things Fall Apart* and *Beloved* direct attention to, and also demand that we begin the chapter by addressing and clearing the critical air on, an important intraracial matter that bears directly not just on that intertextuality. It touches also on my suggestion that we reimagine *Things Fall Apart* as a slavery novel, a slavery-undergirded text, or a slavery-colonization narrative. We need to first confront a quandary that has long hovered like a behemoth specter over the landscapes of experiential, cultural, and literary pan-Africanity. That conundrum takes on new currency and urgency given that the year 2019 marks the four-hundredth anniversary of the involuntary arrival, at Point Comfort on Virginia's James River, of the first Africans, described as "20 and odd Negroes," in British North America. Seized from a Portuguese merchant-slaver *São João Bautista* and bartered by the raiding Dutch traders for food and supplies, they would be brought on the English privateer *White Lion*, followed soon after by the *Treasurer,* in late August and a year before the *Mayflower,* to the colony of Jamestown in what was the beginning of a New World and a globally transformative institution of transatlantic slavery. That slavery encounter permanently entwines and, to this day, still haunts Europe, Africa, and the Americas.

I am speaking of the persistent question, broached by Achebe in the introduction, of continental Africans' and African literature's engagement, or supposed failure thereof, with the past/subject of slavery and particularly the transatlantic slave trade, which S. E. Ogude rightly calls "the one single experience that binds all black people together" (21) and Achille Mbembe, in *On the Postcolony,* describes as "the event through which Africa was born to modernity" (13). Or, as that intraracial friction is sometimes bluntly phrased—a directness given cinematographic relief in the movie *Black Panther*—continental Africans, especially West Africans, whose ancestors sold their brothers and sisters into slavery, and modern and contemporary continental African

writers, to whom the legacies of that international mercantilism in black bodies
and labor are also bequeathed, have by and large tended to cultivate a culture
of silence and stoicism on the nightmarish epoch of slavery and the transatlantic slave trade. For Africans and African Americans, *Things Fall Apart* and
Beloved, through separate but linked geographic, disciplinary and canonical
routes, return them to and remind them of those differently located yet sea-
joined "sites of memory" and seismic historical change. Achebe and Morrison
transport them, and us, back to the lived and metonymic *village* and those
originary and interpenetrating moments of racial tragedy and trauma that are,
and have continued to be, variedly remembered and parsed on both sides of
the Atlantic, hence the fissure and the vent. Concerning those pasts, the distinguished historian K. Onwuka Dike noted: "No aspect of West African history
has received fuller treatment, and justifiably so, than the iniquitous transatlantic slave trade. Sir Reginald Coupland stated, with scarcely any exaggeration,
that the treatment of Africa by Christian Europe in the period of the slave trade
constituted 'the greatest crime in history'" (3).

There may well be other African novels that are just as, if not more, apposite
than *Things Fall Apart* for deployment to the task of artistic clarification, topic
ensconcement, and/or affective rebuttal that *that* claim of Africans' impassivity
and quietude demands here. To me, however, none of those other slavery-
centered or slavery subthemed African novels, about which more will be said, is
more directly and substantively complementary to *Beloved* and more nuanced
as an expressive refraction of those charges than *Things Fall Apart.* Reviving
that subject of intraracial discord may seem discursively hackneyed or unwarranted here. It could even detain or distract our analytical progress. But it is
a necessary trip back. I say revitalize simply to emphasize that the present
interrogation is hardly the first time *that* hovering kindred rancor, alongside
its implications for the experience of blackness and the study of Black Atlanticism, as Gilroy fields it, has commanded the attention of Africanists.[1] Nor will
this be the last discursive engagement with that matter of black lives.

As the adjoining discussion will expound, what one surmises immediately,
even on a cursory appraisal of the issue, is not that continental (West) Africans are oblivious to the ghosts and vestigial materiality of slavery and the
transatlantic slave trade. Nor is one's takeaway that canonical African literature and African literary criticism have distanced themselves from the imperatives of collective anamnesis of the transatlantic experience. The research and
evidence suggest much more than the point that they, Africans, or, speaking

broadly, that *we [all], remember differently,* to echo Chimamanda Ngozi Adichie. That was how she subtitled her thoughts on the furor that erupted some time ago among Nigeria's ethnic groups, particularly between the Southwestern Yoruba and their Southeastern Igbo brethren. The outcry was over controversial claims Achebe levels in his memoir *There Was a Country* against Chief Obafemi Awolowo relative to Igbo genocide during the 1967–70 Nigeria-Biafra Civil War, at which time Awolowo was Nigeria's finance minister.[2] Underscored to a far greater degree in the research findings, and as *Things Fall Apart* corroborates, however, are the enduring effects of colonization *and* a more complex picture in which "men and women of the African continent were caught up in a system of oppression in which they were alternately victims and pawns" (Holsey 236). It is those adversarial forces, much more than willful cultural, writerly, or scholarly apathies, that are generally identified as having impacted for years the manner of individual, familial, and literary recognitions of the historical pasts. The same pressures have also overdetermined communal memories, institutional (re)constructions, national monuments to, and in some cases commercialization of, slavery on the continent.

In sifting these vexed issues and particularly the charge, one in which *Things Fall Apart* is implicitly implicated as one of modern African literature's founding and foundational texts, I have found various works particularly helpful. I have in mind here Tunji Osinubi, Bayo Holsey, Laura T. Murphy, and Yogita Goyal's percipient discussions of the Africa-/African literature-and-slavery question. Significantly, Osinubi, Murphy, and Goyal especially have also engaged directly and indirectly in their scholarship with Achebe and Morrison's cultural productions. As a result, their insights and Holsey's probe of the pesky family quarrel are particularly germane.

In his book review "The African Atlantic: West African Literatures and Slavery" (2016), Osinubi comparatively evaluates Matthew J. Christensen's *Rebellious Histories* (2012) and Murphy's *Metaphor and the Slave Trade in West African Literature,* also published in 2012. Of significance is the remark with which Osinubi initiates the critique. He notes that "within African literary and cultural studies, work on the representations of domestic West African slavery or the historical slave trades across the Atlantic and the Sahara has been sparse." This is unlike the ready availability of such narratives, as well as critical scholarship on them, he argues, in Caribbean and American literary canons, both of which appear collaborative (149–50). It is that scarcity of investigative output on the African side of the kinship that Christensen and

Murphy attempt to redress. For our purposes, and with regard to what I will suggest later as the explicability of *Things Fall Apart's* one and only direct reference to the transatlantic slave trade, Osinubi speaks to, among other things, the slavery-colonialism dynamic relative to narrative proper. But he also reminds us of something else, reinforcing Adélékè Adéèkó's remark that slavery not only "untracked Africa from its proper trajectory," but it also instigated the continent's subsequent predicament of remembering and its ambivalent relationship to diaspora (Introduction viii)—an argument Yogita Goyal extends in "Africa and the Black Atlantic" (2014). Osinubi observes that "colonial conquest reconfigured Africa's internal relationship to domestic slavery and the internal slave trades such that scholars of slavery in African literatures must take into account how colonialism impacted how slavery is remembered and represented." In other words, "all accounts of slavery and slave trade must be provincialized, i.e., taken out of any singularizing (North Atlantic or putatively global) narrative and rescaled within a local nexus of meanings and historical mechanisms" (150–51).

It can be proffered that *that* injunction to provincialize the forms, accounts, and memories of slavery is what Bayo Holsey undertakes in her 2008 study *Routes of Remembrance: Refashioning the Slave Trade in Ghana*, which examines a country whose widely promoted and celebrated Year of Return in 2019 marks yet another significant step toward intraracial reunion, reconciliation, and, hopefully, healing. Holsey does not just highlight that pluralization in her title. She also uncovers an infrequently considered yet significant way by which colonial subjugation, as Osinubi asserts, drastically unmoored and altered Africa's interior connection to and communal recollections of domestic slaveries and the transatlantic slave trade. *Routes'* publication coincides with the two-hundredth commemoration of Abolition. In it, Holsey set out to examine not just "what it means to live, quite literally, in the shadows cast" by the slave castles in the West African coastline. She was also curious about what it means to remember and establish subjectivity in Cape Coast and Elmina following the slave trade (2). Soon after she began ransacking for shared remembrances of the trade, a chasm emerged between the subject's popularity with the "tourism" sector and its imperceptibility in other areas of Ghanaian life (2).

And when Holsey dug into that paradox, she uncovered what amounts to house secrecy. She discovered, through the local Ghanaians she interacted with over the years in Elmina and Cape Coast, that the pervasive silence, reluctance, subject-deflation and subject-revision among the people were their attempt at self-insulation from what in today's parlance would be condemned virally as victim-blaming and victim-shaming. The silence and hesitation were the Ghanaians' way of avoiding a re-mark of shame; the re-violation, if you will. This is because the neo-assault and neo-humiliation over slavery were inflicted, mainly and ironically, by the same Christian and civilized Europe that chiefly engineered the mechanics of the transatlantic slave trade. As Holsey points out, the local populations are routinely assaulted with mainstream "European" and "academic historical" accounts of the slave trade. In these renditions, Africans in Africa are discredited as extrinsic to the supposedly humanity-marking "march of progress." To circumvent the taint of the slavery plague, to reenvision and position themselves positively as modern and global subjects, Holsey adds, the local residents attempt proactively to separate themselves from that horrid past and topic. They do that by either deliberately veiling the slavery history or, again consciously, remembering it differently (2–3).

Why fault the locals in these intentional acts of dissimulation, recalibration, and self- and group-reinvention, Holsey seems to ask, when dominant depictions of "European and American histories" are couched as stories of "progress, stressing development, modernization, and capitalism"? And when, unlike Europe (and the United States), Africa is stereotyped "by this 'primitive' past" (read, slavery) that has supposedly stagnated it (3). Why blame them, Holsey insinuates further, when European historians emphasize the trade in textbooks to blemish Africa? (23). Or when the efforts at intraracial reconciliation and black diaspora healing performed on Ghanaian soil proper sometimes (un)wittingly turn into rituals of resentment that peg Ghanaian ancestors as culprits in the trade (234). And when there are discourses, some of them by eminent African Americans, that denigrate the whole of Africa as "a cursed land" as a result of its involvement in the trade.[3] These renditions, Holsey argues, fail to interrogate "Africa's entrapment within the global processes." Instead, they reductively interpret the slave trade as a preamble of Africa's "internal combustion" (4). Through practiced reticence, self-removal, and/or emendation, the illustrative Cape Coast and Elmina locals try to construct reputable histories. The cardinal goals of these alter-native accounts are to thwart communal alterity and subversively insert themselves into and claim a place, their seat, in prevailing discourses of the modern and the global (4).

Instead of fostering dichotomy and animus "between those who were enslaved and those who remained," Holsey urges (237), or merely pushing national projects and diaspora programs that develop glorifying and black triumphalist accounts of slavery through the often symbolic and sometimes problematic racial/family reunions (233–34), we must pluralize slavery. Even more important, we must complicate suffering and melancholy. As Holsey reminds us, "The slave trade has never been solely the history of those who were captured from their homes [and their villages], placed in chains, carried across the sea, and forced to toil on plantations." That racial calamity is also as much about "those in the bondage of the global system of oppression that emerged at the moment of this forced migration," she writes (237).

It can be said, furthermore, that *that* obligation to localize slavery, regionalize slavery discourse, and variegate grief, is also what Laura Murphy finds emblematized in most of the West African literary works she studies. Murphy frames her study as a countermotion to perceptions she finds advanced also by various scholars that West African communities and culture workers have been so engrossed with colonization they have yet to rigorously engage with the transatlantic slave trade. In 2007, Murphy published a pilot essay, "Into the Bush of Ghosts: Specters of the Slave Trade in West African Fiction." In that piece, she introduces the topical spine and discursive schematic of *Metaphors*. Building upon the article, Murphy suggests in *Metaphors* that if academics and the general reader of Anglophone and modern West African fiction have not noted such overt preoccupation with the subject of slavery and the Middle Passage as they would while exploring, for example, the African American antebellum and neo–slave narratives, or their British equivalents, it is because West African writers have tended to *remember differently*. To Murphy, the writers and artists do not seem to have overlooked slavery. Rather, they have adopted distinct modalities of representation, commemoration, and sorrow. As a result, Murphy urges that "we must read into the spaces where the slave trade lies lurking, beyond the layer of explicit historical setting" (1). Highlighting the canonical works of such West African writers as Amos Tutuola, Ben Okri, Ayi Kwei Armah, and Ama Ata Aidoo, Murphy argues that

> memories of the slave trade are overlooked in African literatures because they are not revealed in the forms of overt narrativization so familiar in African American literature. . . . [T]he distant past endures in West African culture and literature in forms of "alternative memory" and metaphorization such as tragic repetition, fear and gossip, and tropes of sufferings, bondage, and impotent sexuality—all of which expose the continued physical as well as psychological legacy of a past

that no individual living now personally experienced. Overt narrativ-
ization, archiving, or even explicit cultural discourse are not necessary
for a collective memory of the transatlantic slave trade to exist in West
Africa. In fact, narratives of that kind are nearly nonexistent in the literature of the twentieth century. (3–4)

Murphy slightly underreads or undercounts the canon on her assumption
that works that overtly engage with slavery are almost nonexistent in West
African literature. Such works may be few, but they are there and have been
longtime titles of the republic of modern and postcolonial African expressive
projects, as profiled below. Osinubi, whose extant scholarship and upcoming
monograph probe this subject even more extensively, also flags that under-
count. He additionally underlines that *Metaphors* does in fact recognize in-text
but then oddly neglects to prioritize two such slavery-driven novels. These are
Syl Cheney-Coker's *The Last Harmattan* (1990) and Obi Akwani's *March of
Ages* (2003), which Murphy, echoed by Osinubi, regards as a kind of prequel
to *Things Fall Apart* (see Osinubi, "African Atlantic" 153). Besides those two
examples, there are other African novels that directly take domestic slavery, its
strands and transmutations *and* the transatlantic slave trade and that epoch's
enduring repercussions, as their major concerns and/or subsidiary topics and
allusions. Some of them, which Osinubi also mentions in the review, include,
nonchronologically: Elechi Amadi's *The Slave* (1978); Buchi Emecheta's *The
Slave Girl* (1977) and *The Bride Price* (1976); Yaw Boateng's *The Return* (1977);
and Achebe's *Things Fall Apart, No Longer at Ease,* and *Arrow of God,* to which
we will return (see also Olaogun). To this list one would also add Emecheta's
The Joys of Motherhood (1979) and Isidore Okpewho's *Call Me by My Rightful
Name* (2004), which Adéèkó in his cited introduction juxtaposes to Carryl
Phillips's *The Atlantic Sound* (2000). There are also, more recently, Ayesha H.
Attah's *The Hundred Wells of Salaga* (2019), Yaa Gyasi's *Homegoing* (2017),
should we take Gyasi's birth in Ghana as justification to include her debut in
that cohort of Anglophone West African slavery-focused or slavery-inflected
narratives, and then Adichie's *Purple Hibiscus* (2003).

In light of this relatively paltry inventory of fictional texts, one would not
be blamed for subscribing to the thesis that West African creative writers have
been disproportionately stressing other subjects of Africans' being-in-the-
world. But as suggested, the specter of slavery lies, subterranean, in African literary history, cultural productions, and intellectual thought. As Helena

Woodard concurs in her own review of *Metaphors*, the tropes "of the slave trade that Murphy locates in select African fiction are potent reminders that alternative ways to assess slavery and to chronicle its past-to-present transmission exist beyond what non-African slave narratives or historical fictions convey" (174–75). That specter nudges the works of newer African writers of fiction and human rights narratives, at home and abroad, as Yogita Goyal has uncovered.

Illustrating the thematic afterlives of slavery and the transatlantic slave trade in contemporary African literary consciousness is the emergence of what Goyal calls "new genres in African literature (such as the modern slave narrative and the child soldier novel) that are widely read and promoted by mainstream cultural institutions, from Oprah Winfrey to Jon Stewart, George Clooney to Angelina Jolie, Nicholas Kristof to Samantha Power." What is perhaps fascinating about this expressive category of globalized slavery, Goyal suggests, is not just the works' instancing of "slavery's circulation in human rights narratives about Africa" that indirectly portray the continent—as Holsey pointed out earlier—as a place of "atrocities" that purportedly necessitate sometimes fetishistic if not voyeuristic Western intercessions. It is also how, as Goyal adds, this genre's "accounts of atrocities like human trafficking, capture in war, debt bondage, forced marriage, the use of child soldier, and sex-trafficking . . . are explicitly modeled on Atlantic slave narratives" like those of Frederick Douglass, Harriet Jacobs, and Olaudah Equiano. Not only do they employ amanuenses, they also prompt questions of neo-abolitionism and "what it means to write a postcolonial experience in an American genre" (49–53). In *Runaway Genres* (2019), Goyal expands on those issues. And in a statement that upholds the extra historical contextualization I mobilize here and equally at the beginning of the other analytical chapters, she reminds us that "too often, contemporary literature is read without sufficient attention to history." Viewed thus as ahistorical, it is sometimes inadequately critiqued "as part of an endless present, or as world literature beyond race and nation" (4).

Achebe knows full well history's impact on and indispensability to narrative, literary criticism, and philosophic erudition, even sophistry. He appreciates as well what it means to tell Africa's pre- and postcolonial stories in the West African genre of the village novel. Like Morrison, who in "The Slave-body and the Blackbody" reminds us what "an old commerce" the selling and owning of people is and how rare it would be to find any group among whose ancestors there were no slaves (75–76), Achebe would not be shocked by humanity's evolved capacities for cruelties. He likely would not be surprised by those wide-ranging horrors disclosed by the subgeneric African and other groups' texts that Goyal examines in *Runaway Genres* and elsewhere. If his shrewd responses to historical acts of Christian/missionary charities to Africa were any indication, however, he likely would counter any discourse—philanthropic, human rights, environmentalist, planetary disease sociology, or otherwise—that so much as seeks to consign Africa to the domains of brutality and destitution. But one doubts he would have been inclined to dictate a generic, thematic, and/or aesthetic blueprint to other African authors, even as dire as Goyal's findings seem to frame and extend the canonical problematic.

If there is one specific issue from the past that Achebe was unequivocal about, nonetheless, it is *that* unwieldy subject of transatlantic slave trade and Africa's role in it. Even more noteworthy than his expected candor on the topic is his thought on Morrison's project in *Beloved*. And there is also what, as I earlier suggested and will address later, he left unsaid in his view about Sethe. As some of the earlier-enumerated African novels and especially *Things Fall Apart* show, domestic slavery and the transatlantic slave trade are sometimes unmistakably the focal topics. And at other times, having mutated into other forms of lived reality and having become "a synonym" for all kinds of discourses and debates, as Morrison argues,[4] slavery is tucked seamlessly into African fiction's contexts, subtexts, and settings. It is sometimes masked in themes, plots, characters, symbols, and allusions. While *Beloved*, though an African American novel, illustrates the former instance of thematic focality, *Things Fall Apart* exemplifies the latter case of topic diffusion and dissimulation.

B(l)ack-to-B(l)ack Village Stories:
Texts, Contexts, Subtexts, Intertexts

Achebe and Morrison may not have known early on how *Things Fall Apart* and *Beloved* would fare in the domains of public reading, aesthetic valuation, and even pedagogy. But they were certain about a few things, at least. First and foremost, as indicated in the previous chapter, they knew the stories were needed. They were commissioned, though not by the Earth Goddess Ala directly or necessarily, but by the necessity of rectifying black plight on *her* earth. The two authors knew, too, their novels were and are expressly about the village or, as Morrison put it, about the black neighborhood, community, the tribe. Achebe and Morrison also, similarly, initially envisioned the two stories of black people's backstories as trilogies, the evolutionary paths, narrative maps, and overarching themes of which we traced in the introduction. And, they correspondingly positioned the novels as interventions on distortions of black lives in canonical writings and discourses, white and black, but especially in Western philosophic, travel, sentimental, realist, and modernist texts. A good number of those texts take black subjectivity and black racial experience in Africa, the United States, and other diasporic locations as points of interest. And in some cases, blackness is expedient canvas.

Braided in the interpositions but requiring more attention, however, are *Things Fall Apart* and *Beloved*'s contexts and parallel standings as historically informed village novels. Or, as Robert M. Wren writes of *Things Fall Apart*, "it is fictionalised history" (*Achebe's World* 13). Morrison's model for Sethe is the slave Margaret Garner. Morrison stated that in order to give her imagination free rein, she intentionally did not conduct additional research on the Garner story beyond her chance encounter with a nineteenth-century article on the event while editing *The Black Book*. For representational accuracy, "she and an assistant did extensive research into slavery, abolitionism, Cincinnati in the 1850s and '60s, how much things cost and where streets were" (Kastor 56). Unlike the historical Garner, or the historical Umuchu priest[5] who modeled the Chief Priest Ezeulu in *Arrow of God*, there is no direct historical figure (I don't mean a fictional *foil* such as Joyce Cary's character Mister Johnson) for *Things Fall Apart*'s Okonkwo. However, as others have also pointed out, many of the events in the novel, and in the trilogy's other installments, are historically inspired. As with Morrison's encounter with the newspaper publication on Garner, Achebe, in writing *Things Fall Apart*, may have been exposed to and influenced by textual and thematic antecedents, in this instance, and as Wren writes, P. Amaury Talbot's *In the Shadow of the Bush* (1912), *Some Nigerian Fertility Cults* (1927), *Tribes of the Niger Delta* (1932), and Talbot's four-volume *The Peoples of Southern Nigeria* (1926). Achebe said that in writing *Things Fall Apart* he did not undertake formal "research in the library." Rather, he relied on information "largely picked up" randomly and from "listening to old people— and what I learned from my father." He admits, however, that the eminent missionary G. T. Basden may have served as his image for Mr. Brown in *Things Fall Apart*. And, as Wren additionally suggests, the real-life Dr. J. F. Stewart, whose killing drew disproportionate British revenge, appears to be the prototype for the novel's white man on the bicycle killed in Abame, a murder for which the Abame community is exterminated (*Achebe's World* 13).

This brings us (back) to the village sphere. Or rather, it redirects us to the village novel, particularly what I am suggesting are *Beloved*'s manifestations of key elements of that West African subgenre. To the general Morrison reader accustomed to viewing the novel through the centuries-old conventions of African American and American fiction, New World slavery, and neo–slave narratives, this new notion of *Beloved* as a village novel may sound counter-intuitive. Evidence for the claim is suffused in the story, however. But if that proof seems inconspicuous, it is because it is obscured by the slavery sub-ject itself and the formal innovations. It is concealed, to be more exact, by *Beloved*'s "America" setting, its elliptical locations, cascading stories, and those framed stories' associated polyvocality that disperses narrational gaze. And it is screened, concomitantly, by the unsubtle, nonlinear structure that scrambles the timelines of events. This is unlike *Things Fall Apart*'s delineated Igbo "vil-lage"/"Africa" setting of Umuofia and Mbanta and the novel's fewer but more fluid narrative discontinuities. *Things Fall Apart*'s temporal fluctuations do not obstruct to the same degree as in *Beloved*. Reflecting the W. B. Yeats poem that Achebe adapts for his title and theme of historical cycles—a poem also exploited by Morrison in her master's thesis, with Philip Page (1992) positing the circle as a motif in *Beloved*—the narrative shifts in *Things Fall Apart* do not interfere with our straightforward grasp of the patterns and sequences of his-torical changes tracked in the text.

To help us decipher particularly *Beloved*'s patterning after village literature, we need to recall the earlier discussion of narrative form and Griswold's con-ceptualization. The first of the village novel's attributes to consider is its prime concern to "preserve the memory of a world that is passing." I want to and will spend some time in this chapter addressing the two novels' historical settings and thematic interests, both of which tie directly to the stories' overarching preoccupations with the question of "the past," the always already changing village and ancestral past. If we follow Achebe's own timeline, other reasoned calculations, and additional historical research, a composite picture emerges of *Things Fall Apart* and *Beloved*'s near-perfect alignment in their narrated and extratextual settings. In that 1962 interview with Lewis Nkosi, Achebe esti-mates that his triptych spans about a hundred years. If marked from that 1962, or the 1958 of *Things Fall Apart*'s publication, the timeframe situates the three works' initiating action, staged in *Things Fall Apart*, around the 1850s and/or the 1860s, with Kwame Anthony Appiah noting, as earlier mentioned, that the Igbo encounter with the British imperial exploration occurred in the 1870s,

almost thirty years prior to de facto colonization. Robert Wren earlier speculated that the Okonkwo–Amalinze the Cat wrestling contest occurred around
1875. To G. D. Killam, the novel is set "between 1850 and 1900" (13).

Let us dabble in periodizing arithmetic with these dates and with the novel's
unnarrated historical events. We will return to some of those events in more
specificity later. If Okonkwo is eighteen when he defeats Amalinze, and if,
hypothetically, his father, Unoka, had him when he, Unoka, was also eighteen
years or, let us say, twenty years, that places the Unoka-Okonkwo genealogical line thirty-six years prior to 1876, which means around 1837, 1839. Now,
should we add to that date Unoka's own father *and* the narrator's as well as the
Umuofia and Mbanta men's attributory invocations of their ancestors and oral
history—for instance: Okonkwo's uncle Uchendu is said to be the oldest living
descendant of "Okolo, who had lived about two hundred years before" (165)—
then the novel's narrated and unrepresented temporalities stretch further and
further backward. It backtracks, at the very least, into the 1850s, the period of
the Fugitive Slave Act in the United States.

It is historically and critically significant that the novel does take place also in
the 1850s, as deducted in Achebe, Killam, and my speculated timelines, rather
than in the customarily assumed 1890s. This is because it was in 1856, as Steven
Weisenburger details in *Modern Medea*, that Margaret Garner escaped with her
young family from the Kentucky slave plantation of her master, A. K. Gaines.
Through the Underground Railroad, she ended up in Cincinnati, Ohio. There,
upon discovery by Gaines and federal marshals, she set about trying to kill all
four of her children, succeeding with one, for she would rather they were dead
than condemned to suffer the brutalities of slavery. Margaret was tried, not for
the killing, but instead for stolen property, because prosecuting her for murder
would have opened that can of worms the Enlightenment dreaded. It would
inevitably have directed attention to, and compelled the state of Kentucky and
the peculiar institution at large to speak of and acknowledge, one or two ancillary and inconvenient truths. That would include *her* humanity, motherhood,
rights, rationale, family, freedom, labor, and time. And it possibly would have
led, consequentially, to a discussion of *her* body. For as Robert F. Reid-Pharr
writes, "during the antebellum period . . . the black body [to which he adds the
black household] came to operate—for blacks—as a primary site in the negotiation of slavery and white supremacy" (6). Speaking of blackness and time,
Simon Gikandi has observed how in *Things Fall Apart*, for instance, Achebe
not only affirms African subjectivity and the African body. He also summons

with aplomb a panoply of time- and event-markers. With them Achebe further illuminates "the tripartite relationship between the subject, culture, and time," hence confuting the European fallacy that Africans are atemporal, lacking a consciousness of time and *their* time (*Reading Chinua Achebe* 28–29).

It is perhaps evident what I am getting at here, namely, that consistent with the village novel's paramount intent, *Things Fall Apart* and *Beloved* reimagine the intertwined worlds of slavery/colonization and slavery. To evoke Achebe: both works are acts of atonement with the past. They were penned to grapple with two complicated and still-painful epochs in black racial and world history. They were written to (re)invest black body and life with matter; to return to black humanity the dignity and agency wrested from it during slavery and colonization. In short, what I am attempting to demonstrate is that *Things Fall Apart* and *Beloved* so align and connect at the times and topics of domestic and transatlantic slaveries that one could, as postulated, call *Things Fall Apart* a slavery novel. In the same way the idea of *Beloved* as a village novel would seem curious to some, depicting *Things Fall Apart* as suggested could also appear generically incongruous. But a modal misalliance it is not. In fact, all of Carl D. Malmgren's slightly modified descriptors of *Beloved* apply to both texts. He calls *Beloved* "part ghost[/spirit-child] story, part historical novel, part slave narrative, part love story" (97). Keeping our sights squarely on the village novel's defining project of memorialization, consider, first, *Things Fall Apart*.

We cannot but be struck by the parallels in the historical occurrences on both sides of the Atlantic at the time of Garner's slave rebellion. The 1850s and afterward in the New World witnessed the passage and execution of a stiffer Fugitive Slave Law enacted to thwart slave revolts effected through tightly plotted, daring, but sometimes unsuccessful slave escapes from southern plantations and masters. "Eighteen seventy-four," Morrison writes in *Beloved*, "and whitefolks were still on the loose": with lynching, widespread arson, violence to black children, and rapes of black women (180). In the Old World, in the Niger Delta (or Bight of Biafra) area, between the years 1850 and 1875, virtually all the fishing-villages-turned-city-states in the territory experienced various forms of domestic unrest instigated by freed former slaves, according to K. Onwuka Dike (153). In his chapter "The Slave Revolts," Dike reminds us not only that there also existed large-scale plantations cultivated by slave labor in the Bight of Biafra, specifically in the Efik territory's hinterland. Thousands of slaves escaped to these plantations and transformed one of them into a blood-covenanted fugitive-slave fortress. These slaves/ex-slaves did not accept their abjection and supposed lot in life. As Dike explains, there were many domestic slave insurgencies against entitled former African middlemen and masters. Years back, and incredulously, or perhaps unsurprisingly, these masters had rejected and continued afterward to resist Abolition. They opposed it simply because slave trading and slaves had been the cornerstones of their economic, social, and political power. Aware of their innate humanity and overall worth and aggrieved about their continued stigmatization and exclusion despite their manumission, financial successes, and rising political clout, the ex-slaves continually rebelled. Many ran away—as in the New World—founding or helping to found communities that remind one not only of the Britain-imbricated Maroon societies of Jamaica about two centuries earlier, but also of *Beloved*'s black Cincinnati.

The promulgation of the harsher Fugitive Slave Law in America did not deter resolute slaves like Margaret Garner from efforts to flee an exploitative and dehumanizing institution. So too, according to Dike, did concurrent British attempt to conciliate the master-slave impasse in Old Calabar with a treaty that amounts to a Fugitive Slave Act fail to end the slave revolts (156–65). Writing about the rebellions in "The Blood Men of Old Calabar—a Slave Revolt of the Nineteenth Century?," Ute Röschenthaler observes that the uprising, started in 1850 by slaves "working on the plantations of the deceased Duke Town ruler Ephraim" and restarted after King Archibong's death, continued intermittently until the onset of British colonial regime in 1884 (450). The beneficiaries of international slavery and the domestic slave systems in the Bight of Biafra and America resented Abolition and slave emancipation. They instead sought to sustain the inhumane practice.

But the stark difference between "the plantation slavery of the New World and the domestic slavery as practiced in the Niger Delta," as Dike couches it (37), cannot be ignored. Nor should it be overstated. For whereas slaves in the New World, say, Garner/Sethe, are considered chattel or "capital goods" and are not freed by their oppressive labor, in the Niger Delta, "the wealth produced by a slave eventually set him free" (37). Wealth put the slave on a path to social integration and class ascendancy. "Much of what made New World slavery exceptional" was pigmentation, Morrison reflects in "The Slavebody and the Blackbody." It was "the highly identifiable racial signs of its population in which skin color, primarily but not exclusively, interfered with the ability of subsequent generations to merge into the nonslave population" (76).

The 1959 American edition of *Things Fall Apart*, subtitled "The Story of a Strong Man," includes a critically significant blurb by Achebe. "My main interest," Achebe pronounces in the promotional text, "is in the life of I[g]bo communities in the past. I have chosen a hinterland community far from the coastal peoples who have been debased by their participation in the cruelties of the slave trade." In this declaration, Achebe identifies and describes the story's chronotopic location/temporal setting to include or imply the larger Bight of Biafra area of which Dike writes above. As the historian G. Ugo Nwokeji observes in *The Slave Trade and Culture in the Bight of Biafra* (2010), these same densely populated hinterland Igbo village-communities, of which the fictional Umuofia and Mbanta are examples, demographically made up a significant portion of the Bight of Biafra region that "supplied an estimated 13 percent of all captives exported between 1551 and 1850"—"probably the largest single African group arriving in North America and several Caribbean destinations for much of the eighteenth century" (xiii).

The seamless commingling of slavery, colonization, religion, and racism, and the pernicious impact of these forces on the subsequent cultural and literary memorialization of slavery in that region and elsewhere in Africa are not a matter of debate. F. C. Ekechi helps drive that point home, especially as it pertains to missionary ideology and activity not only in the Igbo experience but also Africa in general. Early in his study *Missionary Enterprise and Rivalry in Igboland,* Ekechi dates missionary incursion in Igboland to later in the nineteenth century, following pioneering efforts of the Church Missionary Society (CMS). Established in 1799, Ekechi writes, the CMS (the religious organization that many years later would convert and train Achebe's father, Isaiah Achebe, as one of Ogidi's and Igboland's earliest Anglican catechists) "selected Africa as one of the spheres of its evangelical operation, and the Negro race in particular." The CMS couched its choice of Africa and black people altruistically, Ekechi remarks. It suggested that it did so out of sympathy, because it felt so sorry for the really awful things slavery had done to Africans and their benighted descendants. But there is more to that story. For underlying "this CMS rationale for going to Africa" for proselytization, Ekechi states, "is the pervasive nineteenth-century European notion that the introduction of Christianity would be the panacea for Africa's wretchedness and woe" (1).

The ancillary endpoint of that proselytization story, that missionary and conversion narrative, as it were, is British imperial expansionism in West Africa. As Ekechi maintains, the church, the state, and mercantilism were inseparable. The mission was rather intimately imbricated with business. It interplayed with the enormous political, industrial, technological, and commercial developments taking place in Europe at the time. Pushed aggressively by Thomas Fowell Buxton, the proposition that the establishment of legitimate trading relationship with Africans would aid the cause of abolition and conclusively suppress the transatlantic slave trade unraveled as a pretext and precursor to British market expansionism and the imposition of multiprong colonial regime (1–2). It is well known that the transatlantic slave trade and slavery continued past its initial paper-Abolition in 1807 in the British colonies. That was the case in Igboland and elsewhere. As Kenneth Morgan writes:

> The British and American abolition of their respective slave trades in 1807 and 1808 largely decimated the Anglophone involvement in the slave trade at the Bight of Biafra. But this did not stop slave trafficking in that region by other flags to supply the sugar and coffee plantations of Brazil, Cuba, Puerto Rico, and the French Caribbean. . . . During the nineteenth century, the commercial organization of the slave trade at the Bight of Biafra extended the methods used in earlier periods. Aro traders continued their role as intermediaries and undertook wars and raids in central and northern Igbo areas to procure slaves. They hired mercenaries as warriors and plundered villages for slaves both for internal use and for the trans-Atlantic slave trade. They retained links with canoemen and connections with traders near the coast who liaised with European slave ship captains. ("Trans-Atlantic Slave Trade" 90)

For our purposes, however, and as Ekechi indicates (1), none of this—the CMS missionary project/the Niger Expedition, the economic inroads into the Niger territories, and the imperial military incursions into and governmental foothold in Igboland, to which one would add the slave captivities and trading before that—would have been possible without the Niger River. As Dike writes, "Throughout Europe the event [the Lander brothers' discovery, through Badagry, of the access/termination point and flow path of the Niger in 1830] was hailed as one of cardinal importance." It was "epoch-making," changing British activity "from exploration to commerce." Next to the Nile and the Congo River, the Niger River is Africa's third-longest waterway. And, "like the more famous Congo," Dike adds, "the Niger was considered a dazzling prize by the competing powers—Britain, France, and Germany" (18).

On that watery setting lies another of the many ancillary sites and fluid moments of kinship and memory/memorialization of the past between *Things rivers*

Fall Apart and *Beloved*. Both books and the separated black lives they celebrate have *known* rivers. To channel Langston Hughes's "The Negro Speaks of Rivers," they have "known rivers ancient as the world and older than the / flow of human blood in human veins." And their "souls" may very well "have grown deep like the rivers" (Rampersad and Ruessel 23). For the African-descended Margaret Garner, *Beloved*'s character Sethe, and other free and fugitive slaves, the Ohio River, which merges with the Mississippi River, was contradictory in its location, history, and function. It was, among other things, a major navigational stretch of the Underground Railroad but also the route of repatriation of recaptured escapees and path of shipment of slaves sold to the Deep South, as Matthew Salafia also discusses in *Slavery's Borderland* (2013). As Morrison points out in *Beloved*, the Ohio River is where the Klan patrolled for "black blood" (66). Similarly for *Things Fall Apart*'s Okonkwo, Umuofia and Mbanta villages, the Igbo and their neighbors at large, the Niger River, which Hughes unfortunately omits from his inventory of Africa-connected big seas and which, like the Ohio River, is also confluential in its merger with the Benue River, was also a double-edged contact zone, as explained below.

The Niger empties into the Atlantic Ocean. "In its 2,600-mile journey from the Futa Jalon Mountains through the savannahs, scrublands, and desert and then southward through the tropical forests, finally losing itself in a thousand digressions in the Bight of Biafra," Achebe writes, "the River Niger sees many lands and diverse human settlements, old and new, picturesque and ordinary" ("Onitsha" 126). It helps link Nigeria's southeastern and southwestern villages and towns and also, for our purposes, the country's north and south, just as the Ohio River fluidly divides but also binds free and slave states. The Niger helped open Igbo hinterland, in this case, to the outside world and vice versa. But it was also, contradictorily, serviceable to rivalrous, coastal human trafficking and international slave-trading, in an unbalanced commerce about which Elizabeth Isichei remarks in *A History of Igbo People*, "anyone studying the records of what was imported into the Delta and I[g]boland in return cannot but be struck by the extraordinary inequality of the exchange" (50). While "the triangular trade contributed vastly to the wealth of Europe," Isichei continues, "for the African societies it touched, the trade was a disaster" (42). It was markedly so, she adds, for the Igbo, whom it robbed of villages, blood, and bloodlines, "of many of her members, in the prime of life, and the children they would have had. We can only speculate as to the contributions they would have made to Igbo life had they remained" (45). Concurs Mbembe in *Necropolitics*: "The slave trade thrived on its hemorrhaging and draining of the most useful arms and most vital energies of the slave-providing societies" (10). The Niger resourced the colonial civilizational expeditions and the Christian missions. In Achebe's fictional rememorying, these imperial operations and conversion quests ultimately make their ways to the villages of Umuofia and Mbanta and other Igbo locales of Achebe's stories. They would set in motion not only chains of sweeping imperial practices and discourses. They also would provoke historic resistances that adversely alter Igbo-African villages and culminate in untold tragedies.

Water/the Niger River—that long, deep, timeless, meandering, and interminable fount of life and history that fluidly links (with) the Atlantic Ocean that links with the Mississippi River that links with the Ohio River that interconnects the past and passing black worlds of Sethe's African mother and Sethe and Baby Suggs and Sethe's husband Halle and their children and the villager Unoka and his unnamed wife and their son and the farmer Okonkwo and his three wives and eight children—technically gets, and *is*, the last word in *Things Fall Apart*. There, it is invoked at different narrative points as "the Great River." It is dredged up literarily by the novel's British District Commissioner to mark the geographic scope but, ironically, the narrowness of his vision and that of his planned travelogue "The Pacification of the Primitive Tribes of the Lower Niger," which *Things Fall Apart* always already entraps. We will return to that point later in this chapter. In "The African Oceans—Tracing the Sea as Memory of Slavery in South African Literature and Culture," Gabeba Baderoon elongates the maritime theme and semiosis. She connects the Atlantic and the other African big sea, the Indian Ocean. She describes both as "the oceans of the middle passage, but also of cosmology, memory, and desire, tracked in the movement, language, and culture of enslaved and dominated people. . . . [T]he descendants of slaves and serfs in South Africa," Baderoon observes, "made a new place where the two African oceans meet" (91; see also Wardi).

Besides *Things Fall Apart* and *Beloved*'s meeting at the time and aquatic locations of captivity, my proposition that *Things Fall Apart*, Achebe's archetypal village novel, be viewed also as a slavery narrative finds added support in other confluences. Elaborated below, the junctions include multiple allusions in the story to slavery. There is also Achebe's earlier-mentioned assessment of *Beloved* and Sethe's infanticides. And equally as significant, though discussed toward the end of this chapter, is an attributed complementarity, an inferred antiphony between *Things Fall Apart* and *Beloved* relative to what I am calling the two works' "narrative and knowledge gaps" on transatlantic slavery and ancestry questions.

As Tunji Osinubi has also identified, there are several moments and spaces in *Things Fall Apart* where slavery and transatlantic-slave-trade *talk* lurk; encrypted, to echo Laura Murphy. These are the narrative junctures in which, as Osinubi denominates, the omniscient narrator engages directly with, references, and/or hints at "slavery," or at other *slaveries* in authorial intimation of slavery's topologies in Igboland in the forms and structures of kinship, bondage, sociocultural alterity, propertization, and ownership. Others are references to firearms, possibly "guns obtained from the white [slave] traders" (Talbot 184), although the narrator suggests that a crafty blacksmith, a migrant/stranger who had lived in Umuofia for years, made Okonkwo a rusty gun, perhaps the one with which he nearly kills his wife, Ojiugo. The clues also include intimations of Umuofia's warlikeness. Wars were the second major source of slaves, next only to kidnapping (Isichei, *History* 45). Other hints are the Ikemefuna/cult slavery substory; the issue of outcasts/*osu* system; the invocation of slavery in the song Kotma *of the ash buttocks;* the subject of loss of sovereignty; the story of Abame that points to the violent subjugation of the historical Aro slave traders; and references to lazy children.[6] Concerning the last group, Wren writes that "the lazy, the indolent, the illegitimate" were in the past "trad[ed] off" as a matter of practice to ease the burdens of overpopulation on communities. He explains that there are even late twentieth-century attributions of low ethics among youths to the stoppage of the slave trade. "The threat of sale to an unknown fate encouraged dutiful behaviour in children. If a child was sold," Wren adds, "he would perforce come into the hands of the Aro" (*Achebe's World* 60).

A few more instances are missing in Osinubi's brilliant analysis. One is *ogbanje*. Evoked multiple times also in *Arrow of God*, this mythic syndrome is popularized in *Things Fall Apart* in the Ezinma story and also in the briefly narrated experience of a young, new Christian and mother of an *ogbanje* child. With published allusions to and records of the phenomenon's occurrence dating to as far back as 1857 and 1894, most explorations of the *ogbanje*, the Igbo strain of the spirit-children/born-to-die myth, do not establish direct connections between slavery and the advent of the belief. As I explicate in *A Spirit of Dialogue*, however, there are subtle ties between slavery and the *abiku*, the Yoruba variant of the experience. There are also associations between mothers' and children's *ogbanje* condition and sickle cell anemia, and between this malaria-implicated, genetic, and often fatal hemoglobin illness *and* the ordeals of enslaved women with multiple child mortalities, as well as with slaves' beliefs in and attitudes toward malevolent spirits, abnormal births, child naming, life, death, interments, and reincarnations in the American South.[7]

The other narrative spot Osinubi misses in which slavery or transatlantic slavery discourse is atomized and screened in the novel is in the historical reference with which Uncle Uchendu attempts to hearten his despondent nephew, Okonkwo. Uncle Uchendu reminds him how much more dire his sentence of exile could have been. "You think you are the greatest sufferer in the world?," Uchendu asks. "Do you know that men are sometimes banished for life?" (135). Unanswered in the novel are the questions: Whatever happened to those forced exiles Uchendu mentions who served life sentences for whatever capital crimes? Did all or some of them fall into the waiting hands of the Abame/Abam warriors and savvy slave traders? Were they helplessly sucked into the vast slave-trading networks of the Aro—a system at the center of which was the purportedly man-devouring "Aro Chuk[w]u Oracle which was universally respected and feared throughout I[g]boland, and in fact by every tribe in eastern Nigeria" where it was held as "the highest court of appeal"? (Dike 37–38, 41). Did the men, for self and familial refuge, entreat deital protection and become *osu,* cult slaves? Severed from the shielding ties of kinship, their means of livelihood constrained or razed, did the men become slaves, as Elizabeth Isichei writes relative to domestic slavery in Igboland, "through economic necessity[?]. Debt could force a man to pawn himself or his child" (*History* 49).

Furthermore, Dike points out that "the system of obtaining slaves by use of oracular devices was fairly widespread in the I[g]bo country." And other than "the Chukwu at Aro-Chukwu, there were other such oracles." Like associates or deputies, these other oracles simply augmented "the work of the all-powerful Aro Oracle, undoubtedly the dominant power in the country" (40). As such, would it be unreasonable to assume that Umuofia's powerful medium and arbiter, the Oracle of the Hills and the Caves or whatever its historical models—which by then would have been subordinate and assistive to the dictatorial and terrorizing Aro Oracle—is implicated in domestic slavery and the Atlantic slave trade? Could it, aided by Priestess Chielo's human predecessors and models, have colluded in the elaborate slavery scheme by readily convicting and condemning to bondage people who wound up, by way of the ubiquitous Aro merchants, in the Niger Delta Atlantic slave markets? (see also Wren,

Achebe's World 24). With its Calabar and Bonny commercial hubs, the Delta, "from the seventeenth century onwards," became "the most important slave mart in West Africa, equaling the trade of all West Africa put together" (Dike 25, 28–29).

More so, the Umuofians are said to be near-mortally afraid of the dark. It is likely that the unavailability of modern electrification in the village, public lighting, heavy forestation, and cosmological attitudes to spirits/the supernatural helped give rise to the Umuofians' reflexive if not primal reactions to pitch darkness, as Achebe writes. That the Umuofia villagers of the story are preindustrial in Western definition and today's measurements does not, however, mean they lack indigenous fire-making implements and broad lighting technology, concept of space illumination, and nighttime event planning and staging. We are told, for instance, that, at nightfall, during the elaborate and long festivities associated with Akueke Obierika's daughter's marriage to Ibe, "burning torches were set on wooden tripods" to floodlight the venue and create appropriate ambiance (118). Yet, could the Umuofians' fear of the dark also have been survivalist reflex? In short, could it have been because of their long, experiential—or passed-on— knowledge and memory of nocturnal and ambushing slave kidnappers?

The other narrative clues are sheathed machetes and the *iga*, or handcuffs. Could self-protection from kidnappers and raiders, or the memories of slave-raiding wars of not long ago then also have contributed to the widespread practice of men wearing sheathed machetes on short and long trips even during peacetime? A climate of fear and deep distrust of even one's own neighbor pervaded Igbo life in the nineteenth century (Isichei, *History*, 64–65). The optics of the handcuffs' force over "violent criminals" are clear and arresting. And those manacles are generally dreaded as "the most deadly of the white man's weapons," *Arrow of God's* narrator records (153). The white man and white power, figured in the District Commissioner, use the *iga* to shackle, subdue, and humiliate six Umuofia leaders, including Okonkwo. He, through his native guards, equally deploys it to terrify hesitant Umuaroans into divulging Ezeulu's residence in *Arrow of God*. Handcuffs—a significant part of "the contemporary prison experience [that] is the violent continuation of chattel slavery and colonialism endured by Black ancestors in Africa and in the African Diaspora" (M. Nagel 136)—may well have been fastened on Obi Okonkwo upon his arrest in *No Longer at Ease*. So, could the Igbo Umuofia villagers' dread of the *iga* have initially arisen from the people's collective unconscious of the widespread use, during slavery, of iron locks and contraptions, among the other technological advances in steel and metal conceived and designed specifically for bodily restraint during the Atlantic passage and plantation enslavement proper in the Old and New Worlds? Recall Paul D, who was subjected to that inhumane and traumatizing assault, remembering that iron bits were unsparingly used on adults and children; on the mouths of "Men, boys, little girls, women" (71).

Consider this also. The white man's very presence in Umuofia/Igboland is slavery-predicated. That is not in dispute. However, what is diligently structured in the novel as Umuofia village's idyllic precolonial moment—the period before direct evangelical and imperial contact—is made possible by the transatlantic slave trade. Put another way: that historically accurate prelapsarian epoch would not have been possible or lasted as long without help, namely, the indirect intervention of those multitribal coastal peoples/Atlantic slave traders in the Bight of Biafra whom Achebe, in the 1959-edition blurb mentioned earlier, viewed as "debased" by their involvement in the horrors of the international slave trade. For as Dike argues, in addition to the Igbo people's indigenous location in the forest belt and the high mortality of European "merchant-adventurers" who regularly succumbed to malaria before the discovery of quinine by the legendary British naval surgeon Dr. William Balfour Baikie, it was those same Niger Delta peoples whose population advantage, economic monopolism, territorial protectionism, and organized armed resistance long hindered British invasion. Although the advent of the steam engine and reinvigorated British naval effort subsequently opened the inland territories to commerce, evangelism, and colonial rule, the protracted and often armed opposition by the coastal peoples delayed imperial penetration into the interior (Dike 1–18, 7, 27, 37). It is this resistance and delay that shielded the fictionalized Umuofias, Mbantas, and Umuaros of Igboland from immediate colonial encounter and conquest.

Of the foregoing narrative interstices and extratextual histories where slavery, as "the past," and the discourse that it engenders are veiled in and transposable into *Things Fall Apart*, Okonkwo's expiatory exile to his mother's village, Mbanta, prompts the novel's one and only explicit reference to the transatlantic slave trade. Readers will recall Obierika, Okonkwo's greatest friend, visiting him there two years into his seven-year banishment. It is during his first trip that Obierika, strategically situated as a proxy narrator, apprises Okonkwo of major developments in his absence, especially the British massacre of Abame. Says Obierika to Okonkwo and Uchendu: "We have heard stories about white men who made the powerful guns and strong drinks and took slaves away across the seas, but no one thought the stories were true." To which the wise Uchendu replies: "There is no story that is not true," a conclusion he reaches, citing the universe's breadth and, more specifically, its cultural and cosmologic diversity (140–41). Given how subtly yet deeply this instance of subject-invocation interconnects *Things Fall Apart* and *Beloved,* how dialectically it positions both texts as historical continuum and much more, I will return to it at the end of this chapter in my discussion of the novels' deftly stylized and widely celebrated closings.

Styling (in) the Village (Novel): Structure, Cosmology, Character, Language

The following are of interest to me in this section, especially with our attention refocused now on both texts: *Things Fall Apart* and *Beloved*'s form, their—particularly *Beloved*'s—expressions of the village novel plot; Morrison's representations of the Cincinnati freed-slave community/the Sethe household and family *and* their Africa-inspirited villagism; and Achebe and Morrison's comparable depictions of their main village characters, Okonkwo and Sethe, in terms of generation, spectrality, (ancestral) haunting, and ontology. Examined also are both authors' figurations of their village- and villagers-impacting white characters—Mr. Brown and Mr. Smith, in *Things Fall Apart,* and Amy Denver, the Garners, the Bodwins, and Schoolteacher, in *Beloved.* Fascinating, too, are Achebe and Morrison's allied, authorial fidelities to village linguistic autochthony; and, in closing, the two novels' much-discussed endings.

In addition to expositing, as recalled earlier, that one of the village novel's core precepts and agendas is narrative preservation—but certainly not idealization and/or fossilization—of a world or a time that is past or passing, Griswold also contends that the genre generally adopts a five-part mythic plot. The arrangement basically includes periods of "traditional stability," "disturbance from outside," "attempted restoration," "climax," and "disintegration or reintegration." This essentially before-and-after theme and plot sequence is so obvious in *Things Fall Apart* it would be rehashing a critically hackneyed trope to unfurl it in its mimetic breadth in the narration. Arguably, even readers new to Achebe and to the novel would have no problem whatsoever identifying those contours. That pre-and-post structure is summarized in Obierika's memorable and often-quoted articulation of the story's title and thesis: The white man "came quietly and peaceably with his religion." He "put a knife on the things that held us together and we have fallen apart" (176).

Although *Beloved* also adopts a pre-and-post narrative axis, that layout is additionally obstructed from easy reader and critical view by the novel's formal design, as suggested earlier. It is obfuscated by, though still lurking in, the story's disjointed organization, its numerous and intersecting stories, multiperspectival diegesis, stream of consciousness, countless allusions, denials of material information, and deferments of nominal contexts, among other techniques. Untangling that chronology and the Obierika-type theme-plot overview requires that we keep in mind this crucial point: *Beloved*'s main character/story is not exactly Sethe/Sethe's. Instead, and as in *Things Fall Apart*, the protagonist is the ancestor-antedating village. *Beloved*'s hero and heroine is the Cincinnati community of freed slaves. As does Okonkwo, around whose abject beginning, improbable meteoric rise, and tragic end Achebe frames Umuofia village's story, Sethe functions connectively as well. She is a vehicle through which Morrison humanizes, historicizes, and mediates the losses and fortunes, and the deepest psychic drives, of that inchoate New World black village.

At its most skeletal, *Beloved*'s village-novel mythic plot—the outline of Sethe's substory, as it were—unfolds in the following linear permutation. First, there is the period of "traditional stability," covering Sethe's story from her early life and enslavement in Garner's Kentucky *Sweet Home* through her escape to Cincinnati and her first four weeks living with Baby Suggs in the home of Scottish abolitionists, the Bodwins. Two things should be clarified right away. One: conceptual "stability" does not mean halcyon temporality. Two: although the enactment of the 1850 Fugitive Slave Act, which Sethe reacted to roughly as "the Misery" (171), is a watershed setback to slaves, it is also a strengthening of the earlier, 1793 Fugitive Slave Act passed by Congress. Thus, I view the new and stiffer iteration of that law as part of slavery's larger pattern/tradition/rhythm of legal restrictions and codes; in short, the topsy-turvy world to which slaves had had to habituate themselves. It is an upside-down life to which they, albeit painfully, had adapted and "stabilize[d]" their unfree and regularly violated black human bodies, spirits, and existences. In contrast to this period of "traditional stability," I interpret the novel's period of "disturbance from outside" as covering Beloved's early spiritual visitations of/intrusions into *and* in 124 Bluestone Road; Paul D's arrival there; and Beloved's subsequent, corporeal manifestation and habitation in the house. The time of "attempted restoration" marks Sethe and Denver's obsessive but unsuccessful efforts to reabsorb and ingratiate the spiteful Beloved and reestablish famil-ial/kinship bonds. Beloved's exponentially growing malevolence and her clear threat to Sethe's life, which lead to the village women's collective intervention, are the novel's "climax." The exorcism of Beloved, the return of Paul D and the ancient dog Here Boy, as well as Denver's mental growth, implied future educational pursuits at Oberlin, and her full immersion in the socioeconomic and cultural life of black Cincinnati cover the plot's phase of "disintegration or reintegration."

What is further notable about the *Things Fall Apart* and *Beloved* story lines is that *Beloved* actually has its own character-articulated plot synopsis. That rundown is supplemented by Ella's theme-crystalizing and equally memorable insistence on equity between past and present, and between Sethe's crime and her prolonged punishment by both Beloved and the village. As with the Obi-erika summative statement above, the *Beloved* narrative passage in question bridges all five mythic sequences of the village-novel plot. It also speaks, more significantly, to rapid and irreversible change. It highlights how quickly things fall apart, so to speak, for fugitive Sethe but with possibilities of her familial renewal and full personal reintegration in Cincinnati's black village community (173–76). Fascinatingly, it is Sethe herself to whom Morrison delegates that chronological plot précis. We find it in Sethe's two-paragraph introspection on her "twenty-eight days" of innocence, indeed of short-lived bliss. That interior monologue is also the high point of the village novel's/*Beloved*'s structural stage of "traditional stability." Sethe's recollection of this prelapsarian interlude is of her "having women friends, a mother-in-law, and all her children together; of being part of a neighborhood; of, in fact, having neighbors at all to call her own—all that was gone and would never come back" (173). Now, suddenly, she says, she is alienated by these previously cordial members of the village after she stoically kills her "crawling already?" daughter barely a month after Stamp Paid rescues and, along with Ella, helps resettle them.

But the question is, why? Other than their disapprobation of Sethe's infan-ticide and their responsorial contempt for her complicated personality, what else explains the people's attitude, their deep resentment? The answer is that the novel in which they are characters is village literature. It is that Morrison paints their community of free slaves as a village, an African village, inexactly (re)constituted in the New World. It cannot be lost on us how Achebe and Morrison purposefully and comparably set their stories in geographic out-skirts. Like stories set in the sea islands—for instance Julie Dash's *Daughters of the Dust,* Gloria Naylor's *Mama Day,* and partly Paule Marshall's *Praisesong for the Widow*—Achebe and Morrison situate the narratives outside locations that are already heavily contaminated by white presence. The goal here arguably is to suggest the areas' minimal disturbance and their preservation of African cultural inheritances and worldview. Umuofia is located away from the Delta/ Atlantic coast and black Cincinnati is, inferably, situated outside of the down-town, the city center proper.

We recall here Achebe and Morrison's aligned positions that villagism, or village sensibilities, generally and inevitably follow (their) rural peasants down to towns. This would be even more the case with *Beloved's* mid- to late nineteenth-century African American characters. Though consigned to a small neighborhood outside the then-emerging midwestern city of Cincinnati, they are perhaps at most three or so generations removed from their originary Afri-can homeland. They may now be "town" dwellers. They may even be said to be living in "Cincinnati." But their ways are villagist. Cincinnati is bigger, more populous, urban, and racially whiter than Carolina, as Baby Suggs recalls. She was first enslaved in Carolina by a Whitlow. And her freedom, after sixty years in bondage, was financially procured by her son Halle. He is the only remain-ing of her "dead and gone" children: Patty, Famous, Johny, Rosa Lee, Tyree, Nancy, and Ardelia.

To Garner—Baby Suggs's next and now-former owner who admits he bought her cheap because of her age and physical infirmity—Cincinnati is "a city of water." It is a sweet place, or rather a sweet home, modern and industrial (142–43). Garner, the slave-collector whom Shirley A. Stave calls "a represen-tation of the God of Genesis" ("From Eden" 110), is acutely and deitally blind to the fact that all Baby Suggs, a cobbler, desired is self-ownership and self-determination. She would trade Cincinnati city for her freedom, husband, and children. A few pages later, Cincinnati, as filtered through former slaves and fellow villagers Paul D and Stamp Paid's consciousness, is "still pig port in the minds of Ohioans. Its main job was to receive, slaughter and ship up the river the hogs that Northerners did not want to live without" (154). Antebellum Cincinnati, the "slaughter and riverboat capital," may provide its free and freed African-descended black residents employment in "killing, cutting, skinning, case packing and saving offal" (155). Its black community is even said to have two graveyards and six churches. Yet, though physically located in and sub-sumed under plantation economy and logic, and the broader social universe of their Euro-American captors and masters, the slaves' world—essentially an

African/village world—is extrinsic. It existed outside of that planter universe, especially culturally, ontologically, and religiously.

In addition, we may recall verbatim Wendy Griswold's conceptualization earlier that the village, permeated by religion and always already complicated and transitioning, is characteristically "thick with human relationships, with rivalry, jealousy, support, sanctions, desire, bitterness, respect, contempt." Echoing, for instance, M. M. Green's firsthand observations about the village of Umueke Agbaja discussed in the previous chapter, Griswold pictures the village as a place "where little goes unobserved, where what is observed is commented upon, and where 'transparency' is a virtue, secretiveness a sin." The village novel, inscribed in a language felicitous to its environment and its characters' vernaculars, as George Nyamndi adds, also features individuals or rather, and generally, a major character grappling with the tensions between individual desires, pasts, actions, and opinions *and* the collective mores and pressures of his or her village community. These principles are enshrined in paradoxically rigid-and-flexible customs and traditions. Adhering to a relativist cosmos that embraces sacred and secular modes of knowledge and ontological variety, the village is marked, equally, by heterogeneity and ambiguities. As episteme and motif, this miscellany and ambivalence can irrigate characterization and formal experimentation in modernist fiction. It can also brace the postmodernist narrative's predispositions toward irresolution. The village is also indicated by villagers' tendencies toward fatalism.

Things Fall Apart and *Beloved* validate those dimensions of (the village novel's) style. As interesting as the two novels' overlaps of spatiotemporal settings and preoccupation with "the past" are, their connections at the above village sites are even more captivating in breadth and depth. Consider these few examples. Genealogy and generations—which are consolidating fabrics of kinship and the village and also important aspects of the West African village novel—are major subjects in both stories and in Achebe and Morrison's other novels as well. In the present texts, slavery and colonization, as well as other existential circumstances, tear at the roots of the novels' black families and kinship ties on both sides of the Atlantic. Yet, the significance and structures of those filiations are not lost on the people of Umuofia, Mbanta, and the other imbricated villages. Nor are they inconsequential to *Beloved*'s black Cincinnati even under enormous stress from the white world. It is worth recalling here also Elizabeth Isichei's earlier remark about the devastating impact of the transatlantic slave trade (and domestic slaveries). Isichei may well have been speaking of *Beloved*'s subthesis, its characters, their experiences, and African America at large. Morrison's personal experience of being identified as a Wofford kin by her walk finds antecedence and resonance in *Beloved*. It echoes in Paul D's wondering about the ghost-child-woman *Beloved*'s "people" (234–35); Baby Suggs's insinuations of diaspora in her remark about familial dispersal and potential reunification; and in the Bodwins' housekeeper Janey Wagon asking Denver, "You Baby Suggs' kin, ain't you?" (253). It can be argued that, at its heart and formal shape, *Beloved* is about family; about ancestry and kinship: of (African/black) lineages severed, lost, gained, thwarted, extended, mixed, and improvised. It is about that kinship Christianized and redefined by the twin forces of slavery and colonization, the latter impact of which Achebe renders memorably in Nwoye's story and the rift that the white man's religion—alongside other propellants—causes between Nwoye and his father, Okonkwo.

Ancestors and/or their surrogates—central to formations and structures of kinship—are staples of the village and village novels. Thus, Achebe and Morrison's comparable positioning of such "timeless" people as major aspects of *Things Fall Apart* and *Beloved*'s villagism is noteworthy. But even more critically fascinating are the two authors' analogous depictions of the stories of the novels' central, village families as one of genealogical and generational histories, bridges, ruptures, and futures. We are offered in those representations another glimpse into Achebe and Morrison's "concord of sensibilities," to channel Ralph Ellison ("World" 131). The two familial ancestors—Sethe's unnamed African mother and Okonkwo's father, Unoka—are "marked," but in different ways. Sethe's mother, an enslaved African who is said to have spoken a now-lost African language, is raped on the slave ship, as well as burnt and branded with a technological advance in steel and trade-marking: a hot iron that left a "circle and a cross" mark on her rib (61). Afraid of blood in war and a pacifist potentially against slave-raiding, Unoka is "branded" unmanly and weak by his son and others. But although both ancestors appear narratively minor, they are hugely consequential figures in both stories; more narratively consequential, however, than Okonkwo's unnamed and dead mother. They constitute, or rather *embody*, truncated but looming (black) absences, memories, and legacies. They are metaphors of "the pasts" against which Okonkwo and Sethe must (re)construct and navigate their personal identities, present lives, familial futures, and social histories. Like "Beloved," Unoka and Sethe's mother are, in effect, "ghosts," if by ghost we mean—as Juda Bennett writes, evoking Derrida's *hauntology*—"everything . . . history, memory, text, and, indeed, the world as we perceive it. Nothing escapes the problem of presence/absence. Nothing is without ghost effects" (*Ghosts* 4).

That is to say, then, it is not just the slave-villager Sethe and her 124 Blue-stone Road home that are haunted and "possessed" by a slavery-related and restive memory. Umuofia villager Okonkwo and his village household are also haunted, directly and indirectly, in the form of Unoka as "an apparition" from the past. Unoka appears as (a) spirit *possessing*/haunting Okonkwo. An undead, a returning spirit, a repeating history of inerasable *other, difference,* and existential philosophy, Unoka is a still-determinative recollection. He is a cellular, perhaps genetic, memory that in part inflames Okonkwo's dominant emotion since childhood, fear: "the fear of failure and of weakness . . . the fear of himself, lest he should be found to resemble his father" (13). His father the paradox: to him, the lazy and deadbeat dad whose blood and chromosomes run in his veins; the gifted but poor yet merry and lucid artist; improvident and a debtor; a possible alcoholic that may have passed on/transferred that addiction (to palm-wine) to Okonkwo. According to the narrator, Okonkwo "was possessed" by this pesky *ghost,* this "fear of his father's contemptible life and shameful death" (18).

But what is much more astounding about the *Things Fall Apart–Beloved* intertextuality is that Sethe and Okonkwo's hauntings also stem compatibly from a village and cultural taboo—child-murder—and the trauma it exacts. Neil Ten Kortenaar is one critic who has noted that "*Things Fall Apart* displays a fascination with child-murder that can only be described as obsessive." He also keenly recognizes that *Things Fall Apart* and *Beloved* share a concern with trauma resultant from "a parent's killing of a child" (776–77). Of the many deaths—homicides, infanticides, filicides, suicides, and other fatalities—that occur collectively or are implied in the novels, Sethe's murder of her daughter Beloved and Okonkwo's killing of his "son" Ikemefuna and his murder of the District Commissioner's messenger are some of the most far-reaching. They are turning points in both characters' lives, and for their village communities and the narratives as a whole. This claim is not intended to undervalue those other deaths in the texts: lynchings in *Beloved*; the deaths by wars, drought, and imperial violence in *Things Fall Apart*; Sethe's mother's inferred infanticide on the slave ship; Baby Suggs's infanticides by refusing to nurse the babies she bore through rapes by white men; Ella's inferred child murder; Okonkwo's accidental murder of a kinsman Ogbuefi Ezeudu's sixteen-year-old son during Ezeudu's funeral; his near-fatal shooting of his wife, Ojiugo, during the Week of

Peace; his attempted suffocation of Nwoye; and his threat to wipe out the missionaries. Nonetheless, just as Sethe is dogged psychically by childhood and adult wounds, Okonkwo is also scarred by a childhood and adult past/ghost, Unoka. But he is combated and tortured by three or so other specters that are equally historically or slavery-linked. They include the haunting memory of Ikemefuna. The other is his memory of his humiliating and violent incarceration by the white District Commissioner during which time his black back and body, like Sethe's, is stigmatared—scarified and scribed on—by the warden's whip. And, lastly, is the memory of the District Commissioner's messenger.

It is beyond remarkable that any two, sea-separated village characters, in this case Sethe and Okonkwo, can exhibit this level of profile resemblances. For here, again, lies another set of their shared attributes, the questions: Whom did they kill? Why? What are the familial and village repercussions of the murders? And, what are the Umuofia and black Cincinnati villages' reactions to them? We have noted that, in murdering Beloved and Ikemefuna, Sethe and Okonkwo killed their respective children: Sethe, her biological "child," and Okonkwo, his adopted "son." But here is the more profound point. Okonkwo murders in Ikemefuna his or rather what—as in Sethe's case—could be deemed his family's "best thing" at the time. He murders his own "beloved" and "crawling-already? baby" son. Without discounting Ezinma's spiritual connection to and enormous (motherly) influence on Okonkwo, it is the cult slave, Ikemefuna, Okonkwo's ninth child, so to speak, who does not only positively transform the familial atmosphere of the Okonkwo household soon upon his arrival (read, his birth) in Umuofia village. He also endears himself to Okonkwo, whom he calls "father." He influences Nwoye as well. We are told both boys so bonded Ikemefuna "was like an elder brother to Nwoye, and from the very first seemed to have kindled a new life in the younger boy" (52).

If by "crawling-already" or *already crawling* we mean—following Baby Suggs's description of Beloved's infancy to the just-arrived Sethe—a baby/child advancing faster than normal in its milestones of physical, kinetic, and mental abilities; if by that we mean, in short, a smart-already baby, as Baby Suggs says of infant Beloved (93–94): then the "baby"-"child" Ikemefuna fits that portrait. He is the picture of uncommon intelligence, adroitness, creativity, nimbleness, and adaptability. The narrator asserts that Ikemefuna—as though *a new baby, an infant*—"grew rapidly like a yam tendril in the rainy season, and was full of the sap of life" (54). He "had an endless stock of folk tales. Even those which Nwoye knew already were told with a new freshness and the local flavor of a different clan" (34). Sethe kills Beloved two years after her birth. Haunted by Unoka's ghost, Okonkwo murders the beloved Ikemefuna "young," on the third year of his life in the Okonkwo family and Umuofia village, even after the ancestral figure Ogbuefi Ezeudu cautions him against participating in the expiation. The psychic, historical, and racial impulses behind both infanticides are just as stunning. As Kortenaar rightly observes, "at the emotional centre of the novel is the death of Ikemefuna" (776).

Laid bare by the above affecting incidents is another of *Things Fall Apart* and *Beloved*'s inescapable leitmotifs, love. Although the question of primal love is hardly peculiar to the village and villagism, or to the village novel's and village literature's conjoined themes of neighborliness, individual and communal well-being, and balance, it is undoubtedly implicit in those subjects. Encouraged by Morrison's corroborations that love, its semantic fractions, configurations, and performativity are a recurrent topic in her fiction, critics have explored particularly her trilogy through that prism, bringing to the thesis a wealth of insight. For example, speaking with Jane Bakerman in 1977 in one of her much-cited interviews, Morrison declaims: "Beauty, love . . . actually, I think all the time that I write, I'm writing about love or its absence . . . people do all sorts of things, under its name, under its guise" (40–41). Morrison's titular, racial, philosophic, and material distillation of that love premise in her eighth novel, *Love*, is preceded by her treatment of it as an existential, epistemological, and historical conundrum not just in her debut *The Bluest Eye* but particularly in *Beloved*. In it, Paul D views Sethe's mother-love as "too thick," too rigid, compulsive, and destructive. To which Sethe counters that love has to stay resolute or it is no-love. We witness, also, Denver and Beloved's counterpointal loves as they play out (in) their presentness, pieties, and possessiveness.

Extending the *Beloved*/Sethe love template, then, I want to suggest that we add to our normative readings of Okonkwo and his killings of Ikemefuna, the District Commissioner's messenger, and himself. I move that we reimagine the murders not singly as the actions of a villager driven blindly by slavery-connected apparitions, the ghostly fear of weakness and failure. We could also view them as deeds impelled *also* by love. They are consequences of Okonkwo's overpowering—indeed *possessive, jealous,* and thus *excessive*—love of (his) village, his home/motherland, especially of Umuofia's precolonial era. Imbricating herself in questions that disconcerted the Enlightenment, namely, autonomous black humanity and subjectivity and especially the indivisibility of freedom and bondage, Sethe, a slave, murders her child Beloved to exert agency. She *murder* / *love* (handwritten margin notes)

kills to preempt the certainty of that child Beloved being condemned to a dehumanizing life of slavery. And most importantly, she kills out of love. Similarly, Okonkwo commits murders equally agentially but also, subtextually, out of love. A historic and celebrated athlete, a paragon of industry, a onetime head of Umuofia's foreign diplomatic mission, decorated war hero and veteran, one of Umuofia's nine-justices supreme court, dedicated volunteer in his village's national guard, a *palmwine drinker-ed* (to play on Tutuola), polygamist, exile, yet a loving father willing to defy the sacred powers vested in Priestess Chielo to ensure the safety of his sick daughter Ezinma: Okonkwo commits his offenses in loving submission to the Oracle. He perpetrates them, I submit, in loving defense of Umuofia: his home which, to him, would only surrender to the invading locusts and enslaving armies of colonization—as it turns out, literally—over his dead body. Mischaracterized by some as Okonkwo's/African clannishness, (his) patriotism becomes a love-act. It is that love-of-nation, or of a place, or a position and privilege, or *that* defense of sovereignty or a principle deemed sacrosanct or transcendent, for which, for instance, (Aro and other) slave abductors followed assistive and principal oracles and troops follow Oracular orders against declared human or ideological enemies. They pacify such "adversaries" in hills, valleys, and caves, in big cities and small villages, even when and even if the casualties of such love-performances would be innocent, noncombatant, and *crawling-already* babies and children.

Nevertheless, Morrison, through familial, fraternal, and village reactions, points to the presumptiveness and moral indefensibility of Sethe's intemperate, saw-knife and icepick philosophy of love, on mother-love. Achebe, too, deploys the same dialectical channels not only to further complicate Okonkwo, but to render the problematics of his machete-expressions of father-love, fatherland love, and, concomitantly, his masculinist notions of Umuofia citizenship and greatness. Prompted, here, are the village values of interconnectivity, plurality, restraint, and balance. First, we have Denver and Nwoye's uncannily similar intuitiveness and their palpable familial disapprovals of their parents' killings of their beloved, older siblings. We are told, for example, that "As soon as his father walked in, that night, Nwoye knew that Ikemefuna had been killed, and something seemed to give way inside him, like the snapping of a tightened bow. He did not cry. He just hung limp" (61). Comparably, Denver hints she knew instinctively that her mother, whom she says she loves, "killed one of her own daughters"—her sister, whose blood she ingests at the moment of her death. As with Nwoye's debilitation, Denver grows weary. She withdraws into herself and shelters indoors for years. Terrified that they, too, would be harmed by their parents after the infanticides, Nwoye and Denver similarly avoid their father and mother, respectively. Compounded by his uneasiness with his people's forest-disposal and killing of twins, Nwoye post-Ikemefuna's death is so traumatized the agony, loneliness, and grudge drive him to the Christian missionaries. He renounces Okonkwo as his father. That slavery-linked and ghosted/ghostly event also haunts him far into his adulthood. Also querying Okonkwo and Sethe's actions and judgments are their close friends and others in the villages. Obierika, for instance, believes Okonkwo acted unwisely and abominably. He suggests Okonkwo should have space-avoided; that he should have tactfully defied the Oracle by staying at home. Paul D, too, views Sethe's decision as ill-advised and extreme. He also recommends, albeit indelicately, space-avoidance: that, having two feet, Sethe should cautiously have run away instead. Just as troubled by Okonkwo's unilateral killing of the messenger, in this case, is the larger Umuofia village. Implicitly speaking through one of its members, the village wonders aloud, "Why did he do it?" (205)—a question that stunningly recalls Schoolteacher's Nephew, horrified at the site of Sethe's killing of her child in her woodshed, blurting out three times, "What she go and do that for?" (150), as though articulating the collective shock and struggle of the Cincinnati black village with Sethe's infanticidal response. Unlike Baby Suggs's stoicism and nonchalance to the murder, Ella understands Sethe's rage "but not her reaction to it" (276).

Sethe and Okonkwo's slavery-implicated but village-disapproved infanticides (in Okonkwo's case through the elder Ogbuefi Ezeudu) are such big moments in the novels' broader thematic, technical, and philosophic projects, and are so serious in the acts' cosmological and intraracial portentousness, Achebe and Morrison have commented on Sethe. To Morrison, who seems to concur with Ella, Sethe may be justified in her rage. But she still has no right to take Beloved's life. And as his earlier-presented view on Sethe's act conveys (see Botstein), Achebe never exculpates or diminishes Europe's central and sustained roles in the five-century trade in African bodies that depleted the continent of its prime human capital, rendered it more vulnerable to colonial rules, thus doubly making it skid off its paths and destinies in history. Nor does he excuse continental Africans, as suggested in his unease with Africans' culpability in that unspeakable horror. In his analysis of the Sethe-Beloved tragedy, Achebe teases but does not elaborate the analogies I have been sketching above. The Sethe infanticide seems, however, to have reminded him of

Okonkwo's murder of Ikemefuna. Sethe's dilemma—her tacitly sacrificial act in which Beloved's blood is shed for the cause of abolition—discernibly recollects for Achebe Okonkwo and Umuofia's collective repetition of abomination. That is, Okonkwo/Umuofia village executes a sacrilege (the killing of Ikemefuna) to avenge and expiate another cultural breach (Mbaino people's killing of an Umuofia daughter). This racial, ethical, and cosmological paradox helps trigger the returning judgments of a spiteful Beloved/history.

If a vastly changed Umuofia wonders audibly why Okonkwo did it—why, wishing his killing of the white man's messenger in reflexive patriotism, in Sethean resistance and love-rage would incite his downcast village into mounting one last fight against foreign rule—it is also because, like steely Sethe, rigid Okonkwo is often idiosyncratically out of sync. His temperamental and ideological inelasticity is incongruous with the embedded aporias and quicksands of village life in his fatherland. Okonkwo's excessive masculinity and his immutability are inconsistent with the female-spirited and internally contradictory impulses of his Igbo-Umuofia village. His prescription of brutal revolt is also misaligned with the more tactical reaction of his motherland Mbanta village. With its name literally meaning a small place, village, community, nation, people and thus hinting at inherent disadvantages, Mbanta prudently adopts a group-shielding response to, for instance, an Mbanta Christian convert's unprecedented killing of the village's royal python. In short, Okonkwo is mispositioned relative to the broader historic winds sweeping rapidly, and in some cases violently, across many parts of his African world, of which Umuofia and Mbanta are but allegories. Constituted alike ontologically, Sethe and Okonkwo are, then, in this regard, perfect studies for that other important hallmark of village literature. That is, its thematic, figural, and sometimes structural engagement with the age-old struggle between individual and community.

Missy Dehn Kubitschek could not be more astute in her observation, posited as though in reference to Okonkwo and *Things Fall Apart* (minus the postmodernist slant): "*Beloved* specifically investigates what happens when a character refuses a postmodernist world—that is, when a character clings to one interpretation, one meaning, of the past. Unable to change her understanding of a painful past, Sethe becomes its prisoner" (20). Morrison variously stresses that particular villagism point of the ceaselessness of change. They range from her building the novel on multiple generations and the many lives and altered purposes of 124 Bluestone Road to the talk of "the old days" (65). They include as well Denver's disinterest in "the past" and the hint of her future attendance of Oberlin. Her education would, generationally and eventually, situate her as part of the early ferment of the New Negro era.

Achebe and Morrison's village-inspired but also modernist interests in relativity—their decisions to never overexalt any single story, any perception of truth, especially in that individual-community tension—find added confirmation in their novels' tempering if not subversions of Okonkwo and Sethe's dominances as forces in the stories. The resolves are also indicated in how both authors subject to dispute Okonkwo and Sethe's "master" memories and versions of the ghostly *and* spirited pasts. As suggested, Achebe and Morrison realize those goals of ideological contestation and dispersal through their interjections of counterbalancing narratives (see also Jeyifo, "For Chinua"). Even something as mundane, universal, and primordial as love is not conceptually and geographically stable. It is also not functionally uniform, as postulated earlier, and as shown in Morrison's novels. To quote Jean Wyatt, in Morrison's texts love is contingent and sublimated into "a different and surprising shape" (13).

The problem is not just that Okonkwo—as with Sethe's totalizing view of "the past"—is fixated on his narrow interpretation of his own past, figured as the "ghost"/spirit of his father. Nor is the issue merely one of historical disjuncture. That is, the fact that strongman Okonkwo, obsessed with making Umuofia great and widely respected again, loves and defends Umuofia *as-was* and not *as-is now*, in a history-undergirded novel about a slavery-participating republican village and a vanishing age, both of which prioritize temperance and adaptation as an existential imperative. The question is primarily about pride; the unbridled exhibitions of immodesty. Okonkwo, Sethe, and Morrison's eponymous Sula share that trait of conceit in abundance. Sethe's smugness so affronts many black Cincinnatians that they transfer their eighteen-year resentment to her man-friend and squatter Paul D. Likewise, Okonkwo's "brusqueness in dealing with less successful men" is irksome, remarks the narrator (26). His haughtiness piques elders in Umuofia, reminiscent of that charged moment in *Sula* when the elder Eva angrily reminds Sula that "Pride goeth before a fall" (93)—the same judgment against Sethe that Paul D fears he too has imbibed from the townsfolk (171). Umuofia elders remember full well Okonkwo's paternal history and legacy, his lowly beginnings, and crushing early adversities.

That pride would be such a sociocultural anathema in Umuofia and black Cincinnati should not surprise us in light of the cosmologies that frame their moral compasses. Black Umuofia and black Cincinnati align in their African traditions. Both groups subscribe to intuition, medicine, magic, conjure, and hex/fixing. Add to those their beliefs in evil, dreams, spirits, ghosts, reincarnation, telepathy, and signs. Umuofia, Mbanta, and black Cincinnati evince Griswold's picture of the (West African) village discussed earlier: what with their common emphases on elders/ancestral figures discharging the roles of oral historians and guardians and their shared value of collective well-being and group effort. We have also their populations comprising members given to (obviously human) hypocrisy, anger, grievance, and meddling, as Griswold outlines and *Beloved* corroborates.

However, not even the elder, ancestral figure, and unchurched evangelist Baby Suggs, holy—who contemplates color and harmony, preaches black self- and body-love, and is in return beloved and respected—can escape the village's intense intrusiveness, disapprobation, and envy. Her fellow villagers resent her supposed but narratively debunked lucky-slave life. They begrudge her display of purportedly undeserved ostentation. But they forget she spent sixty years in slavery. A body-snatcher and child-stealer, slavery wrecked her physical health. It also robbed her of all but one of her children, whose full human and racial potential would be unrealized, recalling Isichei's observation about slavery's impact. Inadvertently instigated by multitasked old man and long-time Underground Railroad conductor Stamp Paid, Baby Suggs had thrown a "feast for ninety people," with so little, miraculously. The impromptu thanksgiving banquet is to celebrate Sethe's and her three children's safe rescue and arrival in 124 Bluestone Road, but particularly for baby Denver's survival. An old village woman who still farms with hoes, like the Umuofians during their planting and harvesting seasons, Baby Suggs intuits that "Her friends and neighbors were angry at her because she had overstepped, given too much, offended them by excess." They felt insulted by what they saw as her "uncalled-for pride" (135–38). Overtaken by spite, which some of them still hold even during Baby Suggs's death and funeral later (171), they would not alert Baby Suggs to the imminent danger of Schoolteacher's posse of slave patrols headed their way: four new whitefolks that "just rode in," donning "the Look . . . The righteous Look every Negro learned to recognize along with his ma'am's tit" (157). Little wonder, too, Ella's distaste for her former friend Sethe's secretiveness, her reticence and righteous indignation. For eighteen years, Sethe, alienating herself from the village, is further alienated by them, consistent with village's unwritten code of reciprocity. What pains Baby Suggs is losing what used to be the love, counsel, sustenance, and security of the village. This protection is further demonstrated in the village's black women putting aside their grievance with Sethe to save her life and her family from capricious Beloved.

Furthermore, as villages, Umuofia, Mbanta, and black Cincinnati similarly and characteristically have in their midst the socially (marginal)ized, atypical subjectivities and, especially, strangers. But although in general the relationship with strangers may be mutually sustaining, it could also backfire, with repercussions that reverberate. Notice, for example, Umuofia and black Cincinnati's parallel as sanctuaries for fugitives and fugitive slaves, respectively. In *Things Fall Apart*'s rendering, more precisely, Umuofia is a safe haven for what Obierika describes as "a little band of [slavery-forced refugees,] fugitives [that] came into our town" from Abame (137–39), the fictionalized warrior and slave-raiding society of Abam. Abam was literally destroyed by the British in a covert and retaliatory attack executed as part of the wider British military campaign to suppress the African domestic slave trade. But as Obierika also adds: "Most of them [the fugitives] were sons of our land whose mothers had been buried with us. But there were some too [like Morrison's migrating Paul D] who came because they had friends in our town [as are Baby Suggs and Sethe for Paul D], and others who could think of nowhere else open to escape [like the runaways/strangers ferried for twenty years into black Cincinnati by conductors Stamp Paid and his aids]. And so they fled into Umuofia with a woeful story" (138), or rather woeful stories, such as are brought by Baby Suggs, Sethe, and Paul D.

Consider this also. The Sethe–Paul D–Denver early acquaintance with and hospitality to the smooth *stranger-in-the-village*, Beloved, resemble the Mbanta village's initial and unsuspecting reception of the slick *strangers*: the Christian missionaries, whom they provide land/shelter/home, the Evil Forest, for their supposedly lunatic religion. Manipulating their carnivalesque and inspirited worship, Christianity and its missionaries—sly, roving—end up splintering the heart of the host's society. Likewise, Beloved comes as a-spirited-stranger-on-a-mission. She surfaces, fully dressed and barely comprehensible. She arrives as a childlike and sleepy-eyed woman who just "walked out of the [baptismal] water," unnoticed, on the day of carnival (50; see also Elkann 152). It does not end well for Umuofia and Mbanta in their encounters with the baptism-water-carrying, peripatetic, and meddling evangelists, who initially are unintelligible to the locals. Similarly, Sethe's fostering of the time-traveling and devious "Beloved" does not. Or rather, it does not end as anticipated. What is perhaps most remarkable about these two "stranger"/"outsider" intrusions—these inter-positions of chaos into the rhythms of Umuofia life and the rhythmic or "stable" racial and sociocultural tensions of antebellum black Cincinnati—is how they effectuate considerable retrospection *and* change.

Beloved's guileful arrival and infringement in Cincinnati's black village, par-ticularly in its 124 Bluestone Road, prompt complexly stylized excavations of Sethe's memories and the other characters' pasts; their historicity, as it were. Comparably, the wily intrusions of postslavery forces—missionaries, Christi-anity, colonial governance, commerce—pressure Umuofia and Mbanta's reen-gagements with their historicity as well. Subjected to exploratory white gaze and up for re-view now are: the Umuofia and Mbanta senses of and connections to the metaphysical; their relationships to space and time, especially their prior cognition of physical distances and their sense of their geographical boundaries and their deitally linked four-day market calendar and cycle Eke, Oye, Afo, and Nkwo soon to become a seven-day week, Monday through Sunday. Other things now reappraised, or to be reassessed, are the strengths and/or intended contin-gencies of village practices inscribed in chalk- and *uli*-hieroglyphics and also in the people's kinship patterns, political philosophies, and legal codes; their sys-tems of land ownership and tenure; the topographies of their sacred sites; and their diet. Also exposed to further alteration are the processes of their interethnic and regional economies and their indigenous art/aesthetic forms, their musical instruments, music genres, and dance styles that would soon be combined with if not complicated by Christian, Western, and diasporic forms. And, subjected to the new dispensations is, last though not least, their multidialect and tonal Igbo language. It would be orthographied for scripture-translation, religious instruction, church hymnals, indigenized proselytization, colonial pedagogy, and governance. Although always already contaminated and changing, the vil-lage (Umuofia, Mbanta, and their countless literals) would undergo such trans-formations in the now up-close presences of the old-new, paradoxical stranger, whites, who for long were pushed back by the Niger Delta coastal peoples.

"They Got Me Out of Jail." "They Also Put You in It."

It would be an oversight to conclude the chapter without engaging, at some depth, with the uniformities of Achebe and Morrison's depictions of the two novels' major white characters. As far as the stories' villagers are concerned, those whites, while clearly impactful, are strangers and curiosities at best. Or they are, at worst, frightening if not sometimes deadly contradictions, as the below memorable dialectical exchange between Sethe and Baby Suggs intimates:

> "They got me out of jail," Sethe once told Baby Suggs.
>
> "They also put you in it," she answered.
>
> "They drove you 'cross the river."
>
> "On my son's back."
>
> "They gave you this house."
>
> "Nobody *gave* me nothing."
>
> "I got a job from them."
>
> "He got a cook from them, girl."
>
> "Oh, some of them do all right by us."
>
> "And every time it's a surprise, ain't it?"
>
> "You didn't used to talk this way."
>
> "Don't box with me. There's more of us they drowned than there is all of them ever lived from the start of time. Lay down your sword. This ain't a battle; it's a rout." (244)

In works of consequence such as *Things Fall Apart* and *Beloved,* it would have been easy, in the hands of reckless and lesser-gifted novelists, to lose the restraint and ironic distance that are often crucial guardrails against sensationalism. In other words, it would have been effortless for a literary propagandist to idealize blacks and black characters while invalidating the human complexity of whites. Part of that intricacy, as staged by the two texts and substantiated by history and our contemporary moment, is white folks' undeniable capacity for empathy, compassion, generosity, introspection and change but also, sometimes, for life-altering duplicity. The divestment of that depth is what many racist white travelers, anthropologists, scientists, historians, political leaders, writers, and even ordinary white citizens, many of whom (have) never set foot on African soil, meted out to and still target at Africans and their descendants. "For a long time, in the Western imagination," Mbembe writes, "Africa was an unknowable land. But that hardly prevented philosophers, naturalists, geographers, missionaries, writers, or really anyone at all from making pronouncements about one or another aspect of its geography, or about the lives, habits, and customs of its inhabitants" (*Critique* 70). These purveyors of knowledge and truth about *others* left behind tracts, imagery, sentiments, and social theories that have continued, as capricious ghosts, to torment particularly black-white relations in Europe, United States, and other parts of the world.

I am concerned here with *Things Fall Apart*'s two colonial expatriates: the missionaries Mr. Brown and his successor, the Reverend James Smith, on the one hand and, on the other hand, *Beloved*'s enslaver-colonizers the Garners, Mr. Garner's replacement in Sweet Home—his in-law Schoolteacher, the abolitionist Bodwins, and Amy Denver. A vigilant reading of both novels cannot miss Morrison's troping of Sweet Home as a plantation-colony. She paints it as a New World dominion where Emperor Garner and his Empress, Lillian Garner, rule over their benighted African villagers/natives. Sweet Home, in which the Garners experiment with and alphabetize their male slaves, translates also as a colonial laboratory project reminiscent of Valerian Street's Caribbean paradise L'Arbe de la Croix in *Tar Baby*. Equally apparent are the consistent ironies in, and the surficial strategic differences between, the acts of kindness that Mr. Brown, Amy Denver, the Garners, and the Bodwins collectively show the texts' African people *and* Mr. Smith's and Schoolteacher's ruthlessness. Through these, Achebe and Morrison shed light on the absurd *white mythologies* of civilized slavery and beneficent imperium, to evoke Michael Young.

Things Fall Apart's narrator suggests that Mr. Smith's binarism, overt racism, apocalyptic oratory and wrath could present him as the more pernicious of an insidious British colonial campaign and a Christian evangelical dyad; the bad cop, if you will. However, just as Sethe's fellow fugitive Amy Denver's apparent inheritance and seeming habitual use of racial epithet and her view of (Sethe's) black face as "ugly" cannot diminish the shared humanity she shows Sethe in helping her deliver her baby (78–85); just as, conversely, the Bodwins' liberalism and charity do not cover racism's palimpsestry in the minstrel figurine Denver finds in their home; and just as the new religion's daring rescue and restoration of life, dignity, and promise both to Umuofia's discarded twins and the village's various outcasts cannot be denied; so, too, does Mr. Brown's geniality, his "policy of compromise and accommodation" (184), fail to conceal his savior complex. It does not mask the authoritative bearing, as well as the whiff of absolutism and finality, in his monotheism. His diplomacy does not veil the racial, religious, and civilizational hierarchy that spurred and emboldened his long-distance missionary journey and presence in Igboland-Africa in the first place. Notice that the amiable Mr. Brown initially planned to mount a direct, inferably violent assault on Umuofia religion before settling for entreaty and prophesy. "Achebe portrays good white men as well," writes Robert Wren, "the Reverend Mr Brown is obviously a good man—it does not matter; Brown is no less disruptive than [George] Allen," the District Commissioner (*Achebe's World* 82).

In addition, Smith and Brown's social capital, their gendered mark of cultural respect "Mr.," is denied the black men/ex-slave Stamp Paid and the Garners' Pauls A, D, and F. Similarly, "Mr." is unavailable to Halle and Sixo—the wild and Africa-born slave who, though lynched by burning at Schoolteacher's behest, will live on when his pregnant lover Patsy, The Thirty-Mile Woman, delivers his child. Relatedly, reminiscent of the captive African women in the Cape Coast Castle, women whose bodies are exploited by their enslaving English husbands who do not call them "wives" but instead "wenches" in Yaa Gyasi's *Homegoing* (19–23), Garner does not address Baby Suggs as "Baby Suggs" or regard her as "Mrs. Suggs." He would rather she identify and be identified as a slave, Jenny Whitlow. That is the name on her bill of sale given to her by her previous Kentucky owner, Whitlow. As part of the oracle-foretold white locusts on the way, the cordial and historically representative Mr. Brown helped map the land, racially profile the native adversary, and disarticulate his sociocultural institutions. Mr. Brown and his ilk prepared the stage for that historic, asymmetrical exchange in which, as the saying goes, Africans were bequeathed the Bible, trinkets, cheap drinks, cheap guns, foreign tongues and names, while forfeiting priceless assets, including their religions, freedoms, villages, artifacts, and lands. Not only do invaluable African works of art, looted during colonization and sold at auctions, presently adorn Western homes and museums, unrepatriated. But also, even today, Ashleigh Harris writes, Africa's bountiful lands—ironically, tracts of earth from the Dark Continent—are being acquired "on a massive scale" by exploiting "foreign investors," by wealthy foreign nations, whose agricultural productions and water supplies have been jeopardized by insatiable, local consumer demands and global market volatility (2–3).

Morrison highlights, furthermore, the historical and sometimes fluid intertwining of black and white women's lives in Sethe and Baby Suggs's nursing of the plantation mistress, Mrs. Garner. She illustrates it also in Amy Denver's commemoration in Denver's birth and name. That slavery-robbed recognition "Mr." is respectfully returned to Paul D by Denver, Sethe's once-withdrawn child whom it takes a village to raise. Denver is parented by the village, by the resilient collective to not be shamed or stunted by slavery's ravages (Story 26). The reader may recall the moment that Denver, now confidently venturing outside, greets Paul D, "Good morning, Mr. D" (266). And in Joshua (self-renamed Stamp Paid) powerlessly handing over his wife, Vashti, to his master's young son for his sexual misuse, and Schoolteacher's Nephew violently stealing Sethe's milk—a natural resource and life-sustaining nutrient so primal and priceless the Igbo immortalize it in this proverb evoked in *Things Fall Apart*: "A child cannot pay for its mother's milk" (166)—Morrison extends that sordid connection. She hints not just broadly at the histories of black women and white children, who grew and grow up to become white men and women. She calls to mind, more particularly, wet-nursing: the dehumanizing, exploitative, class-demarcating, and power-projecting practice, especially in the antebellum South, of lactating enslaved mothers compelled to breastfeed, or forcibly milked for, their owners' white infants at the nutritional expense of their own babies (West and Knight). Through the above Sethe–Baby Suggs argument, Morrison spotlights the Mr. Brown-perfidy of the Garners' magnanimity; their running of "a special kind of slavery" (140) that is evidently a chimera but also a subterfuge for extractivism.

It is true the sick Mrs. Garner gives Sethe a pair of earrings for her slave wedding to Halle. We also hear that she is distraught by Sethe's report of being physically and sexually violated by her nephew. But not only is it the case that Baby Suggs and Sethe are not recognized as "Mrs.," as stated. It is also Mrs. Garner who sells Paul F for Sweet Home's financial upkeep upon her husband the Emperor's death. We are reminded of Senhor D'Ortega's expedient commoditization of Florens and her mother to the slavery-hating and conscientious Jacob Vaark in settlement of a debt in Morrison's *A Mercy*. It is the now-widowed Mrs. Garner that brings to Sweet Home a merciless Schoolteacher as the plantation-colony's new administrator, its Mr. Smith of *Things Fall Apart*. Mrs. Garner is goaded by other white women into feeling unsafe on a plantation colony and institutional white space populated by black bodies, by plotting native-slaves. Tacit in the white sisterhood's prodding of Lillian Garner is what Crystal N. Feimster, in her study *Southern Horrors* (2009), describes as southern white women's pervasive deployment of the arresting simulacrum of the "'black rapist'" (127). This is a powerful trope that Rebecca Fenton, whom Feimster profiles alongside antilynching crusader Ida B. Wells, aggressively and deliberately employed to incite legal and mob violence against black men.

That "past," that trope, survives, literarily and literally. For as Sandra Gunning also writes in *Race, Rape, and Lynching* (1996), the post–Civil War idea of "the black as beast," in short, "The frightening drama of lynching, of black rape and white victimhood, the endless questions about the moral and legal nature of lynching: these issues made their imprint on American literature at the turn of the [twentieth] century" (3–17). That trope is also incarnated in what is now dubbed variously as "going Karen," doing "BBQ Becky," etc.—all, designating incidents of some white American women who, feeling "unsafe" and particularly entitled to protection, and who knowing full well the historical and socioracial power of their public fright, "fragility," and "tears" (DiAngelo 131–39), are caught on video calling police officers on especially unarmed black men and sometimes black children. In many instances, these calls have had deadly results, as evinced in the unrest-sparking and high-profile police killings, with impunity, of black men, women, and black boys in recent American history. To Morrison and Achebe, and as K. Onwuka Dike's earlier discussion of slavery and the slave trade in the Niger Delta also corroborates, the not-so-shocking irony is that even the most Christian of slave traders, slave masters, doting plantation mistresses, and imperial colonizers in America and Africa would resolve their ethical and gendered crossroads in favor of self, capital, profit, and white supremacy. As Silvia Wynter writes, "New World Black slaves were the first form of that superexploited variant of labor—native labor—which the non-West would provide for the production process dominated by the West" (47).

The Sethe–Baby Suggs contention no doubt speaks to the improbity of enslaver-colonizer charity. But it also extends what Ibram X. Kendi, in his work *Stamped from the Beginning* (2016), calls the "dueling duality" of America's history. By that he means the convergences, the patterned contiguities, of the nation's "racial progress" and "progression of racism" (x–xi). For black people and people of color in general: anyone that witnessed America's election of Republican Party's presidential candidate Donald Trump in 2016 to succeed America's first and two-time black commander in chief, President Barack Obama, or the interlocking events of January 6, 2021, would not need to know about *Things Fall Apart* and *Beloved,* or for that matter read the works of Cotton Mather, Thomas Jefferson, William Lloyd Garrison, W. E. B. Du Bois, and Angela Davis, whom Kendi discusses, in order to grasp his primary thesis about the inherent pleiotropism and paradoxes of America's racial history, particularly. And, the infamy of that day, including the unambiguous display of racial double standard in American law and its enforcement, may stupefy the young villager Sethe. But one doubts that her old mother-in-law, Baby Suggs, holy, prophetic, and "prophesying" (Haywood 2003), would be surprised by them, by that manysidedness and fusion of things, old and new.

On that January 6, racial history, signaling progress, was made in America; but so, too, was its twin, racial setback. The state of Georgia—whose racism and antiblack violence had decades earlier driven Morrison's paternal grandfather and Georgia-native to Lorain, Ohio—elected two Democrats: a Jewish candidate Jon Ossoff and a black minister, Rev. Raphael Warnock, to the U.S. Senate. As Maya King and Teresa Wiltz put it in their article "How Raphael Warnock Fused Old and New South to Win Georgia," published the morning of January 6 in the online news magazine *Politico.com.*: "Raphael Warnock's victory Tuesday night is historic, heralding a litany of firsts," one of them being and preceded by the election, two months earlier, of Democratic Party senator Kamala Harris, vice president Joseph Biden's running mate, as the nation's first woman, African American and South Asian woman, and woman-of-color vice president-elect. "In a Senate that remains almost solely the province of white men," King and Wiltz assert about Warnock, "he'll be the first Black Democrat from Georgia, the first Black Democrat from the South, the first Black pastor and only the second Black senator ever elected from a state below the Mason-Dixon line since Reconstruction." Just hours later, as a stupefied and weary world watched on live television, the U.S. Capitol Building, where members of Congress were in session to certify the Electoral College votes, was stormed in a deadly breach by thousands of armed, domestic insurrectionists, many of whom openly admitted to being incited by love of nation and by loyalty to the defeated and outgoing president, Donald Trump.

Perhaps most critically significant, the *perceptibility* of that complexity, of the confluence of joy and sorrow in the cadence of the dispute between Sethe and Baby Suggs, whose black bodies have been breached by slavery, points also to that other skill that helped catapult Achebe and Morrison to literary fame, namely, their mastery of the master's tongue. If, as George Nyamndi posited earlier, the village novel is equally identified by its vernacular, then Achebe and Morrison's much-explored attention to the undulations of African/black speech cultures in the two works is a hefty achievement, as others have also noted. The late Abiola Irele writes: *Things Fall Apart* "testifies to an aesthetic project that consists in fashioning a new language appropriate to its setting, which serves therefore to give life and substance to the narrative content and thus to enforce the novelist's initial gesture of cultural reclamation" ("Crisis" 454). The Umuofia and Mbanta villagers, in the story's middle- to late nineteenth-century, precolonial setting, would have been speaking a variation or different dialects of Igbo language. And, the dialogues of *Beloved*'s mid- to late nineteenth-century African American characters are an inflected form of their masters' English language. Those accented conversations, however, share with Achebe's English rendition of Igbo oral/aural interlocutions rhythm, imaging, pitch, humor, idiom, and philosophical depth. A student researching the linguistic dimensions of both novels would have much to work with.

Even though there are moments of linguistically calibrated levity in *Things Fall Apart*, and even with some critics debatably describing *Beloved*'s plot as melodramatic in parts, in my view nothing is profligate or purposeless in the two village novels. For both stories are about racial loss, mourning, and resilience. The character Beloved is "the cumulative spirit of loss" due to slavery. She is the embodiment of "the omnipresence of that loss" (Gillespie 80). It is, thus, Achebe's ear for and faithful rendition in English of Igbo modes of expressing that help make *felt* the pathos in Obierika's voice as he delivers those haunting lines of *Things Fall Apart*. It is, likewise, Morrison's superior command of the English language, her "elevated" prose as she calls it (Elkann 168), indeed her virtuoso, griot storytelling that accounts for the characters' and narrators' discernible timbres and altogether the visceral power of the story's various turning points, most especially the chilling moments of Sethe's infanticide. The Obierika grief reflex is so palpable and transcendent it may as well have been hand-scripted by Morrison herself about *and* for Sethe. "That man was one of the greatest men in Umuofia," Obierika indicts the District Commissioner and his native-catching posse at the site of Okonkwo's suicide. "You drove him to kill himself; and now he will be buried like a dog" (208). "That woman was one of the bravest and proudest black women we know. A daughter, devoted wife, daughter-in-law, mother, neighbor, and friend," Morrison could have imagined Baby Suggs, Stamp Paid, Paul D, and Ella confronting Schoolteacher and his slave-catching posse as the sheriff, impassively dismissing onlookers, takes Sethe away for prosecution. "You drove her to kill herself in her best thing. And now she will be caged like a dog."

I have wondered elsewhere why the white man wants Okonkwo's corpse brought to the courthouse. One could easily picture Okonkwo's black body towering and dangling over him like a "strange fruit"[8] from its hanging tree. Judging from the portentous examples in *Things Fall Apart*—of the man hanged for killing a missionary and the character Aneto who is also hanged under colonial law for accidentally killing Oduche over a land dispute—it is clear how, in slavery and postslavery America and in post-Abolition and colonial Africa, the white man and white justice saw not just a traumatizing and societally destabilizing carceral regime (M. Nagel 135–46), but particularly black-neck-and-asphyxiation, lynching/death, as the proper penalty for black-male contraventions. What is also logical, as I contended, is that the white man demands Okonkwo's body not in plans for a deserved state funeral. Perhaps, I speculated, "he intends to examine it closely and prosecute it posthumously, and possibly also take fetishistic, [and] authoritative notes and diagrams if not black-and-white pictures for his memoir and for Anthropology, Ethnology, Anatomy, and Psychology. He foreseeably would misuse it as a deterrent against future native unruliness about the pacification, by turning it, preinterment, into an ethnological freak show, into that 'terrible spectacle,' that 'horrible exhibition,' that Frederick Douglass talks about (Hartman 3–4)."[9]

Or maybe he will emulate *Beloved*'s Schoolteacher. Maybe he will instruct his obliging assistants and enforcers to find a black pen and draw a black line on a white sheet of paper and, unbelievably, group on either section Ezinma's father Okonkwo's animal and human characteristics, starting with his ruptured neck that cannot breathe, again. For the British, as Toyin Falola diligently historicizes in his study *Colonialism and Violence in Nigeria* (2009), imperial violence, which often elicited native counterviolence, was not just a tool of conquest. It was also calculated, ultimately, to humiliate and permanently scar the native.

In the End: No One Believed the Stories Are True; They Are Not Stories to Pass On . . .

As we absorb the anger laced with sorrow in Obierika's voice, and the funerary chill in the narrator's subdued utterances as Sethe is led away by the sheriff, we cannot but be struck by *Things Fall Apart* and *Beloved*'s ironic closings. These endings have for years intrigued readers and critics of both works.[10] In *Things Fall Apart*, the District Commissioner, whose name we learn is George Allen in *Arrow of God*, and into whose prosecutorial gaze and voice Achebe shifts the novel's coda, ruminates on the monograph he is planning to write. "Anyone who has read or taught this novel can testify to the outrageous reductionism of . . . [that] last paragraph," writes Jules Chametzky (3). In it, the commissioner intends to trivialize the *already-told* and memorable life/history of Okonkwo and his Igbo-Umuofia village. Ironically, whatever facile picture of Okonkwo and/or Africa he concocts for circulation in imperial and postimperial archives and/or for schools, teachers, and pupils will already and always be suspect. It will be prone to dissection and rebuttal by its *containing* antecedent, *Things Fall Apart*. Similarly, at *Beloved*'s ending, the omniscient consciousness laments ominously and lyrically that the obsessing history, figure, story, idea, and name that is Beloved, a spirit-child, and that is Sethe as well, is already subject to Okonkwo's fate. It is susceptible to untenable disregard and discontinuance; a casualty, it seems, of the (village's) progressive march back to normalcy and into futurity. To them, the village people, everyone, then and now, as the narrator reports, Beloved "was not" and "is not" "a story to pass on" (274–75). As with *Things Fall Apart* and the anticipated reception of the District Commissioner's upcoming story-book, whatever the enslaver-colonizer's incomplete or distorted version of the events or for that matter the village's disremembering of them, we—*Beloved's* implied larger audience—cannot unread, unhear, and unknow what we just encountered in the novel's preceding 275 pages.

These plot endings are actually one of the two novels' most compelling intertextualities. As hinted above, the endings are, fundamentally, palimpsests. They are about memory and commemoration: about whether *and* what we elect to privilege and sustain, or discredit and erase. Witnessed also in *Beloved* although sometimes not as pointedly stated in it, those questions of narrative reception and audience dubiety, credence, and skepticism are a leitmotif in *Things Fall Apart*. For widespread in *Things Fall Apart* are all kinds of direct and indirect references to stories. The stories are paradigmatic of (Umuofia) village's oral and multiperspectival culture. In the novel, stories are engrafted. Or rather, like slavery, they *lurk*: in names, naming, and praisenames. They are cloaked in conversations, proverbs, prophecies, myths, legends, and songs/music. Stories are invented, borrowed, shared, mediated, critiqued, affirmed, contested, retold, recirculated, etc.

Consider a few of the examples most pertinent to the present postulation. Obierika tells Okonkwo that, in the Aneto lynching mentioned above, the leaders of Aneto's family who are imprisoned with him but released after his hanging are so shaken by the occurrence they are still dumbstruck and unable to narrate their brutal experiences in the hands of the white man. The second instance pertains—as in *Beloved*—to the belief in/question of spirit children. We are told that Mr. Smith was enraged by the story that one of his new converts had permitted her husband to lacerate their deceased baby, who was divined as an *ogbanje,* in the hope of thwarting the child/spirit's rebirth. Even though the story of those hardy and returnee spirit-children is corroborated by his most steadfast converts, Smith still distrusts it. He instead regards it as part of the devil's earthly machinations to demoralize and misguide people. "Those who believed such stories," he says, "were unworthy of the Lord's table" (185). To Smith, then, *this*—the African (*ogbanje*) belief *and* the circulating story of that particular *ogbanje* child—*is not a story to pass on.* It is not Fact, not Truth, in short not a village narrative and epistemology, that should persist or be preserved.

Of the examples, Obierika's sharing with Okonkwo and Uncle Uchendu the received story and history of the transatlantic slave trade is perhaps the most remarkable. "We have heard stories about white men who made the powerful guns and strong drinks and took slaves away across the seas," says Obierika "but no one thought the stories were true." I want to advance an uncommon reading of that statement. Affirmed by the venerable Uncle Uchendu, the Obierika assertion/narrative depicts transatlantic slavery in terms of westward theft of black bodies. This theft occurs at the intersection of, among other things, white military violence and what Elizabeth Isichei argues would have been really cheap, diluted, and peppered drinks, for instance "Brandy and rum," and routinely inferior and improperly aimed weapons, such as imported "Dane guns and muskets" (Isichei, *History* 50). I suggest, one, that *that* Obierika statement, alongside the other intratextual evocations of skepticism, anticipates but also elasticizes *Things Fall Apart*'s ending. That ending is stylized to communicate, through irony, the problematics of colonial amanuensis and translation of African/black histories and stories. Two, and perhaps more important, the assertion has a relationship of reportage and ambiguity to those concluding, lyrical lines of *Beloved*. Obierika's utterance hints at widespread knowledge, in and around Umuofia, of the existence of slavery and the social category of "slaves." It turns saliently, however, on its undertone of incredulity and uncertain continuance: "but no one thought the stories were true."

That is, as with the semantic aporia of *Beloved*'s "It was not a story to pass on" and "This is not a story to pass on," Obierika's reportage is equally contrapuntal and cross-signifying. It infers that people, the villagers, doubted what they heard and seemed to relegate it to the domains of the supposed fantastical, unsourced, and unverifiable. But it also implies *not* that the people were questioning the veracities. Rather, it hints that, to them, the hearers—who are presumably hinterland Igbo and not the Delta coastal peoples used to seeing the docked slave ships and are thus likely more knowledgeable about the transatlantic journeys—the very notion that slaves were being violently transported across the seas, likely not to be seen again, is an aberration. It constitutes a completely different order of atrocity. To the Umuofians and their neighbors, who by the way would have been intimately familiar with an even more gruesome act such as human sacrifice, the transatlantic trade is an unimaginable and peerless horror. It is a horror so gripping one shudders even at the thought of its truthfulness. One shivers at the potential of that abomination being repeated and retold; in short, of it being passed on and rememoried. However, given its realness, that it did indeed occur, as Uncle Uchendu contends, its acknowledgment is both unavoidable and crucial. But the storied tragedies—a catastrophic "cheapening of human life" as Elizabeth Isichei calls slavery (*History* 48), one in which the Igbo-Umuofian-Africans were paradoxically victims and active participants—ought not to be repeated in history.

In a book review "Slavery and the African Imagination," Abiola Irele submits that, because of Achebe's ironic distance from the events of *Things Fall Apart*, he, Achebe, should not be connected personally to the story and its villagism, its "structures of belief in indigenous Igbo culture, evident throughout the novel" (434). I see it differently. My take is that, consistent with Achebe's questioning of various aspects of the (Igbo-African) historical and ancestral pasts, he was dispatching vicariously through Obierika his view of slavery and the transatlantic slave trade in particular as a Morrisonian "unspeakable thing." He sees it as an abomination that must not recur, a point implicit in his reading earlier of Sethe's infanticide.

Therefore, my argument is that the Obierika statement marks a major "gap." Like the other notable "silences" in the novel such as the name of Okonkwo's mother, the names of his four other sons, and the fate of the girl brought with Ikemefuna to Umuofia, the assertion constitutes a significant historical, narrative and epistemological ellipsis in *Things Fall Apart*. In other words, as to the haunting question/"call" insinuated in *Things Fall Apart* but unanswered in *and* unanswerable *by* the text—namely, Whatever happened to those Igbo and other Africans captured, commoditized, transported unmercifully across the big seas, exiled, and dis-homed?—*Beloved* volunteers an answer. It texts this "response": *Here* are their stories. *Here*, reimagined in *Beloved*/Beloved, are the calamities that befell them during the Middle Passage, en route to and in the so-called New World. *Here* is what occurred after they left Igboland, the River Niger, the Calabar River, the Bight of Biafra, the Bight of Benin, Elmina, Cape Coast, Goree Island, the Indian Ocean and the other egresses on Africa's Atlantic shores. *Here* is how they survived and tried, in the beginning, in the midst of their suffering, and in spite of their suffering, and no matter their different, originary homes and lands, to remake a village. *Here* is how they tried to become a people, to have a name, to marry and forge new homes and families and kinships, and to dare love and breathe, again. *Beloved*/Beloved reinvests spirit, flesh, voice, and a collective name "the beloved" to those unnamed slaves and their descendants—sixty million and more, in Morrison's estimation—some of whom Obierika mentions in passing and whose full stories are *passed on,* untold and untellable, in *Things Fall Apart.* Morrison, in essence, recovers and reposi- tions the missing link in *Things Fall Apart.* She fills the ellipsis. As the left grids of the "bookends" and "continuum," *Beloved* and its prequel, *A Mercy,* become, together, shall we say, the New World or more specifically the historical and thematic "prequel" to *Things Fall Apart, No Longer at Ease,* and *Arrow of God,* the second and third segments of Achebe's trilogy in which he returns to the tributary subjects of cult slavery, domestic bondage, and federacy.

As *Beloved*'s racial, literary, and ideological kin, *Things Fall Apart*—in reci- procity, village-style—also helps Morrison close what I construe as an equally important narrative and knowledge "gap" in her story. The lacuna is registered here as a moment of tacit jab at Africa, a subtle poke that *Beloved* only partly amends, and on the spot. "White people believed," Stamp Paid reflects at one point, "that whatever the manners, under every dark skin was a jungle. Swift unnavigable waters, swinging screaming baboons, sleeping snakes, red gums ready for their sweet white blood" (198). Stamp Paid believes it is pointless for blacks to try to convince whites of black humanity, intelligence, and compas- sion. He also counter-charges that whatever jungle there is to speak of is the jungle that has debased whites who ought to be cognizant that the "screaming baboon lived under their own white skin; the red gums were their own" (198– 99). But then, he infers, notably, there is also "the jungle blacks brought with them to this place from the other (livable) place" (198).

Morrison's multidirectional signifyin(g) on "jungle" in Stamp Paid's intro- spection is clear. But one cannot mistake, however, her inferable authorial need to intrude directly into Stamp Paid's thought on nameless Africa. Without Morri- son's and the narrator's parenthetical emendation, it would have read: "the jungle blacks brought with them to this place from the other place." The operative terms here being "jungle" and continental namelessness. Hinted in that statement, even with the bracketed authorial tweak, are many slaves' and African Americans' unremembering of home/ancestry. Laced in it are (their) misapprehensions about and ambivalences toward Africa, where, as Saidiya Hartman writes in *Lose Your Mother,* many present-day African Americans and continental Afri- cans feel like "strangers" to each other (3–9). Along those lines, then, is Stamp Paid wondering—in Countee Cullen's memorable poetic line—"What is Africa to me?" To *Paradise*'s character Patricia Best, the answer is, Nothing.

I argue, however, that in addition to offering the fundamentals for Griswold's theorization of the village novel, *Things Fall Apart*—by way of its locational irony of "Umuofia" (bush or jungle people) and the rebuttal story it tells of a rather complicated Igboland—indirectly writes back to Stamp Paid. It debunks the Conrad-evoking racist ideas about Africa embedded in Paid's riposte. Just as *Beloved* answers perhaps the most crucial question raised on transatlantic slavery but unanswered either by Obierika's referendum or *Things Fall Apart*, so, too, does *Things Fall Apart* intervene in *Beloved*. It helps redress the inculcated psychic injury underneath Stamp Paid's cogitation. And as stylized story and historical novel, it also helps close the equally significant narrative and knowledge gaps of *Beloved*, especially with regard to Africa as a cultureless and "historyless people" (Wynter 46).

Career-defining, *Things Fall Apart* and *Beloved* vaulted their authors, as eagles, to the high summit of Ogbuefi Odogwu's majestic iroko tree. The works took them to the apexes of literature-dom. From there, with pen, pencil, and paper in hand, and a denigrated English language, they continued to inscribe sophisticated yet accessible village stories of imperfect but hardly uncultured and uncivilized black pasts and present (see also Samatar). Altered but inerasable, those rooted pasts are *passed on,* untraced yet traceable. They are kept alive and relevant, sometimes. And at other moments, they are necessarily held at bay, as the always-already dynamic village—which precedes, trumps, and outlives any one ancestor, or ancestral figure—tries to survive, regroup, and transcend those heavy rains of black history. As time passes, some members of the village stay put. But others move to the city, pulled by, among other things, sheer hope and the quest for a better life. There, in the city, they live in-between worlds, bringing the village/their villagism with them. There, they find themselves grappling with differently located modernities, freedoms, music, and generational changes. Or they encounter themselves contending, still, with slavery- and colonization-implicated past declarations and decisions of founders and priests.

3

Slavery, Migration, Urbanity, Kindred Black Music, and the Anomies of New Village Black Subjectivities

No Longer at Ease and Jazz

The Sociologist, the Philanthropist, the Race-Reader are not unaware of the New Negro.
—ALAIN LOCKE, "The New Negro"

The twentieth-century African . . . exists . . . between the Old and the New Africans.
—NNAMDI AZIKIWE, *Renascent Africa*

Like their exhaustively sampled classics and village novels *Things Fall Apart* and *Beloved* that are bridged in the previous chapter, Achebe and Morrison's respective village-city stories *No Longer at Ease* and *Jazz* have also drawn vast attention. As earlier stated, however, I am not aware of any other engaged pairing of these second and equally complementary series of the trilogies. Unjazzlike, so to speak, the critical standard, a pattern unvaried until now, has been to investigate the two works either in terms of their corresponding modernist and postmodernist tendencies. Or their disciplinary, national, continental, and immediate generational boundaries or, especially in Achebe's case, relative to the white imaginary. Speaking of Achebe, it can be argued that the interlocking factors of Britain's slavery and imperial enterprises in Nigeria, his titular and epigraphic debts to T. S. Eliot's "The Journey of the Magi," *No Longer at Ease*'s protagonist Obi Okonkwo's 1950s educational voyage to England, and Achebe's much-discussed rebuttals of British colonial administrator Joyce Cary's *Mister Johnson* have overdetermined the dominant, longitudinal but legitimate framings of *No Longer at Ease*'s path-crossings as largely ones between former empire and ex-colony, Europe and Africa. And not, I dare say, between Nigeria-Africa and the United States. Particularly interesting is that *Jazz*— whose kernel is James Van Der Zee's picture-story of a murdered girl in his collection *The Harlem Book of the Dead*—is deemed "one of Morrison's boldest narrative experiments."[1] In fact, Morrison calls *Jazz*, not *Beloved*, her "best novel" (Elkann 158). But *No Longer at Ease*, which is just as technically inventive and thematically dense, is often considered the least acclaimed of Achebe's five novels (see Babalola 139). The reasons given for that critical underassessment generally swing, oscillating from assertions that *No Longer at Ease*'s preoccupations are not epic but facile to claims that its narrative tone is pedestrian and specious. But although this chapter adds to the scholarship on both texts, my goal here is to orient the hermeneutical and interlocutory compass in a decidedly more transatlantic, latitudinal direction.

In what follows, then, I spotlight some truly remarkable proximities of *No Longer at Ease* and *Jazz*. The two are stories that, in addition to their cosmological gestures and scriptural immersions, also instantiate the earlier theorization of the village-imbricated and -accented city novel as a conjunctional genre concerned with locational, temporal, and experiential intermediations. It is, in a nutshell, and for our purposes, a subgenre[2] about essentially village people migrated to cities, their "new" urban locales, subjectivities, and sensibilities imbued with and modulated by villagism. I will begin by taking a more expansive look at the two novels' spatial backdrops and temporal linkages. But I will touch on, first and unavoidably, the interplays of *No Longer at Ease* and Achebe's fourth and next city-village novel, *A Man of the People* (1966), then Lagos and New York's analogous histories of slavery, and the domestic and international migrations that interlink both works. Those postslavery and historic mass movements of formerly rural black people into the new/modern eras as renascent[3] subjects on both sides of the Atlantic mediate also the nations (Nigeria and the United States), as well as the racial experiences and the literatures of which the texts speak. Later in the chapter, I engage more concertedly with the novels' related villagism. And, much afterward—*still* as imputed elements of village literature—I illuminate their "love" zones.[4] I then unpack their portraits of *the City,* their sound systems (especially their highlife and jazz atmospherics) and their multiperspectival narrations that reinforce the stories' thematic and structural tributaries.

A Sankofic Overture: Scrolling Forward but Texting Backward, Village-Style

Delving right away into the focal novels' transatlantic alliances should be the logical next move. However, as indicated, the significant locational, temporal, and semiotic contiguities of *No Longer at Ease* and *A Man of the People,* and thus indirectly also between *A Man of the People* and *Jazz,* demand that I skip a bit and instead begin with a few retrospective notes on *A Man of the People.* With its spatial scenes and focal timeframes of 1950s and 1960s Lagos and its migration plot and metaphors of music, especially highlife, *A Man of the People* can be seen as *No Longer at Ease*'s collaborative and/or extension text. A reader unacquainted with Achebe's America-permeated biography and his multiplex canon but closely juxtaposing these two works will notice something fascinating.

There is what I previewed in the introduction, but am rephrasing and elaborating here, as "Achebe's narratively widening transatlantic gaze," his westward expansion and fictional turn. Or, to be more precise, his increased *narrative engagement,* from the debut novel and the short story "Vengeful Creditor" to *Anthills of the Savannah,* with "America" as a content-laden subject, as hinted and begun particularly in Obierika's story in *Things Fall Apart* about slaves transported (westward) across the sea. This hemispheric and historical shift is marked by Achebe's inclusion of white and black American characters. It is also indicated by his direct scrutiny and parody of America's postslavery, post–World War II socioeconomic, political, and cultural activities in and influences on a fast-changing Nigeria. Additionally attributive of the turn is his evocation of African America and its history proper. Whereas the extent of *No Longer at Ease*'s explicit mention of materials America includes the narrator's nonchronological references to imported merchandise and insignias of modernity and globalization, from electricity and automobile to beverages and the telephone, in *A Man of the People* the "America" presences are now quite pronounced. Unlike the lowly "old Ford" referenced in *Arrow of God* (150), the said signs, in addition to hints at America as a vacation destination for the postcolonial nouveau riche, are educational/institutional/textual (Harvard, American encyclopedia). They are also as material and symbolic as the big, land-cruising, and stature-boosting American Cadillac invoked in *A Man* and given a prominent spatiotemporal role in Morrison's *Paradise*.

Nonetheless, the America presences in *A Man of the People* play out in the context of Achebe's satirizing of Nigeria's ill-fated and short-lived postindependence experimentations in colonial modernity, multiethnic and multifaith nationhood, British-styled parliamentary democracy, and western capitalism. The novel features, for example, a young, white American couple, Jean and John, whom the former villager, educator, and cynical first-person narrator Odili Samalu surmises "were both in their different ways excellent ambassadors" of America. As Odili learns shortly upon meeting them, John "was one of a team of experts at that time advising our government on how to improve its image in America" (44). In this "America subplot," Achebe depicts the couple as surveilling. They are harbingers of then-inchoate but imminent full-blown neocolonialism yet to befall Nigeria and by extension other newly independent African nation-states during the Cold War. Jean and John are impertinent, with the sexually liberated Jean being brazenly flirtatious and adulterous.

With its heavy backdrop of highlife music, Jean's casual interracial sex with the native Odili has historical precedents that track back to the international slave trade and slavery. Odili's shock at Jean and John's temerity anticipates Beatrice's disbelief and irritation at the unrebuked rudeness and "domineering" behavior His Excellency and his cabinet members suffer at the hands of a young American United Press reporter, Miss Lou Cranford (*Anthills* 68–74). Just as the "cheeky girl from Arizona" and too-eager feminist Lou calls Major Ossai "Johnson" and Chief of Staff General Lango "Ahmed," with the men tolerating the insolence with "nothing but grins of satisfaction" (*Anthills* 71), Jean and John also address the former villager and quasi-literate Chief Nanga, the nation's minister of culture, and his wife so familiarly. They call them by their Christian names "Micah" and "Margaret." Dumbfounded even more by Nanga's enchantment with that cultural impudence that occurs in his ministerial residence, Odili translates the moment as symptomatic of the wider racial and psychic scar inflicted on Africans by the colonial encounter (44), and definitely by slavery as well. Aside from the novel's cast of British and other European characters whose cousins dot the landscapes of African history, fiction and drama of the cultural nationalism, postindependence, and military eras and beyond, we also have another American couple. But there is also, even more notably, an unnamed, middle-aged African American character that, as Odili learns, is significantly writing a book on Nigeria. In addition, like Odili, the reader will find interesting John's effort to rehabilitate America's image abroad. This narrative campaign is preceded literally by successive U.S. administrations' and the CIA's 1950s and 1960s charm-offensive overseas during the Cold War after the world witnessed, on television, America's brutalizing of its black citizens and civil rights activists (see Von Eschen 2004). Equally remarkable, however, is John's attempt to revise some unpleasant chapters of America's history. He downplays the racial underpinnings of and the statistics on lynching: a horrendous experience Morrison marks in *Beloved* and *Jazz*.

I suggest that, staged and reflected in *A Man of the People*, particularly in Jean's dinner party at which are a white American couple, a British couple, an African American, and an African, Odili, is Achebe's broadened Atlanticism. The party is both historic and historical. As I will further argue, it is also narratively antedated in Obi Okonkwo's return trip to Nigeria and in Achebe's voyagal stops, in the novel, at the major slavery-era cities and ports that Morrison would call sites of memory deserving of benches by the road. The gathering (re)convenes, under one roof, the descendants and citizens of the major societies/countries/subcontinents that were entangled in the transatlantic slave trade systems and are further bound by colonization.

Furthermore, for the African American writer whom a white American man accosts respectfully, having mistaken him for an *"authentic"* African (*A Man* 52), his presence in Nigeria and Africa can be seen as a homecoming. It also reads as a flipside of these three illustrative, transatlantic trips: African students' journeys to the United States in the 1920s and interwar years; Achebe's own UNESCO-sponsored 1963 trip to and travels in the United States following his publication of *No Longer at Ease;* and the migration to and return from the United States of the character Reginald "Reggie" Okong. As Christopher Oriko, the first of *Anthills of the Savannah*'s multiple witness-narrators, sneeringly discloses: Okong, in their fictional nation of Kangan, "had attracted the attention of American Baptist missionaries from Ohio who were engaged in belated but obdurate evangelism in his district. They saw a great future in him." After grooming him, Oriko adds, they "ordained him at the age of 26," with big leadership plans for him in their local ministry. We are told that Okong then strategizes his way to the United States. To gain admission and expedite things, he misrepresents his "Grade Three Teachers' Certificate" as equal to "two years of Junior College." And, against the efforts of his disappointed sponsors, the Ohio Baptists, to get him deported, he—wily and resilient—graduates early from "a southern Black college." He returns to Kangan four years later with a

Ph.D. from an unnamed American university, becomes a professor of political affairs at Kangan University, and now His Excellency's Commissioner for Home Affairs (10–12). The African American writer's visit to ancestry recalls also and extends the transatlantic and "reverse" journeys of other blacks from England, America, the Caribbean, and South American nations. As elucidated below, they had traveled to Africa, some to resettle, since the early nineteenth century and as the winds of independence swept across the continent. What is particularly intriguing is the possibility of the African American writer having traveled to Lagos from one of the cities of the Great Black Migration. As Isabel Wilkerson states, that unprecedented, voluntary mass relocation "would not end until the 1970s." It was the first real dawning of black America's own independence, "when the South finally began to change—the whites-only signs came down, the all-white schools opened up, and everyone could vote," she writes (10). Could the writer have come to Lagos from (*Jazz's*) Harlem, New York; Baltimore, East St. Louis, Springfield, or Virginia?

Atlantic Lagos and New York: Interfacing B(l)ack Stories of Slaveries Past and (Great Black) Migrations

Returning to base, consider, first and relatedly, these additional extracontextual commonalities. *No Longer at Ease* and *Jazz* are stories set mostly in major cities that are shaped and connected by their village indentations. But they are also linked, more especially, by their determinative past histories of slavery. Although the novels are focused on the core events of different periods in Nigerian-African and African American histories—the 1950s for *No Longer at Ease*, and the 1920s for *Jazz*—we should not be misled by the temporal gap and seeming generational misalignment. *No Longer at Ease's* constituent stories and historical references stretch further back to pre-twentieth century and before the early twentieth century's Pan-Africanism and the interwar periods. We hear, significantly, of Isaac Okonkwo's trusted "old books and papers" that date back to 1908 and 1920, for instance. Nonetheless, the two narratives are about the same general watersheds of cultural, intellectual, and ontological (re)awakenings in twentieth-century Africa and African America, but with their incubations in the second half of the nineteenth century. Both works are concerned, more precisely, with the coinciding dawns of new eras of African descendants in the Old and New Worlds, called aspirationally the "New African" age in Africa and the "New Negro" epoch in America. Alain Locke sought to give expression and coherence to this New Negro moment in his edited volume of the same title. That landmark 1925 publication made strong impressions not just on South African intellectuals but also, particularly, on the work *Renascent Africa* by Nigeria's postindependence Governor General Dr. Nnamdi Azikiwe, whose racial stirrings and career in journalism, for instance, have precursors in nineteenth-century Lagos.

Underneath the newness and renascence, below the spatial expanses, concrete edifices, then-expanding economies, and enthralling modernities of *No Longer at Ease*'s Lagos and *Jazz*'s Harlem/New York are intersecting histories of international and also, in the case of Lagos, domestic slaveries. Lying but restive outside the pages and narrative consciousness of both texts, these analytically important historical backgrounds are parts of the stories of where the heavy rains began to beat black people in general. The histories have essentially been "passed on," as in built and painted over. This is particularly the case with the scholarship and social commentary on *No Longer at Ease*. In their discussions of the novel, critics and cultural commentators have generally taken the 1950s and the theaters of British colonization and Nigeria's nationalist movement, and not their forerunners—the stages of transatlantic or local slaveries—as additional points of contextual departure.

Nevertheless, before the centrally situated Abuja became Nigeria's Federal Capital Territory, Lagos held that position for decades. Located in Yorubaland and the Bight of Benin and better known to its indigenous inhabitants as "Eko," with its current name deriving from "the Portuguese word for 'lagoon,'" Lagos was the seat of colonial government, Robert S. Smith writes in *The Lagos Consulate 1851–1861* (1979). It would become not just Nigeria's capital at independence, rivaling if not upstaging many of its West African and African peers. It also grew as the nation's commercial and financial axis. As the country's premier cultural center, it would additionally gain fictional notoriety through works such as Cypril Ekwensi's *People of the City* (see also Emenyonu, *Cyprian*). To Chris Dunton: Lagos has become a "City of Words." It is "by the early years of the twenty-first century . . . one of the world's preeminent fictionalized cities, as with London and Paris more than a hundred years before" (68). And before its latest repackaging and exportation to regional, continental, and global markets by Nollywood, Africa Magic programming, and Afrobeat, its "importance as a center for music" had grown "as Decca, EMI, and other record companies established recording studios in the city as they expanded their operations in Africa" (Stewart 101). If, to *Jazz*'s southern migrants and African Americans in general, Harlem—which according to James Weldon Johnson "has changed from Dutch to Irish to Jewish to Negro"—is "the Negro metropolis," "capital," and "Mecca" (*Black Manhattan* 1), to many Nigerians of Obi's preceding, immediate, and later generations, Lagos, if not a bohemia, was at least their own mecca. Lagos was in vogue, to channel David Levering Lewis's title *When Harlem Was in Vogue* (1991). And it has stayed in vogue, for good and ill.

Smith additionally asserts, however, that the "town and island" Lagos had previously been territorially inconsequential relative to other Yoruba states. That was "until the rise of the slave trade there in the eighteenth century" boosted its significance (*Lagos Consulate* 2–3). Like New York's, this history of Lagos as a major international and regional slave port in West Africa is not always thrust to the fore, as asserted. That relegation of the history to anteriority occurred not just in the forward-facing and midcentury nationalist euphoria and expectancy. But it has also continued in much of contemporary Nigeria's consciousness. As Olakunle George succinctly puts it, "The convenient bracketing of creolization at the very foundation of Nigeria's major city reveals the society's failure to truly engage the past of African complicity in the Middle Passage" (17–18). It is to that glossed-over but lurking history—further exemplified for instance in the story of "great woman" but also prominent slave trader Madame Tinubu after whom Tinubu Square and Iyalode Quarters are named in Lagos and Abeokuta, respectively (Yemitan 74)—to which Chimamanda Ngozi Adichie alludes in her piece on Lagos in *Esquire* magazine. She observes: "There are some things of conventional touristic appeal" in Lagos. One of them is "the last gasp of Brazilian architecture in the oldest parts of Lagos, houses built by formerly enslaved Africans who, starting in the 1830s, returned from Brazil and settled in Lagos." The breadth and depth of that Old World history that subtends the colonial, new, urban, and vibrant Lagos are the foci of Kristin Mann's study *Slavery and the Birth of an African City* (2007). That history is also the subject of, particularly, chapter 6—"Politics, Slavery, Servitude, and the Construction of Yoruba Identity"—of *The African Diaspora* (2013) by the eminent historian Toyin Falola.

It cannot be lost on George, Mann, Adichie, Falola, and *No Longer at Ease's* readers that it is to the slavery-tied Freetown, Sierra Leone, to which the elderly African woman Mrs. Wright, one of Obi Okonkwo's fellow passengers on the English merchant boat MV *Sasa*, is headed. More than three decades before Paul Gilroy theoretically popularized the Atlantic-ship-as-trope (16–17), Achebe had painted, through *No Longer at Ease*, a picture of the aesthetic, narrative, and philosophical possibilities of *ship,* England's ship in this case, as well as its implications for the history and study of the black diaspora and Atlantic modernity. The MV *Sasa* may well be a (former) British slave ship with white crew, white passengers, and manumitted Africans on board. Were no Africans—Obi, Clara, Mrs. Wright, and Stephen Udom—but rather white men only seated round the ship's "big central table" for breakfast (27), the gathering would conjure images of the 1884–85 Berlin Conference and the Scramble for Africa *and* the Treaty of Versailles. However, what is fascinating also about Mrs. Wright's journey—Achebe describes her suggestively as "returning to Freetown" (26)— is its resonances of reverse Middle Passage, the voluntary returns of the slaves Mann discusses. One is reminded of the middle-aged widow Mrs. Avey Johnson's own symbolic reversal of the Middle Passage journey in Paule Marshall's *Praisesong for the Widow.* Could Mrs. Wright's parents and family be Sierra Leoneans of Nigerian extraction? In addition, the British mail and cargo boats mentioned in *No Longer at Ease* can be seen as the twentieth-century technological and maritime descendants of the nineteenth-century, slavery-era, and interdicting British cruisers Mann describes. By 1850, Robert S. Smith asserts, "some two dozen" of the cruisers were patrolling the coast, deployed there by Britain as part of its intensified naval campaign "to hunt Portuguese, American, French, and Cuban slavers and to impose anti-slavery treaties on the coastal chiefs" (2). But what further links *No Longer at Ease* and *Jazz,* and West African, British, and African American/American histories are these English cities and sites that Achebe rememories in the novel: London, Liverpool, and Liverpool's Harrington Dock.

Like Lagos and New York, London and Liverpool were major ports in the transatlantic slave trade and slavery. For not only is London's deep involvement in the trade detailed in James A. Rawley's *London, Metropolis of the Slave Trade* (2003), but also, as Kenneth Morgan argues in "Liverpool's Dominance in the British Slave Trade, 1740–1807" (2007) and Anthony Tibbles reinforces more recently in his illustrated work *Liverpool and the Slave Trade* (2018), Liverpool's ships, merchants, and financiers were responsible for transporting untold numbers of disinclined Africans to the Americas. This was a centuries-spanning, inhumane preoccupation on which Liverpool's economic foundations were laid. As David Fleming, the director of Liverpool's National Museums, states emphatically in his foreword to Tibbles's book, "The fact is that Liverpool," surpassing Bristol, "was the European Capital of the Transatlantic Slave Trade 250 years before it became the European Capital of Culture" (vi). Furthermore, is it possible that Harrington Dock, which was a part of the Liverpool port system, serviced the so-called "legitimate" commercial and other corporate interests of the hitherto slave-trading merchants? Did *No Longer at Ease*'s High Court Judge Mr. Justice William Galloway and Obi's colonialist boss Mr. Green set sail for Africa from a London, Liverpool, or Bristol port? Another of the novel's seafaring British expatriates, Mr. Jones, works for the United Africa Company (UAC) (27). And did the UAC's commercial history not include palm oil trade that swapped the trade in African human beings? Hard to miss are Achebe's references to palm oil and palm kernel as though insinuating, additionally, their significances relative to slavery, modern technology, modern commerce, and globalization. "Before gold and diamonds were discovered in South Africa in the 1880s," Falola contends, "no region in Africa was more attractive to the European powers than Nigeria." Two of the major reasons for this irresistibility of the country to empire were the already-entrenched trade in palm oil and palm kernels (*Colonialism* 1).

What is indisputable, however, is that the imperial presences in Lagos of Galloway, Green, Marie Tomlinson, John Macmillan (an imperial attaché in northern Nigeria with a namesake in *Arrow of God*), and the other Europeans in the novel are set in motion years ago by slavery, both domestic and transatlantic. Mr. Green's colonialist projection that Obi may be "bone-lazy" (74) and that Africans are climate-impaired, ethically lapsed, irredeemable by colonial education, and "sapped mentally and physically" (3–4) has roots in slavery. It also has cognates in British evangelization and civilizational propaganda. In *Arrow of God*, Mr. Wright also believes many of the age-grade and gang laborers in his Okperi-to-Umuaro road project are "bone lazy and could only respond to severe handling." In addition to viewing them as "quite amusing," "loyal as pet dogs," and instinctually musical, Wright also "distrust[s] all uppity natives" (76–78). He calls the gang "black monkeys" (83). In *The Missionary Impact on Modern Nigeria*, E. A. Ayandele observes, among other things, that the African's supposed racial wretchedness and the imperative to civilize and save his soul underpinned slavery. Those supposed racial deficiencies equally informed Britain's militarized antislavery campaigns and its aggressive missionary crusades in Yorubaland, Igboland, and elsewhere in the country. Green's deflection and bigotry get a layering of pathos. For, in extending and reading them through the lens of Ellen Thorp's *Ladder of Bones*, the compunction felt by the British to abolish the slave trade in 1807 can be likened to episodes of medieval morality plays, ones in which the British—African slave traders' and slaveholders' partners-in-crime—suddenly got religion. They forsook evil and colonial violence, as the saying goes. "The revelations of the cruelties of the slave trade had aroused in the conscience of Britain a deep sense of guilty responsibility towards the negro," Thorp says of Britain's remorse. The disclosures stirred in the repentant and magnanimous British "a conviction that it was the natural duty to succor those whose lives and homes had been shattered by the slave traffic" (34–35).

The Mr. Green–parroted European vilification of Africa and the doctrine of white messianism were calculated. They were so sustained and impactful that the desire to counter them absorbed the handful of enlightened, late eighteenth- and early nineteenth-century African American emigrationists and missionaries, as Wilson Jeremiah Moses discusses in *The Golden Age of Black Nationalism* (15–17). Also, as James T. Campbell conveys in *Middle Passages*, but especially as David Levering Lewis comments in his preface to the study, an early through late twentieth-century strand of African American Ethiopianism speaks to that very propaganda. It also prompts the provocative question "What is Africa to me?" that Countee Cullen loops in his poem "Heritage." It betrays, on one hand, an internalized apocryphal narrative about Africa's supposed backwardness. And, on the other, it evokes what Yekutiel Gershoni terms "African American avant-gardism" (60–68). Both intraracial quandaries further underscore the fault lines of African and African American kinship.

David Levering Lewis mentions also how, revivified by the formal British establishment of Sierra Leone as a crown colony to resettle freed slaves from Nova Scotia and Jamaica at the end of the eighteenth century, some literate "American free people of color" started "contemplating the ancestral homeland as their Zion. Emigrationist fever spread among the free populations of Baltimore, Philadelphia, Boston, and Newport." They had seen themselves as "strangers and outcasts in a strange land," America. And when, at the turn of the nineteenth century, many of them embarked on their journeys to Africa, Lewis states, "they brought along their own version of racial superiority: Ethiopianism" (xiii): that biblical anthem of racial solidarity and promise that acquired its injunction from Psalm 68:31 "Ethiopia shall stretch forth her hands to God." Abyssinia/Ethiopianism resonated in different forms across Africa. Lewis adds that "African American notables conceived of themselves as forming the vanguard of an African 'race' rising to greatness *under Negro American tutelage.*" Even as they insisted on their American nativity and citizenship while vigorously opposing the efforts of the American Colonization Society (ACS) to forcibly repatriate or slyly deport them to Africa, "go [to Africa] they did" in notable numbers, Lewis writes (xii–xiv; my italics; see also Bruce 135–74).

The return of the emigrationists anticipate(d) the literary arrival, in 1960s Lagos, of the African American writer in *A Man of the People*. So did the journeys of other African Americans. In the two decades before the American Civil War, they had set sail from New York and settled in the U.S.-founded Liberia. And from Liberia many relocated to Lagos, to their ancestral Yorubaland. Describing the returnees in his study *Victorian Lagos* (1977), the late Michael J. C. Echeruo writes: "Whether they were repatriates from Brazil," Cuba, and other parts of the "Americas, immigrants from Sierra Leone and Liberia or simply educated migrants from Egbaland, these men were a force in setting Lagos apart as the youngest and fastest-growing community on the West Coast" (16). They may have brought along their model of Ethiopianism and worldliness, one tinted by the then-prevailing "Victorian idea of evolutionary development" and class, as well as the broader Manichean logic and racial prejudices of Europe. But they also were confronted, initially and afterward, by something autochthonous; something deeper that, to Echeruo, could not be easily defined and disentangled by the hackneyed "'conflict of cultures'" or "'clash of cultures'" thesis of modern sociology, or even by mere notion of "disorientation" (40). As "men who had grown up in foreign lands" and had found themselves at "the cross-roads of civilization" that marked the century in many parts of the world, the returnees had to contend further, in Lagos, with such simple yet profound dilemmas as "what names to adopt, what clothes to wear or how many wives to marry" (35–36).

Be that as it may, it is not just the slavery-connected and -colored port cities of Old Calabar, Lagos, Freetown, London, and Liverpool that are invoked in *No Longer at Ease* as the sites of memory for Africans and their Atlantic descendants. The Bay of Biscay, which Achebe also sights and cites in this narrative rewind of history, links the coasts of the slave-trading and colonizing nations of France and Spain. Achebe also flags that other Christian European country, Portugal. Portugal was a major imperial nation and leader in the international slave trade with historical connections to America and Brazil. The narrator records that at sunset the MV *Sasa* "anchored at Funchal," the largest and capital city of Portugal's Madeiras, also mentioned directly in the text.

We cannot overlook the visual power, historical significance, and generational audacity of Obi and Clara going ashore, joined and flanked by John Macmillan. Obi and Clara stroll along the city's "cobbled streets," idling and enjoying its weather and ordering its wine. They are entertained by its harbor vendor/folk wine-historian, after which they survey its botanical art, curated in its famed "little gardens and parks" (32). And they do all that not as merchandise, spectacles, oddities, and/or subalterns. Rather, they are in Portugal as *persons*: black, village-rooted, *new* African, free, educated, cosmopolitan, and adventurous, or rather *explorers*. Perhaps in earlier centuries, as Portugal's economy deepened its dependence on slave trading and slave labor, Obi and Clara's African ancestors would have had different social designations, legal statuses, and limited mobility in that nation. Heightening that historic import of the Portugal moment and Obi's four-year residency in England is the fact that those two 1950s events occur, to use Ellen Thorp's description, "almost exactly a century after Lagos had come into the orbit of British power." This was "power personified . . . by a British queen." It was in 1853 that Benjamin Campbell famously took up his post at Lagos as the first British consul, writes Thorp, corroborated by Robert S. Smith in the chapter "Mr Consul Campbell" of his book *The Lagos Consulate* (66–90). In 1953, Thorp argues, Campbell's specter would have been stunned by another group of Nigerians—spokespersons of Nigeria's major political parties— who assembled confidently as freemen and freewomen and not slaves outside of London's Carlton House Terrace. They were there to *demand* their nation's immediate political sovereignty before 1956. Their presences would also have rattled "the ghosts of others, seamen and captains, slave-traders and factors, consuls and governors and missionaries" (15–17).

Furthermore, should we ascribe a higher historical meaning and purpose to the two narrative moments noted above, then we cannot continue to critically treat as mere motion sickness Obi's dizziness and top-heaviness, as well as the insomnia and indigestion experienced by the Sierra Leonean Mrs. Wright. Recall the ancestrally instigated restlessness and dyspepsia suffered by Harlem's Avey (Avatara) Johnson on board the cruise/slave ship *Bianca Pride* in Marshall's *Praisesong*. As previously speculated, could Mrs. Wright be a direct descendant of the African slaves recaptured and resettled in Freetown? Although the earlier-mentioned Brazilian artisanal imprint on Old Lagos's structures may not mark this particular site of memory and mourning, there is also what Achebe refers to as "the vast Lagos cemetery" (20). Described as interstitial, located between and separating Lagos mainland and Ikoyi, this hallowed site ties Nigeria-Africa and (black) America, and *No Longer at Ease* and *Jazz*. Like other African creative writers whose long and diverse engagements with the war theme earned the subject a special issue, number 26, of *African*

Literature Today, as the journal's editor, Ernest N. Emenyonu, discusses in his introduction to the volume ("War" xi–xiv), Achebe memorializes Nigeria's servicemen. He commemorates particularly the heroic, traveled, and suddenly worldly Igbo soldiers of World War II. It is these veteran fighters who initiated Obi to the idea of Lagos as a city of lights and motorcars. But the interment ground, the Lagos cemetery, is said to be the resting place of some of Nigeria's World War I troops who were part of the much larger group of African soldiers ensnarled in that war. Fighting on the sides of their colonizers the British, the French, and the Germans, and sometimes deployed by them on the continent in other colonial land-grab missions, thousands of Africans, soldiers and civilians, perished during this European conflict.[5] It is the end of that war, whose centenary was marked in 2018, that those World War I soldiers' fellow officers and black brothers in New York, the 369th Regiment, are celebrating in Harlem, as recalled in *Jazz.* But the ironies here are also staggering. Although it was never intended, to recall James Baldwin, that African and African American soldiers should ever meet, meet they did, but in a foreign conflict. This was a conflict in which they fought to preserve democracy abroad while subjugated under colonization and Jim Crow at home.

In the case of *Jazz:* the passed-on memories of her grandmother True Belle's slavery by Vera Louise Gray in Baltimore are seared in Violet's consciousness as she grows up in Vesper County, Virginia. Also, the deaths of her sister and brother-in-law (Dorcas's parents) during the 1917 East St. Louis race riots haunt the seamstress Alice Manfred. Yet, both women likely would not have known beforehand the whole or the deeper racial-slavery history of the North, specifically New York, to which they migrated from the South. Violet and Joe relocated there by train in 1906. In addition, it is true that, as we noted with Achebe, Morrison filters slavery discourse into *Jazz* through a series of contrived narrative events but also by way of reimagined and seamlessly interwoven historical sites and occurrences. Those slavery-moored subjects and incidents include, nonchronologically, the ascription of the character Wild as Beloved's (re)incarnation *and* Joe's mother; the miscegenation substory of Golden Gray's illicit conception and birth as the son of a young white girl, Vera Louise Gray, and an equally young black boy, Henry LesTroy; and the references to white vigilante violence, the threat of which forces Violet's father to abandon his wife and young family. The other subtexts are Violet's experience of picking cotton and her hard life with her mother, Rose Dear, and her three siblings in their Virginia sharecropper cabin, in which Rose Dear commits suicide; the burning of Vienna in 1893; and Joe and Violet riding a Jim Crow car on their way to Rome in 1906. Add to those allusions the southern white angst at black migration; Harlem's real estate conflicts that culminated in white flight; the Red Summer riots of 1919 backdated by Joe to 1917, when he is almost killed by a white man who hit him with a pipe; a lynching; and the march by World War I's 369th black regiment, among others.

Still, as intimated above, I do not recall any explicit and engaged mention in *Jazz* of "slavery" in New York. But as many studies have demonstrated,[6] slavery was rooted in the state and the city. It festered until abolition in the nineteenth century. Not only was "New York's prosperity . . . wedded to the South," Bordewich writes in *Bound for Canaan*. And not only was "racism . . . virulent" in the city. But also the thousands of fugitive slaves there "were at the mercy of an informal and shifting ring that was known to abolitionists as the 'New York Kidnapping Club.'" The club "included professional slave hunters, city constables, local lawyers, and allegedly the city recorder" (168–69). However, as is the case with *No Longer at Ease*'s seeming silence on slavery (in Lagos), Morrison's reasons for resorting to clues appear evident. The "silence" simulates the deceptive veneer of New York, in the popular imagination, as a sanctuary or "The City of Refuge," as Rudolph Fisher calls it eponymously in his 1926 short story. The silence also intimates how, for many blacks of the New Negro age who are merely two or so generations postbellum, their racial interpellation and cultural catholicity entailed a concerted disencumbering. Interpreted through the always forward-facing, technocentric, and color-unblind prism of Euro-America, progress to them presupposed sustained *forgetting*. It demanded the repression of their supposedly shameful African village heritage and painful racial pasts. But the village, "the past," survives. It *lurks*, sometimes in muted and mutated forms, as *No Longer at Ease*'s Umuofians in Lagos and *Jazz*'s African American and diaspora characters in New York similarly realize.

It would be negligent to proceed to *No Longer at Ease* and *Jazz*'s other major nexuses without touching on two critical and interlocked points that an attentive reading of both novels' spatial and historical contexts would not ignore. I submitted earlier that, despite the (seeming) generational disjuncture of the novels' 1950s and 1920s settings and focuses, the two narratives are fundamentally about black modernities, located on different sides of the Atlantic though not quite separately occurring. In short, they are about the not-so-sudden and not-unheralded emergences of *renascent* or new black Atlantic subjectivities: the "New Nigerian"/"New African" persona and movement and their counterpart and influence: the "New Negro"/"New Negro" movement, as well as the migrations and cultural blooms that informed both eras.

The New Negro Renaissance, the New Nigerian/New African Renascence

Ntongela Masilela's tracing, to the 1880s, of the contemporaneous beginnings of the "New African" movement, especially as it pertains to South Africa, and Echeruo's additional observation, recalled partly below, about those black-Victorian elite of Lagos in the second half of the nineteenth century, unquestionably suggest a need to backdate the commonly assumed commencement of twentieth-century African literary and intellectual activity. In his work on Southern African intellectual history, *The Historical Figures of the New African Movement* (2014), Masilela connects this emergence to the Xhosa and Zulu intelligentsia. But he links the inception particularly to "The Regeneration of Africa," an essay published in the *Journal of Royal African Society* (July 1906) by Pixley ka Isaka Seme. Among his other acclaims, Seme was one of South Africa's first lawyers and a key architect of the African National Congress, for which the multigroup New African movement was the "intellectual" and "cultural" component.

Attributing the notion of New African movement to Seme, Masilela explains that the effort's paramount goal was the establishment of the roots of modernity in South Africa. It spanned "over a century from about 1862 (Tiyo Soga) to 1960 (Ezekiel Mphahlele)," he calculates. And the project "consisted of writers, political and religious leaders, artists, teachers, scientists who called themselves New Africans, specifically *New African intellectuals*." This was to differentiate them from "the *Old Africans* since they were engaged with creating knowledge of modernity (new ideas, new newspapers, new perspectives, new objectives, new formulations)." Masilela stresses, however, that even as those New African intellectuals did not want to feel constrained by *the past*, by "the old ways of traditional societies," they did not outright dismiss bygone values, the age-old village modes of knowing and doing. Rather, they sought to find ways of integrating them with the new realities and the group's progressive agendas (1–8). Echeruo summarizes the following, among other things, in his conclusion: "The fact that these members of the Lagos elite were Africans is not for us as important as the fact that they," like their South African cousins "were, in effect, a new kind of African. True, some of them were descendants of slaves," and they also had certain advantages of history and education over the local Nigerians. "What gave a special character to these new Africans," however, "was the fact that they were in a profound, not a polemical sense, Africans of a Victorian persuasion" (111).

Of special significance, as the above and upcoming discussion indicates, however, is the impact of African American history, experience, and intellectual thought—more precisely the nominal and conceptual influence of the 1920s and 1930s New Negro movement—on its African cousins and, indirectly, on *No Longer at Ease*. A close friend of Alain Locke's and also his fellow Oxford University student, Masilela writes, Seme appeared to have duplicated the coinage "New African movement" not from Locke's *The New Negro*. He seems to have leased it from a precursor text, Booker T. Washington's *A New Negro for a New Century* (280). What drew the South African intelligentsia of the 1920s to the New Negro idea was not just their glowing perception of United States' nineteenth-century economic advancement, which, to them, was evident in cities built and skyscrapers erected. It was also what they viewed (rightly or wrongly) as African American successes barely fifty years post-Emancipation. As the South African intellectuals reasoned, African Americans had made remarkable religious, educational, political, institutional, and cultural strides, particularly with the internationalization of jazz and the Africa-influenced Charleston dance. If they could make such gains that rapidly, they asked, why not continental Africans who had not suffered the repressions of New World slavery (282–83), or at least in the same ways and degrees, as the preceding discussions in chapter 2 have attempted to show. Centered in Harlem, with its overlapping ferment in Washington, DC (Moses, "Lost World"), the New Negro Renaissance, which scarcely altered the quotidian concerns of the city's ordinary blacks, would shape the New African movement that lasted into the 1950s and 1960s. It would also inspire the Paris-based and much-studied Negritude movement led by Léopold Senghor and Aimé Césaire.

We discover in *No Longer at Ease* and *Jazz* varying gestures to the characteristic rifts of *town* and *gown; the chasm between intellectual culture and movement, as it were, and* the masses. On reading *Jazz*, for example, one finds that the mundane events narrated are historically concurrent with the music-impacted New Negro movement/Harlem Renaissance proper. As Alain Elkann notes Morrison as saying, she "never used the word jazz" in the narration (158). Even more, the literary and visual art side of that cultural and philosophic rebirth is purposely downplayed in the novel. It occurs outside the narration. This is unlike what obtains in such Harlem Renaissance novels and romans à clef as Nella Larsen's *Quicksand,* George Schuyler's *Black No More,* Wallace Thurman's *The Blacker the Berry* . . . and *Infants of the Spring,* and Claude McKay's *Home to Harlem* (see also Dickson-Carr). Just as Morrison topically subordinates "jazz" and "New York slavery" in *Jazz,* the phrase "Harlem Renaissance" is also not mentioned in-text.

This is largely because Morrison's main interest was the Harlem villagers, the folk. However, toward the end of the novel, and in her own narrative/ implicit solo improvisation that helps provide for Joe, Violet, and the audience the sorely needed missing links in the Dorcas mystery, Dorcas's friend Felice recalls that her father read some of the period's magazines and journals. They include *"Amsterdam,* the *Age, The Crisis, The Messenger,* the *Worker"* (199). *Opportunity Magazine* is also mentioned. *Jazz's* ordinary blacks appear barely aware of and impacted by the Renaissance's art, literature, and theoretical debates. They are tied, existentially, however, to the period's racial, political, socioeconomic, and global climates. Aaron Douglas, a Topeka, Kansas, transplant to Harlem and one of the Renaissance's premier artists and illustrators, puts it incisively. Ordinary blacks at the time, "the man in the street," he reflects, may not have been aware of or felt the Renaissance's "cultural" and "spiritual" experience. Yet, they were indirect participants in it, and their input may well be greater, he argues. For their lives were key to the very premise of Renaissance (119). As Violet, Joe, Alice Manfred, Dorcas, her friends Felice and Acton, the dancing brothers, and the patrons of nightclubs and Rent Parties show, they knew of, consumed, were imagined, sustained and moved by, at least, the period's race records.

No Longer at Ease is, likewise, tasked with imaging but also unraveling a mid-twentieth-century renascent, continental, and by extension racial subjectivity. This modern village subjectivity is constituted largely by, but also beset with, the hurdles of urbanity, cultural alienation, and a consequential ethical turn. Undertaken by Achebe, that authorial goal of epochal representation has a parallel in the bemused reactions and the at times pointed critiques of the earlier-illustrated Harlem Renaissance novels to the gendered ambivalences, moral judgments, and historical miscues of the New Negro. Consistent, then, with Achebe's sentiment, shared by others, that the "Nigerian"—that turn-of-the-century imperial and geographic construct—is an Azikiwean renascent African, *No Longer at Ease* attempts to map the complicated project of that New Nigerian/New African subject in a new nation. Unlike Morrison's focus on ordinary blacks and migrant southern villagers in *Jazz,* Achebe centers the travails of a cultural and intellectual elite: Obi Okonkwo and his cohort. However, the narration still follows *Things Fall Apart*'s template of instantiating the village-community's foundationality, as well as the counterpoint of self-versus-group. For although elite and pivotal, Obi's private story—like Joe and Violet's—is entwined with other stories. It is riffed in the broader and constitutive experiences and stories of the equally ordinary, southeastern Igbo-Umuofia village-community of Lagos. The earliest members of this notoriously peripatetic ethnic community may have begun their migrations to northern Nigeria and, for our purposes, westward to Lagos, as early as the 1920s, if not before. Like *Jazz*'s southern migrants drawn also westward and northward, to New York especially, by, among other things, the ecological disaster of the boll weevil devastation of crops, the ensuing economic hardship and the peculiar horrors of the Jim Crow era, this transplanted Igbo-Umuofia collective views itself in exilic and survivalist terms. They see themselves as economic migrants to and outsiders in Lagos. It is also through the Obi headlining plot that Achebe mediates (or passes on/continues) the legacies of ancestral and still-agrarian Umuofia village and its villagism.

Together with *A Man of the People, No Longer at Ease* also hints, then, at what can be called a Nigerian Cultural and Intellectual Renascence. This would be in line with that renascence's Atlantic cousin's renaissance overwritten in *Jazz* and its subcontinental cousins' movement in South Africa, as Masilela historicizes. It would also align with, for instance, Azikiwe's grand vision[7] of a new continental order and ontology, and the insistence of his fellow Igbo-Nigerian statesman and educator Mbonu Ojike on the centrality of art to the New African and Africa, its cultural rebirth, and its goals of adaptive industrialization (*My Africa* 222–23). Preceded by over millennia-spanning oral tradition, as well as literary and cultural moments in Africa that include the introduction and presence of Arabic and Western scripts, slave autobiographies (Irele, "Chronology" xii–xxii; Gérard, Foreword), and imprints of the nineteenth-century Lagos Press (Echeruo 1–13), this behind-the-text and mid-twentieth-century cultural and intellectual renascence—an explosion, with a small "e," of works of culture, imagination, and thought—occurred quite notably in the 1940s, 1950s, and 1960s, if not earlier. It assumed the form of emergent traditions of pamphleteering largely energized by now-internationalized and returning Nigerian World War II soldiers, as Emmanuel N. Obiechina details in his studies *Language and Theme* (1990) and *Culture, Tradition and Society in the West African Novel* (1974),[8] and as Terri Ochiagha further contends in her works "Decolonizing the Mind Onitsha-Style" (2015) and *Achebe and Friends at Umuahia* (2015). The renascence also took the shape of quantitative and qualitative rise in indigenous language and modernist literary output in English. It additionally found expression in art, modern journalism, music, entertainment, and sports. College-educated, English major, poet, aesthetic theorist, literary analyst, music critic, cultural observer, public intellectual, civil servant, race leader, and most definitely a player in that "Naija Renascence," as it would be christened today, Obi Okonkwo, far more than Clara, is the Nigerian/West African literary complement to his illustrative South African contemporaries. A renascence man, he also mirrors the 1920s idealistic and (inter)nationalistic New Negro of whom Alain Locke speaks.

In keeping with his concern with generational hurdles and missteps, Achebe suggests, however, that the problem with the New African, the new urban intellectual, the working class, and their idealism, is not just the ephemerality of that utopianism. The character Sam Okoli glimpses that transience in Obi. Nor is the problem that *that* coterie may be tenuously gilded and culturally ambivalent. The issue is their villagist meddling and sanctimony. This reminds one of their New Negro cousins' flaunted rectitude and their own villagist intrusiveness, as *Jazz, Things Fall Apart,* and *Beloved* dramatize. Obi believes strongly in the ostensible messianism, or is it the Ethiopianism, of the new university-educated and book-knowing cohort. His faith in them—in an age of "progress" when knowledge-capital is displacing war- and strength-economy—finds a prelude in his father's trust in white modernity. Isaac is enamored of the *newer* technologies of signification and dissemination. He is particularly fond of modern print, the indelible *uli,* as he deems the "written word" (144–45); fundamentally text/text-ing, long known to and practiced by his Igbo people in their *nsibidi* scripts.

Obi's conviction also calls to mind W. E. B. Du Bois's antecedent proposition of and confidence in the Talented Tenth as racial avant-garde. As indicated, *Jazz* does not narratively reproduce those literary exchanges on the purpose, tenor, and direction of African American art, culture, and letters that played out on the pages of Locke's *The New Negro* and also in such printed, canonical Harlem Renaissance essays as Du Bois's "Criteria of Negro Art," Locke's "Art or Propaganda?," Hughes's "The Negro Artist and The Racial Mountain," and George Schuyler's "The Negro Art Hokum," among others. In contrast, *No Longer at Ease* provides, in-text, a platform for such an intellectual and aesthetic discourse, especially the epistemological confrontation between Africa and

Europe. It cleverly creates space, a forum, as it were, for an encounter that is about cultural decolonization, particularly literary and aesthetic sovereignties.

What I am trying to suggest here, as others have differently observed, is that what presents as mere intertextuality—a casual and multisubject dialogic between Obi and "the Chairman of the [Public Service] Commission, a fat jolly Englishman [who] was very keen on modern poetry and the modern novel"—has broader ramifications, besides its literary anticipation of the literal 1960s conferences on African art. That intratextual conversation on themes "from Graham Greene to Tutuola" (44–45) brings to mind those Harlem Renaissance romans à clef and their interior literary debates mentioned earlier. In addition, the Obi-Chairman conference is born of the then-nascent Nigerian literary and cultural renaissance/renascence occurring literarily and simultaneously outside the pages of the novel. Most importantly, like Hughes's landmark manifesto "The Negro Artist and the Racial Mountain," the Obi counterphilosophy of tragedy is a rejection of the racial mountain erected against Africa, African art, artists, and thought by Victorian and, more broadly, white intellectual paternalism. Extended in that comparably instructive moment in *A Man of the People* when the narrator Odili and others intervene in the misrecognition, diminishment, and critical misappropriation of African sculpture, particularly by an Englishman and a French writer (50–51), Obi's erudition serves also to refute if not implode the mountainous genre-categorization, highbrow critical and philosophic theory, especially formalism, and concept-proprietorship. In short, Obi is challenging the cultures of taste—to channel Simon Gikandi—by which and from which Europe and Anglo-America have historically subjugated their *others* and excluded their *elsewheres*.

Essentially a declaration of independence, Obi's alter-native principle of art and culture refuses the imposed authority and limitations of Western formalist definitions of poetry and the modern novel. It pries open a door of fraternity that legitimates the literary modernity, cosmological undercurrents, and social purposiveness of atypical and sometimes critically misjudged African works. That includes *No Longer at Ease* itself and its national precursors, for instance, Cypril Ekwensi's novels, as well as the pioneering, early to midcentury Yoruba-language stories of D. O. Fagunwa and, especially, Amos Tutuola's fabulations, which Morrison positively cites among her African literary influences. Reminiscent of *Anthills'* career-switching Professor Okong, village-born and Lagos-resident Obi may have abandoned law to study English, to the utter disappointment but ultimate acceptance of his pragmatic Umuofia village, who had invested their hard-earned money to sponsor his overseas education. They had hoped that, as lawyer, he would help them settle land cases. In his counterhypothesis, however, Obi is formulating another kind of law, one that, following Du Bois, can be titled "Criteria of Black African Art." He is helping frame the blueprints for the critical and pedagogic appreciation of his people's mbarist cultural production for which Ala, the Earth Goddess, is muse, patron, and adjudicator. In fact, it is not just *Things Fall Apart* (Innes, *Chinua Achebe* 50) but also *Jazz* that indirectly buttress Obi's aesthetic disposition. His theory of tragedy finds intertextual validation and human practicality in *Jazz* or, more precisely, in Joe Trace's circular depression post Dorcas's death. As Obi theorizes, suicide is an easy way out of the tragic. Actual tragedy is never settled, he postulates. To him, it continues, recursive, like blues, "hopelessly forever . . . in a corner, in an untidy spot" (45–46). Joe would know.

Further grounding and interlinking *No Longer at Ease* and *Jazz,* and concomitantly Achebe's Nigeria and Morrison's African America, are, as hinted, the contacts of some of the major figures of the two black Atlantic generations and renaissance/renascence movements. In his autobiography, *My Odyssey* (1970), for example, Nnamdi Azikiwe reflects on, among other subjects, his westward migration to the United States in 1925—the temporal epicenter of the New Negro movement and *Jazz.* Of historical significance here is Azikiwe's adjustment time in Harlem and his immersion in the insurgent New Negro experience and thought that informed his *Renascent Africa.* And of additional interest are his personal meetings and pan-African relationships with Alain Locke, Du Bois, and Hughes (see Obiwu). As does Masilela in his discussion earlier, Azikiwe acknowledges the impact of the New Negro Renaissance. He notes how "the New Negro movement started by [the Jamaican Marcus] Garvey, and garbed in the robe of intellectualism by Locke and DuBois, like the mustard seed had sprouted many times over and extended to Africa" (*My Odyssey* 143–44).

It is worth noting that the two renascent/New Nigerians/New Africans— the fictional yet era-symbolizing Obi Okonkwo and the literal pan-Africanist Nnamdi Azikiwe—would have been present and operating in Nigeria/West Africa at the same 1950s moment. However, it is the then about fifty-four-year-old and (black) America-trained Nnamdi, and not the twenty-five-year-old, younger, and Britain-educated Obi, who galvanizes positive change. It is he, the New Negro–inspired Azikiwe, who leaves a grander legacy for his ancestral Igbo lineage of Onitsha. It is also the older Azikiwe who, after departing America and initiating his distinguished career in journalism in then–Gold

Coast (Ghana), makes a more lasting impression on his subcontinent's socio-cultural, political, and intellectual effervescence, as did his predecessors, Ghana's own New African J. E. Casely Hayford and, particularly, the proprietors and editors of the various gazettes that comprised the nineteenth- and early twentieth-century Lagos Press. In her study *Histories of Dirt* (2020), especially in the section "African Newspapers, the 'Great Unofficial Public,' and Plague in Colonial Lagos," Stephanie Newell offers insightful observations that both reinforce and extend Echeruo's discussion. Besides addressing more specifically the Lagos Press's anticolonial radicalism that irked the British imperial administration, as well as its social engagement and wider influence, Newell reminds us that, "in the absence of political representation, educated Africans' chief mode of public expression was the press." And, "simply by existing as vehicles to carry colonial subjects' commentaries on government to the rest of the world," Newell adds, "African newspapers had the potential to erode colonialism using the language of the dominant power" (43–44).

Achebe observes that through his newspaper, the *West African Pilot*, Azikiwe not only made a big impact on life in Lagos. He also influenced Nigeria's modern journalism through a tradition of nation-building narratives and hard commentary. This heritage is taken up literarily by *Anthills'* character Ikem Oshodi. In *Reading Chinua Achebe*, Simon Gikandi calls Ikem "Achebe's example of an African deeply involved in the intellectual project of postcolonialism" (131). Achebe tacitly nods toward the legend, whose nickname "Zik" was Americans' abbreviation of Azikiwe, according to Mbonu Ojike (*My Africa* 224). We may recall an elder mispronouncing Isaac Okonkwo's name as "Azik" (59). In short, to Achebe, the Zik-footprint on Nigerian politics, broadcasting, publishing, higher education, intelligentsia, and even highlife music is vast ("Sweet"). So enormous, in fact, that upon his return to Nigeria in 1937 after a nine-year odyssey, Azikiwe—veritably a renaissance and renascence man—was serenaded by Igbo musicians who cut a well-liked "phonographic" track titled "'Egwu Zik'" (Zik Music) to mark the return, as Ojike remembers in his *My Africa* (224). In *I Have Two Countries* (1947), which as *My Africa's* sequel recounts his own travel in 1939 to America for higher education, Ojike calls Zik "the evangelist of a New Africa." He also asserts, "He showed me the way to America. He is my hero," one whose *West African Pilot*, in circulation in late 1930s New York and elsewhere in America, irked the British expats in the United States, such as one "Dr. Thomas Jesse Jones, director of the Phelps-Stokes Fund," who knew of and admitted liking Zik better as a student there

(19–20). That Dr. K. O. Mbadiwe, another America-trained Igbo-Nigerian nationalist and political heavyweight, "remained politically number two in the eastern region [of Nigeria] behind Azikiwe" (Lynch 6), drives home the point of Zik's massive gravitas.

Zik's New Negro/New Nigerian/New African spirit and his trailblazing radicalism bring us to African American critic Gerald Early. It also strengthens our appreciation of *No Longer at Ease, Jazz,* and their leitmotifs of pressure between youth and age, passivity and rebellion, as hinted above. These tropes are routinely mentioned by Achebe and Morrison critics relative to the two novels. In "The Harlem Renaissance and the New Negro," the second section of his introduction to Countee Cullen's collected writings *My Soul's High Song,* Early argues that it is erroneous to see the Harlem Renaissance and the New Negro movement as one and the same. He views the Harlem Renaissance, which he dates between 1915 and 1929, as a "phase, a kind of peak moment," of the broader "New Negro Movement." He times the wider movement more expansively between 1908 and 1938. Early clearly does not diminish the Renaissance's intellectual vigor. But to him, the New Negro archetypal spirit is embodied more forcefully and spectacularly in ontological audacity and dissent. He finds that counterhegemonic punch in his symbol of the New Negro, "Jack Johnson, the first black heavy weight boxing champion." As Early discusses, Johnson, among other things, openly subverted racial and sexual codes through sexual liaisons with and interracial marriages to white women. The nationalistic race leaders reproached Jackson. But Early lauds him as "the famous black badman of blues songs and folktales raised to a national icon" (24–27). "After defeating retired champion Jim Jeffries, 'the great white hope,' in 1910," James Burns and Abel A. Bartley write, Johnson "was known to more people and made more money than any black American before him. No black sports figure would rival his celebrity until it was eclipsed by Muhammad Ali" (223).

It would be impossible to miss or mistake the parallels between (1) Early's idea of the boxer Jack Johnson as modeling the New Negro epochal ontology and psyche, (2) Zik's epigraphic renascent African vis-à-vis imperialism, and (3) *No Longer at Ease's* Old African–versus–New African vocabulary and categories. Obi's paradigm of the Old African is the character Mr. Omo, the administrative assistant whom the imperialist Mr. Green publicly chastises and humiliates. To Obi, Omo is subservient and hampered by "colonial mentality" (46). We also can view all revolting slaves, as well as Obi's own grandfather Okonkwo of *Things Fall Apart,* and *Arrow of God's* Ezeulu discussed in the next chapter, as literary forerunners of modern New Blackness, racial insubordination, and self-rule. But we cannot forget Obi's account of one particular New African quintessence and precursor. His name is Mr. Simeon Nduka, a school headmaster. His gendered, implicitly apocalyptic, and racially deconstructive battle with white supremacy is the tale of legends, Obi recalls in the late 1950s.

As Obi retells it, around 1937 and in the intensity of colonization when "throw[ing] a white man was like unmasking an ancestral spirit," Mr. Nduka, a skilled wrestler and fascinatingly Jack Johnson's racial cousin and fellow athlete across the Atlantic, set off pandemonium when he tackled to the floor the irascible and violent inspector of schools, Mr. Jones. Jones sought to perpetuate the philosophy and practice of white dominance. He misread the direction of world history. He must have been unfamiliar with the Igbo ethos of freedom of speech and thus their distaste for vocal erasure and imposed white authority when he unnecessarily commanded Mr. Nduka to "Shup up!" and followed the verbal toxicity and public indignity "with a slap" (74–75), leading to his downfall and unraveling. I am thinking, also, of Jack Johnson's other cousin, the world boxing champion and the New Nigerian/New African Richard Ihetu "Dick Tiger" who defeated the white American Gene Fullmer (see Adeyinka). And before Dick Tiger, we had the inspiring rebel Nwanyeruwa and her fellow women of the 1929–30 Women's War against British taxation during the Great Depression, or the "world depression" years, as Elizabeth Isichei calls it (*History* 150–59). "Updating" *Arrow of God*, in which the contemporaneous, late-1920s event is not marked, as further discussed in the next chapter, Achebe commemorates this Nigerian-African women's uprising in *Anthills of the Savannah* (84). On the other side of the Atlantic in 1926, African American women took to arms, self-protection, and retaliation against white injustice (*Jazz* 77–78).

It is equally a notable convergence of idiosyncrasies that Obi and Joe's demonstrations of new-age revolutionary agitation similarly tend to be more cerebral than Jack Jackson and Simon Nduka militant. Obi's renascence, his anticolonial disturbance and New African agency, takes the subtle forms of riffed or restyled gestures. They include his literary/intellectual debate and theorizing; his anti-British letter to Hitler, written at age eleven, for which his disappointed white teacher tearfully brands him "a disgrace to the British Empire" (9); and his sartorial indecorum at a semi-official cultural ceremony organized in his honor. We also have his reversion to an underwhelming English diction when his people expect Zik-type oratorical fireworks. Add to that his *going village*. He and his economist friend Christopher resort back to eating pounded yam, *garri,* and *egusi* soup with their fingers. And then there is Obi's bucking of his people's age-old *osu* custom in an exercise of contrarian, modern romance. Joe, comparably, construes new blackness, or at least his interpretation of its grammar, not in outright combat or confrontation, but in jazz improvisational frequencies, so to speak. He constructs it relative to continual self-reinventions; to reconstitutions of one's same black self in its varying familial circumstances, forced and/or voluntary migrations, village-city localities, and sociocultural sustenance. If the New Negro and the renascent/New African subjectivities are ultimately about "change," Joe, who claims (in hints of African cosmology) that he has been reborn seven times, views himself as *the* pattern. He sees himself as the living evidence of racial revival and transformation, from village to the city.

The Village, Village People, Villagism, in Lagos and Harlem, New York

Further firming up *No Longer at Ease* and *Jazz's* kinship is a generative postulation Achebe and Morrison congruently advance in the two texts. Discernible from the foregoing discussion and perhaps already familiar to readers, that point is that the novels' southeastern Igbo-Nigerian and the southern African American migrant communities of Lagos and Harlem/New York are, still, fundamentally villagist, as suggested in Obi and Christopher's *going village,* or rather their *return-to-village* modality in the city. To both authors and works, Black Atlantic modernities are not total. They are neither lineal, insular, nor mechanistic. Nor are they completely hemispheric, undeviating, and deterministic, regardless of the fatalism implied in Clara's hum of "*Che sarà sarà*" during her drive with Obi to her seamstress (19). In short, as Tsitsi Ella Jaji points out, "What it means to be 'modern' is a vexed question in Africa" (14). *No Longer at Ease's* interlacing of African cosmological precepts and *Jazz's* interweaving of those same tenets, as well as distinctly African American outlooks on life, find expressions in both works' consistent treatments of the migrant communities' preservations of their villagism in Atlantic Lagos and New York. As connectors, those cultural continuities are critical to the formal constitutions of the two trilogies as trilogies.

In *No Longer at Ease,* to start with, instances of villagism-modernity dialectic abound. Following is a random clustering of salient samples. But I will, afterward, engage more in depth with a couple of more profound representations.

As we will also find with *Jazz*, and have already noted in the efforts by former slaves in *Beloved* to consolidate or at least syncretize African village sensibili-ties, perhaps the most significant cultural transfer is prompted by geographic dislocation. That transfer is the Umuofia villagers' attempt to reimagine com-munity and reconstitute "Umuofia" in Lagos through the formation of the Umuofia Progressive Union (UPU). Replicated from its village origination, the organization's paramount goal is to promote the general welfare of its members. It does this while also maintaining what Raphael Chijioke Njoku, if studying the UPU case, would describe as a pan-Umuofia identity and consciousness. In "The Making of Igbo Ethnicity in the Nigerian Setting: Colonialism, Iden-tity, and the Politics of Difference," Njoku addresses, among other things, the subject of the existence of a precolonial "pan-Igbo identity." More pertinently, he also touches on what would be one of the many historical antecedents to the fictional UPU, namely, the much broader but "nascent Igbo State Union in Lagos." Following his return home after his medical studies in Scotland, Dr. Akanu Ibiam, "the first Igbo missionary doctor," joined this organization, which began in the 1930s if not earlier (266).

More so, although they are cultural hybrids, but particularly multilingual in their fluency in Igbo, English, pidgin, and quite likely some Yoruba, the Umu-ofians of Lagos sustain their vernacular. This oral culture is demonstrated in their effortless resort to proverbs; their meandering conversation, code switch-ing, imagistic vocabulary, signifying, antiphony, co-signing, and inferred loud-talking. They maintain their villagist reverence for age, without abrogating their (vocal) autonomy, for which Mr. Nduka topples Mr. Jones. The village tradi-tions of palm-wine drinking and of welcoming guests with kolanut and the cul-ture of hospitality remain intact. Wedding ceremonies may have changed with the introduction of the invitation card and the card's *RSVP* requesting attendee-acknowledgment in French language. *The book* and book knowledge, in addi-tion to new technologies of voice recording and sound transmission, may be displacing or have largely supplanted the traditional storytellers and informal education promoted by Obi's mother. But the following ideals and strongholds, thriving in the Umuofia village proper, survive the cultural transplantation and suturing in Lagos: emphasis on kinship, personal autonomy, and industry; women's music group; and the custom of personal and/or group condolence visits. And, in addition to collective intervention, distaste for unbridled pride, and the proclivity for equity, there is also their tendency to pry. But perhaps the most unaltered in this self-collective tightrope of villagism is the UPU members' capacity for unsubtle umbrage and reproach, but also for reasoned restraint, as Obi and Clara experience (4–5, 181–82).

Jazz's southern migrants in New York also exhibit the same stubbornly persistent village mind-sets enumerated below. *Jazz* does not overly dramatize the transatlantic, intraracial, and multicultural composition of the era's, as well as New York's, black populace. Locke highlights that diasporic makeup in "The New Negro." He recognizes Harlem's geographic attraction, physical reunification, and its facilitation of a pan-racial consciousness, identity, and voice for the slavery-dispersed blacks from the American South, the Caribbean, and Africa (represented by the South African intellectuals, as well as Azikiwe and his and later cohorts of Africans from across the continent). There is mention in *Jazz* of a part of town described curiously as "stink[y] . . . Mulberry Street and Little Africa." But then the novel does not include or refer whatsoever to continental Africans, who, it must be admitted, may have been numerically and thus culturally inconspicuous. On reflection, I am not aware of any postslavery and post-Reconstruction continental African characters in Morrison's fiction.[9] At any rate, is the "Little Africa" a slight, a real but small city block of *Africans*, or an Africa-centric sentiment and Harlem commune? It bears stating that, although practically effaced in the novel, there is nothing little about "Africa" in the grand scheme of the era. "Africa" looms large as a paradox in the image-(re)making of the period's art and music with which *Jazz* is embedded and in dialogue (see Kirschke). "Africa" also lurks behind the racial memory, mentality, and complicated *newness* of the novel's New Negroes. As Nathan Irving Huggins puts it in his study *Harlem Renaissance*, "Africa was an essential enigma in this culture-building enterprise" by African American intellectuals (78–79).

In the same way it intermingles other facets of the epoch's contexts and history, *Jazz* suggests that internationality through, for example, the character Malvonne. Malvonne casually references affluent "West Indians" of "the 300 block of Edgecomb Avenue." She also peruses the era-defining contents of the Post Office letters stolen by her nephew William Younger, whom she nicknamed "Sweetness." Like the letters Macmillan and migrant Clara write home to England and Nigeria, respectively, from the ship MV *Sasa*, some of the homebound mails looted by Sweetness belong to migrant black southerners and colonial West Indians in New York. This narrative shrinkage also of Harlem's English-speaking Caribbean population and its contribution to the era would not escape Françoise Charras. Charras has drawn attention to black nationalism's subordination of Caribbean immigrants' noteworthy numbers and input during the period (271). Nevertheless, Morrison hints at the migrant community's linguistic plurality, as does Achebe in *No Longer at Ease*. She also captures the push-factors that particularize the migrants' generational back-stories of escape from "want and violence" that date back to and "crested in the 1870s; the '80s; the '90s" (33).

Having found themselves in Harlem, New York, however, *Jazz's* diverse and pioneering migrants and the native black population try to regroup. They strive to forge, outside the exigencies of daily new living, what can be seen as a bustling village-community and its atmosphere. Continuing the goals and long traditions of the "spate of mutual benefit societies" that were estab-lished, according to Dickson Bruce, "in almost all of America's major cities between 1800 and 1810, with more to come in the ensuing decades" (93), *Jazz's* blacks exude a sense of group cohesion and collective survival by building new institutions or strengthening existing ones. We are told that in Harlem there is "every club, organization, group, order, union, society, brotherhood, sisterhood or association imaginable" (10). Reminiscent of *No Longer at Ease's* Umuofia Progressive Union, *Jazz's* black women of Salem Baptist, for example, organize the Salem Women's Club (SWC). Like the metropolitan UPU whose president at meetings cautions its young members against Lagos's dangerous "sweetness" (94), the SWC holds meetings. A pragmatic group, it prioritizes its members' tabled adversities, apparently in keeping with its aims of fiscal discipline and provincialized racial uplift. Accordingly, as pressing as is the matter of Violet's "craziness" and financial alterity, the SWC defers financially assisting her. This is like the UPU that has to vet but ultimately endorses the murky request for a loan by the Post Office messenger Joshua Udo, who "had been sacked for sleeping while on duty" (90). Instead of shoring Violet, the SWC "mobiliz[es]" to help the more dire and urgent case of a "burnt-out family[]" (4), as do the Umuofians who "had taxed themselves mercilessly to raise eight hundred pounds" to urgently educate Obi in England (112). Also evocative of the UPU's expectant financial/business "investment" in Obi (36), *Jazz's* narrator mentions that another village-modeled and self-determining union, the Civic Daughters club, meets to plan a "Thanksgiving fund raiser for the National Negro Business League" (69). Add to that mutual sustenance the community's neighborliness: the material, emotional, and spiritual support other families provide True Belle's daughter Rose Dear and her children.

Living their lives in between worlds, as Griswold theorized of the city novel, *Jazz's* New York migrant black community members maintain other

Africanisms. An instance is the Africa-derived villagist tradition of respect for age. Equally transplanted with them is their subscription to superstitious knowledge about spirits, fixing, signs, dreams, and numbers. They denominate diabolism not in warring philosophical abstractions. To them, "evil" manifests concretely, in white racism and violence, as well as in egregious acts by otherwise decent persons. That would include Joe's murder of his teenage mistress Dorcas, Violet's retaliatory yet indecorous disruption of Dorcas's funeral and her mutilation of the girl's face, as well as Violet's very strange, public attempt to steal a baby. Evoking the image in *No Longer at Ease* of the old English manageress of the eatery Palm Grove and her companion parrot, Violet's nurturing of a consort parrot would count for them as additional sign of her village-accommodated oddity. Morrison suggests that, perhaps other than the ideals of collectivism, regard for age, and allowance of intuited epistemology, nothing more markedly showcases the community's villagism than their hypercriticism and hatred of pride. Just as evidential are their capacity for envy, spite, and judgment by the young and old alike.

Deserving a closer and unorthodox look among Achebe and Morrison's deployments of villagism are their sometimes subtle yet synergic linkages of Obi and Joe with animism. Specifically, they associate both city men with the metaphysicality and semiosis of trees, mythic life journeys, and "spirit"/ spiritual rebirth and reincarnation. In many African villages and towns, and as Jesmyn Ward also powerfully fictionalizes in *Sing, Unburied, Sing* (2017), trees are considered (con)junctional sites of the secular and the sacred. They are seen especially as the abodes and rendezvouses of both benevolent and capricious spirits.[10] I contend that, veiled in the lyricism, dreamscape, imagery, and romantic conceit of Obi's tree-theme nostalgic poem written in England is his spirituality. This spirituality is placed and played in diaphony to his modernist skepticism about facets of his African cosmos. Subsumed in the poem are what colonial Christianity and education fear from and try assiduously to suppress in natives, namely, the eruptions of village funk.[11] Christian conversion is kept agitated by and thus must continually guard against this undead, this sudden release and revival of the native's alleged primitivism. Along with his father Isaac, Obi, whom David Carroll calls "a black Englishman" (68), is likely more ancestral and superstitious than let on by his learned performance of the binaries of white gaze and white thought-circuitry.

Because Morrison often noiselessly conscripts and interweaves African cosmologies and African American cultures *and* Christianity, it is not confounding that *Jazz* does not inordinately annotate her similar connection of Joe, particularly, with village trees. Nor are we surprised that she does not accentuate her figuration of him as a spirit's child (Wild's son) *and* a spirit-child, one that is restless, un-homed, and deceptively innocuous; a contract/vow breaker. However, a culturally steeped interpretation of the novel, especially an analysis grounded in the corpus of "spirit-children" literature, concept-theorization, and overall discourse, for instance, cannot but intuit and ascribe a deeper subtext to Morrison's preternatural representation of Joe. "He has double eyes. Each one a different color," recalls Felice. "A sad one that lets you look inside him, and a clear one that looks inside you" (206). Joe would remind Achebe readers also of the multisighted diviner known as "'the man of the four eyes'" in the short story "Chike's School Days" (39).

Joe is also a *visitor* in another family's home. Rhonda Williams named the adoptee Joe "Joseph" after her father. But by intentionally leaving out a surname she also let him know, *and lets it be known,* that he is actually not their biological baby, their "natural child" (123). Augmenting that inference are the circumstances of Joe and Violet's first meeting. Then a seventeen-year-old village girl, Violet appears animist in her remark about the potential danger of one relaxing under a tree at night. Analogous to Obi's poeticized desire to evening-dream under a tree, and anticipating Dovey's encounter with Friend in *Paradise,* Violet—believing "trees [could] turn[] out to be full of spirits idling the night away," or spirits passing by—"chose to spread her blanket . . . under a handsome black walnut." This walnut is located "*at the edge of the woods* bordering the acres of cotton." And what happens?: "a man [read, the site's embodied and occupant spirit] fell out of the tree above her head and landed at her side." From then on, that man, Joe, as if declaring his *possession* of the spot, names that walnut "our tree," his and Violet's, although it is said he and his half brother Victory Williams also used to sleep in it (see *Jazz* 103, 105, 30). Interestingly, it is also under a tree that Obi's ethereal poem portrays him as a spirited romantic. Joe and Violet's relationship begins its upswing under a tree, a walnut tree. Obi and Clara's love story marks its downturn from it. For it is "under the tall frangipani tree," and remarkably also "*at the edge of the swimming pool*"—with spirits also linked with bodies of water—that Clara tearfully dashes Obi's dream. She informs him she cannot marry him because she is an *osu* (*Jazz* 80, 31; *my italics*).

Inextricable from their tree-ties, Obi and Joe undergo mythic-level life journeys and change. Obi's homecoming takes sixteen days, or four market weeks, of sea travel. But also, as one Umuofia elder reads it: "Without doubt," Obi has "visited the land of spirits," and is evidently transfigured by it. To another elder, he is "a little child returned," *born-again* and anew, after and "from wrestling in the spirit world" (58–59). C. L. Innes's observation is keen: "Obi's story, though set chiefly in Lagos, is structured around a series of journeys, each of which takes him and the reader to a deeper and more complex understanding of the culture which has formed Obi as well as the degree to which he has grown away from it." According to Innes, "The first is his journey from Umuofia to Lagos; the second the voyage back from England to Lagos. The third and fourth journeys are the most significant—the two trips back to Umuofia—for the difference between these two trips marks the change that takes place in Obi" (*Chinua Achebe* 50). Underreported here by Innes, perhaps, is what should sequentially be Obi's second trip: his journey from Lagos to England. Similarly, however, Joe's *renaissance* is self-chronicled as profound personal change, as *rebirth*, in seven life-journey acts. The possibility that *returned* Obi is someone's reincarnation is ironic because Obi disbelieves in metempsychosis. That clue that he is a reborn spirit comes from the village elder Ogbuefi Odogwu.

Multifunctioning in the narrative as generational memory, culture-bearer, oral historian, and one of the novel's many surrogate narrators and translators of the (seeming) occult, Odogwu implicitly casts a divination, just moments before he couples *Things Fall Apart* and *No Longer at Ease*. He voices back from the dead, so to speak, Umuofia's greatness and the men he and probably other Umuofians honor as that village's towering figures. He names, among them, "Okonkwo, Ezeudu, Obierika, Okolo, Nwosu," "Ndu, Nwosisi, Ikedi, Obika." Notice: no mention of Okonkwo's father, Unoka. Nevertheless, much to Obi's discomfiture and to his modernist skepticism about traditional village epistemology from which his friend Joseph suggests his Western education has alienated him, Odogwu pronounces that he, Obi, "is Ogbuefi Okonkwo come back. He is Okonkwo *kpom-kwem*, exact, perfect." The gnostic Odogwu apostrophizes that Isaac's Christianity also espouses life-death cycles. In *Things Fall Apart*, Okonkwo threatens that he will haunt from the grave any of his children who follow Nwoye's example of forsaking and un-loving the gods of their ancestors. And if the Okonkwo curse on Nwoye as a result of the Nwoye betrayal serves to communicate the depth of his hurt, rage, and disappointment, is it possible Okonkwo reincarnated in Obi? Any chance that he is further making good on the ultimatum by doubly punishing Nwoye through the dishonor of his son, New African Obi's music-aided forbidden love with, and marital interest in, an *osu*?

Two-Timing and Double Time: Village Love and Illicit Loving
in *The City*, and on the Afro Beats of Highlife and Jazz

Also inseparable from the foregoing are Achebe and Morrison's analogous takes on a posited but not exclusively village-literature motif, love,[12] taboo love, to be more exact. The other ancillary subject in the subgenre's peripheral vision is *the City*. Then there is music, itself a cultural mainstay of the village proper and sometimes a major theme or subtheme in village and city narratives. In *Love and Narrative Form in Toni Morrison's Later Novels* (2017), Jean Wyatt maps the thesis that, in Morrison's works, particularly in the later, less realistically rendered and more subtly didactic novels from *Beloved* to *God Help the Child*, "the peculiarities of narrative structure—its gaps, discontinuities, and surprises—bring a reader to question his or her own fixed beliefs about love" (2; see also Loris). As the previous chapter's engagement with the subject helps to demonstrate, and as the foregoing and present discussion shows, that zone of love, along with betrayal, in this case, is also a masterfully stylized but unfortunately a critically underleveraged leitmotif in Achebe's village and city stories. Helen Chukwuma's "Love and Motherhood in Chinua Achebe's Novels" is a departure from the critical dearth. An illuminating discussion, it should spur more interest in the topic, even though the specific topic of "love" does not get a much-deserved exploration either in Chukwuma's essay or the edited collection's index.[13]

To channel in low frequency one of maestro Barry White's sublime orchestra compositions, Achebe and Morrison have in one way or another been engaged with "Love's Theme." They have been preoccupied with *ije love* (love's vicissitudes), as Nigerian music legend Nelly Uchendu—who played Ikemefuna's mother in Nigerian Television Authority's production of *Things Fall Apart* in 1986—would lyricize it in her evergreen hit "Love Nwantiti": a track that award-winning jazz singer Somi refreshes in her 2014 album *The Lagos Music Salon*. Nonetheless, although predated by, for instance, Cyprian Ekwensi's pioneering treatments of the subject in modern Nigerian and West African literature, Obi's adventures in generational and outlaw love and loving in Lagos relative to modernity, ethnic-unity, and nation-building have their thematic, cultural, and structural debuts in Achebe's earlier stories. They have been sampled in Achebe's ironic take on the love and "marriage question" in Nnaemeka and Nene Atang's intertribal romance in his 1952 village short story "Marriage Is a Private Affair." Even more, Obi Okonkwo's life's path to love, so to speak, is modeled after its literary double. It is heralded by another "Michael Obi," aged twenty-six and connected with the village-city, tradition-modernity tensions in Achebe's short story "Dead Men's Path" (1953).

The above Achebe village short stories are then, by way of this study, in conversation with *Jazz* and the rest of Morrison's love (sub)stories. However, *No Longer at Ease* and *Jazz* exhibit some of their strongest affinities in Obi's love affair with Clara, and Joe's with Violet and later Dorcas. It is through those tales on love, and of love, that Achebe and Morrison comparably broach one of the most unwieldy and often artistically tackled issues that persist among Igbo-Africans and African Americans. As Black Feminist theorist Ann duCille points out in *The Coupling Convention*, "the marriage plot" was always considered "a convention of the white middle class" (3); perhaps no longer. The issue and plot linger even as both groups, Africans and African Americans, continue to navigate their journeys from slavery and imperial colonization to independence, from slavery and Jim Crow segregation to freedom, and among both groups from the South/country/village to the city.

I am simply suggesting that Achebe and Morrison are propounding this exact thesis in both texts: that the contingencies of "choice" and "disruptive individuality" are perhaps one of the last remaining conundrums, if not *the* test, of Atlantic modernities among Africans and African Americans (see also Schappell 82–83; Bouson 163; Alwes). These self-versus-group pressures, the history and breadth of which Nathan Irvin Huggins attempts to detail in his *Black Odyssey*'s chapter "The Slave Community" (154–82), are sifted in both narratives. Although it is a core theme of village novels, the precarity is, however, deliberately not totally and *satisfyingly* resolved by the two texts. It is not settled by the novels' village- and love-implicated acts of transgressions: by Obi, Clara, Joe, and Violet, whose parallel age brackets cannot go unnoticed. Obi is twenty-five and guesses Clara is twenty-three, but she could be twenty-five as well. Doubling those ages, or times, Joe and Violet are fifty. The already worldly wise girls—*No Longer at Ease*'s Elsie Mark and *Jazz*'s Dorcas—are about eighteen.

Like its canonical antecedents and its village-city narrative cohort, *No Longer at Ease* metacritiques and in parts satirizes (Babalola 139) the shallowness of affection in New Age, midcentury Lagos. Achebe dramatizes that generational hurdle and misstep, that bungling, as it were, in the superficial relationships of characters such as Joseph Okeke, the Honorable Sam Okoli, and Christopher. To these New Africans, new cosmopolitans, these former-villagers-turned-city-men and -playboys, the women Joy, Bisi, Florence, Elsie Mark, and preengagement Clara—though conscious participants in the love game—are considered "new finds," to use Joseph's opinion of his rotating girlfriends. Add to that list the not-exactly-innocent Irish missionaries, the girls Pat and Nora. *Jazz*, likewise, engages with what Morrison structures in the novel as urbanity's muddling of emotions and passions. But as the narrator reflects and regrets, "Little of that makes for love," or for a loving black relationship, although "it does pump desire. The woman who churned a man's blood as she leaned all alone on a fence by a country road might not expect even to catch his eye in the City" (34). And as the Joe-Dorcas-Aston love crossroads further illustrates, not even younger (black) urbans are shielded from love's village-trickster, or shall we say its Esu Elegbara, capacities to (mis)interpret disparate passions and induce copulation but also to sow mischief and discord with relish.

Besides imagining himself as part of an educated "handful of men at the top" rescuing the nescient Nigerian masses (50)—a Du Boisian Talented Tenth, if not indeed a Race Man (Carby 4–6)—Obi fancies himself a revolutionary. He adjudges himself a generational change-agent who enjoys the chance to box with and hopefully vanquish the limitations of village and other past orthodoxies. Though critically perceived as unheroic, "a wilting puppet" and "weakling" (Ogwude 334), Obi considers himself a cultural iconoclast. He sees himself as a rebel, one who, on learning a new bride-price ordinance that corrects for changes in women's educational and cultural statuses has hiked the customary payment, declaims he would not pay even a small amount to marry. Most of all, Obi reckons himself, and intends to prove he is, a radical-in-love and a radical-lover in an emergent country where, as Christopher hypothesizes, "love" is a Western construct and thus nonexistent. Thus, believing himself a self, modern, and free, a national "pioneer" who helped integrate racially segregated housing in Ikoyi, Obi hopes to strike the first blow in a righteous war. His is a crusade born of outrage and indignation. He hopes to dismantle what, unlike Christopher, he concludes is an absurd *osu* custom—a passed-on prohibition against marriage between a freeborn and a girl "simply because her great-great-great-great-grandfather had been dedicated to serve a god, thereby setting himself apart and turning his descendants into [*osu*] a forbidden caste to the end of Time" (82).

But, *still* requiring the authorization of village tradition in private parental consent and also the validation of the larger village group in communal affirmation, his modern/New Nigerian/New African quest to trailblaze in love and culture is thwarted. Like Joe Trace bound to and spun by City track, Obi is bound by what Michelle C. Loris calls "the external social context" of love (53).

He is derailed and spun by a slavery-steeled *osu* track laid in the village centuries ago. Readers will remember Obi's downward spiral as his conservative village parents expectedly oppose his experimental agency. And, his familial tensions mount with his mother's death. Obi suffers psychosomatic illness caused by long stretches of relationship stress. His love blues are intensified by his cascaded money blues, which Clara attempts unsuccessfully to help him assuage with a loan that he, in the recklessness of modern youth, loses to thieves. His incarcerating depression evolves into hard thought and, later, stoicism and apathy. Obi's ordeals find a marked analogy in Joe's house arrest, emotional torture, and introspections—his own love-blues relieved somewhat by Felice's visits and clarifying disclosures about young Dorcas's coldness, deviousness, insecurities, insatiability, and two-timing. It cannot be lost on us the parities between Obi's futile letter to Clara written as he "nowadays spent all his time in bed," essentially in a corner, ironically living out his own theory of real tragedy (178–79) *and* Joe's purgatorial dishevelment and soliloquies to Violet and the dead Dorcas. Both men's melancholia and apologia are queried in this *updated,* cynical rejoinder by *No Longer at Ease*'s narrator: "What comfort did a dead man [or dead woman] derive from the knowledge that his [or her] murderer was in sackcloth and ashes?" (178).

Without question, Obi's village predicament is myriad and affecting. He even perceives himself as having died and been reborn after the guilt stage of his mourning. But we cannot ignore the equally *individualizing* and thus choice-imperative of Clara's implied infanticide. Clara's intent to "find a way out" (163), her decision to abort their baby, is a Sethe moment. Either bring into the world a child that is already condemned by Old World domestic slavery to follow the condition of the *osu* mother, as in New World chattel slavery. Or, out of love, but also in gendered exercise of maternal agency, save the baby infanticidally from a predetermined future of caste alterity. However, as with Sethe's tough choice that "has enormous cosmic and psychological consequences for the parent" (Story 21), Clara would perhaps have to contend with a theological and ethical question. The problematic, admitted by Morrison, is one of authority. Who conveyed her, Sethe, a Creator prerogative to deny the unborn child its own life and chances? Even though the character "mad" Amos marries an *osu*, Sarah, in Achebe's "Chike's School Days," Achebe intended the Obi-Clara cultural impasse to further symbolize the limbo status of the *osu* system and question in Igboland especially at the time. Nonetheless, Clara's radical election of abortion over motherhood is prompted not just by self-love.

It appears driven also by altruism if not indeed her love of Obi. Her telling him she is calling off their engagement "because she did not want to ruin his life" (141) recalls Dorcas's anomalous, and some might say perplexing, resolve to protect Joe, her shooter, by withholding his identity. Obi pays for the abortion. But will he readily and ultimately embrace the vicarious village stigma, the cultural *othering*, of osu parenthood, as does the vanguard Christian convert Amos that defies his mother Elizabeth's grief and the ancestors' anger? Like Eloe that—as place (village) and idea (the past)—constitutes perhaps the most consequential barrier between the multiply reincarnated and traditionalist Son and the modern, citified Jadine in *Tar Baby*, the osu issue, the narrator surmises, is Isaac's son Obi's most daunting predicament.

That Clara loses what would have been her first child and also spends five weeks in the hospital due to complications from the abortion speaks to the human cost of the civilizational clashes. It expresses the Baldwinian price of the ticket, in this case the ticket to modernity; the competing pulls, as it were, of bondage and freedom, of Old *and* Renascent Africa and blackness. Coupled with that tragedy is a potential Obi-Clara family doomed from the outset, as Clara knew deep down, its unraveling expedited by villagist meddling unhinged by Joseph Okeke. In its burden, the osu custom, as narrated, is apathetic to its victims' résumés and suffering. For instance, it cares less about Clara's humanity. It is disinterested that she possesses the very personal qualities and has also accrued such academic and professional feathers that Igbo culture, particularly modern and achievement-enchanted Igbo sensibility, would expect of and/or admire in its children. Clara appears compassionate and family-centered, as amply evident in her relationship with Obi and in her sharing her home with her first cousin in Yaba. She is educated, discerning, resilient, gainfully employed, beautiful, witty, and unaging, like Sula—an ever-youth for which Obi likens her to timeless music. She is also self-aware, fertile and, upon all that, a *been-to* (see Lawson 2–3). Take away the osu mark, and she easily anticipates *Anthills'* Beatrice—another Achebe female force linked with deity. A member of Nigeria's postindependence generation of leaders, Clara has the potential to become what the Igbo to this day proudly call "*Ada eji aga mba*," in loose translation: a daughter of stature, the kind one takes on a distant journey; akin to praise-naming Henry LesTroy Hunters Hunter. Just as a disillusioned Alice Manfred moves back to Springfield in *Jazz*'s end, Clara, likely equally disenchanted, and cast and caste off from collective kinship, leaves Lagos immediately upon being discharged from the hospital, her whereabouts hauntingly unknown.

And here are, perhaps, some of *No Longer at Ease*'s most profound and love-connected ironies. Does Isaac Okonkwo know, as Elizabeth Isichei states, that although the Igbo attitude to the *osu* would harden to one of paradoxical "reverence and abhorrence," the *osu* were initially "regarded with respect and honour"? It would not be until the nineteenth century when "their numbers expanded" that "their status deteriorated dramatically" to the extent "they became outcasts, feared and despised"? (*History* 47–48). Also, were the lives of playboys Joseph Okeke and Christopher, or that of the UPU member who disparages Clara as "a useless girl," on the line at the hospital where Clara works the essential frontlines, chances are no one would first ask about her gender and genealogy, her (cultural) identity, and caste. No one would recommend that urgent, lifesaving treatment be delayed or discontinued because, well, the supervising nurse, or perhaps the doctor, lab technician, pharmacist, or paramedic is an *osu*. Does Isaac Okonkwo know that, on the ship, *osu* Clara helped heal and save the life of his sick son Obi with Avomine tablets? The Umuofians in Lagos and, particularly, Obi's Christian but cultural-conservative parents still subscribe to the *osu* custom which, Francis A. Arinze also reminds us, however, "did not exist in all parts of I[g]boland" (92). But the Lagos village Umuofians seem unperturbed by, or appear at least not to have considered, the potential of nonprocreational sex and thus blood-mixing and caste-crossing having already occurred between the *osu* and their freeborn son, as Clara and Obi's conventional coupling and intercourse show.

Perhaps unbeknownst to them, Umuofia village's pantheon of heroes and statesmen is already impure, in that it includes the man "Nwosu," literally an *Osu's Offspring*/descendant, remembered fondly by the elder Ogbuefi Odogwu. Even more: the New Nigerian/New African—the Obis and *A Man of the People*'s Odilis—can always trespass the slavery-gestated and once-restricted sexual color line by frolicking and casually sleeping with white women and white girls in England and Lagos. Also, the traditionalist Joseph can brag about sleeping with a virgin Joy, his girlfriend for five months. All of that is sanctioned and part of *the new*. But as the end to his affair with Clara clearly telegraphs, Obi better nip that quest to marry and father a child with Clara—the novel's sign of ruptured kinship and cultural unbelonging; indeed, a site of Igbo cosmological dilemma and imperfection. In his most tactical argument against the marriage, Isaac Okonkwo counterinvokes the same biblical enlightenment Obi cites in a subtle dig on his father's and the culture's double-dealing, or at least the appearance of it. Drawing upon the book of Leviticus, Isaac contends that

"Naaman, captain of the host of Syria, was a great man and honorable, he was also a mighty man of valor, but he was a leper." And *"Osu,"* he adds emphatically and brutally, "is like leprosy in the mind of our people" (152).

The Naaman-aware Methodist Church that founded Igboland's Uzuakoli Leprosy Colony, the courageous British missionary doctors and Igbo humanitarians who, at the time of Isaac's statement, worked at the hospital, and that hospital's historically most prominent patient and one of Igboland's and Nigeria's most well-known victims of that deforming disease, Ikoli Harcourt Whyte—whose mother's name, ironically, is Hannah—would have things to say to Achebe's Isaac, Hannah, and Joseph. For instead of signifying revulsion in Igbo psyche, as the many contemptuous references to leprosy in *Arrow of God* also suggest, Harcourt Whyte, a prolific composer even with his impaired fingers, was celebrated at home and abroad. Like Claude McKay's New Negro Renaissance poem "If We Must Die" that is said to have been quoted by Prime Minister Churchill to rally British troops during World War II with Churchill unaware the poet was black, Whyte's music gave succor to Ndi-Igbo and more notably Igbo-Biafran soldiers during the Nigeria-Biafra Civil War (Achinivu 99–104). Whyte was embraced for composing what many who know his songs, for instance the track *"Atula Egwu"* ("Don't Be Afraid") and several others, would agree are some of the most touching hymns in the Igbo choral suite to this day. Born around 1905, diagnosed with leprosy as a teenager, Whyte personified dignity and steadfastness, which he showed his fellow patients and choir. He was, in a very real sense, a renascent New Nigerian. He was a New African in his vanguardism, legacy, and most of all his brave leadership of fellow ostracized patients in a successful revolt against brotherly betrayal and eviction from their secluded settlement. Whyte may have *died* when leprosy struck and debilitated him, just as the fettering *osu* custom scarred Clara. But in music he experienced and experiences *rebirth*.

It is also not only New Negro rebellion against what he, too, deems a manacling custom but the desire for a new personal freedom and racial order that equally propel Joe's taboo affair with Dorcas. The same undergirds of *individuation* or agency could be said to inform Violet's equally taboo response to that affair, more specifically her spontaneous commission of an abomination to expiate another, as does Sethe. In his interior monologue that collapses biography, testament, "diary," and palpable intimate talk with the deceased Dorcas, whose picture and memory have consumed him and Violet since her murder, Joe makes revealing and gendered admissions. He hints that he felt constrained by *tradition,* by the convention of virtuous living in his observance of monogamy as his wife's Change of Life stales their marriage. Hindered even more by the afterlives of America's past of plantation slavery and its persistent custom of racism, he needed to exhale. He craved self-assertion, to break the rules by doing wrong, even for once. As with Obi's admission to ignorance about the depth of love's mystery and power until Clara, Joe confesses to the same naiveté. But he intimates it is on the impulse of youth, or largely because he failed to locate Wild, the supposed mother who abandoned him, that he got married.

In what reminds us of Elsie Mark and the other scholarship applicants' collective deployments of pressure, seduction, and most of all bribery to compromise Obi and secure his assistance, Joe nimbly breaks Malvonne's moral resistance and entangles her in his corruption scheme. With the application of "improper influence," which is how *No Longer at Ease*'s Christopher conceptualizes bribery (138)—specifically the promise of regular and discrete bribes and appliance repairs for Malvonne—Joe convinces her to rent him her nephew Sweetness's room to commit adultery, or to break a union-vow, a *pact,* in spirit-child mode and register. To justify the individuating amorality for which Manfred calls him "nasty" and a "dog" (evoking pejoratives cast deterrently at spirit-children *ogbanje* and *abiku*), Joe levels allegations against his wife. He claims Violet cares less about him now and more about her ritualized birds, especially the parrot that tells her "I love you." He accuses her of cooking unappetizing pork, unbearable silence at home, and physical distance (44–49). Like Isaac Okonkwo's recourse to scripture, Joe evokes a biblical precursor and archetype "Adam [who] ate the apple and its core" and gladly vacates Eden "a rich man," apprised of hitherto impermissible knowledge that is both heavenly and beatific (133).

Joe also confesses to being inspirited by risk, the thrill of danger and recklessness. Obi is as well, especially had he successfully persuaded his parents with *modern* logic, married his fiancé Clara, defied his ancestors, and forever bucked a stifling village tradition. He cannot abide a system that, to him, consigns a healthy *and* modern person as a leper just for being an *osu.* In Joe's case, the hazard *and* the thrill are magnified by Dorcas's tender age, his morality and marriage, the possibility of discovery and, yes, race. To him, as to Obi, it is ultimately about (his modern and radical black) subjectivity; about one's or that black individual's choice and daring. It is about "the picking out, the choosing" for oneself, Joe reasons (133–35), especially as a black man and a black person in America. A member of an Africa-descended group essentially *osu-fied* in America—transgenerationally marked and relegated to what Isabel Wilkerson calls "historically" the nation's "lowest caste" (*Caste* 6)—Joe laments that he has always *complied*. He has mostly done right by his nation, one whose "unseen skeleton," Wilkerson adds, is "a caste system that is central to its operation" (17). He has even overadhered to the nation's Protestant ethic of hard work, thrift, abstinence, and economic success in property ownership that is trampled by white hatred. He does not "drink, smoke, gamble or tithe," he says (49), and yet. And, the City, the living City, can vouch for him on that. It can testify to his faith in *progress*, just as it can attest to Obi's and without question Clara's (initial) idealism.

New African Obi and New Negro Joe, particularly, may be village-hampered. In Joe's case, as stated, he is additionally hobbled by race. But one thing their citification has done, other than subject them to Du Boisian double consciousness, is further potentiate their risk-taking. With the "c" in "city" uppercased/personified in *Jazz*, the City incentivizes the two village men's willingness to "gamble"—in jazz mode. It should be noted that Achebe and Morrison are not the first or only African and diaspora writers to explore and complicate the City, especially relative to modernity, migration, subjectivity, and (un)belonging. As such, *No Longer at Ease* and *Jazz* follow closely the same universal script in terms of the migrants' or refugees' or the general newcomer's perceptions of their host nations and/or their immediate city environments, to which they have moved after hearing often-exaggerated stories of the City. The new arrival typically has an initial and stock sense of wonder, followed by an awakening and, in the long run, the "negotiation of a possible return, be it physical or psychological. The longing or yearning for a return," Cajetan Iheka and Jack Taylor add, "is often connected with," among other things, "the migrants' exclusion or limited access to the social and economic resources of their new environment" (6).

From Achebe and Morrison's earlier-discussed views on city-village interfaces in African and African American experiences to the literary criticisms on *No Longer at Ease* and *Jazz*, so much has been discoursed on urbanization in the two stories. As such, it would be unproductive to rehash details of each text's fine texturing of the City. Suffice it to state generally, however, that in addition to analogously limning vivid images of the layouts, structures, local colors, and even class and resource disparities of the two biggest cities of their nations, Lagos and New York respectively, Achebe and Morrison also represent them uniformly as inherently dialectical. They paint them as very "plastic" and melodramatic, to lease Jonathan Raban's very apt descriptors (2, 9). Among other things, the City in each story is expansive but shrunk by locomotion and wayfaring. It entices yet distances; congregates but also fragments and estranges. It encourages striving yet stifles dreams. It inculcates ostentation by day and escapism by night in glitzy cinemas, eateries, parties, and dancehalls. Cleverly corrupting, it cultivates decadence and infidelities among its old and abides sin and obsession by its young. It is sexually licensing but binding of the unwary newcomer. It plays coy and plays *players*, needling and spinning them. In its forward-orientation it aims for historical amnesia, the repression and ultimately erasure of its and its residents' pasts. It is sobering in its ethnic and racial strife, among other conflicts. Recall, for instance, Joseph remarking that Syrians "own everything in Lagos" (38) and the race riots in New York and elsewhere. But the City can also underwhelm in its congestion, unsanitariness, danger, and, perhaps most of all, its persistent pockets of village rurality and its incubations of commercial mendacity, false divinities, and political charlatans. As the young, southeastern migrant and street performer Elvis in Chris Abani's *GraceLand* wonders: how could the city, how could Lagos, specifically, be such "half slum, half paradise. How could a place be so ugly and violent yet beautiful at the same time?" (7).

The above penultimate assertion is of historical and critical import. We have, in *No Longer at Ease*, the spectacle of charismatic City racketeers in a car, peddling Long Life Mixture as elixir to blaring music and an enraptured street audience in metropolitan Onitsha (54–55). This parallels *Jazz*'s recalls of the legendary Father Divine feeding hungry and disabled veterans from his wagon in music-saturated Harlem and Violet's purchase of and faith in "malts full of Dr. Dee's Nerve and Flesh Builder" (196–97). Note, too, the semblance of a voyeuristic police officer—seemingly in the colonial government's campaign to suppress vice, especially escalating marital infidelities at beaches—mistaking Clara for a prostitute and asking Obi, with whom she is seated in a car on Lagos's Victoria Beach Road, "Is she your wife?" "Where you pick am?" (85) *and* the 1920s antivice movement in New York State. It is against the backdrop of this movement that *Jazz* is set and Joe's trysts with Dorcas occur and assume broader historical significance. In Morrison's *Love*, a beach- and Police-heads–connected marital affair, in which a twenty-nine-year-old wife "furrowed in the sand with her neighbor's husband," ends tragically (5). One of Obi's neighbors is said to routinely bring "an African prostitute home on Saturday nights" (102) in what is a thriving underground economy. With respect to that decades-long New York offensive against vice, William E. Nelson writes that "Although a loosening of sexual standards may have occurred in society at large during the 1920s, strong pressures for legal enforcement of Victorian sexual norms remained." The Prohibition did not just target "rape, prostitution, pornography, homosexuality, and gender-related violence." It also "sent private investigators out to monitor places of prostitution and sought legislation to facilitate the arrest of the male customers of prostitutes" (265, 269).

But if one thing remains intractable to the hypocrisies of city law, surveillance, prohibition, and policing, and is steadfastly patronized by its customers, female and male, old and young, urbanized or villagist, it is music. As indicated in its multiple fusions in *No Longer at Ease* and *Jazz,* and notably its functional integrations in numerous aspects of African and African American cultural experiences (Ekwueme 128–32; Ojike, *My Africa* 224–25), music is a major component of both authors' village heritages and their literary works. And it plays a huge role, more broadly, in black people's existences and creativities in the diaspora. In Achebe's case, music is surprisingly a critically understudied element of his artistic vision.[14] Obi's Clara-connected reminder that "music should not be dated" (31) hints at an authorial sense of music's timelessness. But the cue signals also music's assortment, vitality, and borderlessness, as signified further in the diversity, occasions, and technical serviceability of music and extramusical indices in Achebe's other texts. As a whole, his fiction and occasionally his commentaries are spiced with references to European, Christian, African American, Caribbean, and Italian music: hymnals, devotionals, spiritual tunes, blues, jazz, calypso, orchestra, waltz, brass band, etc. The bulk of his catalogue and lyrical samples are, however, traditional Igbo-African music and music-making. The suite includes village recitatives, women's birth/fertility songs, folk lullabies, children's play and mischievous songs, masquerade chants, incantatory humming, and dirges, as well as seasonal rain songs, ceremonial tunes, celebratory ditties, praise-songs, and satirical melodies. Others are the bird Eneke Ntulukpa's derisive song, unscripted traders' songs, market-women's instrumentals, and, especially, work songs,[15] whose spontaneous, antiphonal compositions—as *Arrow of God* illustrates (56, 81–82, 211)—evince some of the African roots of New World and diaspora black music, in this instance jazz.

With regard to *No Longer at Ease* and *Jazz*'s music *instrumentation,* the reader will notice structural parallels exemplified in these randomly sorted narrative plates. In *No Longer at Ease,* we hear of Obi and Hon. Sam Okoli's big radiograms; the Lagos nightclub Imperial; Bisi's faddish buying of new records; the new rage of nightlife and dancing; memorable descriptions of dance scenes;

street drumming; waltz, blues, and sacred songs. In *Jazz*, there is mention of Victrola Impossible phonograph; Lincoln Theater; the nightclubs Mexico and Indigo; Felice's continued but trendy purchases of records; the new craze of nightclubbing and dancing; depictions of dance scenes; street drumming; blues, and spirituals. But it is in Achebe and Morrison's collective activations of high-life and jazz—sinful "race music," as a disapproving Alice Manfred would call them (79)—that the two novels' music notations and synthesis reach their peak amplification and sociocultural seditiousness.

It is quite remarkable that *No Longer at Ease* and *Jazz*'s focal music would also be what Emmanuel Obiechina calls "democratically oriented" (79) forms that counter Victorian imperiousness, respectability, and censure. They are also, most importantly, forms that define the sociohistorical zeitgeists of the novels' New Nigerian/New African and New Negro eras. The point I am trying to (im)press here is not simply about the striking coincidence of highlife and jazz's respective centralities to the two narratives and also to black Atlantic moder-nities. Nor is it just that Achebe and Morrison generally deploy the genres to interplay village and city, and texts and contexts, as other reviewers have even more eloquently observed. For not only do highlife and blues-toned jazz chal-lenge the earlier-mentioned prohibitions against vice. Not only do they defy the nomad logic of Victorian morality that inspirited the interdictions in Lagos and New York. But also, the two forms help create the ambiences of seduction for Obi, Joe, and some of the other characters' related ethical improprieties.

Rather, what I am proposing is that the major intersectionality at play here is the evolutionary continuum of Africa–world music, particularly the interac-tions, cross-illumination, and -amplification of twentieth-century West Afri-can, Afro-Caribbean, and particularly African American *musical* and *showbiz* histories. At play are the mid-twentieth-century culture wars in Nigeria that are inevitably brought back to memory by the mediation of *No Longer at Ease*, *A Man of the People*, and *Jazz*. Morrison scholars and jazz/*Jazz* critics have engaged duly with especially the novel's blues and jazz contexts and cadences. They have also noted how—to repurpose Robert Cataliotti's apposite claim— Morrison's "attraction to the [titular] music," like other black writers' interests in it, "surely lies in its sense of communal" or, shall we say, its village "heri-tage, its original and masterful techniques, its seductive," African/Afro *beats* "rhythmic sophistication and its spontaneous improvisational brilliance" (x). Substantial information exists, then, including contrarian *Jazz* criticism,[16] for students, nonspecialists, or anyone else exploring the novel's music outfitting.

However, with respect to *No Longer at Ease,* or *A Man of the People* for that matter, even the most percipient discussions of the work(s) have tended to generalize the novels' overt musical inflections, let alone the musical history Achebe overlays in the texts.[17] To help close that rotating gap, I want to venture some thoughts on what is narratively veiled *and* critically skipped in Achebe's long play on music.

Like Morrison's *Jazz, No Longer at Ease* is also actually about the Jazz Age. Or more precisely, it is about the golden age of jazz in Nigeria. It is cryptically concerned with a period of societally and literarily impactful musical innovation and cross-fertilization that lurks behind the novel's immediate temporality and musical embroidery. Unstated in the novel, but likely familiar to scholars of Nigerian and West African music, is that Robert Olabinjo "Bobby" Benson (1921–1983)—a real, renascent New Nigerian/New African and an avant-garde musician whose calypso-inflected, big-band highlife hits "Nylon Dress" and "Gentleman Bobby" Achebe samples—also played jazz. Parts of the tracks' lyrics are quoted in the novel. But the latter title's cautionary story line of guitarist Bobby's innocence in an untoward encounter with a female fan who spontaneously gave him a kiss during a show to her husband's displeasure and intervention is seamlessly parsed in-text, with the *adjudicating* narrator siding with the applauding patrons in holding Bobby blameless in the implied infidelity and zeitgeist affair (127–29).

Nevertheless, Benson, who had stints as a boxer and a tailor, began his transformative music and variety-entertainment career experimenting with jazz and other forms. Readers interested in exploring his life but especially highlife music relative to twentieth-century West Africa will find these studies listed in the bibliography additionally helpful: Amoah-Ramey; Collins (all); Plageman; Oti; and Kelley. To me, however, *Jazz in Nigeria* (1984) by Benson's friend Bassey Ita and John Collins's *Highlife Giants: West African Dance Band Pioneers* (2016) collectively offer perhaps the most critically pertinent and engaging discussion of Benson's life, legacy, and jazz's arrival and evolution to the point of spurring both a jazz epoch in Nigeria's cultural history and a culture war. Ultimately won by highlife, as Ita explains below, the debate thrust in tension jazz and highlife/highlife dance style. It also placed in contest, as Achebe ingeniously implies, highlife and such other forms as waltz and foxtrots. Ita describes the older Benson, who owned the popular Lagos nightclub Caban Bamboo, as sporting a "silvery Imperial Major beard" (23). Did Achebe meet or know (the older) Benson? Did he at some point visit and/or socialize at Caban Bamboo? And is Benson's beard the fount of *No Longer at Ease*'s nightclub, Imperial, in which the Benson classics mentioned above are performed in the novel?

To Plageman and Collins, the earliest gestations of the West African urban, hybrid, socially conscious, and popular dance music later categorized as highlife in the 1920s can be traced back to the 1890s and to Sierra Leone and Ghana. To Ita, Nigerians started playing jazz more notably in the 1940s, but as early as the 1920s (see *Highlife Giants* 20). And the genre would come to dominate the nation's ballroom and urban music scene to the point that Ita, too, calls the time "our local Jazz Age" (20; see also Jaji 14). "Down to the late forties," Ita writes, Nigerian orchestras "played mainly ballroom dance music but nearly all the musicians played jazz as well" (14), including the venerable Hubert Ogunde, who pioneered the Yoruba Travelling Theatre and used "jazz, swing and calypso" as his shows' musical accompaniment (*Highlife Giants* 128–29). Even Sango's highlife in Ekwensi's *People of the City* is said to sound as though he "were modeling his style after Louis Armstrong" (28). To Achebe, Armstrong's instrumentation and singing recall "masquerades, the masked spirits, talking, singing," (un)consciously translating in new sound "very ancient music from Africa" (Morrow 1991).

As his evidence that "the Jazz bug had eaten in deep" in Nigeria, Ita points to the proliferation of brass bands. The army, the mission schools, and even churches, all had them (15–16)—a development recorded in *No Longer at Ease* in the existence of an Umuofia Ladies' Vocal Orchestra and the C.M.S. Central School Umuofia's brass band that plays "Old Calabar." Benson had been abroad since joining the British Merchant Navy service of World War II. However, after narrowly escaping death when their boat was torpedoed by Germans, after surviving his prisoner-of-war experiences in an Italian camp, and after leaving "the UK for United States where, for a while, he appeared in films and on stage" (*Highlife Giants* 125), he would return to Nigeria with numerous show business ideas. He had been urged home in 1947 and also was financially backed by his older brother, the erstwhile "nationalist politician, civilian minister," and Ikorodu town's first lawyer T. O. S. Benson (Ita 23). Benson's showbiz ideas led to his formation in Lagos, with his Scottish–West Indian wife, Cassandra, of the Bobby and Casandra Theatrical Party show in 1948. Although their standard routines, continued from their original London templates, included, interestingly, blackface "minstrel-type shows," with the couple dancing "the jitterbug and kangaroo to jazz and boogie-woogie music" played on gramophone records (*Highlife Giants* 126), and although the emergent "intellectual jazz . . . called Bebop" counterpointed the swing form that drove Benson's influential entertainment, he still said of himself: "I am a Jazzman till tomorrow. Whatever the music I play, you'll sense jazz feelings and elements" (Ita 18–19).

Ita calls the multi-instrumentalist and trend-setting Benson a "deservedly acclaimed Father of Nigerian music," one whose cultural influence and business acumen seemed to undo the era's mental and moral inhibitions and fore-sightedly broke "the ancient barrier between hotelier and musician" (21–23). Penny M. Von Eschen seconds that valuation of Benson's legacy (234). The two years that the Benson live-band Jam Session Orchestra lasted were the furthest any jazz ensemble went in the nation, the period being jazz's "finest hour" in Nigeria, Ita adds. Benson's establishment of Nigerian Jazz Club in 1952 or 1953, Britain-trained tenor saxophonist Chris Ajilo's founding of the Agil Jazz Club in 1955, and other attempts made to recapture the glory days' interest level in jazz were flatly unsuccessful. The reason, Ita believes, was what unfurled as the culture war, or "the War of Form," as he phrases it. It was a conflict in which the Miles Davis–emulating Nigerian jazzmen "went to war with their audience," and "all to a man they lost their battles." The jazzmen did not merely forsake swing and embrace the upstart, cerebral, technically baffling, and largely undanceable modern jazz/bebop. They also arrogantly trivialized highlife as essentially a *village, native,* and lowbrow art. They forgot, too, Ita cites Zeal Onyia as lamenting, that their audience, "the Nigerian public[,] is a dancing one, always going for the boisterous and emotional element of music." Killed practically by the inflexible jazzmen themselves, Ita declares, Nigerian jazz was also a victim of history. It lost both the culture/formal war and most of its following to the once-besmirched highlife. *Going-village,* so to speak, the audience now overwhelmingly preferred highlife, in tune with the era's nationalism and its spirit of self-governance and cultural decolonization. Any hope Nigeria's Jazz Age had of salvaging the form lay, significantly, in complementation and change; in fusing jazz and highlife styles and beats. This sonic bridge was soundly built in Nigerian highlife musicians' adaptation of "the 12-bar blues form of Jazz as their standard form," Ita notes (24–28).

It is critically significant that Achebe came of age and literary prominence, and particularly that he wrote *No Longer at Ease,* during this Nigerian Jazz Age/jazz-highlife apex. Also, it is not inconceivable that he may have played some part in cementing highlife's supersedence of modern jazz as the national music, or one of the national musics, through his powerful 1950s position in radio, specifically his work at the narratively invoked Nigerian Broadcasting Service (NBS), formerly the Nigerian Broadcasting Corporation, established in 1954. To Zeal Onyia, Ita adds, it was "'the NBC [that] killed Jazz'" through its programing emphasis on Afro or "local sounds and beats," as well as talks. But Ita is adamant that the sonic supplantation resulted from sweeping historical shifts and the Nigerian jazzmen's musical anachronism (28). In addition, Achebe's narrative rendition of the nightclub sets obfuscates, perhaps intentionally. We are unsure as to whether it is Bobby Benson performing his reflexive titles, which would have included the 1952 hit track "Taxi Driver," or if it is another band playing those *sinful* and grooving black songs, consumed by alcohol-downing, cigarette-smoking, and generally unrepressed Lagosians. One of them—bucking in plain sight Victoria's/Victorian rectitude and disapproval—is indecently wearing a pellucid and brassiere-revealing blouse!

But what is just as glaring is Achebe's advancing of the novel's project of cultural nationalism through the promotion of highlife music and its indigeneity, danceability, performer-audience interaction, and generational appositeness. Thus, it is not by accident that, in stark contrast to their instinctive and ebullient reactions to the highlife numbers' lyrics and messages, Imperial's patrons and dancers tellingly retire to their seats to drink, smoke, and relax when the band plays rather pensive and poignant forms. They also do the same when the band switches to invasive imperial cultural transfers that foster mimicry in the native (see Ojike, *My Africa* 228–30). Foxtrot and quickstep, both of which Achebe mentions and memorializes in the novel, are "based on the dance music of North American blacks [that] began to hit Africa," John Collins writes. "Ironically," Collins introspects, "they were introduced mainly by whites, who had gone crazy over these new dance tunes and began disseminating them as sheet music and on old wax cylindrical records" ("Musical" 26).

And lastly, in what recalls Rudolf Fisher's celebrated Harlem Renaissance essay "The Caucasian Storms Harlem" (1927), we have in the *No Longer at Ease* interracial club scene a case of "The Caucasian Storms Lagos." In the piece, Fisher reflects sardonically on what is more succinctly tagged today as cultural appropriation. He remembers the sudden white fascination with and invasion of several popular and once-black Harlem restaurants of his youth. But these are joints in which he now feels alien, a curiosity, even blue. Like Fisher, Achebe subjects to multiple, satirizing black gazes the spectacle of white imperial slumming in an *African* cabaret. In this sociocultural space ironically called Imperial—kindred to *Jazz's* Mexico and Indigo—the supposedly low-brow, West African, urban-village music, highlife, takes center stage (128).

Coda on a High, Life Note: On the Polyphonic Amplification of the (Villager's) Fall

It speaks volumes about Achebe and Morrison's geniuses that they could harvest the slavery-implanted seeds and the village-grounding theses of culture-contact and moral dilemmas, featuring on center stage the New Nigerian/New African Obi and Clara and their Atlantic literary cousins and predecessors the New Negro Joe and Violet, and then spin those germinal tales. They weave the tales and threads into high-stakes dramas on life, on the human condition, especially the quandary of (village) love and betrayal. But if the narratives are arresting, it is not simply because of the respective core conflicts, as compelling and axial as they are. Or is it due to music's major roles in them. If the works are moving, it is precisely because of Achebe and Morrison's executions of the storytelling act—an acuity that, in Achebe's case, undercuts critical imputation of technical inferiority to *No Longer at Ease* relative to Achebe's other novels, as mentioned earlier. I would therefore like to conclude the chapter on those thoughts, beginning however with a few summative observations on the novels and their renascent/renaissance protagonists. I close out with a few notes also on the stories' plots and points of view—those old-fashioned tools of story-telling without which both narratives lose their village-novel generic imprint, their modernist electricity, and their biblically informed ethical charges.

Perhaps nothing helps to more strongly connect the two novels' ironies and intensify their affects than Achebe and Morrison's permeations of the stories in scripture. Repurposing, or shall we say localizing, the biblical allegory and trope of Fall-from-Eden, both authors, as ethically driven village novelists, stage the Obi and Joe sagas compatibly as many-sided life lessons. They frame them as the enlightening tragedies of flawed, originally village people who, among other things, succumbed to secular sweetness and stresses. These leading villagers-turned-urbans are additionally betrayed by a cavalier modernity. In his case, Obi is jostled by what Frantz Fanon unpacks as the "pitfalls of national consciousness" (148–205) and Basil Davidson discusses as "the curse of the nation-state." Obi and Joe are in many ways, then, victims of modernity in general and black Atlantic modernities, more specifically. These modernities, brash and cousins all, overpromised newness, freedom, aggressive agency, and *youth* leadership. But like overexperimental bebop, they inadequately simulated the intransigence of the old—the village, the past—which they strive to usurp and upstage. Nor did the modernities sufficiently prepare for the fragilities of new foundations and the relativities of forward-focused progress.

Looking (back)ward and more closely on it now, it makes sense that Obi and Joe are firstborn sons; in Joe's instance, an only child and son, should we allow that *Beloved's* enigmatic, roving, and elusive Wild is his mother? Also, both men's names are most apt and cohering. Their names, Obi and Joseph, are circumstantial and testimonial. Or more precisely, they are parental-experiential appellations rooted in traditional (African) onomastics and also in scripture. In the book of Genesis, Jacob and Rachel's young son Joseph is sold into slavery by his half brothers. He is betrayed by them and abandoned in Egypt, where, ironically, he rises to near-Pharaonic power. As the originary *one-left-behind-by-family* who informs Joe's ascription to himself the surname Trace, the biblical Joseph occupies a special place in his parents' hearts and the family's bloodline. His ordeal is immortalized in music, in the gospel-accented track "Brother" in the reggae great Jimmy Cliff's 1974 hit album *Music Maker.*

Similarly, Obi is beloved. His full name, Obiajulu, means the heart (Obi) *or* "the mind at last is at rest" (7). He was born after his mother—who is also training and other-mothering their relatives Joy and Mercy in housekeeping— had already borne four daughters. She would altogether have eight children, including Janet, Esther, Agnes, and Obi's immediate older sister. This older sister's similar, gender-compensatory name "Nwanyidinma—'a girl is also good'" presages the character Beatrice Okoh's father naming her "Nwanyibuife—A female is also something" in *Anthills* (79). Then we have Obi, Eunice, and John. Obi's carefully chosen baptismal name, Michael, complements his first-son and lead-role status. For, like the high-achieving biblical Joseph, youthful "Michael" is viewed as a triumphal archangel: *a vanguard-of-the-race,* the race of angels. Also attributed with mercy and clarity in biblical lore, "Michael" reinforces the Igbo Obiajulu's connotation of spiritual and emotional *alleviation.* This is especially so for Obi's father, who, following the birth of Nwayidinma, had begun worrying and wondering—like the Morgan men in *Paradise*—if he would have no male heirs in a culture that prizes male progenies.

Fascinatingly, Achebe nominally inverts that archetypal Joseph plot and narrative, though retaining the trope of betrayal. *No Longer at Ease's* own Joe—Joseph Okeke—Obi's countryman, classmate, and friend at whose Lagos residence he stays some days en route to England, is portrayed in the novel as epitomizing that special category of friendship. The Igbo call it "*enyi di ka nwanne*" (friend who is like sibling/relative). In his pride in Obi, in his conviviality, hospitality, and unsolicited counsel to him, and, perhaps most significant, his protectiveness, Joseph may as well be Obi's blood and older brother. But to Obi's disappointment, it is *Joseph* who—believing his Life experience outmatches young Obi's Book-knowledge—alerts Isaac to Clara. It is he who also apprises the UPU president of the affair, now sacrificed, in hopes of forestalling a cosmological catastrophe that an Obi marriage to an *osu* supposedly would unleash. New-era Joseph betrays Obi in a fraternal double-cross worthy of Stamp Paid and Paul D, a conceptual perversion that arguably would be inconceivable between and to *Things Fall Apart*'s Old School great friends Okonkwo and Obierika and *Arrow of God*'s Ezeulu and Akuebue. As with the personal impact and narrative utility of True Belle's divulgence of Hunters Hunter's cabin to Golden Gray, however, that Josephite betrayal is also a significant turning point of events, particularly for Obi.

In city villagers Obi and Joe's failings *and* falls from Edenic grace, Achebe and Morrison maintain the treachery overtone of the Joseph archetype. The Lagos high court judge's admonition to Obi is encapsulating. To him, Obi is "a young man" of coveted high "education and brilliant promise" (2). Evidence of Obi's virtues and prospects is clear throughout the narrative. Yet, dangerously blurring the boundaries of virtue in an upturned world of competing village and urban regimes of values, he deliberately takes bribes and cheats on Clara. But although he deserves credit for his cultural daring and sympathy for his blues, he fails. His tragic fall—his rather excessive (modern)ist experimentation in pattern-deviation—sounds quite like the defeat of the self-unrestrained improvisational soloist/artist in a community-oriented jazz/mbari village festival. Likewise, Morrison figures Joe as smart, resilient, honorable, mild, and harmless. He is a villager and a hunter, a "Country boy" turned "country man" (129). A man of Paul D's blessedness; a model thrifty but drifty man, one who sells women's Cleopatra products, while his wife, an itinerant beautician, used to style their hair. Incredulous that such an exceptional man could have killed her niece, however, Alice Manfred reconsiders Joe's public image. She judges him as disappointing. "He *knew* wrong wasn't right," she says, "and did it anyway" (73–74).

We learn at the chronological ending of *No Longer at Ease* that Clara, violated and betrayed by Joseph and Obi, is out of Obi's life. And we are told, contrastively in *Jazz*, that Joe and Violet, for whom life has never really been at ease, are gradually rebuilding their lives and marriage—one that has known traumas, including Violet's abortion (109). It is however evident that, as is sometimes the case with village lore, the two novels' central and complicated stories cannot be told in the linear fashion of "realism and reality" (Gikandi, *Reading Chinua Achebe* 80). This helps explain the works' fractured and open-ended plots. Their comparable structures mirror the ruptures of modernity, the confusions of the modern psyche, and the ambiguities of the modern novel. And just as significant is that the stories are so intricate that there cannot be absolutes. As Gikandi writes of *No Longer at Ease*: "There is no resolution here" (*Reading Chinua Achebe* 91). There are no totalized or totalizing reasons for the whys: the keynotes and multiply reprised riddles that analogously open the stories. "I cannot understand why he did it," wonders *No Longer at Ease's* exasperated British Council man (3). But he may as well be talking about Joe's murder of Dorcas and Violet's desecration of her corpse at the girl's funeral: both, village taboos consolidating the narrative as "recurring point[s] of return and reference" (Furman 86). The Council man is speaking also for the author. He is opining for all those pondering, in the village and the city, in the court of public opinion, why Obi takes the bribes. Those are an ethical frailty for which he, though outwardly stoic and nonchalant in court, now sits in imperial judgment, facing jail time. The Council man speaks relatedly for those asking, as does *Jazz's* narrator, why Malvonne, too, takes bribes; why she corrupts her soul by facilitating Joe's betrayal of Violet. But because the full answers, or the possibilities of answers to the *whys*, are dispersed and constituted throughout all the pages of both novels, we the reader-audience-voyeur-witness-and-judge, the Morrisonian chorus held in suspense, must wait. Unhurried, village-style, we must be delayed through the entire stories for possible explanations of the "mysteries."

Furthermore, propositions abound as to the identity and behavior of *Jazz's* narrator. Is it really the book talking, as Morrison herself has suggested in her foreword to *Love* (x–xi) and in interviews with Elissa Schappell (54), Salman Rushdie (52) and elsewhere, thus calling to mind Henry Louis Gates's trope of the Talking Book in African American literary experience? Or is the narrator a different consciousness? If different, is it male or female? etc. To Chad Jewett, jazz itself is the narrator (445). Nevertheless, one is struck by the idiosyncratic constants between *No Longer at Ease* and *Jazz's* narrations and multiple narrators. *No Longer at Ease* adopts the framing structure of books within a book (Obi's ongoing diary and the other books summoned in-text) *and* stories within a story/stories. In this schema, both the narrator and the various confounded constituencies with stakes in Obi's scandalous *osu*-crisis and in his bribery trial offer contradictory and sometimes real-time witness accounts. "[F]orced to fall back on dubious metaphysical or semantic games" (Gikandi, *Reading Chinua Achebe* 91), they espouse convictions and fabricate even more sensational stories on the issues. Similarly, *Jazz* integrates conventional narration, solo improvisations, polyvocal sections, and interior monologues.

Interestingly, however, there are a number of other peculiar mannerisms shared by *No Longer at Ease*'s narration/narrator(s) and *Jazz*'s. We arrive at those intertextual particularities by way of *Jazz*'s narrator's very first utterance, this truth-claim: "Sth, I know that woman." Not only is that sound "sth" premiered twice in *Beloved*. But also, in the first of the two *Beloved* references—"a *sth* when she misses the needle's eye"—the phrase's association with a needle, one, expresses the narrator's replication of the quiet sound made by a woman needling alone. That is how the muttered word *"mine"* sounds to Stamp Paid as he reaches 124 Bluestone's steps (173, 185). And two, it reminds us of the contact-sound of a turntable's tonearm and needle lowered on a record's groove. Sight, letter, sign, and sound are aligned and mutually resonated, hence *Jazz*'s epigraph. That modernist and Imperial declaration of certainty—"Sth, *I know* that woman," *that* (corrupt)ed and crazy black woman Violet—is echoed in Mr. Green's patronizing, first narrative assertions: "I can" say with unalterable, imperial "facts" why Obi did it. I can authoritatively explain why he took bribes, because *I know* him and his race as corrupt (3–4).

But the apparent irony is that *Jazz*'s narrator and Mr. Green know far less about their black subjects–protagonists than they assume. It is that idea, the assumption of the simpleness of the (black) village and villager, the Country person, the native, that Achebe and Morrison successfully discredit in both novels, which are also, as indicated earlier, books about books. In other words, "book"/ *the* book/book's-*knowledge*/writing, is a metaphor in the two works. Philip Rogers also makes that point particularly about *No Longer at Ease* (165–66). Madhu Dubey posits that in *Jazz* "the printed book is shown to be embroiled in the logic of urban commodity spectacle" (131). That spectacle is no less exemplified in the Obi court trial. The narrators' common tendencies in question also include their reflexivity; perspectival shiftiness between omniscience and first-person orientations; positional detachment but also instinctual intrusion; epistemological certainty undercut by self-doubt as normative assumptions are contravened, even betrayed, by *unexpected* character motives, actions, and outcomes. Others are participant-observation; a relaxed, "playful" temperament in tension with cynicism; and perhaps most interestingly, a presentness, a meandering but dramatic immediacy characteristic of oral tradition and village storytelling.

Observe, lastly, how in *No Longer at Ease* and *Jazz* the major actors/characters are announced up front. They are intimated in the opening acts and first chapters of flashbacks. The same is true of the basic conflicts. With the intimations mirroring the key note/keynote emblematic of highlife's song-texts and, relatedly, jazz's paramount principle of variations on a "melody or theme" which jazz musicians call "the head" (Berliner 63), the entireties of the subsequent sections of the novels are then structured as *themes-reveal* or *theses developments*. As with the "detective story," as Morrison says of *Jazz's* schematic (Schappell 80), those sections are arranged as communal inquests (or villagist prying) into the question of *why*. The timeless puzzle is why, putting it theologically, even beloved angels, no longer at ease within the old and the new, in the village and the City, fall apart and from grace. They descend, straight, like furious arrows. To Achebe and Morrison, the answer and consolation may be that the characters are in the end not divine but human. They are shaped by their historical, racial, gendered, and other pasts. They are dwelling in a beguiling world that is far from the confederated havens envisioned by powerful deities, whose foundational wills are hot riddles that defy even priestly interpretations.

4

On Black Village Havens Impelled by History, Impeded by Opposing Visions of the (Past) Wills of Gods and Founders

Arrow of God and Paradise

Wisdom is like a goatskin bag; every man carries his own.
—NWAKA, *Arrow of God*

In *Paradise*, struggles over interpretation [are] in some ways the novel's central drama.
—LINDA J. KRUMHOLZ, "Reading and Insight"

When, in his earlier-cited conversation with Okey Ndibe, Chinua Achebe concluded that African, African American, and, more broadly, black people's globally scattered stories are actually not that disparate and that it was left to especially the continent's descendants on both sides of the Atlantic to continue uncovering and potentiating the connections, those observations were not peculiar or sublime. Nor did they propose a singular diaspora mission. For as shown in the last chapter's discussion of the New Negro and New African movements, for instance, many before Achebe had championed the cause of transatlantic excavations and linkage of black experiences. But perhaps little did Achebe realize how critically fructuous those assertions would be, particularly relative to the hard-to-overstate correspondences of *Arrow of God* and *Paradise*. As is the case with *Things Fall Apart* and *Beloved*, *No Longer at Ease* and *Jazz*, so much of insight and value has also been posited about these last offerings of his and Morrison's century-spanning trilogies. But as with heaven and the dark side of the moon, many aligned parts of those last installments' topographies have yet to be mapped and coordinated.

Nevertheless, if Morrison in *Paradise* is also gesturing to the Achebe trilogy, more specifically to the novels' thematic consistencies—in this case *Arrow of God* and *Paradise's* salient preoccupations with "interpretation": a play on clashing memories, stories, perceptions, truths, and wisdoms commented on by virtually all *Paradise* criticism that I know, including Krumholz's quotation above and reviews that explain the novel relative to Faulkner, for instance Joiner (2010) and Jones (2002)—one of the hints may lie in syntactic polymorphism. It may be laced in the texts' "bow" and "brow" echoes and riffs. In other words, the signals could be checked in the uniformity of furious providential instrumentation. This empyrean *tooling* in both works is implicit in the phrases Arrow of God, "The Bow that shoots at the Sky," and "arrow in the bow of his god" (*Arrow* 151, 191). In *Paradise*, it is tacit in the originary, opaque, and equally titular Oven inscription at the center of a generational and perspectival chasm: "Beware the Furrow of His Brow," "Be the Furrow of His Brow" (93), and "We Are the Furrow of His Brow" (298).

We will get back to that chief and interlinking motif of "contrastive readings" whose narrative paramountcy Achebe warrants by staging it, literally, as the opening scene and time-marking act of *Arrow of God*. Suffice it to assert for now that no sensitive juxtaposition of *Arrow of God* and *Paradise* will miss, as indicated, both novels' nodal plenitude, their vast "web of affiliation" (Gates, *Signifying* xxii). Nor can one mistake especially their gendered divergences. Coming randomly to mind are parallels in these frames: the significances of the two novels in Achebe and Morrison's literary careers and the works' reimagining of factual, intersecting events in Igbo-African and African American histories—a crucial subject/section on which I plan to spend some time. Also fascinating are their similar plot designs, each story opening with a *quest* and also featuring two separately located village worlds, different yet linked, and likewise beset internally with tensions. These are the worlds of Umuaro and Government Hill in Okperi (the latter comprised of Captain Winterbottom, Clarke, Robert, Wade, and Wright, and Winterbottom's three stewards) in *Arrow of God* and those, in *Paradise*, of the Convent and Ruby, the latter's eminent citizens including the Morgan twins, Deacon and Steward. We have also the stories' themes of Old and New World religions and priesthoods. Just as notable are their explorations of varieties of "war" and the tragic repercussions of the past's excessive constraints on the present. Add to those planes the novels' tropes of road projects; the question of male succession; the dramaturgic depictions of the peoples' commemorations of their founding; spirituality; the motif of sin and cleansing; and the subject and practice of sacrifice.

In short, pare *Arrow of God* and *Paradise* down to their barest outlines, strip from them the paddings of structure, spaces, symbols, and the other diversionary schemes of modernist and postmodernist narrations, and what emerges is this chapter's simple thesis, namely, that both projects are clan stories. Or, in Wendy Griswold's conceptualization to which we will return, they are village novels. The two texts are tales of the tribe, of interrelated black attempts at autonomous village, if not utopic, confederations with their mythic narratives of origin. Compelled originally by slavery, the "Umuaro" nation, on one side of the Atlantic, and "Haven" and later "Ruby," on the other, are overdetermined ideas and ideals. "Imagined communities," to channel Benedict Anderson, they are sociohistorical and geographic constructs. Each compact and formation is undone, however, by inevitable and precipitous change, by the perfect-storm confluence of powerful forces from without and, more consequentially, fractures and threats from within. At the end of the stories, the two territorial and religiopolitical amalgams suffer significant institutional impairments and human casualties. These are due partly to the arrogance, pertinacity, and vengeance of the village-towns' principal powerbrokers. Prescient, fearless, agile, even "cosmopolitan" (M. Nagel 142), Ezeulu rejects Winterbottom's/the British administration's offer of his being designated Warrant Chief. But his refusal to alter received tradition and mandate even when demanded by the elders embodying Umuaro; even as he knows various ancient customs in his Igbo world are changing; even as his wives and children face retaliatory hostility; and even as potential famine endangers his high office and his people, forcing them to abandon him and his god Ulu and defect to the promised safeguard of the Christian God—that calculated adamance proves disastrous and long-lastingly afflictive, "like an *ogulu-aro* disease which counts a year and returns to its victim" (*Arrow* 220). So, too, do the rigidity, reprisal, and apoplectic rage[1] of Ruby's New Fathers. Equally remarkable is that the obstinacies are cast as acts of obedience and loyalty. They are couched, particularly by the aggrieved, prideful, and supposedly infallible men, as adherences to "the past," to the village-towns' founding/ foundational gods, ancestors, and *constitutional* principles.

In his reading of *Paradise*, "Furrowing All the Brows," Philip Page notes that a recurrent observation among the initial reviews of the novel, some of which he references, is that it is taxing. To Page, much of the explicatory challenge stems from Morrison escalating the stakes of form, style, and subject from the novel's opening. As Page states (637–38), Morrison, among other things, delays for readers and at times completely denies them, even trips them on, important answers to characters, incidents, and questions, in what Page, in another but related study, calls Morrison's "technique of suspension" (*Dangerous* 33). Page is right; *Paradise* can be daunting. It is my hope, however, that studying it side by side with *Arrow of God* will help further sieve for the reader some of the semiotic cluttering, and the cultural and cosmological *mysteries*, Page mentions. That would include the reader discovering, in *Arrow of God*, not only a model village novel and a narrative with similar density of characters and names. In *Arrow of God*, the reader finds a story that is also centrally concerned with genealogy and legacy, as well as "the convergence of religion and history," as Valerie Smith writes of *Paradise* (89). Or a "transfer of faith," as Robert Wren says of *Arrow of God* ("From Ulu" 28).

Of Texts and Contexts: Interlinking (the) HiStories behind the Village Havens' Stories

In the remainder of this chapter, I will be attempting a multipoint, methodical, and at times discontinuous and definitely uneven elaboration of what I have been outlining above as *Arrow of God* and *Paradise*'s extraordinary affinities. This unstraightforward critical reconstruction of the village havens' stories is necessitated by those stories themselves and also by their telling. And so, just as both novels' plots are nonlinear, so is this discussion of the two narratives. I want to begin that explication, however, with the following titbits that are likely familiar to Achebe and Morrison scholars, critics, and general readers.

For both authors, the two novels are canonical milestones, stature-cementing, and two of their narratives framed around historical substructures, as elucidated shortly below. In Achebe's case, *Arrow of God* is the project that completes his African trilogy. It is his third published novel, but the turn-of-the-century watershed moment it engages with is actually the intermediate grid of his triptych's one-hundred-year radius. And its golden jubilee in 2014 was marked by conferences and symposiums organized in the "US, UK, The Middle East, Asia, and Africa," as Achebe's daughter Nwando chronicles in her entry to the 2017 publication *Illuminations on Chinua Achebe*. Above all, *Arrow of God* continues to command its peak critical prestige. Although perennially overshadowed, and perhaps in sales also, by its globe-trotting older sibling *Things Fall Apart*, it is the work most Achebe scholars recognize as his magnum opus. To help put that crown in a broader perspective, Biodun Jeyifo, in his keynote address to the symposium held at Syracuse University in connection with the jubilee, states: "As far I know and with perhaps the exception of *Things Fall Apart*, this is the first time in modern African literary history that a symposium"—it turns out, one of several—"has been organized and held on a single literary text" ("Intimations" 17). Furthermore, *Arrow of God* is the only one of Achebe's five novels that he said he would find himself revisiting. Unlike his prepublication refinement of *Things Fall Apart*, whose bloated draft manuscript skewed the narrative proportionality of the three-family saga he had envisioned, Achebe had to revise *Arrow of God* postpublication. He remedied in the second release what he felt were some structural flaws in the story's first edition.[2]

Released to great expectations five years after *Jazz*, *Paradise* was the work that further proved—as if extra proof was necessary—that Morrison's 1993 Nobel Prize in Literature was no fluke. Although some early reviews of *Paradise* flagged, as Page suggested, its "heavy-handed foreshadowing and contrived plot devices," its sharp gender dichotomies, and its overtly feminist agenda (D. Smith), there is no doubt that *Paradise* is magisterial. As Justine Tally puts it, it is "vintage Morrison, one more step in the novelistic development of a writer whose concern with language, myth, and the history of black people in the United States has confirmed her, in the words appearing on the cover of *Time* magazine, as 'America's Greatest Storyteller'" ("*Paradise*" *Reconsidered* 12). Other than *The Bluest Eye*, which Morrison in 2018 said she "would like to do over" not only because she "know[s] more now" but also for the fact that she is "smarter" (Elkann 153), *Paradise* is the endeavor Morrison is certain she wanted to revisit and revise some (Mulrine). In addition, like the other four works of the second installments, *Paradise* is informed by history. It is in part inspired by a story Morrison said she heard during a trip she took to Brazil in the 1980s. The story was that some armed men had murdered a group of Candomble-practicing black nuns who sheltered abandoned children in a convent, to the anger of local residents. That this story turned out to be untrue was immaterial to Morrison. It mattered little to her because it touches, critically significantly, indeed fundamentally, on one of *Paradise*'s (and *Arrow of God*'s) major themes: religion. To Morrison, the story "said much about institutional religion and uninstitutional religion, how close they are" (D. Smith n.p.).

As indicated above, *Arrow of God* and *Paradise* internally braid with and extend the generational stories begun respectively in *Things Fall Apart* and *Jazz*. Robert Wren rightly contends that *Things Fall Apart* is such a narrative foundation that it is critical to our fuller comprehension of *Arrow of God*. According to Wren, Achebe took the risk of layering and complicating the latter novel because he could count on his readers' familiarity with the antecedent narrative (*Achebe's World* 91). Marni Gauthier similarly points out that Morrison inserted within *Jazz* the following keynote that anticipates and temporalizes *Paradise:* "The wave of black people running from want and violence crested in the 1870s; the 80s; the 90s but was a steady stream in 1906 when Joe and Violet joined in." *Paradise's* "historical timeline," Gauthier adds, "begins in the 'crest' of that flight. By situating the flight this time as a specifically *northwestern* exodus, Morrison inscribes African Americans in the US mythic history of westward migration" (396).

It is, then, one of those unwritten but definitely noteworthy chapters of black Atlantic history that, at their heydays, the migration-galvanized New Negro movement/Harlem Renaissance and the all-Black town epoch memorialized respectively in *Jazz* and *Paradise* would coincide with the turn-of-the-century era of the Warrant Chief System in Southeast Nigeria dramatized in *Arrow of God*, with Adiele Afigbo's research discussed below and S. A. Nnolim's booklet *History of Umuchu* together providing Achebe additional archival and structural support.[3] What to my knowledge has not been critically considered and may actually be far more edifying than the more obvious parallel of the focal novels' temporal settings, however, are the easily overlooked congruities of the racial, historical, and cultural dimensions of Indirect Rule and all-Black town experiences. Those congruencies start coming into fuller and crisper view as one goes interpretively granular, so to speak. They magnify, in short, as one starts meditating on subtleties and reconciling the respective empirical assessments of at least two important studies on the origins, character, and twilights of the subjects. I have in mind here Adiele Afigbo's authoritative *The Warrant Chiefs* (1972) and Hannibal B. Johnson's richly illustrated monograph *Acres of Aspiration*, published in 2002, with a foreword by Michael Eric Dyson.

Let us stipulate for now that, underneath the topical variance of "Indirect Rule" and "all-Black town" and the two periods' locational separations, are racially charged and interrelated events long set in motion by, and thus having as one of their driving coefficients, Britain. Not only the Britain-connected transatlantic slave trade and domestic slaveries, but the blueprints of nation/ nation-building and governance that the British transplanted in Southeast Nigeria and colonial North America, to the close replication by kindred-descendants of slaves and former British subjects on either side of the Atlantic. Although students of West African colonial history, Achebe readers, and more broadly critics of modern African literature are likely sufficiently familiar with the Warrant Chief System, some readers of Kindred Spirits may be new to Arrow of God and the said Indirect Rule. As such, revisiting and perhaps more importantly annotating pertinent parts of Afigbo's and, afterward, Johnson's discussions are crucial to a better understanding of, and an attempt to relate, the institutions and projects of Indirect Rule and all-Black towns.

As Afigbo explains, the Warrant Chief System is one of the various forms and implementations of Indirect Rule. And Indirect Rule itself, later known as Native Administration, cannot be fully comprehended outside of the larger complex of British Christianizing, civilizational, economic, cultural, administrative, and nation-building efforts in West Africa (1–6). In fact, as another scholar of the subject, Michael Crowther, avers in The History of Nigeria (1978)—and reinforced in Arrow of God's Captain Winterbottom—the whole colonial reformist enterprise and its afterlives are rooted in racism and white paternalism. They are grounded in British convictions about the native's innate primitiveness, childlikeness, and inferiority (215–16). Although Afigbo engages tangentially with America, it should be pointed out that imperial Britain had earlier deployed the inverse practice—Direct Rule—in its slaveholding Crown Colonies in America. Relatedly, when Winterbottom and Clarke denigrate their colonized subjects, with Winterbottom concluding that what should be primal ambition and abuse of power are instead a racial particularity, "a trait in the character of the negro" (108), he consigns black humanity outside the chain of being. He implies not just (black) Africans but also their descendants in the United States and elsewhere in the diaspora.

Nevertheless, according to Afigbo, British imperial control in West Africa started—as we may recall from our discussion of Things Fall Apart and Beloved—in the coastal districts marked as "Crown Colonies." Afigbo asserts that the Crown Colony approach was the initial notion of Direct Rule in which British institutions and notions of government were established and enforced. Under its counterpart, Indirect Rule, those premises and practices were intentionally precluded. In their places, the British exploited autochthonous institutions (4–5). Afigbo points out that in their attempt to execute Indirect Rule in Southeast Nigeria, to deploy it among the Igbo and their neighbors (the Ibibio, Ijo, and Ogoja peoples), "the British selected certain natives who they thought were traditional chiefs and gave them certificates of recognition and authority called warrants. The warrant entitled each of these men to sit in the Native Court from time to time to judge cases. It also empowered him to assume within the community he represented executive and judicial powers which were novel both in degree and territorial scope" (6–7).

Charged with nation-building and native stewardship, Sir Frederick Lugard returned to Nigeria in 1912 to administer the imperial mandate, Afigbo notes. In his effort to discharge that assignment of amalgamating the country's Northern and Southern protectorates, he decided to create an identical governmental arrangement by extending to Nigeria's Southeast, between 1914 and 1919, the model of Indirect Rule already at work in and better suited to the emirate North and monarchical Southwest. In doing so, Lugard had put in place what could be regarded as an administrative oxymoron. And nothing, following his departure from Nigeria, better illustrates the insensitivity of this superimposed administrative reform, Afigbo contends, as have other historians, than the institution in 1928 of direct taxation that culminated in the Women's Riot of 1929. Unsurprisingly, the Warrant Chief System imploded for reasons of cultural misalliance, Afigbo surmises. It seemed doomed from the start because its guiding assumptions were not aboriginal. Nor was the System, as a model of sociopolitical and economic engineering, psychically healthy for the people (xi–xii). Foisted on a well-known, democratic Igbo people and their neighbors, the System was "a blatant failure," Crowther remarks (215). This is especially because, as Afigbo further contends and concurs, it created, in the Warrant Chiefs, the court clerks, and the court messengers, government-backed tyrants [like *Arrow of God*'s Okperi paramount chief James Ikedi with unprecedented powers]. As Afigbo reflects, "The very idea of a man, no matter what he was called, who had powers to 'issue' orders to his village and/or its neighbours or to a whole clan was a political novelty." "For the first time in the people's history," he punctuates, "a scrap of paper" and, just as important, the positional interpretation of the inscription on that paper, "had the power to change the course of events" (256, 258).

The Indirect Rule/Warrant Chief System experiment was not just racially underpinned and also usurping and unpopular in its political, cultural, and economic impacts. The high human cost of its ultimately unsuccessful career was notably gendered as well. Afigbo writes that, in the "bloody encounter between the troops and the women," a confrontation in which "machine-gun and rifle" were used in the arguably sacrificial "slaughters," many women lost their lives (241, 243). Crowther, who also gives fairly detailed attention to those historic upheavals, reflects on how the Commissions of Inquiry and the hundreds of reports that the civil unrests prompted helped paint a definitive picture of the programs' blindness, failures, and futility. But a consequence of British imperial rule and those policy blunders was a deepening, in Nigeria, of the thirst for independence, Crowther remarks. British indelicate governmentality intensified a "new spirit of nationalism" spearheaded by Nigerian student associations, one of whose founders, the little-celebrated Ladipo Solanke, was the organizations' flag bearer and indefatigable agitator. Solanke held these reins until Dr. Nnamdi Azikiwe's return from the United States (212–18). As we may recall from the previous chapter, Azikiwe, who would later become Nigeria's governor general at independence and who had landed in Harlem in the mid-1920s, was inspired by the New Negro movement and epoch. From it he would learn about and personally witness the effect, on black America, of the Great Black Migration. It was this historic mass movement that, in America's Midwest, irrigated the foundations and founding of all-Black towns.

Arrow of God invokes various pre-twentieth-century historical occurrences, and its narrative scope extends to the 1920s decade of the Women's War. But, although we learn, especially through Winterbottom's grudges and judgment, about the absurdities, abuses, dangers, and utter futility of the Warrant Chief/ Indirect Rule system in Igboland, and although we hear also about illegal taxation funneled to appointees and about a "very adverse report" "by the Secretary for Native Affairs on Indirect Rule in Eastern Nigeria" (180), the women rioters' murders are not, unfortunately, covered and commemorated in the novel. And this appears to be because, occurring as they did in 1929, they fall outside the early to mid-1920s endpoints of the novel's historical attention, as deductible in events precisely dated and hinted at by Winterbottom around 1921 and 1923 (109), with the unprecedented tragic consequences of his Warrant Chief conflicts with Ezeulu, and between Ezeulu and his people, occurring perhaps just months after those conflicts erupt. Nonetheless, the transgressive and evocatively armed-and-dangerous women rioters (Azikiwe's New, Renascent Africans who fight back) were immolated for the preservation of imperial regime. Perhaps a more accurate reading of it is that the women *agentially* put their lives on the line. And many among them paid the ultimate price for the eradication of a slavery-connected foreign rule that is also, paradoxically, bound with the "founding" of the idea and experiment that is Nigeria.

At that turn of the century when the nation-building, British imperial government was implementing its misguided administrative policies among Nigeria's Southeastern Igbo, some of whom may have already begun, in trickles, a westward economic migration to the colonial capital of Lagos, as *No Longer at Ease* suggests, masses of free blacks in the United States were also North- and Midwest-bound from the South. The phylogeny and intersections of the "all-Black towns" they established and the Indirect Rule/Warrant Chief System become much clearer if we additionally stipulate that both institutions arose under the fraternal climates of racism, slavery, and colonization. That clarity is enhanced if we also view the two epochs' conjunctions from at least two discrete but still-overlapping standpoints. One is "land." Two is what I am calling "the black/native's self-determining rereading and reapplication"—in Africa and in African America—of those *scraps of paper* Afigbo speaks of. Which is to say: as in the Igbo cautionary axiom about role-modeling, depicted in the proverb about calves internalizing and replicating what their mother the she-goat does as it chews grass, the native diligently followed the enslaver-colonizer's prototypes of governmental actions and economic power. The native then repeated them, with a *native difference.*

A planetary resource without which slavery, colonization, or empire was possible and sustainable anywhere, the economy of "land" unifies Indirect Rule and the all-Black town movement. And while "land" is implicit in the former logic and practice, it is explicit in the latter. Either way, land is central to colonization and the native's multiprong resistance to it, in this case in Africa, as Jomo Kenyatta's *Facing Mount Kenya* (1962) and Ngũgĩ wa Thiong'o's *Weep Not, Child* (1964) illustrate in Kenya's related experience. Land/ territory is also indispensable to colonization and slavery, as Morrison demonstrates in *A Mercy.* Land is crucial, even more so, to the multiply dispossessed southern black migrants' counterpositional aspirations to rootedness and self-empowerment—or Direct Self-Rule—in the Midwest and literally postcolonial North America at large. Recall how, in his chat with Clarke, Winterbottom appears frustrated that the British are not, and inferably should have been, as blatant, combative, and perhaps militaristic as their neighbor France's civilizational mission and land robberies. "Look at the French," he laments. "They are not ashamed to teach their culture to backward races under their charge.

Their attitude to the native ruler is clear," he opines. "They say to him: 'This land has belonged to you because you have been strong enough to hold it. By the same token, it now belongs to us. If you are not satisfied come out and fight us'" (35–36). Not only is Winterbottom's underplaying of the British land-grab and political meddling counteracted by the "many oracles [who] prophesied" accurately that "the white man had come to take over the land and rule" (*Arrow* 43) and by historical facts such as the Nigeria-Biafra Civil War. And not only is it blunted by the colonial regime's intervention in the Umuaro-Okperi land conflict in *Arrow of God* and—as *Things Fall Apart* imparts—in the District Commissioner and his unscrupulous court clerks "judg[ing land] cases in ignorance" of Umuofia's customs and introducing capital punishment in boundary disputes (174–76). But also, whatever spin empire gives imperialism, the underlying goal of colonization remains land/territorial dominion and natural-resource expropriation (Fanon 159).

Furthermore, the social death to which slavery subjects the enslaved is one of tragic severance from primal blood ties and the appurtenances of kinship, as Orlando Patterson contends in *Slavery and Social Death*. But it is also one of the slave's forced separation from (physical, ancestral, spiritual, and cosmologic) homeland, or home *and* land. "The fundamental feature of slavery, in law," Patterson argues, "was the fact that the slave could not be a proprietor: he or she was, quintessentially, a property-less person. From this fundamental disability flowed, both in legal and socioeconomic terms, all the other manifold disabilities of the slave." The master may and did indeed sometimes allow the slave "a *peculium*," an "investment by the master of a partial, and temporary, capacity in his slave to possess and enjoy a given range of goods." However, this peculium should not be confused with "genuine property" ownership, Patterson cautions. This is because—like the little goat of which a child is granted provisional stewardship but which the child mistakes for permanent ownership in Igbo proverb—the peculium was contingent. It was indeed transient, like Warrant Chieftaincy. It "never included *all* the proprietary capacities. The master always reserved a claim on the possessions of the slave." The "usufruct could be withdrawn at any time" (182). In short, the inability to truly own wealth-accumulating property (in this case habitational and agricultural land) was the severest of the slave's handicaps, Patterson declares (186). And even when, among other things, blacks in America completely paid for and *legally* owned property, that legality was in innumerable instances rescinded. The land was stolen by force, deceit, and/or denial. Afterward, the history and ensuing storying of that blatant theft, and its afterlives in sharecropping and the peonage and penal systems, are slanted and/or erased by the contract breakers, as Vann R. Newkirk II writes in the *Atlantic's* September 2019 lead piece "The Great Land Robbery: The Shameful Story of How 1 Million Black Families Have Been Ripped from Their Farms."

That foundational travesty, that economic loss and racial cross, is the crux of Michael Eric Dyson's foreword to Johnson's *Acres of Aspiration*. Dyson notes, among other things, that "the hunger for home has been a constant theme of black life. Since Africans were ripped from their native shores and brought to America in chains," he states, "the search for a place to call our own has ignited dreams of a black homestead" (vii). Dyson may as well be introducing not just *Acres* but also *Sula,* in which we are told how an honorable white farmer betrays his illiterate slave with rocky and infertile land and, years later, urban renewal razes that thriving and complex black village neighborhood of the Bottom for the construction of the Medallion City Golf Course. He could have been presenting Colson Whitehead's *The Underground Railroad,* where not acres but rather tiny pieces of dirt earth to call their own on the Randall plantation mean a lot to the novel's slaves, especially the protagonist, Cora.

In *Acres,* Johnson profiles Edward P. McCabe, whom he calls "The Father of the All-Black Town Movement." It is clear, however, that McCabe's life, career, and death are but a snippet of the much-larger picture Johnson paints of a landmark African American initiative. The McCabe legend is also ancillary to the broader event that Johnson, at the study's conclusion, calls "a great tsunami of forces that would engulf, if not wholly submerge," that black midwestern and land-centered ambition (203). Interweaving excerpts from African American literary, historical, cultural, and sociological works, biblical verses, passages from the U.S. Constitution, and lines by American leaders, among other intertextualities, Johnson takes us through that protracted journey brought to an end by a combination of factors. They include white resistance, industrial expansion, and urban renewal, all of which thwarted the ambition of the pioneers and overwhelmed the enclaves' agrarian economy.

Johnson traces the story of Oklahoma's all-Black town movement to the very core of American history, Native American experience of mass removal, and to the cultural and blood ties long shared by that state's Native American and African American populations. He dates the movement's highpoint between 1890 and 1910. However, he situates its first steps in 1619 with the arrival, in the English colony of Virginia, of the first Africans severed from their "motherland,

culture, and family" (1); shipped "away across the seas" by white men, as Obierika mourns in *Things Fall Apart*. We follow *Acres* into the history of "Brooklyn,
Illinois [that] lays claim to being the oldest Black town in America" (6), one
whose motto is "FOUNDED BY CHANCE, Sustained by Courage," as Sundiata Keita Cha-Jua writes in his study of that village town. "According to oral tradition, during the 1820s a band of eleven families, consisting of free persons of
color and fugitive slaves, led by 'Mother' Priscilla Baltimore, fled the slave state
of Missouri, crossed the Mississippi River, and settled in the wilderness in St.
Clair County, Illinois," an enclave that would become Brooklyn, with that name
given to it in 1837 "when five white men platted the land." But it would eventually go from a biracial town to an all-Black community with ensuing white flight.
And many African Americans would come to know it, not by its confusing official designation Brooklyn, but popularly as Lovejoy (Chu-Jua 1–2, 6). We rejoin
Johnson as he discursively crosses to the Edward P. McCabe story. We journey
along as he revisits the tragic 1921 Tulsa Race Riots (now in its one-hundredth
anniversary) and then makes a meditative stop on the future of all-Black towns,
many of which, listed in the appendix, are now described as "All-Black 'Ghost
Towns' in Oklahoma." The resonant statements and descriptions outlined
below stand out to me. They are critical to a broader, comparative understanding of *Arrow of God* and *Paradise*, whose narratives not only capture their related
kernels of Indirect Rule and all-Black town. They also thematically append to
and aesthetically reinterpret those germinal histories.

   We hear in *Acres*, for instance, and as Cha-Jua corroborates (1), that the
above-named Brooklyn started as "a collective of a few "freedom villages"
established by fugitive slaves and free Blacks" (6). Johnson writes that "All-
black towns symbolized a new sense of race consciousness," one propagated
by Booker T. Washington, the ultimate aim being to rehabilitate, through economic command of white respect, "a fragile, collective Black psyche damaged
immeasurably by years of bondage, peonage, and maltreatment." To Washington, Johnson opines, all-Black towns are "laboratories for a grand social
experiment." In addition to hearing in *Acres* also of "Founders" and "founding,"
we learn that the all-Black town endeavor is nationalistic (7–8); or that it is
driven by "protonationalism," as Cha-Jua phrases and defines it: "an ensemble
of political attitudes that represent racial solidarity or commitment to Black
empowerment by organizing Blacks into autonomous organizations, institutions, and communities" (3). Johnson avers that having believed Oklahoma, to
which they escaped from the South's virulent racism, was "the Promised Land,"

and having gotten used to the trappings of full citizenship by living with the Indians, the "Black Creek freedmen, so-called 'Natives,'" who had long resided and prospered in Oklahoma, were later disgruntled by "the onslaught of new Black migrants from the South who arrived later in the nineteenth century." Calling the recent arrivals "'Watchina' or 'State Negroes,'" the Black Creek also were unwelcoming. They derided the new arrivals as too obsequious to whites (24). Johnson refers to the "original . . . families" (34). He talks about how McCabe and others, uplifted by the success of Tulsa's historic Greenwood District, saw Oklahoma as "the African American Utopia."

Like a Warrant Chief's withdrawn scrap of paper, the Warrant, and like a slave's withdrawn peculium, however, that dream would be crushed as Oklahoma in 1907 became the nation's forty-sixth state. To cap the setback, the state's new government instituted Jim Crow actions that entrenched segregation (172). In all, imagining their village community, the African American pioneers who built the all-Black towns had aspired to "create fantasy islands, idyllic safe havens" as firewalls against socioeconomic oppression, Johnson writes (203). And other than the human longing for freedom, they had believed the paramount objective—real proprietorship and not a peculium—warranted the sweat and sacrifice. They were convinced that "land ownership" was fundamental to greater attainments. In short, they had had a dream that, one day, in addition to creating for them the opportunity for self-governance, or what could be interpreted as Direct Self-Rule or *native administration,* land would unstoppably culminate in unqualified citizenship (xii).

Besides the nexus of land, granular rumination would find as well that underneath the Warrant Chief System's debacle and the all-Black town aspiration is *textual reinterpretation.* Animating the debacle and the dream is the colonized native and freeblacks, the slave's and former slave's reading of antecedence. Of significance, then, to the Warrant Chiefs and the pioneering African American all-Black town builders is the transformative power of the *scrap of paper,* in this case, foundational and warranting documents. We are not speaking here of the epistemological subtexts or the ontological impacts of *literacy,* as Ezeulu foresaw. At issue, Ato Quayson argues below, and I concur, is hermeneutics. This is a leitmotif in both novels. For as we know, the twin questions of position(ing) and perspective, or what Dickson Bruce would call "Claims to authority" (94), emblematized the colonizer-colonized and master-slave dynamic.

I am suggesting, in short, that the seal- and signature-activated text of the scrap of paper/Warrant may have been clear in black-and-white. But the British colonial administration and the Igbo appointees (particularly the Warrant Chiefs who overextended their charges) evidently read the document divergently. The British imperial government may have overworded or underworded the Warrant to convey the narrowness of the native appointee's mandate by inscribing that its holder is "subject to the Rules and Regulations drawn up for the guidance of Members of the said Court" (Afigbo 81, sample warrant). In the physical absence of the master who delegated and dictated from a distance under Indirect Rule, the James Ikedis and their historical originals, carrying their goatskin bag of wisdom, hatched their own understanding of matters. They went postmodern, or is it poststructuralist, so to speak. Consequentially meddling with language, the English language imposed on them, they executed the phrase "Rules and Regulations" as open-ended and thus amenable to multiple *other* readings and applications. They superimposed on it the culturally unsanctioned authority they wielded over their egalitarian fellow Igbos. After all, and although the native may not have known it, Lugard himself had also taken liberties with the tasks issued him by the British government. He "gave his assignment a broad interpretation," Afigbo points out (xi).

Similarly, it has been pointed out by many, from researchers and literary critics to legal scholars and especially black clergy, that the slave owner and the slave often maintained contrastive views of the world at large. More specifically, they variably read, with cross-purposes, consequential *scraps of paper*, in this instance the U.S. Constitution and particularly the Bible. From their privileged racial, legal, social, economic and gendered placements, the master and mistress deliberately tweaked and sometimes outright twisted the Constitution, the apocryphal stories of scripture, and other libertarian tracts to suit their aims and calm their nerves. The enslaved, on the other hand, thought about and felt the papers alter-natively. Turning themselves into strict constructionists, they held firm to the Word and the clause, to the letter of the nation's founding documents that speak performatively of life, liberty, and the pursuit of happiness. To which the enslaved, in warranted and paramount jeremiad, append "divine justice."

Additionally, the colonized Warrant Chief and the ex-slave/all-Black town builder followed, or at least attempted to join, the master/the master's class in indulging in concrete rewards of striving. It should be borne in mind here that the British imperial government and Lugard were merely continuing the genealogy of European promulgations of world-transforming declarations, as clearly illustrated in the Portuguese and Spaniards executing the fifteenth-century papal bulls that altogether authorized and set in motion the transatlantic slave trade and the European plundering of foreign lands in Africa and the Americas (Charles and Rah 13–23). Veritably the changing same, or acts of mimicry as Homi Bhabha would more famously couch it (122–23), the Ikedis' power- and money-grabs basically emulate the enslaver and colonizer's standards of material expropriation and good life.

Apparently, Edward P. McCabe was humanly not immune to the Warrant Chiefs' hunger for class, power, and property or the English colonists' and their descendants' tribal allegiances and exclusionism. Johnson discusses that not only did McCabe, in spite of growing Indian opposition and relentless white racism, make it "known that he wished to become the appointed governor of the Oklahoma Territory, whether or not it became a Black state" (44). But also, in his iteration of nationalism, or protonationalism, McCabe was "determin[ed] to keep the town of Langston Black." And this resolve "led to extraordinary, though not wholly novel, measures." He "attempted to include restrictive covenants in land titles to prevent the transfer of property to Whites" (42). The English colonists envisioned the New World as a haven and intended the country they built on pillaged Native American property as an exclusively white nation. Consistent in the sense of particularity with which the all-Black towns perceived themselves, and are perceived in history, is those English Pilgrims' and enslavers' view of America as exceptional—an aspiration to which Katrine Dalsgård brings broader context and insight in her piece on *Paradise* "The One All-Black Town Worth the Pain" (2001). This model-replica or source-duplicate dialectic is evident in *Arrow of God*. It is, however, one of *Paradise*'s central concerns. Morrison addresses it rather pointedly at the end of the novel. There, the narrator recalls the story of Deacon Morgan's grandfather Zechariah and his twin brother, Tea. Zechariah was Coffee before changing his name. We are told that "Coffee" could also have been a mispronunciation, or rather a misinterpretation, of "Kofi" (192). Anyway, Zachariah had claimed to have seen with his son Rector a vision of a walking man that both men would interpret and propagate as the master narrative of the slaves' exodus. But after disclosing that the twins' color-line encounter with white power caused an enduring rift between them, the narrator says that the all-Black village-town's Old Fathers/Founders thought they had outplotted, outperceived, and "outfoxed the whiteman when in fact they imitate him" (306).

On the Mechanics of (Village Novel) Narration:
Plot, Points of View

Arrow of God and *Paradise* achieve verisimilitude by staying close to history and culture. But, as did founders Lugard and McCabe, Achebe and Morrison gave those respective contexts of Indirect Rule in Igboland and all-Black town endeavor in America very broad titular, thematic, aesthetic, political, and phil-osophical interpretations. We may recall Afigbo noting that Lugard took liber-ties with his imperial Call. He left a consequential policy footprint on Nigeria's twentieth-century coming-of-age story as an amalgam-and-invention in 1914 and as a federation in 1960; an alliance that, like the American Union, would fall apart in civil war. That Nigeria-Biafra Civil War at home and over land was in the same turbulent 1960s decade of *Arrow of God*'s publication and of decol-onization movement in Africa. Both aligned with the Vietnam War, the civil rights struggle, second wave feminism, as well as the nationalist, anticolonial, Afrocentric, and militant agitations of the youth-driven Black Power movement revisited in *Paradise*. As the foregoing discussion has been indicating, Achebe and Morrison fleshed out of the kernels two tribal stories. When we read both stories as exhibiting benchmark features of the village novel and villagism, among the other elements considered immediately below, the novels' affinities of context, setting, structure, subject, character, and tropes are deepened.

In addition to noting that the historical events rememoried in *Arrow of God* and *Paradise* occurred post-Abolition and post-Reconstruction, we also iden-tify another alignment, this time, the novels' plots. I admire Chinwe Chris-tina Okechukwu's probing analysis of Achebe's rhetorical strategies in *Arrow of God*, an argument she elaborates in her important study *Achebe the Orator* (2002). However, I would beg to differ with Okechukwu's point that the nov-el's diegesis "is not intricate" ("Oratory" 568). With story lines as textured as the themes they tackle, *Arrow of God* and *Paradise* begin similarly with male-centered *quests*. Soon after the openings, they also present the respective foun-dational histories of Umuaro, Haven, and Ruby. As with the architectures of *No Longer at Ease* and *Jazz*, Achebe and Morrison analogously introduce the novels' driving conflicts, conceits, and characters in the first chapters. Achebe names and sketches the major players in the about-to-unfold drama of *Arrow of God*. He virtually presents us most members of the Ezeulu family and other figures, human and divine. Morrison elects racial and nominal suspense instead. In *Paradise*'s prologue, "Ruby," which is the story's end, she withholds most of the names of the novel's major players. She relies instead on clues, apertures, sartorial markers, irony, and sarcasm. She also deploys venues and dates to relate backdrops and intensify anticipation.

In short, as in a detective story's structure, which she likes and mimics also in *Jazz*, or as viewers of the long-running NBC hit television series *Law and Order* would recognize, Morrison first reports an ongoing homicide on *and* at the Convent. She then takes her time *retracing* and *contextualizing*. She methodically divulges the full names, relatives, and experiential circumstances of not just the victims (whose "races" we are baited to guess at our peril, as in "Recitatif") but those of the perpetrators as well. Fascinatingly, this pattern mirrors how the assailants "shoot the white girl first" and are then unhurried with the remaining assaults. The men take their time exploring. Or rather, they eschew haste as they read and interpret—as one does a Book—the Convent's interiority, its wide-open spaces, and its interstitial corners.

As indicated, *Arrow of God* and *Paradise* open with interpretation-connected male *quests* or *searches*. Evidently involving women in different but significant ways and undertaken for various purposes, the hunts have serious existential ramifications for Umuaro and Ruby. Intimately imbricated in the quests are the stories' powerful and power-obsessed male characters: Chief Priest Ezeulu, on the one hand, and the Morgan twins, on the other. The objects-subjects of their intense searches—the new moon, for Ezeulu, and the Convent residents, for the twins and their seven companions—are gendered female in the novels. They are also elusive and mischievous at the moment of the men's quests. Two of the women—the moon-watching Mavis and the amateur astrologer Gigi—are linked with hermeneutics. They are fascinated with the heavens. As is Ezeulu, they are intrigued by the cosmos, by its signs and their significations. Achebe describes the moon—a shifty domain and text—as "play[ing] its game" with Ezeulu (1). Observe as well that these targets of the males' quests are collectively (mis)read as aberrant and suspect. They are misperceived as sinister to the social order for their unorthodox and uncontained *appearances* and *positioning*.

Nevertheless, Achebe and Morrison hint at the gravitational power of the gendered cosmic and human targets over the patriarchal male questers. As Ato Quayson infers (38), the two authors point as well to the women's agencies as percipient interpreters of the sacred, the secular, and the menfolk. Ezeulu's first wife, Okuata, displays that analytic capacity. Before her death, and as her son Edogo later remembers, she *read* Ezeulu's dominant flaw differently as one of control and conformity. These are subjects also at the heart of *Paradise*. His "only fault," Okuata explicated, "was that he expected everyone—his wives, his kinsmen, his children, his friends and even his enemies—to think and act like himself. Anyone who dared to say no to him was an enemy" (93). Ezeulu rejects the possibility of his gaze, his observational and deductive power, aging and failing. He may have kept watch for the new moon, in accordance with his priestly duties. But it is Ugoye, the younger of his wives—who include Ojiugo, Matefi, and the dead Okuata—who in the new moon's abnormal posture and gesture foresees an evil portent. Ugoye accurately albeit unwittingly divines the existential crossroads ahead for Umuaro. Achebe skillfully albeit disjointedly plots the paths to that crisis, as does Morrison in *Paradise*'s case.

As with the tragedies of *Things Fall Apart* and *Beloved*, *No Longer at Ease* and *Jazz*, the epic dramas of *Arrow of God* and *Paradise* inferably could not be told as captivatingly in linear fashion, as I cautioned earlier. Which helps explain the circumstantiality of the trilogies' final installments. In "Another Look at *Arrow of God*," Alastair Niven contends—as though in reference to *Paradise*—that *Arrow of God* skips. Its narration "jumps thirty years," she calculates. It goes "from the 1890's to the early 1920's" (57). Although *Paradise*'s narrative present is July 1976, the story also jumps. It shifts among events that occur in different years, but most significantly those of 1889. That was when, as Morrison writes, 158 Mississippi "Freedmen who stood tall" founded what their descendants would view as "the one all-black town worth the pain" (5). Those freedmen and others may have called their amalgam a "town." But I want to propose, and will be elaborating relative to both novels, that what they created in the 1880s was a village. What they passed on to their heirs—at the same moment the Southeastern Igbo–Umuaro saga is unfolding on the other side of the Atlantic—is a village community. Or it is, at the very least, an atmosphere, experience, and cosmologic sensibility that could be additionally understood from the standpoint of *villagism*.

Recalling Wendy Griswold to the Village Square

It is helpful at this time to recall Wendy Griswold on the village novel. Unlike the city novel that, for our purposes, is mostly preoccupied with a life lived in between worlds (one of those worlds being the village, both geographically and as consciousness and praxis), the main task of the village novel, which is conventionally set in rural environments, is maintenance. Its primary purpose, Griswold suggested, is the enshrinement of the consciousness of a passing world. Just as helpful is her description of the village proper. Concurring with

George Nyamndi that "setting" and "the vernacular" are among the genre's core features, Griswold describes the village as characterized by density of human connections, competition, resentment, compassion, prohibitions, longing, regard, and scorn. Village is a place, she states, where privacy is rare; prying is routine; and accessibility is prized over reticence. The village assumes the sociocultural and political attributes of "community," she writes. To Griswold, if there is a single descriptor that best captures "village," the "African village" in this case—an idea, arrangement, and experience expansively reimagined in the Nigerian/West African novel on which I argue Morrison bases her declarative that she writes "village literature"—that qualifier would be *complicated*. That is what we have in Umuaro and Haven-Ruby.

Achebe and Morrison's creations of Umuaro and Haven-Ruby village communities are analogously historically grounded. The two "laboratory," protonationalistic but now foundationally cracked and crises-engulfed formations are products of the Atlantic slave trade and slavery. When the constitutive families of six villages—Umuachala, Umunneora, Umuagu, Umuezeani, Umuogwugwu, and Umuisiuzo—entered into an alliance, the larger village union they established and named "Umuaro" was racially homogeneous but idiosyncratically and ideologically heterogeneous. Precolonial "Umuaro" was, in effect, an all-Black town, a freedom village. It was a land formation whose beleaguered Southeastern Igbo citizens must have thought of initially as a Paradise, a Haven, the Promised Land, a utopia, even if that sensibility of fortress and the idyll was neither permanent, nor could it possibly have been expressed in ornate English prose, the poetic imagery of John Milton, or Christian eschatological terminologies.

While six villages constitute Umuaro, fifteen families are reported to forge the Ruby village alliance. As we may recall, Hannibal Johnson described Brooklyn, one of the earliest and archetypal all-Black towns, as "a collective of a few 'freedom villages.'" In Morrison's rendering, Ruby's precursor, Haven, was at the time of its founding in 1890 not just a village. Like Umuaro and its six mother-villages and their Old Fathers, Haven had also been very agrarian. It was a community whose Old Fathers had relied heavily on "subsistence farming" before its severe population and economic decline (6). As with the black community's relegation at the outskirts of Cincinnati city, a location that bespeaks village and enables preservation or syncretism of Africanisms in *Beloved*, Ruby's own location, ninety miles or so removed from the next town and about twenty miles removed from the Convent, serves to intimate its rurality. It indicates as well Ruby's potential incubation of remnants of

African cultures and cosmologies transplanted by the Founders/Old Fathers from the South. Ruby is "a sleepy town with three churches within one mile of one another," the narrator says, "but nothing to serve a traveler: no diner, no police, no gas station, no public phone, no movie house, no hospital" (12). It is interesting, then, that "Umuaro" and "Ruby"—the latter founded in 1948 after World War II by the New Fathers and named after the dead sister of the twins Deacon and Steward Morgan—may not exit, or have existed, if not for the respective demises of the original homesteads.

As with Brooklyn, whose origin, names, and earliest black settlement "are the subjects of myth and error," of fading memories and discrepant narratives (Cha-Jua 31, 37), there are at least two major but competing versions of the Umuaro origin story. For Haven and Ruby, there is one dominant and recycled account, or interpretation, of the alliance's beginnings in supposedly distinctive (racial) ingenuity and superhuman perseverance. We are told, through Ezeulu's embittered retrospection on Umuaro's land-settlement, its territorial quest and expansion, as read and passed on to him by his father:

> In the very distant past, when lizards were still few and far between, the six villages—Umuachala, Umunneora, Umuagu, Umuezeani, Umuog-wugwu and Umuisiuzo—lived as different peoples, and each worshipped its own deity. Then the hired soldiers of Abam used to strike in the dead of night, set fire to the houses and carry men, women and children into slavery. Things were so bad for the six villages that their leaders came together to save themselves. They hired a strong team of medicine-men to install a common deity for them. This deity which the fathers of the six villages made was called Ulu. Half of the medicine was buried at a place which became Nkwo market and the other half was thrown into the stream which became Mili Ulu. The six villages then took the name of Umuaro, and the priest of Ulu became their Chief Priest. From that day they were never again beaten by an enemy. (14–15)

This assumed, authoritative Ezeulu rendition of an ideal—Umuaro's found-ing—is partial if not a self-serving misrepresentation. That is according to Nwaka, Ezeulu's nemesis. Nwaka is fortified and bolstered by his childhood friend and Ezeulu's rival priest Ezidemili. He is also strengthened by his ambi-tion, wealth, word-ownership, and institutional knowledge. Perhaps most of all, he feels epistemologically singular because of the imputed authority of his father's equally supposedly indisputable account of the historical past. As

Nwaka claims in his prowar rebuttal: "My father told me a different story. He told me that Okperi people were wanderers. He told me three or four different places where they sojourned for a while and moved on. They were driven away by Umuofia, then by Abame and Aninta. Would they go today and claim those sites?" (16). For our purposes, one of the most critically significant parts of the Nwaka record of Umuaro's formation is its inclusion of pilgrimage: the impact of slavery-implicated domestic migration in the land settlement and the alliance's homestead foundation. Notice, then, how in the Nwaka retelling, the same and potentially traumatizing and incensing experiences of brotherly snobbery suffered by Okperi's forebears closely match what Morrison portrays in *Paradise* as the "Disallowing." That is, the hurtful rebuff, ridicule, even violence, that Haven's migrating Old Fathers remember experiencing at the hands of their fellow blacks, among other groups. This Disallowing speaks also to the assault, disrespect, and unwelcoming that Ruby's founders, the World War II African American soldiers, experienced upon their return home.

Like Umuaro's mythic histories and triumphal stories, Haven and Ruby's have also been passed down by oral tradition. They are circulated in supposedly unretouched village narratives. The stories are told and re-cited by the Old and New Fathers, especially the Morgan twins, Steward and Deacon. Its parts are dispersed throughout *Paradise* but are later researched and amended by Patricia Best in order to close their gendered gaps. The Haven story is of ex-slaves drifting westward in search, not of a peculium or usufruct, but of a livable, own home. Reminiscent of (seeming dizygotic twins) Ezeulu and Nwaka's dependencies on their memories and on their invocations of equally conflicting ancestral archives, we are told that the Morgan twins, who collectively

> remember the details of everything that ever happened . . . have never forgotten the message or the specifics of any story, especially the one told them by their grandfather—the man who put the words in the Oven's black mouth. A story that explained why neither the founders of Haven nor their descendants could tolerate anybody but themselves. On the journey from Mississippi and two Louisiana parishes to Oklahoma, the one hundred and fifty-eight freedmen were unwelcome on each grain of soil from Yazoo to Fort Smith. Turned away by rich Choctaw and poor whites, chased away by yard dogs, jeered at by camp prostitutes and their children, they were nevertheless unprepared for the aggressive discouragement they received from negro towns already being built. (13)

Nevertheless, besides land, three other things seem to have been priorities both to Umuaro's founders and Haven's Old and Ruby's New Founders and Fathers, namely, religion, freedom, and security. It seems apparent that, in their needs to become a people or rather *peoples* following the village towns' founding, the Old and New Fathers of Umuaro and of Haven and Ruby are introspective. They realize the importance of group survival, tradition, and protection, besides the imperative of psychic rehabilitation from the collective trauma of slavery. For every word of Hannibal B. Johnson's description of the offered rationale for all-Black towns applies to the constitutive but formerly separate six villages and families of Umuaro. As Johnson stated, the village-towns were established to rebuild "a fragile, collective Black psyche damaged immeasurably by years of bondage, peonage, and maltreatment" by Abam warriors, in Umuaro's case. The founders collectively appear to appreciate the significance of custom and *institutions* in group identity, cohesion, and continuance.

This brings us to the Ulu-Oven relations. It directs our attention to their domestic location, cosmologic affinities, and institutional power. Morrison often interweaves African modes of thought in her works. Building upon that knowledge, I want to stipulate that the Oven likely has a basis in actual history. One possible model is the "big dugout . . . [an] eighteen by twenty feet . . . fireplace . . . several families . . . cooked at" when they moved to Oklahoma in the 1880s and 1890s, as recalled by Edna, the eldest daughter of Ralph Ellison's adopted grandfather, the pioneering J[efferson] D[avis] Randolph (Anderson, "Ralph"). Ellison in fact hints at the makeshift and raced stove at least twice in *Invisible Man*: one, in the Harlem yam seller's "improvised oven" (218) and, two, in the Invisible Man's sarcastic retort to a racially presumptuous kinship question by Brother Jack at both men's first encounter (292). But I also want to argue that what Morrison presents as the Oven could also be read as an "Ulu." We can, even at the risk of critical stretch, view it additionally as an Ulu-type syncretistic (African) village divinity and shrine; an institution, practice, and inheritance re-visioned in the New World. The nature-attuned Old Fathers of Haven and the evidently churchgoing New Fathers of Ruby prioritize the cultural establishment and consecration of this important, unifying, and sustaining (village) "deity."

I proposed earlier that we reimagine the Achebe and Morrison trilogies as a continuum, which would make *Arrow of God* and *Paradise* bookends. If, as ascribed, *Beloved* responds to Obierika's question-call in *Things Fall Apart* as to what happened to the captive Igbo-Africans shipped westward, *Paradise*, I suggest, implicitly completes *Arrow of God*. It does so by indirectly participating in the discourse that Albert Raboteau terms "The Death of the Gods." This hypothesis on Africanism was famously debated by Melville Herskovits and Franklin Frazier, and arbitrated by Raboteau in his study *Slave Religion* (43–92). Because of the conditions of captivity, the Middle Passage, plantation slavery proper, and slave Christianization, Old World community-instituted oracles such as the dreaded Ibini Ukpabi of Arochukwu and village gods such as the fictionalized Igbo-African deities Idemili, Ogwugwu, Eru, Udo, Ngwu, Ojukwu, Ulu, and the countless others—as well as, significantly, the rituals associated with them in the Old World—may not have been diligently taken apart, piece by piece, and solemnly relocated to new sites in the New World. They may not have been transplanted to North America with their essences, names, priests, and devotees intact. This is the case with the reassembled "deity" Oven. Its transposition hints at the transplantation of African traditional/village religions and cultural institutions and practices to the New World.

African gods, spirits, shrines, and totems may not have lived on in British North America. However, as *Paradise* implies, in dialogue with *Arrow of God*, the religious and sociocultural propensities of those gods' New World incarnations in the Oven and the Preacher—more specifically the Christian churches' reverends and ministers—cause one to wonder if those Old World gods and metaphysics did indeed "die." Ulu and the Oven are powerful cultural signifiers. They are heritages and symbols whose functional correspondences are striking. Like the biblical and deital Ark of the Covenant associated with Israelites' bondage and exodus, Ulu and the Oven occupy revered places in the peoples' survivals, spirituality, and secular imaginations. Indicating the Oven's Ibini Ukpabi/Long Juju awe is its rededication: the care with which, after World War II, Ruby's New Fathers, "veterans all . . . took it apart, carrying the bricks, the hearthstone and its iron plate two hundred and forty miles west." As with the village festivities that attended Ulu's hallowing, one of the Morgan twins remembers while inside the Convent "the ceremony they'd had when the Oven's iron lip was recemented into place and its worn letters polished for all to see" (6). And again like Ulu, the mouthed Oven is figured as *animate*, a *provider, protector, savior,* and *survivor.* But it is also, paradoxically, a riddle and a devourer. It is "the god that kills and saves" its supplicants (*Arrow* 71). The "killing" is read also as Ulu and the Oven's shared potency to foment new acrimonies and also exacerbate old domestic feuds to the level of unwarranted lethal crises among a people, as Umuaro and Ruby's respective in- and out-fighting shows. We hear that "No family needed more than a simple cookstove as long as the Oven was alive." And that even at a time of spiraling modernity and change "the Oven stayed alive" (15). Like Umuaro, Haven and Ruby may be populated by opinionated folks who hate dictation. But as I will further discuss, they are invested in that attempt to forge a village community by inaugurating (religious) festivals and rituals centered around the Oven and its spatial expanse. This is exemplified in the wandering Old Fathers' habit of gathering the village around the Oven. They bring slaughtered livestock and game to the agape and oracular Oven almost sacrificially (15), like Old World deities' priests. Or, more exactly, like Ezeulu seemingly sacrificially placing one of the sacred yams on top of his smoldering log fire (3).

Concerning the sacral, Old World village healers and priests, whom William M. Banks interestingly describes as "intellectual workers" and who, as he suggests, were foundational to black intellectual class and project (3–21), may not have arrived in the New World intact, in their original forms and garments, as earlier asserted. But as researchers such as Banks and others have suggested, they, or at least their essences, took new forms in plantation conjurers and, later, in Christian preachers. In *The Souls of Black Folks'* chapter "On the Faith of the Fathers," for example, W. E. B. Du Bois asserts this about the black preacher, as though familiarly depicting Ezeulu: "The Preacher is the most unique personality developed by the Negro on American soil. A leader, a politician, an orator, a 'boss,' an intriguer, an idealist,—all these he is, and ever, too, the centre of a group of men, now twenty, now a thousand in number. The combination of a certain adroitness with deep-seated earnestness, of tact with consummate ability, gave him his preëminence, and helps him maintain it. The type, of course, varies according to time and place" (120).

Notice, then, the commonalities and *continuities* of institution, profile, and temperament between the New and Old World religions, priests, and *worshippers* in both novels. These mutually antagonizing three denominations featured in *Paradise*—the (black) Baptists, Methodists, and Pentecostals—become, shall we say, the New World incarnations of, or parallels to, the three polarized religions serving Ulu, Idemili, and the Christian God in *Arrow of God*, as Annie Gagiano charts, noting also the other intense frictions among Umuaroans (85–86). We hear that Ruby's Baptist, Methodist, and Pentecostal congregations are at odds. These rivalrous Ruby priest-ministers—the Africa-embracing Baptist preacher Reverend Pulliam and the Methodist church's traditionalist pastor, Reverend Misner—resemble *Arrow of God's* competing priests Ezeulu and Ezidemili. Nicholas Brown sees in their rift "the conflict between the priest of an autochthonous god and the priest of a synthetic god" (111). Achebe and Morrison comment, additionally, on the impact of material burden and influence in religious practice through these other parallels. There is, on one hand, the fraternity between *Arrow of God*'s physically smallish, charcoal-black, and aggrieved priest Ezidemili and the wealthy, flamboyant, and attractive Nwaka; and, on the other, the comradery between *Paradise*'s Reverend Pulliam and the ostentatious banker and debonair Deek. Nwaka's considerable financial weight in Umuaro brings to mind the Morgan twins Steward and Deek's sheer control over Ruby's economy.

Separate from though connected to Ulu and the Oven, the other earliest-cohering village traditions for Umuaro and Ruby are commemorative rituals. Take Umuaro's first. Umuaro has two major, calendrical festivals besides village-specific and smaller ceremonies. The first of the two big rituals is the planting season's Festival of the Pumpkin Leaves. During this rite, also called Feast of the Pumpkin Leaves, Ezeulu cleanses the six villages prior to their planting of crops. Not only does Ezeulu have to reenact, during the festival, "the First Coming of Ulu and how each of the four Days put obstacles in his way" (71). But also the occasion's highlight is a ritual race, the *ogbazulobodo*, which Ezeulu used to run in his youth but which now falls on his son Obika, with tragic consequences at the end of the novel. The second major ritual is the harvest season's and census-related Feast of the New Yam. Erasing spirit-human, sacred-profane binaries, this feast congregates divinities and mortals in one spot. Occurring at the temporal junctions of preceding and incoming years, the feast heralds major harvesting of crops. It recollects for the six-village federation its inaugural unification as well as its ongoing gratitude to Ulu for rescuing the villages from Abam attacks and captivity. This amalgamation, virtually an Umuaro Independence Day, is re-created at each New Yam feast.

For Ruby, their ritual is what one can call the Ceremony of the Horse Race. Hinting at the centrality of horses to the life and economy of Oklahoma territory, Morrison describes the festival simply as "a horse race" originated and organized by "a man named Ossie" (10). It also entails, fascinatingly, Ruby people taking items to the venue. The atmospherics at the Umuaro Festival of the Pumpkin Leaves and the Ruby Horse Race are palpable. Just as we are told that "the [Umuaro] market place was filling up steadily with men and women from every quarter" (67), so too do we hear that from every corner of Ruby, "from army-issue tents, half-finished houses and freshly cleared land people rode in, bringing what they had" (10). What Umuaro women have and bring in abundance to the celebration are the pumpkin leaves used for "the general and all-embracing rite" (68) in which the women also run their own race, after Ezeulu's. And what Umuaro men donate to the New Yam observance are yams, from which Ezeulu chooses the thirteen sacred tubers he eats. In Ruby, the people bring what could also be regarded as harvests: "stored-away things and things got up on the spot" (10). Umuaro's Festival of the Pumpkin Leaves—whose religious essence and cultural pageantry remind one of Easter and Christ's Passion—reaches its crescendo in ritual running: the climatic reenactment by Ezeulu of Ulu's immanence and his ordainment as Ulu's priest and a sacrificial lamb. So, too, is Ruby's Ceremony of the Horse Race capped by a run, a competitive three-person horse race.

On close examination, even more remarkable similarities emerge between these village community cerebrations relative to such matters as their purposes, locations, attendances, main events, and ambiences, etc. All three festivals—The Feast of the Pumpkin Leaves, the Feast of the New Yam, and the Ceremony of the Horse Race—are not just carnivalesque and spiritual moments. In fact, *Arrow of God*'s narrator calls Umuaro's Festival of the Pumpkin Leaves "the spectacle" (69). Each of them also implicitly doubles as cleansing and thanksgiving, more explicitly stated in *Arrow of God* than in *Paradise*. As reconciliatory village events, the festivals take place in open grounds: at "the center of the market place" for Umuaro (71) and at "the center of town" for Ruby (10). The Pumpkin Leaves festival and the Horse Race are *pathway*-related and inceptions. Marked, for Umuaro, is Ulu's original consecration and installment. And for Ruby, it is the celebration of the clearing of a path and the coming and christening of the people's first major and *connective* arterial, which we learn is Central Avenue. Later, new streets will intersect this principal arterial, forming multiple crossroads/metaphoric crosses. Finessing that trope of intersections, *Paradise* discloses that a single major road leads from and connects Ruby to the Convent. And while Ruby's first-ever village festival is linked to this road's Ulu-like coming, the commemoration or as Patricia Best puts it "the official story" of the town's founding continues years later. It is proclaimed "from pulpits, in Sunday school classes and ceremonial speeches" (188). At their Nativity Play at Calvary Baptist Church—perhaps modeled after the historic Calvary Baptist Church, Oklahoma City, founded in 1921—the children, wearing masks, reenact the passed-on story of the Disallowing: the Original families' rejection by their fellow blacks in Fairly.

One listening to an exchange between Patricia Best and Richard Misner at that Christmas event cannot but conclude that it gives the Achebe statement at the beginning of this chapter an added level of urgency. A moment of dramatic irony occurs when Patricia and Misner, who co-teach the children "Negro History," engage in the poet Countee Cullen's "What Is Africa to Me?" argument. To Patricia, who is of course unaware of the depth of Africa's historical, religious, and cultural tinting and unification of *Paradise*, Africa is an irrelevant past. I would like to use that debate (206–10), itself an extension of the Herskovits-Frazier intellectual heavyweight rumble on the jungle,[4] as an access point. I want to reframe it as pathway into additional exploration of *Paradise*'s village-literature conception, particularly Ruby's villagism, among which is *offering* or sacrifice, a hot theme *Paradise* and *Arrow of God* share.

Villagism: A Portal to Portals, the Portal of Portality

Besides these tenets of villagism—the ancestral/cosmological subtexts of the Oven; Haven and Ruby's establishment; the Horse Race; the town's kinship ties and oral tradition; and the prying—the impresses of African traditional religions are decipherable also in other loci, objects, and viewpoints. Perhaps unbeknownst to Patricia, who, ironically, is studying the people's Africa-transferred oral tradition, the extra traces include, for instance, the syncretic displays and rituals of the Convent women's spirituality. The village gossip that Ruby people had heard that the Convent women, or one or some of them, may be animists or something is confirmed when the father-and-son duo of the firing squad descends to the Convent's chapel. The men's cryptically anthropological (re)search and incredulity record the residents' religious syncretism, exemplified in their seeming idol worship, use of candles, and practice of food offerings (or sacrifices). I argue as well that the supposedly strange occurrence Philip Page notes as a *Paradise* "mystery," namely, an unidentified man cutting a path through Dovey's yard, is a natural-supernatural encounter. The *mystery* is spirit visitation, the first time of which is preceded by what Dovey reads as "a sign." As she looks at the backyard trees from the opened window, she believes she witnesses where "a mighty hand dug deep into a giant sack and threw fistfuls of petals into the air. Or so it seemed. Butterflies. A trembling highway of persimmon-colored wings cut across the green tree-tops forever—then vanished" (90–91). But the main telltale sign—trees—is there, and it appears in other Morrison novels. As discussed previously, trees are viewed in many African cosmologies as the abodes of resident and/or roaming spirits. We noted examples in *No Longer at Ease* and *Jazz* in, for instance, Obi and Violet's respective but analogous encounters under trees and in Jesmyn Ward's skillful play on the trope of afterlife and trees in *Sing, Unburied, Sing*. Also in *Arrow of God*, it is "near the udala tree" that a terrified young Obika encounters a spirit after a flash of lightning. Obika acknowledges seeing it "turn into the Bush That Ruined Little Birds." Ezeulu, co-signing, realizes that the apparition is "the god of wealth," Eru, "the Magnificent, the One that gives wealth to those who find favour with him" (8).

Morrison compresses much that requires unpacking in *Paradise*'s deftly executed village spiritualism, especially in this otherworldly encounter between the affluent Morgan twin Steward's wife, Dovey, and the spirit/man. The first point is junctionality. The man is said to be encroaching on the property. He is said to retire, to vanish, "between the trees" (92). Morrison hints also at *spirit presence, possession*, and haunting, a theme for which Melanie R. Anderson, invoking Derrida's idea of spectrality, perspicaciously calls *Paradise* "a haunted novel" ("What" 308). I say "haunting" in terms of the spirit man assuming spatial residency in the structure and its environs because, fascinatingly, the house is unoccupied. Dovey even admits, or reveals, as much to the man, whom she would come to regard as Friend, and whom she thinks of in terms of a second husband with whom she is having a secret affair. The man's seeming interest or *investment* in the previously rental property and the frequency of his trespass through it are indicative. They seem to imply perhaps that he has some kind of *previous-life* connection to it, to its land, or the area at large. Dovey knows most if not all Ruby families. She believes he is a stranger because, judged by village way of identifying and knowing, he bears no physical resemblance to any Ruby lineage. Pay close attention also to the narrator's description of the property, or rather Dovey telling the man, unprompted, that the house is confiscated but taken off sale-listing by the twins. Who is the man Dovey implies previously owned but lost the property and land? Or who perhaps painfully surrendered it as the slave would the peculium? How old is that structure and what is its history? Could the man be a returnee ghost/spirit from the slavery past, like the eponymous Beloved? It is interesting how, like Beloved appearing to Sethe as a grown woman after the carnival, it is after the heated yet carnivalesque village meeting at Calvary that the man instigates his first contact with Dovey. With the village/attendees split in their perspectives on the Oven's opaque inscriptions, Dovey's view on the wor(l)ds and their contestation is mediatory. She proposes noon, or that the village take the middle ground in the divisive issue.

Novelists are known to duplicate plotlines, repurpose tropes, and some-times genealogize characters. This is evident in Achebe's chronicling of the Okonkwo bloodline and his recalibrations of the inflexible-strongman type. Unlike *No Longer at Ease*'s Catholic convent whose young, secular-minded Irish missionaries Nora and Pat are disallowed by the watchful Mother and Sisters from boundary-crossing, in this case the "infraction" of interracial affairs with African men, *Paradise*'s convent "is a way station, a crossroads, and a meeting place," Anderson adds. Like *Beloved*'s 124 Bluestone Road, it is located "between the human and spiritual realms" and is consequently "home to various supernatural occurrences" ("What" 311–12). Here, I argue, Morrison recycles in the Dovey-and-her-Friend/Second Husband substory the Beloved-as-audience-and-defogger technique. In other words, there is a structural and functional symmetry between Beloved and Friend. Not only are the two ghost-spirit figures figured as *godly*, corporeal, and verbal, even though at their ini-tial meeting Dovey does not see Friend's lips move when he responds to her question. In *Beloved* and *Paradise,* the figures also serve as revelatory devices, or what I call "traveling excavator of buried memories" in my related discus-sion elsewhere of John Edgar Wideman's exploitation of *ogbanje*, the spirit-child belief and concept, in *The Cattle Killing* (see Okonkwo, *Spirit* 125). Just as spirit-child woman Beloved pries open Sethe's and indeed Paul D's repressed memories; just as how in Beloved's presence Sethe starts talking, confessing, justifying, unburying her past, unprompted, so too does Dovey, in Friend's presence. She gets overly chatty, albeit embarrassed, it seems, by her villagist openness. Dovey seems to have found favor with the god Eru-esque man. In short, a close, cultural reader would extrapolate *offering for (deital/spiritual) favor* in Dovey's feeding the man "a slice of bread loaded with apple butter." We are told that, like the ravenous Oven, he devours all of it (92).

As the above and earlier discussion demonstrates, one of the hallmarks of villagism is rational (as in, sensible) subscription to illogicality. In other words, a reconciliatory acceptance of such scientifically questioned and modernity-derided epistemologies as magic, spells, dreams, ghosts, and other folk beliefs. Dovey's sister and Deacon Morgan's wife, Soane, as well as Connie, also actuate that mode of knowing in *Paradise*. In addition to sharing that Soane lost her sons Easter and Scout in Vietnam in 1969, the narrator also depicts Soane as super-stitious, as are Dovey and Umuaroans (see Ogbaa, *Gods* 54). The belief in some African and other cultures about the death-connection and thus ominousness of vultures—a carnivore mentioned by Winterbottom in *Arrow of God*—appears to have survived in the New World. It finds expression in Soane's reading of the sight of buzzards flying over the town as a sign about her dream that K.D.'s marriage to Arnette cannot repair the festering enmity between Ruby's leading families. Also furthering the present claim are Connie's latent magical powers. It is that supernatural gift that had enabled her—at the midwife Lone's urging—to raise Scout from the dead after an accident. Ironically, detractors from Connie's Christian religion (whose founder, Jesus, also archetypically performed the same miracle on Lazarus) ridicule her unorthodox healing and interventionist power. A clairvoyant herself, Lone *knows* about Deacon Morgan's affair with Connie, who used to drug him for sex and taste his blood during intercourse, to his shame and mortification. There is also villagist *spite*, as Griswold conceptualized. One finds multiple displays of bitterness among the characters, from Umuaro to Okperi, and from the Convent to Ruby.

On the other side of rancor-as-villagism is onomastics-as-village-epistemology in Umuaro, Haven, and Ruby. In his study *Gods, Oracles and Divination: Folkways in Chinua Achebe's Novels,* the fourth chapter of which begins with Achebe's statement in *Morning Yet on Creation Day* that "If you want to know how life has treated an Igbo man, a good place to look is the names his children bear"—Kalu Ogbaa engages with the subject of deities. This is of interest to us in this section and is also central to *Arrow of God* and *Paradise.* Ogbaa also affirms Achebe relative to Igbo vernacular and culture of names. He asserts that Africans "know the indispensable part names play in their cultures and societies" and that their creative imaginations give expressions to that knowledge and custom (61). The five converging rubrics into which Ogbaa sorts autochthonous names in Achebe's novels are helpful for a richer understanding of the *Arrow of God–Paradise* kinship. According to Ogbaa, in Achebe's novels there are "Dedicatory Names," "Philosophical Names," "Praise Names," "Allusive Names" given to human beings and in some cases to gods, as well as "Other Names" given, significantly, to "clans and villages, spirits, age group, and place" (63–84). To these classifications—though subsumed under the praise- and allusive-name clusters—Morrison would add discretely "abbreviated" names and particularly "nicknames," which she said were prevalent among African Americans.

I want to suggest not only that "Haven" and "Ruby" are clan names picked by the black people, but that "Oven," like "Ulu," is nominally deital. I want also to hazard an alternative reading of "Umuaro" and the two novels' titles. Ogbaa contends that Umuaro means "'Weighty Community': because Ulu unites the villages that make up the clan and thus gives them strength to fight Abam head-hunters and agonists" (*Gods* 84). But is it not possible that in calling the six-village federation "Umuaro" (literally Aro People or Aro Descendants) with the evocative suffix "aro," Achebe was gesturing to the historical Aro nation? The choice of "aro" makes correlational sense. The Aro historically were a people scattered, like the constituent Umuaro villages. Famously peripatetic, and today constituting an Aro diaspora, they were coalesced—as is Umuaro under Ulu—around their widely respected oracle and protector-deity "Ibini Ukpabi," dubbed "the Long Juju" by the British. It could also be that, with the "aro" suffix, Achebe was trying to imply the fictional village coalition's origins in Aro-connected international slave trade and domestic slaveries, part of the latter being tied to land pressures and destructions of vulnerable communities (Wren, *Those Magical* 60). As such, like (Igbo-African and of course other) children named after the circumstances of their births, "Umuaro" reflects arguably the single-most-impactful historical factor in their amalgamation: the Aro/slave-raiding. The name itself becomes a commemoration. In *Paradise*, it is interesting that the people first considered naming the new town "New Haven." But they ultimately choose "Ruby" in honor of the deceased Ruby, evocative of accounts given of Brooklyn's name (Cha-Jua 31). They opted for Ruby also as though superstitiously mindful of experiential redux. In other words, with most of the other original all-Black towns having nearly turned into ghost towns, they seem afraid of a cycle repeating. Or perhaps they chose "Ruby" in recognition of the imperative of archetype-replica differentiation. That is the whole point—as Ezeulu says his father told him—of Okperi ances-tors cautioning Umuaroans to whom they gave both habitational land and the deities Udo and Ogwugwu against reusing the two gods' names verbatim.

Whatever informed Achebe's choice, the focal novels' sacral and numinous titles are mutually reinforcing and interchangeable. In response to Michel Fabre drawing Achebe's attention, during their interview, to *Arrow of God*'s tit-ular similarity to Conrad's *Arrow of Gold*, Achebe admits to the phrasal resem-blance. But while he notes having earlier addressed his relationship to Conrad's works, "The title, *Arrow of God*," he says, "is explained in the book itself" (Fabre 45–46). Nonetheless, the novel's core concerns and tropes would also stay intact had Achebe called the book simply *Umuaro*. This is because the story of a village, of a people (which is the novel's overarching subject), is far greater than one man, in this case the arrow-of-god, Ezeulu. The same obtains had he titled it *Paradise*. That would be an ironic play on the white man's/the missionaries' Promissory Note of a futuristic Heaven/Haven. That promise partly constitutes Christianity's driving logic for its interpositions on and its displacement/sacrificing of indigenous belief systems and practices for Heaven's sake. Likewise, *Paradise*'s themes would be unaffected had Morrison called it *Arrows of God*. That name would reflect the story's engagement with the sharp-, multipoint, and God-incensing tensions among the three religious orders and their presiding priest-ministers.

The Villagist Idea and Pitfalls of Oblation-as-Panacea

Should "tension" define the village moods of *Arrow of God* and *Paradise*, "sacrifice" would qualify the two texts' undertones. From his earliest short stories to the village novels especially and on to *Anthills of the Savannah*, Achebe has variously engaged with the subject of sacrifice. The close reader will notice the many times and environments—familial, social, historical, religious, cultural, descriptive, etc.—in which he invokes the word "sacrifice" in *Arrow of God*. Likewise, *Paradise* is arguably the only one of Morrison's novels in which she directly drops the word "sacrifice" a few times in the course of narration but more importantly effectuates it as the key introductory action and a narrative thread. Critics may have noted, however, Morrison's hints at sacrifice sometimes in her themes of *offering* and *loss*. Notable examples are found, non-sequentially, in *The Bluest Eye* (in the Pecola Breedlove story), *A Mercy* (in Florens's mother's traumatizing offering of her to the Anglo-Dutch slave trader Jacob Vaark), and in *Sula* and *Song of Solomon*. As with *Paradise* opening with an armed assault, *Sula* particularly begins with racial attack and offering. It starts with violence; a ritualized erasure of black place and space. The story commences with the brutal tearing, uprooting, and sacrifice of the equally slavery-gestated Bottom, which used to be a thriving black village community, for the construction of the Medallion City golf course. There is also the human sacrifice implied in Chicken Little's drowning to calm a restive river; Eva's murder of Plum; and her sacrificing of her leg for familial survival and of her life to douse fire. We can also add to those instances the community's scapegoating of Sula. Earlier in the story, Sula sheds her blood to deter Nel from bullying Irish boys. We have, in *Song of Solomon*, Pilate's self-sacrifice in Milkman's rite of passage into (racial) cognition and manhood, among other examples. And with Orlando Patterson's equation of lynching with ritual sacrifice, then the hangings and killings—for instance, those of slaves recalled in *Beloved*, and the lynching of free blacks such as occurred in all-white town Georgia's Forsyth County in 1912 and exhumed in Patrick Phillips's riveting work *Blood at the Root* (2017)—all take new meaning.

In "Feast of Blood: 'Race,' Religion, and Human Sacrifice in the Postbellum South," the second chapter of his provocative study *Rituals of Blood* (1998), Patterson correlates most antebellum lynching to ritualized human sacrifice. But more importantly, he provides wider historical contexts into oblation. Reinforced by Achille Mbembe, who has called lynching "the arresting, grotesque, and exhibitionist form of racist cruelty" (*Necropolitics* 18), Patterson's insight helps us to further appreciate Achebe and Morrison's structuring of sacrifice in *Arrow of God* and *Paradise*. As Patterson postulates:

> THE RITUAL KILLING of human beings is, of course, the ultimate form of blood-sacrifice. The practice has existed, at some time, among nearly all peoples. Contrary to common belief, it was not confined to the most primitive peoples but tended to be found more among highly advanced premodern peoples. It was evident in all the advanced ancient Near Eastern civilizations, including that of the ancient Hebrews—as the tradition of the Aqedah, or Binding, (i.e., Abraham's binding and offering of his only son, Isaac, as a human sacrifice on Mount Moriah) attests—and throughout pre-Christian Europe. . . . [H]uman sacrifice is closely related to slaveholding. Indeed, among many peoples, ranging from the Northwest Coastal Indians of America to the Aztecs, Ashantis, and Carthaginians, human sacrifice was one of the main reasons for the holding of slaves and the taking of prisoners of war. (181–82)

To his own question as to the semantics of sacrifice and why its cruelest expression "the slaughter of fellow human beings—tends to be among mankind's most sacred rituals?" Patterson answers in two ways. It stems from the widely held significance of blood in human life. It also has to do with the continued ancient belief that its shedding secures "a vital alliance between those united in a blood-bond." Thus, blood is a powerful agent, a solidifier of tribal alliance. According to Patterson, sacrifice is generally viewed as propitiatory, in addition to providing cultural and mental needs of those involved. Attributing the contention to the anthropologists Henri Hubert and Marcel Mauss, Patterson emphasizes sacrifice's very ritual and thus dramatic dimension, with the drama's apex being the victim's killing. Of critical pertinence is that sacrifices generally occurred at established sacred sites or sites made sacred by the acts. And, depending on the reason for the sacrifice or the deity conciliated, the victim would be typecast as embodying either or both of the polarities of virtue and vice. As in the "Human sacrifice" of "African-descended people . . . to appease the Southern gods" for America's unification at the Constitutional Convention (Anderson, *Second*, 28), sacrifice reinforces bonds among sacrificers and between them and their god (182–83).

Francis A. Arinze's earlier-cited *Sacrifice in Ibo Religion* (1970) clearly shows that sacrifice is as much an ancient ritual among the Ashanti of Ghana, whom Patterson references above, as it with the Igbo of Southeast Nigeria. And more important, Arinze, whose study antedates *Rituals of Blood,* agrees generally with Patterson on the character of oblation. But what Arinze brings additionally to the topical table is provinciality. He furnishes layers of culturally specific information that broadens our understanding of the focal novels. He puts redemptive sacrifice in Igboland into two discrete categories. One is to eliminate "abomination." The other is for slighter misdeeds. Arinze explains that "public expiatory sacrifices in an I[g]bo town or village used to assume special solemnity in the sacrifice of scapegoats. A town or a village could heap all its sins on a goat or cow and then offer it to a spirit." This required prior consultation with an oracle, however. "In the old days," he adds, "human beings were used to remove the ills of the multitude in a few places such as Onitsha." Crediting G. Basden's findings, Arinze writes about how "at the solemn feast of *Ofalla,* the yearly appearance of the Obi (King) of Onitsha, the victim was a good-looking girl in her teens." She "was tied with ropes and palm leaves (*omu*), and was dragged round the town to take away its sins, and then down two miles into the River Niger" (34–37).

It needs to be declared that, because of its primacy in *Arrow of God* and *Paradise,* the idea of *offering* has not gone unrecognized in scholarship on both novels. Nor are tropes and subjects of sacrifice scarce in African fiction and literary criticism in general. For as Olakunle George correctly observes, "African literary texts do not just deploy sacrifice as theme." They "also reflect critically on it." In this way, "the texts are more contradictory and suggestive than the writers themselves sometimes intend" (16). Earlier in his discussion, George points us to African writers in whose works the motif is variedly instantiated. They include Soyinka, Cheikh Hamidou Kane, Ahmadou Kourouma, Yvonne Vera, Ngũgĩ wa Thiong'o, Nuruddin Farah, and, of course, Achebe (13), whose *Arrow of God* amply demonstrates what George keenly recognizes as "the costs and ambivalences of sacrifice" (12). Clearly missing in the scholarship on *Arrow of God* and *Paradise,* however, are any comparative readings that touch on

Achebe and Morrison's villagist treatments of the topic and those treatments' counterpoints as well. In both works, sacrifice is consistently purificational and/or political. It is chiefly undertaken as part of cleansing observances. But the most glaring deviation in the texts is about who—outside of such sacrificial objects as animals, food, and money—gets immolated in the ritual, whether communal, actualized, or figurative. Who, in the novels, one must ask, are those human victims marked by Old World priests and villagers and their New World descendants and followers—Christian preachers and congregations—as the sources and personifications of supposed atrocities? The abominations are said to threaten the well-being and continued existences of *the lands* and alliances of Umuaro and Ruby.

The answer is rather obvious. Those actually or symbolically *offered* and "slaughtered" in *Arrow of God* are male. But then we must recall that the contemporaneous bodily and ultimate sacrifices of the 1929 Women's War rebels are not narrated in *Arrow of God*. In *Paradise*, however, the victims are female. We will get to them shortly. Preceded of course by rhetorical invocations and narrative actuations of sacrifices in Achebe's earlier short stories and novels, an index of sacrificial episodes in *Arrow of God* would include the following: the human sacrifice that enabled the creation of Ulu; Ezeulu as scapegoat (the lamb) whose annual ritual "death" in the Festival of the Pumpkin Leaves expunges into the ground Umuaro's communal evil. Ezeulu's exhaustion after the Festival is considered unavoidable and necessary to the sacrifice. Then there is the purification rite at the crossroads required for Obika's new wife, Okuata. It is performed by the medicine man Aniegboka, with the sole purpose of confirming, with all concerned holding their breath, that Okuata is indeed a virgin. In Umuaro, fines or a sacrifice is required of anyone who violates the prohibition against picking fruits from the sacred *udala* tree. The tree is located behind an *okwolo* hut in Umuachala's *ilo*—Umuaro's biggest clearing. We also have the unusual roadside sacrifice using a British coin with King George's head. And there are hints by Umuaro elders of past human sacrifices in the culture (209). Outside of the human sacrifice foundational to Ulu, perhaps the other quite profound offering in *Arrow of God* is Ezeulu's self-admitted sacrifice of his son Oduche. This *loss* is magnified by Obika's death, which "dements the Chief Priest" (Ogbaa, *Gods* 132). And that *loss* also ripples in Ezeulu being sacrificed at the novel's end for Umuaro's survival and group continuance.

Ezeulu sends, or rather *offers*, his teenage son Oduche to join the white man's Christian religion and school. To Ezeulu, the Oduche decision is premeditated,

tactical, and foresighted. But as Oduche's mother and Edogo separately interpret it, and as Ezeulu's friend Akuebue suspects, that judgment/action is tan-
tamount to human sacrifice. My reading is, however, that the Oduche sacrifice
is botched and/or unsuccessful, bringing to mind the ambiguity and irresolution George mentioned. I interpret it as unaccepted by the gods in light of
Oduche's postoblation *aliveness,* his subsequent abominable *activity.* The *offering* is unsuitable also because of Oduche's mother's strenuous objection to Ezeulu's *unilateral* and callous action. It is negated, perhaps, because the goal or
beneficiary of the offering is not the community but Ezeulu alone.

As "sign" of Ezeulu's sacerdotal miscalculation and his human fallibility relative to his choice of victim, Oduche interprets and executes rather broadly
his Call. His mandate is issued, however, not on a warranting scrap of paper.
Rather, it is unambiguously verbalized. Oduche is encouraged in his sacrilege
not only by his culture's and the village-empowering multiperspectivity. He
is buoyed also, particularly, by his own father deputizing him on a mission of
epistemological and religious espionage. Like the boy, in Ezeulu's own proverb,
who discards prudence in favor of irruption, smashing the door with his feet
when his father sends him to steal, Oduche attempts to kill Umuaro's sacred
python. His misdeed adds to the many oven-hot issues confronting Ezeulu,
what with the rancor and jealousy among his wives and children; his daughter Akueke's marital issues; and a first son/sculptor Edogo, who resents his
father's dominance and favoritism and sometimes channels his bitterness and
defiance into carving the images of gods and aggressive-looking masks. Add to
those a handsome, beloved, hot-tempered, alcoholic, and seemingly ill-fated
son, Obika. Obika is whipped on his bare back more than a dozen times by
Mr. Wright. His crime? He arrived late with a parodic swagger at the job site.
Wright's action stuns both Ezeulu and Obika's aggrieved age-group working on
the Okperi-Umuaro road project without pay. There is also Nwafo, the youngest son, with aspirations to Chief Priesthood.

Ezeulu's trusted village undercover-spy-gone-rogue, Oduche is inspirited
by dreams of intellectual power and social prestige. To him, both things are
modeled in one Blackett. Legend has it that although a black man, Blackett, a
West Indian missionary, is more knowledgeable than whites. Oduche is further emboldened by new-convert zeal. He is encouraged, much further, by the
proselytization and cultural antecedent of his new School Teacher, the English-
fluent John Goodcountry. Goodcountry is from the Niger Delta. There, as
Goodcountry apostrophizes, the early Christians demolished shrines and

killed their people's sacred iguana. Against the empirically informed caution by the worldly carpenter and convert Moses Unachukwu, Goodcountry persists in interpreting scripture in binaries. Seated "like a rock" through Unachukwu's objections (48), Goodcountry promises Oduche that at his baptism he "will be called Peter; on this rock will I build my Church" (49). And like *Things Fall Apart's* Mr. Smith, Goodcountry preaches not syncretism of African villagist modes of life and thought *and* Christianity. Instead, he crusades for jurisdictional and theological trespass. He promotes not just aggressive overthrow of indigenous spirituality, as *Things Fall Apart's* Mr. Brown earlier considered. He also embraces radical martyrdom, exemplified for him by one "Joshua Hart, his kinsman, who suffered martyrdom in Bonny" (46–47). Were we to extend Goodcountry's logic: Hart probably now lives in heaven, in paradise, not only with the Supreme Divine and the Old Testament Abraham, Isaac, Jacob, Moses, and Sarah. He also dwells there with Baby Suggs, holy, and beloved Ikemefuna. All are hopefully serenaded by the trumpet-blowing but arrow-and-sword-wielding host of angels, whom Satchmo likely has got accustomed to blues-jazz gumbo, to droning "What Did I Do to Be So Black and Blue" and rocking to its twin "When the Saints Go Marching In."

Back on earth, though, and to village Haven and village novel *Paradise,* Morrison paints a picture of a once-precious stone. She tells the story of a specular gem, a Ruby-rare all-Black town. Its Africa-descended inhabitants, with their forebears sainted by slavery and segregation and having marched in covenant through Louisiana, Mississippi, the midwestern deserts, and *into* a village, are grappling with the high and low notes of existence in a promised land. This is a land that they now believe, or that believes itself, contaminated by evil, human evil. Given how the arc of Ruby's fraught history has all along been bending toward communal "cleansing" and renewal, I want to propose that we see *Paradise's* entire narration as one elaborate drama of cautionary ritual sacrifice. As such, it is a ritual drama that *teaches* and aligns with Patterson, Arinze, George, and *Arrow of God's* sharp points on oblation. In terms of *Paradise's* overt references to "sacrifice," these instances stand out: The reader may recall the moment Steward, who views Reverend Misner as threatening, wonders "if that generation—Misner's and K.D.'s—would have to be sacrificed to get to the next one" (94). It also is telling that Morrison evokes Reverend Cary's sermonic riff on the "sacrifices" Ruby people "make *every* day to live here in God's beauty, His bounty, His peace" at precisely the moment Lone overhears the nine assailants plotting the ambush of, or the *offering* at, the Convent (274).

Consider these. If, according to Patterson, sacrifices generally take place in established consecrated spots or spots consecrated especially by (the) human slaughter, the *Paradise* attack occurs at a "religious" site: the shrine-like Convent. The Ruby ritual also has, conventionally, a scapegoat or, rather, in this case, scapegoats. These are the women at whom aspersions are cast. The women are vilified as bearing "the female malice." Like the objectified, easily expendable (but apparently history-haunting) slaves cast into shallow graves in Ezeulu's proverb, the Convent women are also deemed wastes, "detritus: throwaway people that sometimes blow back into the room after being swept out the door" (4). The sacrificers consider them "diseased" (8), blasphemous (7), "awful" and "strange" (11), "Bitches," "witches," "heifers," and "sluts" (276). More so, the denomination-balkanized citizens of Ruby are warring among themselves. However, they find in the Convent and its occupants a unifying *other* and cause. They locate/interpret in them a common enemy on whom the village-community's inexplicable aberrations are blamed. It seems apparent that harming the women provides the people the psychological function or release Patterson mentions. The climax of ritual sacrifice is the killing of the victim. A period of calm, of order, or one marked at least by the hope or possibility of redemption, ensues.

If we sequence *Paradise*'s narration, those last stages of sacrifice, namely, the victim's death and social catharsis become evident. They could be said to play out in the apocalyptic Convent massacre and the novel's postscript moment of Lone's hope for Ruby's repentance in gracious second chance. The phases would be implied in Deek's introspections on his cruelty, and a disdainful Billie Delia anticipating resurrection, the Second Coming, so to speak, of her friends the Convent women. As though verifying Olakunle George's remark that "the best of African writing . . . reject[s] sacrificial violence (in pagan or modern societies), even as [it] celebrate[s] the *rhetoric* of sacrifice in social relations" (16), Ruby "disintegrates" in its crisis: in its conflicting narratives of and its finger-pointing over the tragic events, particularly over the whereabouts of the Convent women's disappeared bodies. Like the resurrected Christ, the women, however, start making private "spiritual" and "physical" "appearances" to their beloveds. That the women are now making their alive and active bodies/selves manifest in public, postritual attack, is telling. It indicates that, as with Ezeulu's offering of Oduche, the men's sacrifice of the women is botched.

Actualized in *Paradise*, then, as well as in *Arrow of God*, are those interlocking but not always consecutive mythic phases that broadly characterize the village novel plot, as Griswold explained earlier. The stages—"traditional stability," "disturbance from outside," "attempted restoration," "climax," and "disintegration or reintegration"—are realized. In *Arrow of God*, for instance, the denouement is inferred variously. We glean it in Obika's Ezidemili-implicated sacrificial death, as Clement Okafor suggests (213–14). It is hinted, too, subsequently, in the grief-hastened onset of Ezeulu's inherited madness, interpreted variously: by the people, as vindication; and by his nemesis Ezidemili, as cautionary tragedy, a lesson against overreach. To them, his demise, his fall from grace, as it were, testifies to the dictum that no man, no matter his power and prestige, is greater than his people. The other clue is Ulu's not-unprecedented sacrifice and ruin, as foreseen by the elder Ogbuefi Ofoka (212–13). The denouement is additionally reified in the restoration of cosmic and ecological order, as a nearly imperiled Umuaro, rescued before from the slave-raiding Abam, is once again unfettered to harvest its crops. This time, however, the reaping would be under the authority, management, and protection of a new deity: the Christian God in Heaven/haven. In this religious and "divine warfare," as Clement Okafor so aptly describes it, human beings, including Ezeulu himself, are pawns. They are "mere arrows with which the anthropomorphic gods shoot one another" (214). Or lacerate human beings, as Ezeulu recognizes in his threatening assertion that "The gods sometimes use us as a whip" (208). Ezeulu may have avoided the peculium of Lugard's/Winterbottom's Warrant Chieftaincy. But he cannot escape the usufruct circumscriptions of (Igbo) deities and priesthood.

Arrow of God's victims of village sacrifice are male. It is *Paradise*, however, whose spotlighting of female casualties mirrors the female immolation in the Onitsha-Igbo practice Basden recorded in his study that Arinze cites. One thing is clear, though. The nine murderous, God-worshiping and God-fearing men of Ruby, taking liberties with their Christian call, and with their eyes toward h(e)aven, toward paradise, as inheritance, would make a good apostolate for the man-spirit Ezeulu. The men took to heart—or rather, they interpreted literally—the Chief Priest's defense of his Abrahamian Aqedah. As Ezeulu counterargues to his friend Akuebue as to his considered justification for offering Oduche at the sacrificial altars of the white man's colonial education on earth and his Christian religion and its deity in heaven: "A disease that has never been seen before cannot be cured with everyday herbs. When we want to make a charm we look for the animal whose blood can match its power; if a chicken cannot do it we look for a goat or a ram; if that is not sufficient we send for a bull. But sometimes even a bull does not suffice, then we must look for a human" (133).

Or for a woman, for women-being, in the case of Ruby, whose New Fathers may wish to distort or outright delete the Convent Five and the village town's foremothers from history, reminiscent of how women are not featured in Ogbuefi Odogwu's registry of Umuofia stalwarts in *No Longer at Ease*. But through Patricia Best's archival work, her journal that reminds one of Willa Prescott Nedeed's archaeologic activities in Gloria Naylor's *Linden's Hills*, Morrison more directly reconstructs and recovers the subordinated names and stories of Ruby's founding women. Roger Best's daughter, Patricia, recognizes that those women, like her light-skinned, intraracially ostracized, and dead mother, Delia, may have "had only one name[:] Celeste, Olive, Sorrow, Ivlin, Pansy." Or theirs may have been "generalized last names[:] Brown, Smith, Rivers, Stone, Jones" (187). Regardless, like the legendary "Mother" Priscilla Baltimore of Brooklyn village, described by Cha-Jua as a brave and "extraordinary woman" who "was often called to risk her life" for the cause of abolition and thus "deserves a place in the pantheon of courageous African Americans, such as Harriet Tubman and Josiah Henson, who led their people out of bondage" (39–40), the women and mothers Patricia recalls were vital to the fate of the village-founding fifteen families.

Ruby women's strength of arm shows also when they stepped in to contribute to the legal defense fund of the fictionalized four boys whose jailing and prosecution on trumped-up charges led to the historic Norman, Oklahoma, tragedy. The women felt the pain of the boys' mothers. But the men, "Fleetwoods, Pulliam, Sargeant Pearson and the Morgans . . . [were] adamant in their refusal" to financially assist (206). We hear that nine of the fifteen families, among who are the Blackhorses, Beauchamps, Catos, the two DuPres families, plus the Fleetwoods, Floods, Morgans, and the Pooles, were intact at the original exodus. Patricia labels them "8-rock" in reflection of the belief held widely in Haven and Ruby regarding the families' purportedly authentic Africanity. Transgenerationally weaponized and leveraged, the claim is that the families are the chosen lineage, or what *Arrow of God*'s British lieutenant-governor of Nigeria calls "Natural Rulers" in his memorandum to Winterbottom on indirect rule (26). As Patricia hints, no strong reason is advanced for this *natural selection*, so to speak, other than pigmentation, the fifteen families' very dark skin and supposed pure African blood. Paralleled here, ironically inversely, is Winterbottom's subtle skin-bias, his unvoiced equation of Ezeulu's supposed racial *impurity*, the chief priest's "non-negroid" feature—his "very light . . . almost red" skin, which Winterbottom conjectures as the Igbo "in the distant past assimilat[ing] a small non-negroid tribe of the same complexion as the Red Indians" (37–38)—as Ezeulu's potential and distinguishing leadership attribute. Paralleled, also, is a long-accepted premise in Umuaro. Although it is now thrust into dispute by historical developments and, particularly, the Nwaka-led open challenge to Ezeulu: the doxa is that Ezeulu's Umuachala village, said by Nwaka to be the weakest member of the six-village federation, *and* the familial bloodline of the terracotta-skinned Ezeulu, are essentially exceptional. They have long been propagated as the singular pipeline to the Ulu-priesthood of a kingless Igbo-Umuaro. This is a people well known for their cultural plasticity and religious infidelity; indeed, for discarding outdated and/ or inept gods, as the novel's Aninta people demonstrate.

Nevertheless, Ruby village's Founding Mothers are not lost in history, thanks to Patricia Best's recoveries of their sacrifices. Likewise, *Paradise*, in preserving memories of a slavery-impelled but passing Haven and Ruby, identifies the attackers toward the novel's end. Significantly, however, it does that but not before introducing us to the female victims sacrificed by the men. Not before "freez[ing] the action" (Krumholz 22) and taking us through the complicated but narratively detailed lives of the troubled, lost, and supposedly "sinful"/evil women. These are their names and stories: Consolata—a Brazilian orphan gifted with spiritual and healing powers but kidnapped at nine years old by Mother Superior (Mary Magna) and brought to the original Convent. Connie is the Catholic nunnery's oldest residing tenant following Mary's death. She plays a critical role in the women's journeys of self-rehabilitation but is shot in the head by Deacon, against Steward's dissuasion. Mavis Albright: After the accidental but seemingly infanticidal suffocation of her twins, Merle and Pearl, in her husband Frank's green Cadillac that she parks outside to buy Frank hotdogs in Maryland, Mavis, worried that her remaining and resentful children are after her life, escapes in the Cadillac. By chance, she arrives at the Convent. She becomes its second resident and a fugitive. Grace (nicknamed Gigi): Also arrives at the Convent by chance after leaving her imprisoned boyfriend, Mikey Rood. Driven there by Roger Best in his multipurpose wagon-ambulance-hearse, she arrives a day after Mary Magna's death and after a brief encounter at the bus top with K.D., with whom she would have a long sexual affair that he ends both in repulsion and gendered hate. Seneca is traumatized by maternal betrayal. Deserted by her mother, Jean, when she was five years old, Seneca grows up in multiple foster homes. She has to abandon her also-incarcerated boyfriend, Eddie Turtle. Imprisoned in Wichita and an only child whom she dated only six months, Eddie had mistreated her. He wounded her self-image, with all the past ordeals culminating in Seneca's secret self-mutilation. Pallas Truelove: Named Pallas by her father, with her mother, Divine, nicknamed DeeDee, Pallas—sixteen years old, a runaway, betrayed by her boyfriend, Carlos, pregnant and sick—lands at the Convent after catching a ride with Indians. One of whom, an elderly woman, drops her off at a clinic. Billie Delia Cato is Patricia Best and Billie Cato's daughter and best friend to K.D.'s pregnant and college-bound girlfriend, Arnette Fleetwood. Billie encounters Pallas there by chance. She soon hands her over to Mavis at the Convent, where she delivers a baby boy they name Divine. These women are the prey that the men—Steward Morgan, his twin, Deacon, their nephew K.D., Arnold Fleetwood, Jeff Fleetwood, Wisdom Poole, Sergeant Pearson, Harper Jury and his son Menus Jury (285–87)—went to massacre in the multiply repurposed refuge. The Convent, we are told, had been "an embezzler's folly" and a boarding school for Indian girls.

I suggested earlier that when the six founding villages/constitutive families of Umuaro and the founding families of Haven and Ruby agreed to their respective rural confederacies, their priorities appeared to be religion, freedom, and security. And that is besides the even more paramount imperative of their collective psychic healing from slavery's debilitations. For generations, those twin dreams of paradisiac sovereignty and safety seem to have been stably realized for both unions until adverse historic and social changes. In Umuaro's case, the aspirations of security and peace appear actualized. That would be until, inferably, population density, land/agricultural pressures, and prosperity instigate Umuaro's quest for territorial expansion and, concomitantly, a scapegoat. Umuaro's publicly and hotly debated aggression against Okperi reminds us of Ruby's equally intensely debated attack on the Convent. A divided Umuaro holds a heated emergency meeting. It attempts to forestall war through a diplomatic mission to Okperi. But that effort is thwarted by cultural and diplomatic blunders by Umuaro's emissaries. It is hampered by the lead envoy Akukalia's egregious cosmological faux pas of breaking Ebo's *ikenga*.

We learn, similarly, that the supposedly *evil* and h(e)aven-contaminating Convent women were warned but that they rebuffed all the reprimands. With the women allegedly ignoring such caution, the denominations' spokespersons call an urgent village meeting at the Oven to determine a course of action. A confused and fractured Umuaro chooses ultimately, especially at Nwaka's coercion, to wage what turns out to be a reckless assault against Okperi in retaliation for Akukalia's murder. Relatedly, the Ruby church members' resolution-of-blame is a frontal, implicitly religious war, an armed attack at the Convent and women. It is the Umuaro war against Okperi that invites the outside force of British intervention. It also leads to what Ezeulu, who feels a personal and institutional vindication, considers his truthful testimony against Umuaro. But others, especially his detractors, interpret it differently and broadly. They see his solicited attestation as irreparable treachery. As charged by his adversaries, in an inconstant Umuaro-Igbo culture unsuitable for monarchy, for natural rulers: he bore consequential witness against his own people, his village, before Winterbottom, the imperial white man they nickname "Otiji-Egbe," the "Breaker of Guns" (36).

Toward a Closing: The Village World Is (Like)
a Prism Turning and a Mask Dancing

I would like to commence my conclusion by attending to a subject I have all along been skirting relative to the *Arrow of God–Paradise* intertextuality, namely, both novels' consistent takes on "generation" and "change." More specifically, I want to return to the two works' engagements with the question of epochal doubts about the continued relevance, sustainability, and authority of (certain overdetermined) deities, heritages, monuments, institutions, and memories; in short, *pasts*, village pasts, structured by Achebe as Umuaro's weakened Ulu and by Morrison as Haven/Ruby's famished and equally incapacitated Oven. Staying analytically true to both stories' discursivity, I would get around to that issue by way of another portal. I want to address it through another concern to which that inquiry and really this chapter's other subtopics are cross-bolted. Valerie Smith frames the window: "In *Paradise*," she argues, "Morrison grapples with the implications of one question in particular: why do our notions of utopia depend upon separation and exclusion? Why is the idea of paradise as much about those we include as it is about those we keep out?" (86; see also Mulrine 71).

It turns out Achebe has also long been intrigued by that contradiction. Just as Morrison extended the motifs of ambiguous-Will/text (mis)interpretation and Disallowal from *Paradise* to *Love*—specifically in the disputes over Bill Cosey's inconclusive will scrawled on a 1958 menu (79, 88–89) and the story of his utopic Hotel and Resort that was known in the 1940s to blatantly reject lower-class locals on whom it would later depend for survival (41–42)—Achebe appears to have threaded the paradox from *Things Fall Apart* to *Arrow of God*. In *Things Fall Apart*, a story that is also about the puzzling wills and actions of founders, ancestors, gods, and oracles, the implied exceptionalism of the nine-village and militarily rock-solid alliance and experiment that is precolonial "Umuofia" is predicated on exclusions, contrary to the village orthodoxy of inclusivity. Umuofia is built in part on the amalgamation's peripheralization of its *others* and *outcasts*, palimpsests all. This fairly internecine kin-ostracism, which Haven's Founders would quickly recognize and which their conflicted descendants in Ruby are battling to pass on, compounds Umuofia's inherent other fractures. It leaves the village-community, leaves Umuofia, even more open, more vulnerable, to adversarial forces of history, most consequentially those of Empire. Notice, likewise, that the condition of divine possibility, institutional power, cultural prestige and philosophical longevity of *Arrow of God*'s Ulu is the sustained subordination if not the exclusion of the other deities (Idemili, Ogwugwu, Eru, and Udo) and their priests, whose understandable grievances are amplified and exploited by Nwaka.

That the village deities passed over in Ulu's hierarchical elevation are much older divinities makes this a case of what, in the previous chapter, I called the Josephite betrayal. Or what the Igbo, in their timeless sagacity, enshrined in their proverbial logic on love-economy and attention-investment. Ndi-Igbo pronounce that *Alụta agbọghọ achụfuo agadi adịghị nma,* meaning literally: Casting away the old wife because of a new bride is wrong (and, it could also be added, dangerous!). Not only do Achebe and Morrison respectively knit *Arrow of God* and *Paradise* around that ancient and scripture-dramatized problematic of displacement. They also project it as one of the ingrained quagmires of utopia. It is, to them, in short, the bane of federacies, whether village or nation. Just as the scapegoated "Okperi" is said to have existed way before the aggressor "Umuaro," so also do we hear that the Convent antedates the invader Ruby. As part of his play on generations, on age and youth, Achebe makes that *pass-over* dynamic—the lavishing of affection, recognition, even power on the younger and the newer—one of *Arrow of God*'s leitmotifs. He depicts it in the colonial administration headquarters' power play, its costly dismissal of the empirical knowledge of Igboland offered on the paramount chief question by the old, frail, but experienced coaster Winterbottom. But then Winterbottom's will-imposition, his cosmology-impacting thirty-two-day jailing of Ezeulu for rejecting the offer to become Warrant Chief, sets adrift raw feelings and actions that culminate in Ezeulu's and more broadly Umuaro's tragedies. The dynamic reflects also in Winterbottom's resentment of the privileges enjoyed by the smart younger colonial staffers. We find it illustrated in Ezeulu's dignifying of his younger son—the rash, brash, and supposedly manlier Obika—over Obika's more introspective older brother Edogo. We see it in the Chief Priest's risky positioning of his much younger son Nwafo, and not his oldest son, Edogo, on the path to succession to Ulu priesthood.

Paradise is clearly concerned with that subject as well. Just as Ezeulu is uneasy about Edogo possibly assuming the priesthood, the Morgan men are also worried about accession. Deek and Soane lost their two boys, and Steward is childless. We are told that K.D. is the last male in the family's lineage of high-achieving/exceptional men. But like Obika's troubling irascibility, K.D. has anger and judgment issues. His actions routinely prompt questions if not rectification. The Morgan men wonder if Arnold, K.D.'s girlfriend Arnette's father, *should not* be displaced and excluded from his position in the village's cultural configurations of family and extended kinship. They doubt that Arnold would be entitled to anything, any Morgan inheritance whatsoever, if their nephew K.D.'s baby that Arnette has turns out to be a boy.

At issue ultimately in restive Umuaro and Ruby, however, are questions of the generational enshrinement—the preservation and dignifying—of *the past,* or certain pasts, particularly that village/historical *inheritance* or order of things consecrated in Ulu and Oven, respectively. Argues Valerie Smith, again quite incisively: "In the narrative present, the 1970s, the new generation of younger people want to use the oven in the town square as a place where they can congregate, socialize, and engage in political organization." They crave "a usable past," Smith adds, one "that can be shaped and mobilized to serve the needs of the present" (88). As Luther Beauchamp's boys Royal and Destry joltingly put it to their respect-fixated village elders still trapped in the founding stories and texts they inherited from their fathers and grandfathers: the question—equally apposite to *Arrow of God,* Umuaro, and Ulu—is whether to live in crippling fear of god and the past. Or should they check and/or balance deity?

A chief priest hyperaware of the limits imposed on his office and autonomy by his god, itself hyperaware of having a mortal antagonist in a resentful Idemili, Ezeulu is virtually faltered. He is subverted by the potent tag-team of Nwaka's direct and Winterbottom's incidental exposures of Ulu's datedness and enfeebled muscularity, especially by its failure to safeguard Obika. It speaks to the inherent misadventure of the British-instituted Indirect Rule/Warrant Chief System not only that it sought to conscript, impose and catastrophically detain even an unwilling nominee in Ezeulu, but also that Ezeulu himself, wishing dutifully to actualize his interpretation of his role as Ulu's weapon, would refuse to cave to an existential emergency and eat the remaining sacred yams.

He opts instead to let Umuaro suffer; "to hit" it "at its most vulnerable point—the Feast of the New Yam" (202)—simply to avenge, as do Haven's Founders, a personal injury: the humiliation he believed his confused kinsmen subjected him to in their positional neutrality in his war with his "friend" Winterbottom. Equally ironic is that Ulu does not even save Ezeulu from suffering the same madness that struck his mother, originally an Okperi native.

Notice, comparably, that instead of looking inward at their inflexibility, their ingrained conservatism and hubris, for what ails their village community, their havenly kingdom, Ruby's tyrannical male leadership and executioners see themselves as arrows of god. They consider themselves no longer the mentees of the New Testament Christ who pardons and embraces sinners, outlaws, and outcasts, but rather a furious and unforgiving Old Testament god's fire and brimstone, its ap(pointed) instruments to penalize the iniquitous, particularly the allegedly abominable Convent women. They forget their shared history with the women, namely: that, as descendants of maroons, of once-lost and refuge-seeking escapees viewed by marauding southern whites as detritus and skin-color sinners, they too have all along been in a "Convent," a geographic shelter, Oklahoma. Nevertheless, to Ruby's younger generation, the Oven's (deital) coldness and institutional ineffectuality—its subjection and acquiescence to desecration and other forms of misuse and misgivings—are proof enough of its anachronism. To them, the radical youth of the new era, any unpliable past, any "past" whatsoever that renders infeasible and invisible their subjectivity-in-village community, should be troubled, or outright defied and defiled.

Besides corroborating *Arrow of God* and *Paradise* on the cross-cultural commonality of generational dialectic and group-versus-individual skirmish, two of Achebe and Morrison's precursors, Zora Neale Hurston and Ralph Ellison, also remark on another of the two novels' major and land-linked suppositions. Hurston is the daughter of a onetime mayor of Eatonville, Florida, one of the first-chartered all-Black towns in the United States. Ellison himself is a proud Oklahoman, born six years into the statehood of that frontier territory that is *Paradise*'s focus and setting. Besides their shared experience of migration, Hurston and Ellison know one or two things about founders and all-Black towns, especially what necessitated and complicated them. They would concur that part of the challenge presented by efforts to *correct* or reverse the afterlives of collective traumas—be they, as in this case, land-robbery, colonization, and slavery—has to do with the constraining charges of progenitors (*the living dead*) in their literal, ideological, and symbolic manifestations.

Hurston and Ellison's bildungsromane *Their Eyes Were Watching God* and *Invisible Man* bear witness to that. The two works are respectively traversed by that lurking and restless "ghost." We witness *it*, for instance, in the stark, one might say Victorian, directives on men, marriage, and love issued the teenager Janie Crawford by her ever-watchful maternal grandmother, a former slave. It lurks in the references to himself by the character Joe Stark, the all-Black town/village builder, as "I god" in *Their Eyes*. We find that "specter" hovering in *Invisible Man*'s motif of original Founders, white and black, but particularly memorably in the dying grandfather's charge to Invisible Man's father. It expresses in Mr. Norton's creator and messiah complex; in Dr. Bledsoe's ambition, guile, and power play; in Mary Rambo's other-mothering and expectancy of racial salvation from Invisible Man; and in Brother Jack's talk of heroic personal sacrifice. It is there, in short, in the Brotherhood's and Ras the Exhorter's/Destroyer's clashing radicalism and militancy: all passed on not only as (memories of) racial injuries but also dogmas to Ellison's directionless Invisible Man.

To Janie and Invisible Man, both on allegorical journeys of identity-construction (see Sundquist 1–28), that *indirect rule* of the past and its imposed commandments (read, Warrant rules and regulations) can easily morph into a roadblock. Unmoderated, they can turn into long-running hurdles not just to collective transcendence. They are also potential obstacles to the growing black child's or more broadly young black people's individuation and (radical) voice-in-the-village community. They can constitute hopes and impediments, to evoke Achebe; a blessing and a curse, as Invisible Man reads it; in short, as much acres of aspiration to the present and future generations as they are potentially an apparitional encumbrance on paradise. But to *Arrow of God* and *Paradise*, the issue is further aggravated when, speaking literally and metaphorically, stewards of divine orders and ancestral legacies watch a lavishly attired dancing Mask from only one perspective. It is worsened when the custodians of racial possibility and memory and the transmitters of cultural value, on both sides of the Atlantic, taper the spectacular specularity of painting, mbari, diamond and ruby, and the complex polyrhythm of jazz, respectively, to a single ray and note.

And thus it cannot be lost on us that, because of its temporal and spatial specificity, and especially because it is group-/village-sanctified, vested with spirit, force, and legitimacy *by the people*, the deital and institutional Oven is serviceable, or at least supposed to be. It is transitory, again like the man-made Ulu (M. Lewis 84). Both Ulu and the Oven *were* situational, fashioned to be conditional. And nowhere is the Oven's *constitutional* framing and intended amenability to de-construction more evident than in the New Fathers' ability to reengineer and repurpose it; to disassemble the original structure and reinforce its constitutive material. They rebuild and resituate it elsewhere, or elsewheres if necessary, even as, or even if, later, they struggle to (re)interpret its equally man-scripted, originary titular Injunction. If Ruby people do not learn from their Atlantic cousins, Aninta and Umuaro people, and unshield the Oven from constructive criticism and inevitable change in the face of generational propensities and existential crises, it would soon be "a dead god." That remains true, no matter the Oven's human arrows. And it stays true, indeed immutable, regardless of the inhumane circumstances of its original reification, in this case slavery and Jim Crow.

In all, Achebe and Morrison provincialize the dangers of "utopia" in stories of the tribe (see also Tabone). And as ethical and committed novelists, they collaborate in *teaching*. Through the power of storytelling, both authors, like Ogbuefi Odogwu, enlighten their audience, us. Furthermore, *Arrow of God* and *Paradise* seem to have foreseen the ongoing controversies in the United States and other parts of the world over Confederate monuments, slave memorials, colonizer statues, populism, nationalism, and exclusionary immigration policies. Through their globally circulating trilogies and other texts, Achebe and Morrison edify us, not only about history's and the past's presentness. They also awaken us to the sometimes tragic aftermaths of stasis. That lesson is especially poignant for black people in villages and cities on both sides of the Atlantic. Both authors tease out change's village-grounded, epistemic tributaries of reinvention and balance. These are coded, fascinatingly, in Anna Flood's profitable transformation of Ruby's Ace's Grocery with creative updates while preserving its foundation, its ancestry and rootedness in the village.

Conclusion

May the Path Never Close

One hundred years ago, the pathbreaking Renaissance Man and Achebe and Morrison's racial kin, predecessor, and comrade-in-art James Weldon Johnson reflected on a concept with which we began this study. As did Ogbuefi Odogwu in the introduction, Johnson articulated his own definition of greatness, or of cultural preeminence, in this case. In the preface to his landmark anthology *The Book of American Negro Poetry* (1922), he asserts: "A people may become great through many means, but there is only one measure by which its greatness is recognized and acknowledged. The final measure of the greatness of all peoples is the amount and standard of the literature and art they have produced. The world does not know that a people is great until that people produces great literature and art. No people that has produced great literature and art has ever been looked upon by the world as distinctly inferior" (vii).

Achebe and Morrison would recognize the Western historical and philosophical assault, the pressures of racial uplift, and the New Negro generational fervor that stirred Johnson's declaratives. They would detect as well the racial stress, the routine, racism-induced microtensions on the black body and on black life that additionally motivate his nameless, ex–colored man's conscious resort to duplicity, sublimation, and survivalism. Perhaps most of all, they would share Johnson's underscore of the importance of works of imagination to a people's collective identity, cultural dignity, and mental well-being. It is not in doubt, then, what feats of village-matrixed storytelling the two trilogies paired as continuums in this study are. Nor is it even open to debate how much higher in the ladder of cultural attainment Achebe and Morrison personally, and their creative works, have raised and continue to elevate black people everywhere.

But we cannot fully appreciate the communications of those works, particularly the trilogies—*Things Fall Apart* and *Beloved*, *No Longer at Ease* and *Jazz*, *Arrow of God* and *Paradise*—as well as both writers' other cultural productions, without equally knowing their underpinnings of painting, music, mbari, and the dancing Mask.

Nonetheless, in pondering how to conclude this study, not necessarily conventionally whether it has sufficiently met the burdens of its agenda outlined in the introduction, I found myself returning to one extra discovery about the Achebe-Morrison connections. I could not help but be drawn back to the tropes of *openness* and the tones of *futurity* that conclude Achebe and Morrison's final published novels, respectively *Anthills of the Savannah* and *God Help the Child*, which "has already joined Morrison's other texts on syllabi in colleges and universities around the globe" (Eaton et al. xiii). The two stories do not just end with occasions of hope and (generational) continuity—with pregnancies and childbirths. They also stage generational benedictions for the black family, especially for black children and (their) futures, hence Morrison's inferable titular play on one of Billie Holiday's most acclaimed songs, "God Bless the Child"—a Holiday assertion rooted in family, as it were; in the parent-child, mother-daughter relationship of Holiday and her mother, Mom Holiday, as Bud Kliment explains (75). Nevertheless, the two narratives finish with performative prayers, with *affirmations* for life and prosperity that Achebe's Igbo people would call *"igo ofo ndu na oganihu."*

In *Anthills*, for instance, Elewa delivers the late Ikem's baby, a girl, whom the deital daughter Beatrice counterintuitively gives a boy's name "AMAECHINA: *May-the-path-never-close. Ama* for short" (206). In *God Help the Child*, Bride, whose real name is Lula Ann, informs Booker that she is pregnant with his baby, which he welcomes as *their* baby, a joyous news for which Bride's mother, Sweetness, though speaking cynically, ends her interior monologue prayerfully: "Good luck and God help the child" (178). Prior to that moment, however, the narrator *affirms:* "A child. New life. [May she or he be] Immune to evil or illness, protected from kidnap, beatings, rape, racism, insult, hurt, self-loathing, abandonment. [May he or she be] Error-free. All goodness. Minus wrath. . . . So they believe," Amen! (175). Also calling on God to bless (*and* help) the (black) child, themselves assembled, and their allegorical African state of Kangan, Elewa's uncle proceeds with the village normative—the customary ritual prayers, to which the ecumenical audience responds *"Isé!"* on each riff (211–12).

Transposing those narrative affirmations to the current endeavor, my hope, really, as conveyed at the outset, is that *Kindred Spirits* becomes the birth/beginning of, and the prayer is that the path would never close on, a sustained and vibrant Achebe-Morrison comparative scholarship. Because black people, no matter the centuries-long effort to blemish and repress them, obviously have a deeply human and living story to tell, and because that story, though geographically dispersed, must be heard, may the transatlantic paths never close to our critical excavation, pedagogic rediscovery, and cultural reconciliation of them. But also because the present effort, *Kindred Spirits,* is an extension of a hope, or rather the path, paved years ago by others, notably Ernest A. Champion, it is befitting that we gesture backward again, village-style, to his *Mr. Baldwin, I Presume.* "Colonialism in Africa, in Asia, and in other parts of the world and slavery in the United States and the Caribbean have given birth to the very unique phenomenon which we now call racism," argues Champion cogently (xii–xiii). Of even greater significance is Champion's transatlantic and curricular vision. He reminds us that, "for too long, education . . . compartmentalized the study of the African continent and that of the African-American as though the two existed independently" (52). Redressing this balkanization was a subtext of Morrison's publication of *Contemporary African Literature.* As that compilation's editors Edris Makward and Leslie Lacy similarly affirm, indirectly concurring with Achebe, whatever their separations, African and African American writers and writings have long been and will remain kindred.

Those interstices I called the "African literature" and "Chinua Achebe" gaps in Morrison studies, and conversely the infinitesimal critical attention paid to what I variously identified as Achebe's westward expansion, his "broadened Atlanticism," and the "America subplot" of his fiction, and indeed his career, could also have stemmed from the polarization Champion decries and Morrison attempted to help remedy. The lacunas may have resulted from what had been African literature's peripheralization in the North American academy. As Abiola Irele argues, for a long time African literature had "difficulty in finding a proper home" in American university education. It had had a fairly "ambiguous institutional and academic status" within it. That disciplinary Disallowal in paradise, so to speak, appeared poised to continue into the 2000s and beyond, save for the drastic changes to "literary studies in the West, with unsettling effects on the traditional conception of literature and the academic organization of its study" (*African* xiii). Irele appears to be speaking here of "the culture wars," those politics- and policy-shaping "battles that raged during the late 1980s and

1990s" over "the literary canon," Henry Louis Gates Jr. reflects, with "that bat-tleground soon expanded to include heated confrontation over the rise of eth-nic and gender studies programs (African American studies, women's studies, gay studies, etc.) and their proper place in any serious Faculty of Arts and Sci-ences, if, indeed, they should have any place at all as freestanding or even quasi-independent, tenure-granting entities" (*Tradition* 113–14).

It would not be exaggerative to also attribute that transformation Irele men-tions to the "arrival" of the younger generation of African and African-descended writers and artists in Africa, Europe, and the United States. With respect to the United States, Stephanie Li contends that the nation-transcending and canon-blurring works by those new African authors, among whom she highlights Teju Cole, Chimamanda Ngozi Adichie, NoViolet Bulawayo, and Dinaw Mengestu (there are several others), have forced a rethinking of canon, more specifically the conventional borders of African American literature and experience. And just as significant, the works have also further troubled anachronistic as well as prevailing constructions of blackness and belonging, Li postulates (*Pan-African* 2018). That African literature would even be subjected to such unwelcoming in the American academy is somewhat ironic, given that black African bodies, the transatlantic slave trade, "underwrote" that academy, as Craig Steven Wilder reminds us (18). "American colleges were not innocent or passive beneficia-ries of conquest and colonial slavery," Wilder states. With buildings, halls, and endowments at various universities and colleges in the United States tellingly named after former slave traders, slaveholders, secessionists, and imperialists; with monuments, imposing and slyly nondescript, erected on campuses' open spaces, "the academy never stood apart from American slavery—in fact, it stood beside church and state as the third pillar of civilization built on bondage" (11).

Nevertheless, if Champion's pairing of African literature's *Things Fall Apart* and Baldwin's *Go Tell It on the Mountain* (1953) could yield such new knowledge about both texts and about the black experience on both sides of the Atlantic, and if a deeper contextualization and analysis of the Achebe and Morrison triads of texts could uncover such additional and sometimes fluid confluences, one could only imagine the dividends of rigorous, monographic bridging of other African diaspora *and* African authors and texts. Evidence of those poten-tialities abounds in the precedent, contemporaneous, and boundary-crossing scholarship of other comparatists with which *Kindred Spirits* shares broad goals, as stated in the introduction. It is crucial, therefore, that we not misper-ceive the transatlantic comparative project as an entirely and/or exclusionary

African–African American exchange. One of my most enduring memories of my undergraduate studies in English at the University of Nigeria, Nsukka, was our required readings not just in British (medieval through Victorian) texts. It was also, especially, our survey course on American literature, our delving into Caribbean fiction, and my cohort's realization of the many historical, thematic, and stylistic path-crossings of those fields and postcolonial African literatures in English, subsumed at the time under that contested imperial umbrella, Commonwealth literature.

It makes common sense, then, that the literal and literary assault on racism, in its infrastructural manifestation as idea, policy, and practice, be tactical and collaboratively resourced. For the domain of culture, the battle would require the mobilization, on both sides of the Atlantic, of those battalions of "archaeologists" that Achebe believed would be needed to unearth the prejudice-concealed and often-distorted truths of black people and their dispersed yet interrelated stories. It is also my view that in the more specific realm of literature, and as it pertains to Africans and their cousins in the diaspora, that fight against antiblackness may similarly entail more than each national, regional, or subregional literature combating the foe from its corner of the world. Nonetheless, in redirecting modern African literature's general continental focus, as well as its inaugural, longitudinal orientation—its North-South, Europe-Africa gaze and concerns—the increasingly transatlantic scope of recent fiction, art, and criticism by both established and younger generations of African culture and intellectual workers offers added pretexts for more studies like *Kindred Spirits*. And instead of Achebe and Morrison's transitions flattening or regressing pedagogic, scholarly, professional, and institutional activities on both authors, their passing should revitalize those engagements, as the Toni Morrison Society intends to do in her case.

Let me end with what I consider perhaps some of the most fascinating epiphanies in this book. Many readers would of course beg to differ. But here they are. One: the narrative ellipses of and the gap-closings between *Things Fall Apart* and *Beloved*. Two: the (Nigerian) Jazz Age of *No Longer at Ease* and the connections of the New African–New Negro movements relative to that novel and *Jazz*. And three: the eye-opening parallels of Ruby, Haven, and Umuaro (to which one must add Umuofia) as slavery-tied all-Black towns; with Umuaro, especially, arguably envisioned as "haven" perhaps in whatever their Igbo-language phrasing. In any case, it is because of such little findings, in addition to all earlier institutional, cultural, and critical efforts to connect Achebe and Morrison, that I believe the paths of comparative scholarship on the two writers and their canons, now hopefully begun with *Kindred Spirits*, will not close. In the end, it is all about the ancestor-enabling, the city- and modernity-inflecting, village. It is about the villagism that village incubates, and about the village novel and village literature more broadly that narrate and widen village's contextual range and conceptual power on both sides of the Atlantic. And not only is the ancient owner the village and the village is cerebral, as Achebe and Morrison jointly contend. But also the village, almost always, gets the last word.

NOTES

INTRODUCTION

1. See *No Longer at Ease* (59–62) for more on the Odogwu conversation.
2. Morrison's work has been dissected through a plethora of critical idioms: "cultural studies, African Americanist, psychoanalytic, neo-Marxist, linguistic, and feminist methodologies," according to Valerie Smith (1). That is not to mention deconstruction, postmodernism, ecocriticism, biblical studies, Doreatha Drummond Mbalia's Nkrumaism/materialist ideology (15–27), and, as Jennifer Lee Jordan Heinert adds, "New Historicist and semiotic analyses" (1), among many others. In most of the Morrison scholarship—and most dismaying in the books, some of them award-winning studies, that explore her ties to ideological Africa and the underpinnings of African cultural, religious, and spiritual epistemologies in her works, and in some that interrogate her writings through anticolonial and/or postcolonial theoretical and critical apparatuses, with a stress on Morrison's innovative language—"Chinua Achebe" is not indexed at all. See, for example, Tally, *Toni Morrison's "Beloved"*; Zauditu-Selassie; Gillespie; Jennings; and Higgins. And in the few single-author and/or comparative studies of Morrison criticism in which he is mentioned in text, the references are generally perfunctory (see, for example, V. Smith 1; Grewal 7; Marrouchi 256; Adams 81–89; Roynon 2013, 107–11; and Li, *Toni Morrison* 31. Leon Botstein's "Things Fall Together" is quite informing and useful.
3. I have in mind here Said's *Orientalism*; Gates's *The Signifying Monkey*; Mudimbe's *The Invention of Africa* and *The Idea of Africa*; Gilroy's *The Black Atlantic* (though Gilroy's conceptual and historicist sidestepping of Africa has been vigorously questioned); Wilentz's *Binding Cultures*; Falola's numerous edited volumes on diaspora, especially *The Atlantic World, 1450–2000*, Okpewho, Davies, and Mazuri's *The African Diaspora*; Okpewho and Nwezi's *The New African Diaspora*; and Gruesser's *Confluences*. There are several others, however. See Gikandi's *Maps of Englishness* and *Slavery and the Culture of Taste*.
4. See Belcher, *Abyssinia's Samuel Johnson: Ethiopian Thought in the Making of an English Author* (2012).

5. In *Africa in Stereo: Modernism, Music, and Pan-African Solidarity* (2014), Jaji interconnects the histories, cultures, and political experiences of Africa and African America, especially, through music, specifically her paradigm of stereomodernism.

6. Mobilizing the idea of black cosmopolitanism, Nwankwo corresponds African American, Caribbean, and Latin American literature in her book *Black Cosmopolitanism: Racial Consciousness and Transnational Identity in the Nineteenth-Century Americas* (2005).

7. See Goyal, *Runaway Genres: The Global Afterlives of Slavery* (2019).

8. Shane Graham links Langston Hughes to African literary history through the notion of "cultural entanglement" in his recent study *Langston Hughes and the Rise of African and Caribbean Literature* (2020).

9. Compounding the matter is how little institutional, critical, and public fanfare this transcontinental project attracted at its release and has commanded since then, compared to, for instance, the recognitions accorded, deservedly I must add, some recent and comparably landmark works on Baldwin. Eddie S. Glaude Jr.'s *James Baldwin's America and Its Urgent Lessons for Our Own* (2020), Aaron Ngozi Oforlea's *James Baldwin, Toni Morrison and the Rhetorics of Black Male Subjectivity* (2017), Raoul Peck's documentary *I Am Not Your Negro* (2016), Jesmyn Ward's *The Fire This Time: A New Generation Speaks about Race* (2016), and Ta-Nehisi Coates's *Between the World and Me* (2015) come quickly to mind.

10. See, for example, Jeyifo, "Intimations"; N. Brown; Rehm; Beckmann; and P. G. Williams.

11. Consider these somewhat arbitrarily presented and synopsized commonalities: Achebe and Morrison first met, so to speak, in the spirit of modernist ideas and letters, and a world in a state of temporal flux. In about the same year, 1955, that Morrison was completing that much-investigated master's thesis and Achebe had just begun drafting by hand a story he planned as the epic saga of a family's three generations, both authors—young and virtually unknown black writers on both sides of the Atlantic—inscribed the same W. B. Yeats poetic phrase "things fall apart" in their first major creative and academic publications. On page 2 of her thesis's introduction, Morrison writes, "Current isolation is not 'alienation within a stable world, but in a world where 'things fall apart.'" Furthermore, the same transgenerational subjects she explored in that thesis, namely, alienation, exiles, and suicides, are also themes of Achebe's *Things Fall Apart* and *No Longer at Ease*.

And these as well: Achebe and Morrison grew up in nations that have human, economic, and cultural ties that go back centuries. Although Nigeria was a "colony of occupation" and the United States a "settler colony" (Ashcroft,

Griffith, and Tiffin 211), both countries were, nonetheless, former dominions of Britain. Besides their embroilments in the transatlantic slave trade and colonization, Achebe and Morrison's nations each fought a postindependence civil war. The wars pitted each country's northern and (in the case of Nigeria) *Southe*astern regions, with the seceding Souths, in whose geographic borders most of the battles and bloodshed took place, losing in the catastrophic, fracturing, and still-haunting conflicts. As children, Achebe and Morrison were respectively raised in storytelling and Christian (Anglican and mostly Catholic) households that not only bequeathed them love of imaginative creation. They also modeled for them the necessity and possibilities of reconciling the sacred and secular worlds. They came of age and received Western education in parallel years, graduating from college the same year, 1953: Achebe, from the University College, Ibadan, and Morrison, from Howard University. More so, Achebe and Morrison, both of whom engaged in name change, were influential editors (see also D. Williams).

Both authors' views are congruent on the question of modernity and (literary) modernism. They analogously write diligently because, to them, storytelling is not a frivolous act but rather a matter of grave import. They agree on the questions of author-audience relationship; locality versus universality in art; ethics/morality in art; and the issue of authorial responsibility, commitment, and literary/aesthetic objectivity. Their stances are the same on the art-versus-politics debate and on the issue of Western colonialist criticism of their work and that of other black and Third World writers. They interweave material from history, anthropology, folklore, and mythology. Both write with considerable restraint. They uniformly eschew adjectival and adverbial modifiers, and are masters of dialogue and disambiguation. They separately and together have engaged with the tightly interconnected heavy topics of race and slavery and colonization and home and love and betrayal and mercy and memory and (ir)regular members of the community, including (a)typical mothers and spirit children, madmen and "tarred" women, thieves and soldiers, politicians and the proletariat, priests and preachers, among other captivating figures. They write extensively about Christian religion and also pick characters/character names from the Bible. For instance, their novels and short stories invoke nominal "Pilate" and feature characters named Hannah, Joshua, Joseph/"Joe," Michael, Margaret, Jacob, Florens/Florence, Esther, Jean, Elizabeth, Mercy, John, Beatrice, William, Bill, and Mr. Smith. They have been drawn to the Corinthians and have also written of recitative and Desdemona. Their stories feature parrots, esoteric caves, spirit encounters, one-legged old women, hunters, and blacksmiths. They tell stories for and about children, and point comparably to the lasting psychic scars of parental and/or grandparental action and love, or lack thereof, on the present and next generations. And they are also keen social observers, fierce cultural critics, and impactful consciences of their nations.

This book's titular phrase gestures to Ernest A. Champion's identification of the artistic bond between Achebe and James Baldwin.

12. I also owe the modified phrase "low-hanging fruit" to one of the University of Virginia's peer reviewers who evaluated this book's proposal.

13. In her study *The New Jim Crow* (2012), Michelle Alexander reminds us about the metamorphoses and sometimes indecipherable continuities of slavery and Jim Crow in new systemic policies and institutional practices of law and mass incarceration designed to disempower black men, dispossess them of freedom, and consign them to a cyclically subordinated underclass in what Alexander calls "a new racial caste system."

14. I will say more on this in chapter 2.

15. The list includes, in no particular order: John Milton, René Descartes, Mark Twain, William Faulkner, Virginia Woolf, Ernest Hemingway, Willa Cather, Nathaniel Hawthorne, Edgar Allan Poe, Herman Melville, F. Scott Fitzgerald, John Irving, James Joyce, Thomas Hardy, Gabriel García Márquez, E. L. Doctorow, Sinclair Lewis, Zora Neale Hurston, Richard Wright, Ralph Ellison, James Baldwin, Paule Marshall, Gayl Jones, Ben Okri, Camara Laye, Wole Soyinka, J. M. Coetzee, Audre Lorde, Dionne Brand, Thomas Pynchon, Jonathan Safran Foer, Margaret Atwood, Marcel Proust, Jean Rhys, Jamaica Kincaid, Philip Roth, Bobbie Ann Mason, Lee Smith, William Shakespeare, Dante, Henry James, T. S. Eliot, Saul Bellow, Eudora Welty, Maxine Hong Kingston, Leslie Silko, Sarah Orne Jewett, Olaudah Equiano, Frantz Fanon, Ayi Kwei Armah, Ama Ata Aidoo, Tayeb Salih, Leila Aboulela, Alice Walker, Gloria Naylor, Toni Cade Bambara, Phillis Wheatley, Theresa Hak Kyung Cha, Phillis Alesia Perry, Emma Pérez, Paule Gunn Allen, Kathy Acker, Anne Hutchison, Reinhold Niebuhr, Flannery O'Connor, Chimamanda Ngozi Adichie, John Winthrop, Aeschylus, Euripides, the classical tradition, the Bible, among others.

16. This conversation, officially captioned "Reading the Writing: A Conversation between Toni Morrison and Claudia Brodsky," is uploaded on YouTube under the title "Toni Morrison on Language, and the 'White Gaze.'"

17. PEN America, "Tribute to Chinua Achebe," August 8, 2008.

18. In "Faulkner and Joyce in Morrison's *Song of Solomon*," David Cowart argues that, even though Morrison might disapprove of his reading, it is his position that her debts to Faulkner are extensive and incontrovertible.

19. I thank one of the peer reviewers of the manuscript for reminding me of this Foucault caution.

1. "THINGS FALL TOGETHER"

1. The essay could be considered alongside such other pieces as W. E. B. Du Bois's "Criteria of Negro Art," Alain Locke's "The New Negro," Zora Neale Hurston's "Characteristics of Negro Expression," Richard Wright's "Blueprint for Negro Writing," and Larry Neal's "The Black Arts Movement."
2. I am mirroring Henry Louis Gates Jr.'s description of Esu-Elegbara as "the figure of figures."
3. See, for example, Blassingame; Raboteau; Genovese; and Herskovits.
4. These works come immediately to mind: Marouan; Patton; M. Anderson, *Spectrality*; West; Zauditu-Selassie; La Jennings, *Toni Morrison and the Idea of Africa*; and Higgins.
5. Chimamanda Ngozi Adichie's employment of blogs/blogging in *Americanah* and Nnedi Okoroafor's novels come quickly to mind. But for more, see Ivor W. Hartmann's edited volume *AfroSF: Science Fiction by African Writers* (2012).
6. These are assembled from the various Morrison interviews collected in Danille Taylor-Guthrie's *Conversations with Toni Morrison* and Carolyn C. Denard's *Toni Morrison: Conversations*.
7. See Morrison, "Behind the Making" and "Rediscovering"; and Naylor, "A Conversation," 199.
8. See Ezenwa-Ohaeto for the full story, 104–5.
9. For Morrison, see her *Playing in the Dark*; Nobel lecture *The Dancing Mind*; the essays "James Baldwin: His Voice Remembered; Life in His Language"; and the just-cited "Home," as well as countless interviews, most importantly those she had with Mel Watkins, Charles Ruas, Thomas LeClair, Nellie McKay, Bessie Jones and Audrey Vinson, Christina Davis, Salman Rushdie, Elissa Schappell, A. J. Verdelle, and Carolyn C. Denard. And for Achebe, see the essay cited above, and also "English and the African Writer," "Language and the Destiny of Man," "The African Writer and the English Language," "An Image of Africa: Racism in Conrad's *Heart of Darkness*," and "Politics and Politicians of Language in African Literature."
10. See Ezenwa-Ohaeto, *Chinua Achebe*, 46–49; see also Searle 162.
11. N. McKay, 142–46; see also LeClair 120–21.
12. The latter two essays are collected contiguously in his volume *Hopes and Impediments*.
13. See, for instance, Christopher Okonkwo, "Chinua Achebe's Blue Notes."

2. REMEMORYING THE (VILLAGE) PASTS WHERE
THE RAINS BEGAN TO BEAT US

1. In 1996 and 2009, respectively, the journal *Research in African Literatures* published special issues on diaspora and slavery. Edited by Simon Gikandi, volume 27, number 4 (1996) gathers provocative contributions that responded to the gap in concept and historicity contained in Paul Gilroy's then recently published *The Black Atlantic*. Volume 40, number 4 (2009), edited by Adélékè Adéèkó, compiles essays on the theme "Writing Slavery in(to) the African Diaspora." Needless to say, discussion of what I am calling the kindred rancor continues in other studies and environments.

2. This Adichie piece, "Chinua Achebe at 80: 'We Remember Differently,'" appears online in *Premium Times*, November 23, 2012.

3. Many will remember Henry Louis Gates, for instance, making that insinuation of the African continent being cursed some time ago in one of his PBS series.

4. Morrison makes this claim in the essay "The Slavebody and the Blackbody," 76–77.

5. See, for instance, Charles Nnolim, "A Source for 'Arrow of God'" (1977).

6. See Osinubi, "Chinua Achebe and the Uptakes of African Slaveries" for more on this.

7. See Okonkwo, *A Spirit of Dialogue*, introduction and chap. 1.

8. Originally the title of Lewis Allen's protest poem which he showed to Billie Holiday and which will become one of her signature and most haunting songs, "Strange Fruit" is about "lynchings in the South," writes Bud Kliment in *Billie Holiday*, "and the strange fruit of the title refers to the bodies of lynched blacks hanging from the branches of a tree. Holiday was so moved by the poem and, with the help of Sonny White, her accompanist at the time, she adapted it into a song" (64–65).

9. I make this argument in my essay "Chinua Achebe's Blue Note." Please see the article for more.

10. See, for instance, Jeyifo, "For Chinua" (55–56); Phelan (237–38); Perez-Torres (93); and Adéèkó (2011).

3. SLAVERY, MIGRATION, URBANITY, KINDRED BLACK MUSIC,
AND THE ANOMIES OF NEW VILLAGE BLACK SUBJECTIVITIES

1. Valerie Smith makes this point in *Toni Morrison: Writing the Moral Imagination* (84). But there's also a case to be made for *Beloved* in that regard.

2. Morrison relates *Jazz* to a "detective story." She offered this comparison in her interview with Elissa Schappell (80).

3. In his preface to *Renascent Africa*, Nnamdi Azikiwe sketches his vision of Africa's renascence. Seeing renascent Africa as "the Africa of to-day," he describes the renascent African as "exist[ing] in a transitional stage between the Old and the New Africans. He refuses to view his fortune passively. He is articulate. He is destined to usher forth the New Africa" (8–9). Furthermore, Azikiwe outlines these five bases for the philosophy of a New Africa: "Spiritual Balance," "Social Regeneration," "Economic Determinism," "Mental Emancipation," and "National Risorgimento," all in italics (8–11).

4. I am playing on a song title by the Caribbean musician Billy Ocean, "Love Zone."

5. Further research is needed to officially corroborate the statement on the Lagos interment ground, the source of which is an online description of a Lagos veterans cemetery dated to the World War I era. The government is associated with ownership of the lot. However, for more on African soldiers of World War I, please see the Deutsche Welle (DW) online piece "World War I: The 'Black Army' That Marched in from Africa," www.dw.com/en/world-war-i -the-black-army-that-marched-in-from-africa/a-4623927, which is in part the source of my assertions on the subject. While so much has been written over the years about African Americans' centuries-long participation in U.S. and global conflicts, little published history exists on African World War I soldiers. Hopefully correcting this dearth, however, is *White War, Black Soldiers: Two African Accounts of World War I* (2021). This is the George Robb–edited volume of the personal accounts of the conflict by the book's authors and World War I veterans Barkary Diallo and Lamine Senghor.

6. See, for instance, Foner; Bordewich, *Bound for Canaan*; Osofsky; and J. W. Johnson, *Black Manhattan*.

7. Refer to note 3 above.

8. See Obiechina, *Onitsha Market Literature*, for an extended discussion of this tradition of pamphleteering.

9. This realization struck me as I worked on this chapter. If wrong, I would gladly stand corrected.

10. See my previous study *A Spirit of Dialogue* (2008) for more discussion of this.

11. I am playing on the title of Susan Willis's essay on Morrison titled "Eruptions of Funk: Historicizing Toni Morrison," published in *Black American Literature Forum* 6.1 (1982). "Funk" in my usage refers to things Christian missionaries and colonial masters intended to repress in the colonized because they thought them repugnant and primitive.

12. Morrison has said she agrees with her readers that she writes a lot about love. But actually, it is betrayal that "I am always writing about," she amends. "Love is the weather. Betrayal is the lightning that cleaves and reveals it" (see Morrison's foreword to *Love*, x).

13. The various essays collected in this volume examine Achebe's engagement with gender. But the subject of love does not feature in the index, although Chukwuma's essay title suggests it as the focus.

14. I am not aware of sustained discussions of the theme of music in Achebe's fiction.

15. I identified these genres from examining Achebe's novels and short stories.

16. See, for instance, Munton.

17. I am thinking here of, for example, Emmanuel Obiechina's discussion of high-life in *Culture, Tradition and Society in the West African Novel* (79–80).

4. ON BLACK VILLAGE HAVENS IMPELLED BY HISTORY, IMPEDED BY OPPOSING VISIONS OF THE (PAST) WILLS OF GODS AND FOUNDERS

1. I am playing here also on bell hooks's eponymous phrase *Killing Rage: Ending Racism* (1995).

2. See Achebe's "Preface to the Second Edition" of *Arrow of God*; and Wren, "Achebe's Revision of *Arrow of God*" (1976).

3. In *Achebe's World*, Robert Wren addresses Charles Nnolim's article on the hardly coincidental parallels between this 1953 Nnolim booklet about an Umuchu priest who refused Warrant Chieftaincy and *Arrow of God*'s Ezeulu. Wren also believes Afigbo's research on the warrant chiefs for his Ph.D. possibly influenced Achebe (85–86).

4. I am of course playing on the 1974 Ali–Foreman heavyweight fight in Kinshasa, Zaire (now Congo), popularly known as "The Rumble in the Jungle." The pun here is that the intellectual heavyweights Frazier and Herskovits are engaged in a contest over the survival in America of cultural beliefs and practices of Africa, viewed in racist Western imagination as a jungle.

BIBLIOGRAPHY

Abani, Chris. *GraceLand*. London: Picador, 2004.

Achebe, Chinua. "Africa Is People." *Massachusetts Review* 40.3 (1999): 313–21.

———. "African Literature as a Restoration of Celebration." *Chinua Achebe: A Celebration,* edited by Kirsten Holst Petersen and Anna Rutherford. Portsmouth, NH; Heinemann, 1990. 1–10.

———. *Anthills of the Savannah*. New York: Anchor, 1987.

———. *Arrow of God*. New York: Anchor, 1989.

———. *Chike and the River*. Cambridge: Cambridge UP, 1966.

———. "Chike's School Days." *Girls at War and Other Stories.* New York: Fawcett Premier, 1973. 37–42.

———. "Chinua Achebe on Biafra." *Transition* 36 (1968): 31–38.

———. *Christmas in Biafra and Other Poems*. New York: Doubleday, 1973.

———. "Colonialist Criticism." *Hopes and Impediments: Selected Essays.* New York: Anchor, 1988. 68–90.

———. "The Day I Finally Met Baldwin." *Callaloo* 25.2 (2002): 502–4.

———. "Dead Men's Path." *Girls at War and Other Stories.* New York: Fawcett Premier, 1973. 70–74.

———. *The Drum*. Enugu, Nigeria: Fourth Dimension, 1977.

———. "The Education of a British-Protected Child." *The Education of a British-Protected Child: Essays.* London: Penguin, 2009. 3–24.

———. "The Empire Fights Back." *Home and Exile.* New York: Anchor, 2000. 37–72.

———. "English and the African Writer." *Transition* 18 (1965): 27–30.

———. *The Flute*. Enugu, Nigeria: Fourth Dimension, 1977.

———. *Girls at War and Other Stories*. New York: Fawcett Premier, 1973.

———. *Home and Exile*. New York: Anchor, 2000.

———. *Hopes and Impediments: Selected Essays*. New York: Anchor, 1988.

———. "The Igbo World and Its Art." *Hopes and Impediments: Selected Essays.* New York: Anchor, 1988. 63–67.

———. "Impediments to Dialogue between North and South." *Hopes and Impediments: Selected Essays.* New York: Anchor, 1988. 21–29.

———. "The Judge and I Didn't Go to Namibia." *Callaloo* 13.1 (1990): 82–85.

———. *A Man of the People*. New York: Anchor, 1966.

———. "Marriage Is a Private Affair." *Girls at War and Other Stories.* New York: Fawcett Premier, 1973. 22–30.

———. *Morning Yet on Creation Day: Essays.* New York: Anchor, 1976.

———. "Named for Victoria: Queen of England." *Hopes and Impediments: Selected Essays.* New York: Anchor, 1988. 30–39.

———. *No Longer at Ease.* New York: Anchor, 1994.

———. "The Novelist as Teacher." *Hopes and Impediments: Selected Essays.* New York: Anchor, 1988. 40–46.

———. "Onitsha, Gift of the Niger." *Morning Yet on Creation Day: Essays.* New York: Anchor, 1976. 126–30.

———. "Publishing in Africa." *Morning Yet on Creation Day: Essays.* New York: Anchor, 1976. 85–91.

———. "The Role of the Writer in a New Nation." *African Writers on African Writing.* Ed. G. D. Killam. Evanston, IL: Northwestern UP, 1973. 7–13.

———. "Spelling Our Proper Names." *The Education of a British-Protected Child: Essays.* 2009. 54–67.

———. "The Sweet Aroma of Zik's Kitchen: Growing up in the Ambience of a Legend." *The Education of a British-Protected Child: Essays.* New York: Knopf, 2009. 25–34.

———. *There Was a Country: A Personal History of Biafra.* London: Penguin, 2012.

———. "Thoughts on the African Novel." *Hopes and Impediments: Selected Essays.* New York: Anchor, 1988. 91–99.

———. "Today, the Balance of Stories." *Home and Exile.* New York: Anchor, 2000. 73–105.

———. *The Trouble with Nigeria.* Enugu, Nigeria: Fourth Dimension, 1983.

———. "The Truth of Fiction." *Hopes and Impediments: Selected Essays.* New York: Anchor, 1988. 138–53.

———. "Uncle Ben's Choice." *Girls at War and Other Stories.* New York: Fawcett Premier, 1973. 75–82.

———. "What Has Literature Got to Do with It?" *Hopes and Impediments: Selected Essays.* New York: Anchor, 1988. 154–70.

———. "Where Angels Fear to Tread." *Morning Yet on Creation Day: Essays.* New York: Anchor, 1976. 61–64.

———. "The Writer and His Community." *Hopes and Impediments: Selected Essays.* New York: Anchor, 1988. 45–61.

———. *Things Fall Apart.* New York: Anchor, 1994.

Achebe, Nwando. "Global Celebrations of the 50th Anniversary of *Arrow of God*: The Gift of Remembrance." *Illuminations on Chinua Achebe: The Art of Resistance.* Ed. Mĩcere Gĩthae Mũgo and Hebert G. Ruffin II. Trenton, NJ: Africa World, 2017. 147–58.

Achinivu, Achinivu Kanu. *Ikoli Harcourt Whyte: The Man and His Music, A Case of Musical Acculturation in Nigeria.* Hamburg: Verlag der Musikalienhandlung, 1979.

Adams, Anne V. "'I Haven't Seen You in 400 Years!': Chinua Achebe and African American Writing." *Chinua Achebe: Tributes and Reflections.* Ed. Nana Ayebia Clarke and James Currey. Ayebia Clarke, 2014. 81–89.

Adéèkó, Adélékè. "Introduction." *Writing Slavery in(to) the African Diaspora.* Spec. issue of *Research in African Literatures* 40.4 (2009): vii–xi.

———. "Okonkwo, Textual Closure, Colonial Conquest." *Research in African Literatures* 42.2 (2011): 72–86.

Adichie, Chimamanda Ngozi. *Half of a Yellow Sun.* New York: Knopf, 2006.

———. Introduction. *Chinua Achebe: The African Trilogy: Things Fall Apart, No Longer at Ease, Arrow of God.* London: Everyman's Library, 2010. vii–xiii.

———. *Purple Hibiscus.* New York: Anchor, 2003.

———. "Still Becoming: At Home in Lagos with Chimamanda Ngozi Adichie." *Esquire* 4 March 2019. www.esquire.com/uk/culture/a27283913/still -becoming-at-home-in-lagos-with-chimamanda-ngozi-adichie.

Adjaye, David, et al. "Luminous City, Luminous Gallery." *New African Fiction.* Spec. issue of *Transition* 117 (2015): 198–209.

Afigbo, Adiele. *The Abolition of the Slave Trade in Southeastern Nigeria, 1885–1950.* Rochester, NY: U of Rochester P, 2006.

Afrique. "An Interview with Chinua Achebe." *Conversations with Chinua Achebe.* Ed. Bernth Lindfors. Jackson: UP of Mississippi, 1997. 7–10.

Akwani, Obi O. *March of Ages.* Enugu, Nigeria: Fourth Dimension, 2003.

Alexander, Michelle. *The New Jim Crow: Mass Incarceration in the Age of Color Blindness.* Rev. ed. New York: New Press, 2012.

Allen, Brooke. "The Promised Land." *New York Times Books Review* 11 January 1998.

Alwes, Derek. "The Burden of Liberty: Choice in Toni Morrison's Jazz and Toni Cade Bambara's The Salt Eaters." *African American Review* 30.3 (1996): 353–65.

Amadi, Elechi. *The Slave.* Portsmouth, NH: Heinemann, 1978.

Amoah-Ramey, Nana Abena. *Female Highlife Performers in Ghana: Expression, Resistance, and Advocacy.* Lanham, MD: Lexington, 2018.

Andersen, Richard. *Toni Morrison.* New York: Marshall Cavendish Benchmark, 2006.

Anderson, Benedict. *Imagined Communities: Reflections on the Origin and Spread of Nationalism.* London: Verso, 2016.

Anderson, Carol. *The Second: Race and Guns in a Fatally Unequal America.* New York: Bloomsbury, 2021.

———. *White Rage: The Unspoken Truth of Our Racial Divide.* London: Bloomsbury, 2016.

Anderson, Jervis. "Ralph Ellison Goes: The Author of 'Invisible Man' Revisits his Oklahoma Childhood.'" *New Yorker* 22 November 1976.

Anderson, Melanie R. *Spectrality in the Novels of Toni Morrison.* Knoxville: U of Tennessee P, 2013.

——. "'What Would Be on the Other Side?': Spectrality and Spirit Work in Toni Morrison's *Paradise.*" *African American Review* 42.2 (2008): 307–21.

Appiah, Kwame Anthony. Foreword. *The African Trilogy: Things Fall Apart, Arrow of God, No Longer at Ease.* London: Penguin Classics, 2017. vii–xi.

——. Introduction. *Things Fall Apart.* By Chinua Achebe. New York: Knopf, 1992. v–xvii.

Arinze, Francis A. *Sacrifice in Ibo Religion.* Ibadan, Nigeria: Ibadan UP, 1970.

Ashcroft, Bill, Gareth Griffiths, and Helen Tiffin. *Key Concepts in Post-Colonial Studies.* London: Routledge, 1998.

Attah, Ayesha H. *The Hundred Wells of Salaga.* New York: Other P, 2019.

Awkward, Michael. *Inspiriting Influences: Tradition, Revision, and Afro-American Women's Novels.* New York: Columbia UP, 1989.

Ayandele, Emmanuel Ayankami. *The Missionary Impact on Modern Nigeria, 1842–1914: A Political and Social Analysis.* New York: Humanities P, 1967.

Azikiwe, Nnamdi. *My Odyssey: An Autobiography.* New York: Praeger, 1970.

——. *Renascent Africa.* New York: Negro UP, 1969.

Babalola, C. A. "A Reconsideration of Achebe's *No Longer at Ease.*" *Phylon* 47.2 (2nd Qtr. 1986): 139–47.

Baderoon, Gabeba. "The African Oceans—Tracing the Sea as Memory of Slavery in South African Literature and Culture." *Research in African Literatures* 40.4 (2009): 89–107.

Baker, Houston A., Jr. *Modernism and the Harlem Renaissance.* Chicago: U of Chicago P, 1987.

Bakerman, Jane. "The Seams Can't Show: An Interview with Toni Morrison." *Conversations with Toni Morrison.* Ed. Danille Taylor-Guthrie. Jackson: UP of Mississippi, 1994. 30–42.

Baldwin, James. "If Black English Isn't a Language, Then Tell Me, What Is?" *The Price of the Ticket: Collected Nonfiction, 1948–1985.* New York: St. Martin's, 1985. 649–52.

——. "The Language of the Streets." *Literature and the Urban Experience: Essays on the City and Literature.* Ed. Michael C. Jaye and Ann Chalmers Watts. New Brunswick, NJ: Rutgers UP, 1981. 133–37.

——. "Princes and Powers." *The Price of the Ticket: Collected Nonfiction, 1948–1985.* New York: St. Martin's, 1985. 41–63.

Banks, William M. *Black Intellectuals: Race and Responsibility in American Life.* New York: Norton, 1996.

Baptist, Edward E. *The Half Has Never Been Told: Slavery and the Making of American Capitalism.* New York: Basic, 2014.

Baraka, Amiri. "Black Literature and the Afro-American Nation: The Urban Voice." *Literature and the Urban Experience: Essays on the City and Literature.* Ed. Michael C. Jaye and Ann Chalmers Watts. New Brunswick, NJ: Rutgers UP, 1981. 139–59.

Baxter, Lee, and Martha Satz, eds. *Toni Morrison on Mothers and Motherhood.* Ontario, Canada: Demeter, 2017.

Beckmann, Felicia. "The Portrayal of Africana Males in Achebe, Marshall, Morrison, and Wideman." *Journal of Black Studies* 32.4 (2002): 405–21.

Beier, Ulli. *Introduction to African Literature: An Anthology of Critical Writing from Black Orpheus.* Evanston: Northwestern UP, 1967.

Belcher, Wendy Laura. *Abyssinia's Samuel Johnson: Ethiopian Thought in the Making of an English Author.* Oxford: Oxford UP, 2012.

Bennett, Juda. *Toni Morrison and the Queer Pleasure of Ghosts.* Albany: State U of New York P, 2014.

Bennett, Juda, Winnifred Brown-Glaude, Cassandra Jackson, and Piper Kenrix Williams. *The Toni Morrison Book Club.* Madison: U of Wisconsin P, 2020.

Benston, Kimberly W. "I Yam What I Yam: The Topos of (Un)naming in African American Literature." *Black Literature and Literary Theory.* Ed. Henry Louis Gates Jr. New York: Methuen, 1984. 151–72.

Berliner, Paul F. *Thinking in Jazz: The Art of Infinite Improvisation.* Chicago: U of Chicago P, 1994.

Bhabha, Homi K. *The Location of Culture.* London: Routledge, 2006.

Blackburn, Sarah. "*Sula* (1974)." *Toni Morrison: Critical Perspectives Past and Present.* Ed. Henry Louis Gates Jr. and K. A. Appiah. New York: Amistad, 1993. 6–8.

Black Creation Annual. "Conversation with Alice Childress and Toni Morrison." *Conversations with Toni Morrison.* Ed. Danille Taylor-Guthrie. Jackson: UP of Mississippi, 1994. 3–9.

Blassingame, John W. *The Slave Community: Plantation Life in the Antebellum South.* New York: Oxford UP, 1979.

Bloom, Harold. "Editor's Note." *Bloom's Modern Critical Views: Toni Morrison: New Edition.* Ed. Bloom. Bloom's Literary Criticism, 2011. vii.

———. Introduction. *Bloom's Modern Critical Views.* 1–5.

Boateng, Yaw. *The Return: A Novel.* New Yok: Pantheon, 1977.

Booker, M. Keith, ed. *The Chinua Achebe Encyclopedia.* Westport, CT: Greenwood, 2003.

Bordewich, Fergus M. *Bound for Canaan: The Epic Story of the Underground Railroad, America's First Civil Rights Movement.* New York: Amistad, 2006.

Botstein, Leon. "Things Fall Together." *Transition* 89 (2001): 150–65.

Bouson, J. Brooks. *Quiet as It's Kept: Shame, Trauma, and Race in the Novels of Toni Morrison*. Albany: State U of New York P, 2000.

Brodsky, Claudia. "Toni Morrison on Language, Evil, and 'The White Gaze.'" Youtube.com. 8 March 2013. www.youtube.com/watch?v=FAs3E1AgNeM.

Brooks, Jerome. Interview. "Chinua Achebe, The Art of Fiction." *Paris Review* 36.133 (1994): 142–66.

Brooks, Peter. *Reading for the Plot: Design and Intention in Narrative*. Cambridge, MA: Harvard UP, 1984.

Brown, Cecil. "Interview with Toni Morrison." *Toni Morrison: Conversations*. Ed. Carolyn C. Denard. Jackson: UP of Mississippi, 2008. 107–25.

Brown, Nicholas. *Utopian Generations: The Political Horizon of Twentieth-Century Literature*. Princeton, NJ: Princeton UP, 2005.

Bruce, Dickson D., Jr. *The Origins of African American Literature, 1680–1865*. Charlottesville: U of Virginia P, 2001.

Bruck, Peter, and Wolfgang Karrer. *The Afro-American Novel Since 1960*. Amsterdam: B. R. Grüner, 1982.

Burns, James, and Abel A. Bartley. "*The Great White Hope* (1970): A Forgotten Biopic?" *Invented Lives, Imagined Communities: The Biopic and American National Identity*. Ed. William H. Epstein and R. Barton Palmer. State U of New York P, 2016. 223–37.

Burrows, Victoria. *Whiteness and Trauma: The Mother-Daughter Knot in the Fiction of Jean Rhys, Jamaica Kincaid and Toni Morrison*. Palgrave, 2004.

Butler-Evans, Elliott. *Race, Gender, and Desire: Narrative Strategies in the Fiction of Toni Cade Bambara, Toni Morrison, and Alice Walker*. Philadelphia: Temple UP, 1989.

Carby, Hazel V. *Race Men*. Cambridge, MA: Harvard UP, 1998.

Carrasco, Davíd. "Magically Flying with Toni Morrison: Mexico, Gabriel García Márquez, *Song of Solomon*, and *Sula*." Ed. Adrienne Lanier Seward and Justin Tally. Jackson: UP of Mississippi, 2014. 144–56.

Carretta, Vincent. Rev. of *Olaudah Equiano and the Igbo World: History, Society, and Atlantic Connections*, ed. Chima J. Korieh. *Writing Slavery in(to) the African Diaspora*. Spec. issue of *Research in African Literatures* 40.4 (2009): 183–84.

Carroll, David. *Chinua Achebe: Novelist, Poet, Critic*. Houndmills: Macmillan, 1980.

Cataliotti, Robert H. *The Music in African American Fiction*. New York: Garland, 1995.

Challenor, Herchelle Sullivan. "No Longer at Ease: Confrontation at the 12th Annual African Studies Association Meeting at Montreal." *The Crisis of African Studies*. Spec. issue of *Africa Today* 16.5/6 (1969): 4–7.

Chametzky, Jules. *Our Decentralized Literature: Cultural Meditations in Selected Jewish and Southern Writers*. Amherst: U of Massachusetts P, 1986.

Champion, Ernest A. *Mr. Baldwin, I Presume, James Baldwin-Chinua Achebe: A Meeting of the Minds.* Lanham, MD: UP of America, 1995.

Charles, Mark, and Soong-Chan Rah. *Unsettling Truths: The Ongoing, Dehumanizing Legacy of the Doctrine of Discovery.* Downers Grove, IL: InterVarsity, 2019.

Charras, Françoise. "The West Indian Presence in Alain Locke's *The New Negro* (1925)." *Temples of Tomorrow: Looking Back at the Harlem Renaissance.* Ed. Geneviève Fabre and Michael Feith. Bloomington: Indiana UP, 2001. 270–87.

Cheney-Coker, Syl. *The Last Harmattan of Alusine Dunbar.* London: Heinemann, 1990.

Christian, Barbara. "A Conversation on Toni Morrison's Beloved." *Toni Morrison's "Beloved": A Casebook.* Ed. William L. Andrews and Nellie McKay. New York: Oxford UP, 1999. 203–20.

———. "Layered Rhythms: Virginia Woolf and Toni Morrison." *New Black Feminist Criticism, 1985–2000.* Ed. Gloria Bowles, M. Giulia Fabi, and Arlene R. Keizer. Urbana: U of Illinois P, 2007. 127–41.

Christian, Barbara, et al. *Black Women Novelists: The Development of a Tradition, 1892–1976.* Westport, CT: Greenwood, 1980.

Christiansë, Yvette. *Toni Morrison: An Ethical Poetics.* New York: Fordham UP, 2013.

Chu-Jua, Sundiata Keita. *America's First Black Town: Brooklyn, Illinois, 1830–1915.* Urbana and Chicago: U of Illinois P, 2000.

Chukwuma, Helen. "Love and Motherhood in Chinua Achebe's Novels." *Achebe's Women: Imagism and Power.* Ed. Chukwuma. Trenton, NJ: Africa World, 2012. 89–100.

Clarke, Nana Ayebia, and James Curry, eds. *Chinua Achebe: Tributes and Reflections.* Ayebia Clarke, 2014.

Coates, Ta-Nehisi. *Between the World and Me.* New York: Spiegel and Grau, 2015.

Cole, Herbert M. *Mbari: Art and Life among the Owerri Igbo.* Bloomington: Indiana UP, 1982.

Collins, John. "The Early History of West African Highlife Music." Spec. issue of *Popular Music* 8.3 (1989): 221–30.

———. *Highlife Giants: West African Dance Band Pioneers.* Abuja: Cassava Republic P, 2016.

———. "Jazz Feedback to Africa." *American Music* 5.2 (1987): 176–93.

———. "Musical Feedback: African America's Music in Africa." *African Diaspora Studies.* Spec. issue of *Issue: A Journal of Opinion* 24.2 (1996): 26–27.

Conner, Marc C. "Modernity and the Homeless: Toni Morrison and the Fictions of Modernism." *Toni Morrison: Memory and Meaning.* Ed. Adrienne Lanier Seward and Justine Tally. Jackson: UP of Mississippi, 2014. 19–32.

Cosier, Stelamaris. *Bridging the Americas: The Literature of Paule Marshall, Toni Morrison, and Gayl Jones.* Philadelphia: Temple UP, 1991.

Cott, Jonathan. "Chinua Achebe: At the Crossroads." *Conversations with Chinua Achebe*. Ed. Bernth Lindfors. Jackson: UP of Mississippi, 1997. 76–87.

Cowart, David. "Faulkner and Joyce in Morrison's *Song of Solomon*." *Bloom's Modern Critical Views*, 7–18.

Crowther, Michael. *The History of Nigeria*. London: Faber and Faber, 1978.

C-Span 2. "In-Depth: Toni Morrison." February 4, 2001.

Cullen, Countee. "Heritage." *My Soul's High Song: The Collected Writings of Countee Cullen, Voice of the Harlem Renaissance*. Ed. Gerald Early. New York: Anchor, 1991. 104–8.

Currey, James. *Africa Writes Back: The African Writers Series and the Launch of African Literature*. Woodbridge, Suffolk, UK: James Currey, 2008.

———. "Chinua Achebe, the African Writers Series and the Establishment of African Literature." *African Affairs* 102.409 (2003): 575–85.

———. "Literary Publishing after Nigerian Independence; Mbari as Celebration." *(in)Visibility in African Cultures*. Spec. issue, *Research in African Literatures* 44.2 (2013): 8–16.

Dalsgård, Katrine. "The One All-Black Town Worth the Pain: (African) American Exceptionalism, Historical Narration, and the Critique of Nationhood in Toni Morrison's *Paradise*." *African American Review* 32.2 (2001): 233–48.

Danticat, Edwidge. *Create Dangerously: The Immigrant Artist at Work*. New York: Vintage, 2010.

Davidson, Basil. *The Black Man's Burden: Africa and the Curse of the Nation-State*. New York: Times Books, 1992.

Davis, Christina. "An Interview with Toni Morrison." *Conversations with Toni Morrison*. Ed. Danielle Taylor-Guthrie. Jackson: UP of Mississippi, 1994. 223–33.

Denard, Carolyn. "Blacks, Modernism, and the American South: An Interview with Toni Morrison." *Toni Morrison: Conversations*. Ed. Denard. Jackson: UP of Mississippi, 2008. 178–95.

———. "The Long, High Gaze: The Mythical Consciousness of Toni Morrison and William Faulkner." *Unflinching Gaze: Morrison and Faulkner Re-Envisioned*. Ed. Carol A. Kolmerten et al. Jackson: U of Mississippi P, 1997. 17–30.

DiAngelo, Robin. *White Fragility: Why It's So Hard for White People to Talk about Racism*. Boston: Beacon, 2018.

Dickson-Carr, Darryl. *African-American Satire: The Sacredly Profane Novel*. Columbia: U of Missouri P, 2001.

Dike, K. Onwuka. *Trade and Politics in the Niger Delta, 1830–1885: An Introduction to the Economic and Political History of Nigeria*. Glasgow: Oxford UP, 1956.

Douglas, Aaron. "Aaron Douglas Chats about the Harlem Renaissance." *The Portable Harlem Renaissance Reader*. Ed. David Levering Lewis. London: Penguin, 1994. 118–27.

Dreifus, Claudia. "Chloe Wofford Talks about Toni Morrison." *Toni Morrison: Conversations.* Ed. Carolyn C. Denard. Jackson: UP of Mississippi, 2008. 98–106.

Du Bois, W. E. B. "Criteria of Negro Art." *Within the Circle: An Anthology of African American Literary Criticism from the Harlem Renaissance to the Present.* Ed. Angelyn Mitchell. Durham, NC: Duke UP, 1994. 60–68.

———. "Of the Faith of the Fathers." *The Souls of Black Folk: Authoritative Text, Contexts, Criticism.* Ed. Henry Louis Gates Jr. and Terri Hume Oliver. New York: Norton, 1999.

Dubey, Madhu. *Signs and Cities: Black Literary Postmodernism.* Chicago: U of Chicago P, 2003.

duCille, Ann. *The Coupling Convention: Sex, Text, and Tradition in Black Women's Fiction.* New York: Oxford UP, 1993.

Dunbar, Paul L. "We Wear the Mask." *Call and Response: The Riverside Anthology of the African American Literary Tradition.* Ed. Patricia Liggins Hill et al. Boston: Houghton Mifflin, 1998. 615.

Dunton, Chris. "Entropy and Energy: Lagos as City of Words." *Research in African Literatures* 39.2 (2008): 68–78.

Durrant, Sam. *Postcolonial Narrative and the Work of Mourning: J. M. Coetzee, Wilson Harris, and Toni Morrison.* Albany: State U of New York P, 2004.

Dussere, Erik. *Balancing the Books: Faulkner, Morrison, and the Economies of Slavery.* New York: Routledge, 2003.

Duvall, John N. "Morrison and the (Faulknerian Dark) House of Fiction." *Faulkner and Morrison.* Ed. Robert W. Hamblin and Christopher Rieger. Cape Girardeau: Southeast Missouri State UP, 2013. 19–35.

———. "Toni Morrison and the Anxiety of Faulknerian Influence." *Unflinching Gaze: Morrison and Faulkner Re-Envisioned.* Ed. Carol A. Kolmerten et al. Jackson: U of Mississippi P, 1997. 3–16.

Dyson, Michael Eric. Foreword: "The Hunger for Home." *Acres of Inspiration: The All-Black Towns in Oklahoma.* By Hannibal B. Johnson. Austin, TX: Eakin, 2002. vii–x.

Early, Gerald. Introduction. *My Soul's High Song: The Collected Works of Countee Cullen, Voice of the Harlem Renaissance.* Ed. Early. New York: Anchor, 1991. 3–73.

Eaton, Alice Know, et al. Introduction. *New Critical Essays on Toni Morrison's God Help the Child.* Ed. Eaton et al. Jackson: U of Mississippi P, 2020. ix–xiii.

Ebeogu, Afam. "The Igbo Home in Achebe's Fiction." *Emerging Perspectives on Chinua Achebe. Vol. 2: ISINKA, the Artistic Purpose: Chinua Achebe and the Theory of African Literature.* Ed. Ernest N. Emenyonu and Iniobong I. Uko. Trenton, NJ: Africa World, 2004. 169–84.

Echeruo, Michael J. C. *Victorian Lagos: Aspects of Nineteenth Century Lagos Life.* London: Macmillan Education Limited, 1977.

Egar, Emmanuel Edame. *The Rhetorical Implications of Chinua Achebe's Things Fall Apart*. Lanham, MD: UP of America, 2000.

Egejuru, Phanuel Akubueze. *Chinua Achebe: Pure and Simple, an Oral Biography*. Lagos, Nigeria: Malthouse, 2001.

Eichelberger, Julia. *Prophets of Recognition: Ideology and the Individual Novels by Ralph Ellison, Toni Morrison, Saul Bellow, and Eudora Welty*. Baton Rouge: Louisiana State UP, 1999.

Ekechi, F. K. *Missionary Enterprise and Rivalry in Igboland 1857–1914*. London: Frank Cass, 1972.

Eko, Ebele. "Chinua Achebe and His Critics: Reception [of] His Novels in English and American Reviews." *Studies in Black Literature* 6.3 (1975): 14–20.

Ekwensi, Cyprian. *People of the City*. London: Heinemann, 1963.

Ekwueme, Lazarus E. N. "African-Music Retentions in the New World." *Black Experience in Music* 2.2 (1974): 128–44.

Elkann, Alain. "The Last Interview." *Toni Morrison: The Last Interview and Other Conversations*. Brooklyn, NY: Melville House, 2020. 145–70.

Ellison, Ralph. *Invisible Man*. New York: Vintage, 1952.

———. "The World and the Jug." *Shadow and Act*. Quality Paperback Book Club, 1953. 107–43.

Emecheta, Buchi. *The Bride Price*. New York: G. Braziller, 1976.

———. *The Joys of Motherhood*. London: Heinemann, 1972.

———. *The Slave Girl*. London: Allison and Busby, 1977.

Emenyonu, Ernest N. "Chinua Achebe and the Problematics of Writing in Indigenous Nigerian Languages: Towards the Resolution of Igbo Language Predicament." *Remembering a Legend: Chinua Achebe*. Ed. Emenyonu and Charles E. Nnolim. New York: African Heritage, 2014. 181–201.

———. *The Literary History of the Igbo Novel: African Literature in African Languages*. London and New York: Routledge, 2020.

———. "War in African Literature: Literary Harvests, Human Tragedies." *African Literature Today* 26 (2008): xi–iv.

Emenyonu, Ernest N., and Pat Emenyonu. "Achebe: Accountable to Our Society." *Conversations with Chinua Achebe*. Ed. Bernth Lindfors. Jackson: UP of Mississippi, 1997. 35–44.

———. *Cyprian Ekwensi*. Evans Brothers, 1974.

Erickson, Daniel. *Ghosts, Metaphor, and History in Toni Morrison's "Beloved" and Gabriel García Márquez's "One Hundred Years of Solitude."* London: Palgrave, 2009.

Ezenwa-Ohaeto. *Chinua Achebe: A Biography*. Woodbridge, Suffolk, UK: James Currey, 1997.

Fabre, Michel. "Chinua Achebe on *Arrow of God.*" *Conversations with Chinua Achebe.* Ed. Bernth Lindfors. Jackson: UP of Mississippi, 1997. 45–51.

Falola, Toyin. *Colonialism and Violence in Nigeria.* Bloomington: Indiana UP, 2009.

———. "Politics, Slavery, Servitude, and the Construction of Yoruba Identity." *The African Diaspora: Slavery, Modernity, and Globalization.* Rochester, NY: U of Rochester P, 2013. 163–86.

Fanon, Frantz. *The Wretched of the Earth.* New York: Grove, 1963.

Feimster, Crystal N. *Southern Horrors: Women and the Politics of Rape and Lynching.* Cambridge, MA: Harvard UP, 2009.

Feng, Pin-chia. *The Female Bildungsroman by Toni Morrison and Maxine Hong Kingston.* New York: Peter Lang, 1999.

Fisher, Rudolph. "The Caucasian Storms Harlem." *The Portable Harlem Renaissance Reader.* Ed. David Levering Lewis. London: Penguin, 1994. 110–17.

———. "The City of Refuge." *The City of Refuge: The Collected Stories of Rudolph Fisher.* Ed. John McCluskey. Columbia: U of Missouri P, 1987. 3–16.

Fleming, David. Foreword. *Liverpool and the Slave Trade.* By Anthony Tibbles. Liverpool, UK: Liverpool UP, 2018. vi.

Foner, Eric. *Gateway to Freedom: The Hidden History of the Underground Railroad.* New York: Norton, 2015.

Foucault, Michel. *The Order of Things: An Archaeology of the Human Sciences.* New York: Vintage, 1994.

Fultz, Lucille P. "Introduction: The Grace and Gravity of Toni Morrison." *Toni Morrison: Paradise, Love, A Mercy.* Ed. Lucille P. Fultz. London: Bloomsbury, 2013. 1–19.

Fuqua, Amy. "'The Furrow of His Brow': Providence and Pragmatism in Toni Morrison's *Paradise.*" *Midwest Quarterly* 54.1 (2012): 38–52.

Furman, Jan. *Toni Morrison's Fiction.* Columbia: U of South Carolina P, 1996.

Gagiano, Annie. *Achebe, Head, Marechera: On Power and Change in Africa.* Boulder, CO: Lynne Rienner, 2000.

Gates, Henry Louis, Jr. "Preface: Toni Morrison (1931–)." *Toni Morrison: Critical Perspectives Past and Present.* Ed. Henry Louis Gates Jr. and K. A. Appiah. New York: Amistad, 1993. ix–xiii.

———. *Signifying Monkey: A Theory of African-American Literary Criticism.* New York: Oxford UP, 1988.

———. *Tradition and the Black Atlantic: Critical Theory in the African Diaspora.* New York: Basic Civitas, 2010.

Gauthier, Marni. "The Other Side of *Paradise*: Toni Morrison's (Un)Making of Mythic History." *African American Review* 39.3 (2005): 395–414.

Genovese, Eugene D. *Roll, Jordan, Roll: The World the Slaves Made*. New York: Vintage, 1976.

George, Olakunle. *African Literature and Social Change: Tribe, Nation, Race*. Bloomington: Indiana UP, 2017.

Gérard, Albert S. Foreword. *African Language Literatures: An Introduction to the Literary History of Sub-Saharan Africa*. Washington DC: Three Continents, 1981. ix–xv.

Gershoni, Yekutiel. *Africans on African-Americans: The Creation and Uses of an African-American Myth*. New York: New York UP, 1997.

Gikandi, Simon. "Africa and the Idea of the Aesthetic: From Eurocentricism to Pan-Africanism." *English Studies in Africa* 43.2 (2000): 19–46.

———. "Chinua Achebe and the Invention of African Culture." *Research in African Literatures* 32.3 (2001): 3–8.

———. *Maps of Englishness: Writing Identity in the Culture of Colonialism*. New York: Columbia UP, 1996.

———. *Reading Chinua Achebe: Language and Ideology in Fiction*. Woodbridge, Suffolk, UK: James Currey, 1991.

———. *Reading the African Novel*. Woodbridge, Suffolk, UK: James Currey, 1987.

———. *Slavery and the Culture of Taste*. Princeton, NJ: Princeton UP, 2011.

———. "Traveling Theory: Ngugi's Return to English." *Research in African Literatures* 31.2 (2000): 194–209.

Gillespie, Carmen. *Critical Companion to Toni Morrison: A Literary Reference to Her Life and Work*. New York: Facts on File, 2008.

Gilroy, Paul. *The Black Atlantic: The Black Atlantic: Modernity and Double Consciousness*. Cambridge, MA: Harvard UP, 1993.

Glaude, Eddie S., Jr. *Begin Again: James Baldwin's America and Its Urgent Lessons for Our Own*. New York: Crown, 2020.

Gorlier, Claudio. "Mbari versus Conrad: Chinua Achebe's Aesthetics." *Emerging Perspectives on Chinua Achebe*. Vol. 2: *ISINKA, the Artistic Purpose: Chinua Achebe and the Theory of African Literature*, ed. Ernest N. Emenyonu and Iniobong I. Uko. Trenton, NJ: Africa World, 2004. 49–55.

Goyal, Yogita. "Africa and the Black Atlantic." *Research in African Literatures* 45.3 (2014): v–xxv.

———. "African Atrocity, American Humanity: Slavery and Its Transnational Afterlives." *Research in African Literatures* 45.3 (2014): 48–71.

———. *Runaway Genres: The Global Afterlives of Slavery*. New York: New York UP, 2019.

Graham, Shane. *Langston Hughes and the Rise of African and Caribbean Literature*. Charlottesville: U of Virginia P, 2020.

Gray, Paul. "Paradise Found." *Time Magazine* 19 January1998.

Green, M. M. *Igbo Village Affairs: Chiefly with Reference to the Village of Umueke Agbaja*. London: Frank Cass, 1964.

Greenfield-Sanders, Timothy. Dir. *Toni Morrison: The Pieces I Am*. 2019.

Grewal, Gurleen. *Circles of Sorrow: The Novels of Toni Morrison*. Baton Rouge: Louisiana State UP, 1998.

Griswold, Wendy. *Bearing Witness: Readers, Writers, and the Novel in Nigeria*. Princeton, NJ: Princeton UP, 2000.

———. "The Writing on the Mud Wall: Nigerian Novels and the Imaginary Village." *American Sociological Review* 57 (1991): 709–24.

Gruesser, John Cullen. *Confluences: Postcolonialism, African American Literary Studies, and the Black Atlantic*. Athens: U of Georgia P, 2005.

Gunning, Sandra. *Race, Rape, and Lynching: The Red Record of American Literature, 1890–1912*. New York: Oxford UP, 1996.

Gyasi, Yaa. *Homegoing*. New York: Vintage, 2016.

Habila, Helon. *Measuring Time: A Novel*. New York: Norton, 2007.

Hackney, Sheldon. "'I Come from People Who Sang All the Time': A Conversation with Toni Morrison." *Conversations with Toni Morrison*. Ed. Danille Taylor-Guthrie. Jackson: UP of Mississippi, 1994. 126–38.

Hakutani, Yoshinobu. *Cross-Cultural Visions in African American Modernism: From Spatial Narrative to Jazz Haiku*. Columbus: Ohio State UP, 2006.

Hakutani, Yoshinobu, and Robert Butler. Introduction. *The City in African-American Literature*. Ed. Hakutani and Butler. Plainsboro, NJ: Associated UP, 1995. 9–18.

Hall, Alice. *Disability and Modern Fiction: Faulkner, Morrison, Coetzee and the Nobel Prize for Literature*. London: Palgrave, 2012.

Hall, Toni. "I Had to Write on the Chaos I Foresaw." *Conversations with Chinua Achebe*. Ed. Bernth Lindfors. Jackson: UP of Mississippi, 1997. 8–26.

Hamblin, Robert W., and Christopher Riegel. *Faulkner and Morrison*. Cape Girardeau: Southeast Missouri State UP, 2013.

Harding, Wendy, and Jacky Martin. *A World of Difference: An Inter-Cultural Study of Toni Morrison's Novels*. Westport, CT: Greenwood, 1994.

Harris, Ashleigh. *Afropolitanism and the Novel: De-realizing Africa*. London: Routledge, 2020.

Harris, Trudier. *The Scary Mason-Dixon Line: African American Writers and the South*. Baton Rouge: Louisiana State UP, 2009.

Hartman, Saidiya. *Lose Your Mother: A Journey along the Atlantic Slave Route*. New York: Farrar, Straus and Giroux, 2008.

Hartmann, Ivor W, ed. *AfroSF: Science Fiction by African Writers*. N.p.: StoryTime Publications, 2012.

Haywood, Chanta. *Prophesying Daughters: Black Women Preachers and the Word, 1823–1913*. Columbia: U of Missouri P, 2003.

Heinert, Jennifer Lee Jordan. *Narrative Conventions and Race in the Novels of Toni Morrison*. London: Routledge, 2009.

Heinze, Denise. *The Dilemma of "Double Consciousness": Toni Morrison's Novels*. Athens: U of Georgia P, 1993.

Henderson, Carol E. *Scarring the Black Body: Race and Representation in African American Literature*. Columbia: U of Missouri P, 2002.

Herskovits, Melville J. *The Myth of the Negro Past*. Boston: Beacon, 1958.

Higgins, Therese E. *Religiosity, Cosmology, and Folklore: The African Influence in the Novels of Toni Morrison*. London: Routledge, 2001.

Hill, Patricia Liggins, ed. *Call and Response: The Riverside Anthology of the African American Literary Tradition*. Boston: Houghton Mifflin, 1988.

Holloway, Karla F. C., and Stephanie A. Demetrakopoulos. *New Dimensions of Spirituality: A Biracial and Bicultural Reading of the Novels of Toni Morrison*. Westport, CT: Greenwood, 1987.

Holsey, Bayo. *Routes of Remembrance: Refashioning the Slave Trade in Ghana*. Chicago: U of Chicago P, 2008.

Houston, Pam. "Pam Houston Talks with Toni Morrison." *Toni Morrison: Conversations*. Ed. Carolyn C. Denard. Jackson: UP of Mississippi, 2008. 228–59.

Howells, William Dean. "Review of *Majors and Minors*." *Howells as Critic*. Ed. Edwin H. Cady. London: Routledge and Kegan Paul, 1973.

Huggins, Nathan Irvin. *Black Odyssey: The Afro-American Ordeal in Slavery*. New York: Pantheon, 1977.

———. *Harlem Renaissance*. London: Oxford UP, 1971.

Hughes, Langston. *An African Treasury: Articles, Essays, Stories, Poems by Black Africans*. New York: Pyramid, 1961.

———. "The Negro Artist and the Racial Mountain." *Within the Circle: An Anthology of African American Literary Criticism from the Harlem Renaissance to the Present*. Ed. Angelyn Mitchell. Durham, NC: Duke UP, 1994. 55–59.

———. *Poems from Black Africa*. Bloomington: Indiana UP, 1963.

Hurston, Zora Neale. "Characteristics of Negro Expression," *Within the Circle: An Anthology of African American Literary Criticism from the Harlem Renaissance to the Present*. Ed. Angelyn Mitchell. Durham, NC: Duke UP, 1994. 79–94.

———. *Their Eyes Were Watching God*. Perennial Classics, 1990.

Iheka, Cajetan, and Jack Taylor. "Introduction: The Migration Turn in African Cultural Productions." *African Migration Narratives: Politics, Race, and Space*. Ed. Iheka and Taylor. Rochester, NY: U of Rochester P, 2018. 1–15.

Imbua, David Lishilinmle. *Intercourse and Crosscurrents in the Atlantic World: Calabar-British Experience, 17th–20th Centuries*. Durham, NC: Carolina Academic, 2012.

Innes, C. L. *Chinua Achebe*. Cambridge: Cambridge UP, 1990.

———. "Chinua Achebe (1930–2013): Obituary, Founding Father of African Fiction Whose Novels Chronicled Nigeria's Troubled History." *Chinua Achebe: Tributes and Reflections*. Ed. Nana Ayebia Clarke and James Currey. Oxfordshire, UK: Ayebia Clarke, 2014. 3–7.

Irele, F. Abiola. *The African Imagination: Literature in Africa and the Black Diaspora*. Oxford: Oxford UP, 2001.

———. "Chronology." *The Cambridge Companion to the African Novel*. Cambridge: Cambridge UP, 2009, pp. xii–xxii.

———. "The Crisis of Cultural Memory in Chinua Achebe's *Things Fall Apart*." *Chinua Achebe. Things Fall Apart: Authoritative Text, Contexts and Criticism*. Ed. Irele. New York: Norton, 2009. 453–91.

———. "Slavery and the African Imagination." *Du Bois Review* 3. 2 (2006): 431–36.

Isichei, Elizabeth. *A History of Igbo People*. New York: St. Martin's, 1976.

———. *The Ibo People and the Europeans: The Genesis of a Relationship—to 1906*. New York: St. Martins, 1973.

Ita, Bassey. *Jazz in Nigeria: An Outline Cultural History*. Lagos: Atiaya Communications, 1984.

Jackson, Tommie Lee. *"High-Topped Shoes" and Other Signifiers of Race, Class, Gender, and Ethnicity in Selected Fiction by William Faulkner and Toni Morrison*. Lanham, MD: UP of America, 2006.

Jaffrey, Zia. "Toni Morrison." *Toni Morrison: Conversations*. Ed. Carolyn C. Denard. Jackson: UP of Mississippi, 2008. 139–54.

Jaji, Tsitsi Ella. *Africa in Stereo: Modernism, Music, and Pan-African Solidarity*. Oxford: Oxford UP, 2014.

JanMohamed, Abdul R. *Manichean Aesthetics: The Politics of Literature in Colonial Africa*. Amherst: U of Massachusetts P, 1983.

Jarrett, Gene Andrew. *Deans and Truants: Race and Realism in American Literature*. Philadelphia: U of Pennsylvania P, 2007.

Jefferson, Williams. *Toni Morrison and the Limits of a Politics of Recognition*. CreateSpace Independent Publishing Platform, 2014.

Jennings, La Vinia Delois, ed. *Margaret Garner: The Premiere Performances of Toni Morrison's Libretto*. Charlottesville: U of Virginia P, 2016.

———. *Toni Morrison and the Idea of Africa*. New York: Cambridge UP, 2008.

Jewett, Chad. "The Modality of Toni Morrison's 'Jazz.'" *African American Review* 48.4 (2015): 445–56.

Jeyifo, Biodun. "*Arrow of God*: Intimations for the Post-Globalization Wave of Writers." *Illuminations on Chinua Achebe: The Art of Resistance*. Ed. Mĩcere Gĩthae Mũgo and Hebert G. Ruffin II. Trenton, NJ: Africa World, 2017. 15–26.

———. "For Chinua Achebe: The Resilience and the Predicament of Obierika." *Chinua Achebe: A Celebration.* Ed. Kirsten Holst Peterson and Anna Rutherford. Sydney: Dangeroo, 1990. 51–70.

Johnson, Hannibal B. *Acres of Inspiration: The All-Black Towns in Oklahoma.* Austin, TX: Eakin, 2002.

Johnson, James Weldon. *Black Manhattan.* Boston: Da Capo, 1958.

———. Preface. *The Book of American Negro Poetry.* Ed. Johnson. New York: Harcourt, Brace, 1922. vii–viii.

Joiner, Jennie J. "The Slow Burn of Masculinity in Faulkner's Hearth and Morrison's Oven." Faulkner in Contemporary Fiction. Spec. issue of *Faulkner Journal* 25.2 (2010): 53–68.

Jones, Bessie W., and Audrey Vinson. "An Interview with Toni Morrison." *Conversations with Toni Morrison.* Ed. Danille Taylor-Guthrie. Jackson: UP of Mississippi, 1994. 171–87.

Jones, Jill C. "The Eye of the Needle: Morrison's 'Paradise, Faulkner's Absalom, Absalom!', and the American Jeremiad." *Faulkner Journal* 17.2 (2002): 3–23.

Kadir, Djelal. "What Does the Comparative Do for Literary History?" *PMLA* 128.3 (2013): 644–51.

Kalu, Anthonia. "African Literature and the Traditional Arts: Speaking Art, Molding Theory." *Research in African Literatures* 31.4 (2000): 48–62.

Kastor, Elizabeth. "Toni Morrison's Beloved Country: The Writer and Her Haunting Tale of Slavery." *Critical Essays on Toni Morrison's Beloved.* Ed. Barbara H. Solomon. Boston: G. K. Hall, 1998. 53–58.

Kendi, Ibram X. *Stamped from the Beginning: The Definitive History of Racist Ideas in America.* New York: Nation Books, 2016.

Kelley, Robin D. G. *Africa Speaks, America Answers.* Cambridge, MA: Harvard UP, 2012.

Ker, David I. *The African Novel and the Modernist Tradition.* New York: Peter Lang, 1998.

Killam, G. D. *The Novels of Chinua Achebe.* Africana P, 1969.

King, Lovalerie, and Lynn Orilla Scott, eds. *James Baldwin and Toni Morrison: Comparative Critical and Theoretical Essays.* New York: Palgrave Macmillan, 2006.

King, Maya, and Teresa Wiltz. "How Raphael Warnock Fused Old and New South to Win Georgia." *Politico.com* 6 January 2021. www.politico.com/news/2021 /01/06/how-raphael-warnock-won-georgia-455320.

Kirschke, Amy H. "Oh Africa! The Influence of African Art during the Harlem Renaissance." *Temples of Tomorrow: Looking Back at the Harlem Renaissance.* Ed. Geneviève Fabre and Michael Feith. Bloomington: Indiana UP, 2001. 73–83.

Kliment, Bud. *Billie Holiday.* New York: Chelsea House, 1990.

Koenen, Anne. "The One Out of Sequence." *Conversations with Toni Morrison*. Ed. Danille Taylor-Guthrie. Jackson: UP of Mississippi, 1994. 67–83.

Kolmerten, Carol A., et al. *Unflinching Gaze: Morrison and Faulkner Re-Envisioned*. Ed. Kolmerten et al. Jackson: U of Mississippi P, 1997.

Kortenaar, Neil Ten. "Becoming African and the Death of Ikemefuna." *University of Toronto Quarterly* 73.2 (2004): 773–94.

Kramer, Barbara. *Toni Morrison: A Biography of a Nobel Prize-Winning Writer*. Berkeley Heights, NJ: Enslow, 2013.

Kronenfeld, J. Z. "The 'Communalistic' African and the 'Individualistic' Westerner: Some Comments on Misleading Generalizations in West Criticism of Soyinka and Achebe." *Research in African Literatures* 6.2 (1975): 199–25.

Krumholz, Linda J. "Reading and Insight in Toni Morrison's *Paradise*." *African American Review* 36.1 (2002): 21–34.

Kubitschek, Missy Dehn. *Toni Morrison: A Critical Companion*. Westport, CT: Greenwood, 1998.

Larsen, Nella. *"Quicksand" and "Passing."* Ed. Deborah E. McDowell. New Brunswick, NJ: Rutgers UP, 1986.

Lawson, William. *The Western Scar: The Theme of the Been-to in West African Fiction*. Columbus: Ohio UP, 1982.

LeClair, Thomas. "'The Language Must Not Sweat': A Conversation with Toni Morrison." *Conversations with Toni Morrison*. Ed. Danille Taylor-Guthrie. Jackson: UP of Mississippi, 1994. 119–28.

Leeming, David. *James Baldwin: A Biography*. New York: Henry Holt, 1994.

Lévi-Strauss, Claude. *The View from Afar*. Trans. Joachim Neugroschel and Phoebe Hoss. New York: Basic, 1985

Lewis, David Levering. Preface. *Middle Passages: African American Journeys to Africa, 1787–2005*. By James T. Campbell. London: Penguin, 2006. ix–xviii.

Lewis, Maureen Warner. "Ezeulu and His God: An Analysis of Chinua Achebe's *Arrow of God*." *Black World* 24.2 (1974): 71–87.

Li, Stephanie. "*FIVE POEMS*: The Gospel According to Toni Morrison." *Callaloo* 34.3 (2011): 899–914.

———. *Pan-African American Literature: Signifyin(g) Immigrants in the Twenty-First Century*. New Brunswick, NJ: Rutgers UP, 2018.

———. *Toni Morrison: A Biography*. Santa Barbara, CA: Greenwood Biographies, 2009.

Lincoln, C. Eric, and Lawrence H. Mamiya. *The Black Church in the African American Experience*. Durham, NC: Duke UP, 1990.

Lindfors, Bernth. "Africa and the Nobel Prize." *The Nobel Prizes in Literature 1967–1987: A Symposium*. Spec. issue of *World Literature Today* 62.2 (1988): 222–24.

——, ed. *Conversations with Chinua Achebe*. Jackson: UP of Mississippi, 1997.

——. *Early Achebe*. Trenton, NJ: Africa World, 2009.

Lindfors, Bernth, et al. "Interview with Chinua Achebe." *Conversations with Chinua Achebe*. Ed. Lindfors. Jackson: UP of Mississippi. 27–34.

Lively, Adam. *Masks: Blackness, Race and the Imagination*. Oxford: Oxford UP, 2000.

Lobodziec, Agnieska. *The Timeless Toni Morrison: The Past and The Present in Toni Morrison's Fiction: A Tribute to Toni Morrison on Occasion of Her 85th Birthday*. Frankfurt: Peter Lang, 2017.

Locke, Alain. "Art or Propaganda?" *African American Literary Criticism, 1773–2000*. Ed. Hazel Arnette Ervin. Woodbridge, CT: Twayne, 1999. 49–50.

——. "The New Negro". *The New Negro*. Ed. Locke. New York: Atheneum, 1992. 3–16.

Loris, Michelle C. "Self and Mutuality: Romantic Love, Desire, Race, and Gender in Toni Morrison's *Jazz*." *Sacred Heart University Review* 14.1 (1994): 53–62.

Lovejoy, Paul E. "Olaudah Equiano or Gustavus Vassa: What's in a Name?" *Igbo in the Atlantic: African Origins and Diasporic Destinations*. Ed. Toyin Falola and Raphael Chijoke Njoku. Bloomington: Indiana UP, 2016. 199–217.

Luszczynska, Ana M. *The Ethics of Community: Nancy, Derrida, Morrison and Menendez*. London: Continuum International, 2014.

Lynch, Hollis R. *K. O. Mbadiwe: A Nigerian Political Biography, 1915–1990*. London: Palgrave Macmillan, 2012.

Lynn, Thomas Jay. *Chinua Achebe and the Politics of Narration: Envisioning Language*. Cham, Switzerland: Palgrave Macmillan, 2017.

Makinde, Adeyinka. *Dick Tiger: The Life and Times of a Boxing Immortal*. Tarentum, PA: World Association, 2004.

Makward, Edris, and Leslie Lacy. Introduction. *Contemporary African Literature*. Ed. Makward and Lacy. New York: Random House, 1972. 1–5.

Malmgren, Carl D. "Mixed Genres and the Logic of Slavery in Toni Morrison's *Beloved*." *Critique: Studies in Contemporary Fiction* 36.2 (1995): 96–106.

Mann, Kristin. *Slavery and the Birth of an African City: Lagos, 1760–1900*. Bloomington: Indiana UP, 2007.

Marouan, Maha. *Witches, Goddesses, and Angry Spirits: The Politics of Spiritual Liberation in African Diaspora Women's Fiction*. Columbus: Ohio State UP, 2013.

Marrouchi, Mustapha. *Signifying with a Vengeance: Theories, Literatures, Storytellers*. Albany: State U of New York P, 2002.

Marshall, Paule. *Praisesong for the Widow*. New York: Plume, 1983.

Masilela, Ntongela. *The Historical Figures of the New African Movement*. Vol. 1. Trenton, NJ: Africa World, 2014.

Mason, Lauren. "Leaving Lagos: Intertextuality and Images in Chris Abani's *Graceland*." *Africa and the Black Atlantic*. Spec. issue of *Research in African Literatures* 45.3 (2014): 206–26.

Matus, Jill. *Toni Morrison*. Manchester, UK: Manchester UP, 1998.

Mbalia, Doreatha Drummond. *Toni Morrison's Developing Class Consciousness*. Selinsgrove, PA: Susquehanna UP, 1991.

Mbembe, Achille. "African Modes of Self-Writing." Translated by Steven Rendall. *Public Culture* 14.1 (2002): 239–73.

———. *Critique of Black Reason*. Trans. Laurent Dubois. Durham, NC: Duke UP, 2017.

———. *On the Postcolony*. Berkeley: U of California P, 2001.

———. *Necropolitics*. Trans. Steven Corcoran. Durham, NC: Duke UP, 2019.

McCluskey, Audrey T. "A Conversation with Toni Morison." *Conversations with Toni Morrison*. Ed. Danille Taylor-Guthrie. Jackson: UP of Mississippi, 1994. 38–43.

McKay, Claude. *Home to Harlem*. Boston: Northeastern UP, 1987.

———. "If We Must Die." *The Portable Harlem Renaissance Reader*. Ed. David Levering Lewis. London: Penguin, 1994. 290.

McKay, Nellie. "An Interview with Toni Morrison." *Conversations with Toni Morrison*. Ed. Danille Taylor-Guthrie. Jackson: UP of Mississippi, 1994. 138–55.

McKee, Patricia. *Producing American Races: Henry James, William Faulkner, Toni Morrison*. Durham, NC: Duke UP, 1999.

Mishkin, Tracy. "Theorizing Literary Influence and African-American Writers." *Literary Influence and African-American Writers: Collected Essays*. Ed. Mishkin. New York: Garland, 1996. 3–17.

Mobley, Marilyn Sanders. *Roots and Mythic Wings in Sarah Orne Jewett and Toni Morrison: The Cultural Function of Narrative*. Baton Rouge: Louisiana State UP, 1991.

Montgomery, Maxine Lavon. Introduction. *Contested Boundaries; New Critical Essays on the Fiction of Toni Morrison*. Ed. Montgomery. Newcastle upon Tyne, UK: Cambridge Scholars P, 2013. 1–11.

Moore, Chioni, and Analee Heath. "A Conversation with Chinua Achebe: On the Fiftieth Anniversary of *Things Fall Apart*." *Transition* 100 (2009): 12–33.

Moore, Geneva Cobb. *Bodily Evidence. Racism, Slavery, and Maternal Power in the Novels of Toni Morrison*. Columbia: U of South Carolina P, 2020.

———. *Maternal Metaphors of Power in African American Women's Literature: From Phillis Wheatley to Toni Morrison*. Columbia: U of South Carolina P, 2017.

Morgan, Edmund S. *American Slavery, American Freedom: The Ordeal of Colonial Virginia*. New York: Norton, 1975.

Morgan, Kenneth. "Liverpool's Dominance in the British Slave Trade, 1740–1807." *Liverpool and the Transatlantic Slave Trade.* Ed. David Richardson et al. Liverpool, UK: Liverpool UP, 2007. 14–42.

———. "The Trans-Atlantic Slave Trade from the Bight of Biafra: An Overview." *Igbo in the Atlantic World: African Origins and Diasporic Destinations.* Ed. Toyin Falola and Raphael Njoku. Bloomington: Indiana UP. 82–98.

Morrison, Jago. *Chinua Achebe.* Manchester, UK: Manchester UP, 2014.

———. "Tradition and Modernity in Chinua Achebe's *African Trilogy.*" *Research in African Literatures* 49.4 (2018): 14–26.

Morrison, Toni. "Behind the Making of *The Black Book.*" *What Moves at the Margin: Selected Nonfiction.* Ed. Carolyn C. Denard. Jackson: UP of Mississippi, 2008. 34–38.

———. *Beloved.* New York: Knopf, 1987.

———. *The Bluest Eye.* New York: Holt, Rinehart and Winston, 1970.

———. "City Limits, Village Values: Concepts of the Neighborhood in Black Fiction." *Literature and the Urban Experience: Essays on the City and Literature.* Ed. Michael C. Jaye and Ann Chalmers Watts. New Brunswick, NJ: Rutgers UP, 1981. 35–43.

———. *The Dancing Mind.* New York: Knopf, 2007.

———. "Faulkner and Women." *Faulkner and Women: Faulkner and Yoknapatawpha, 1985.* Ed. Doreen Fowler and Ann J. Abadie. Jackson: U of Mississippi P, 1985. 295–302.

———. "The Foreigner's Home." *The Source of Self-Regard.* By Morrison. New York: Knopf, 2019. 5–13.

———. Foreword. *Love.* By Morrison. New York: Vintage International, 2005. ix–xii.

———. *God Help the Child.* New York: Knopf, 2015.

———. *Home.* New York: Random House, 2012.

———. "Home." *The House That Race Built: Original Essays by Toni Morrison, Angela Y. Davis, Cornel West, and Others on Black Americans and Politics Today.* Ed. Wahneema Lubianno. New York: Vintage, 1998. 3–12.

———. Introduction. *The Radiance of the King.* By Camara Laye. Trans. James Kirkup. New York: New York Review of Books, 2001. xi–xxiv.

———. "James Baldwin: His Voice Remembered; Life in His Language." *What Moves at the Margin: Selected Nonfiction.* By Morrison. Ed. Carolyn C. Denard. Jackson: UP of Mississippi, 2008. 34–38.

———. *Jazz.* New York: Knopf, 1992.

———. "Life in His Writing." *James Baldwin: The Legacy.* Ed. Quincy Troupe. New York: Simon and Schuster/Touchstone, 1989. 75–78.

———. *The Measure of Our Lives: A Gathering of Wisdom*. New York: Knopf, 2019.

———. "Memory, Creation, and Writing." *Thought* 59.235 (1984): 385–90.

———. *A Mercy*. New York: New York: Vintage International, 2009.

———. *The Origin of Others*. Cambridge, MA: Harvard UP, 2017.

———. *Paradise*. New York: Knopf, 1998.

———. *Playing in the Dark: Whiteness and the Literary Imagination*. New York: Vintage, 1992.

———, ed. *Race-ing Justice, En-gendering Power: Essays on Anita Hill, Clarence Thomas, and the Construction of Social Reality*. New York: Pantheon, 1992.

———. "Recitatif." *Confirmation: An Anthology of African American Women*. Ed. Amiri Baraka (LeRoi Jones). Toronto: Quill, 1983. 243–61.

———. "Rediscovering Black History." *What Moves at the Margin: Selected Nonfiction*. By Morrison. Ed. Carolyn C. Denard. Jackson: UP of Mississippi, 2008. 39–55.

———. "Rootedness: The Ancestor as Foundation." *Black Women Writers, 1950–1980*. Ed. Mari Evans. New York: Anchor Doubleday, 1984. 339–45.

———. "The Site of Memory." *What Moves at the Margin: Selected Nonfiction*. By Morrison. Ed. Carolyn C. Denard. Jackson: UP of Mississippi, 2008. 65–80.

———. "The Slavebody and the Blackbody." *The Source of Self-Regard*. By Morrison. New York: Knopf, 2019. 74–78.

———. *Song of Solomon*. New York: Knopf, 1993.

———. *The Source of Self-Regard*. New York: Knopf, 2019.

———. *Sula*. New York: Knopf, 1993.

———. *Tar Baby*. New York: Knopf, 1993.

———. "The Trouble with Paradise." *The Source of Self-Regard*. By Morrison. New York: Knopf, 2019. 271–79.

———. "Virginia Woolf's and William Faulkner's Treatment of the Alienated." Master's thesis. Cornel U, 1955.

———. *What Moves at the Margin: Selected Nonfiction*. Ed. Carolyn C. Denard. Jackson: UP of Mississippi, 2008.

Morrison, Toni, and Claudia Brodsky Lacour, eds. *Birth of a Nation'hood: Gaze, Script, and Spectacle in the O. J. Simpson Case*. New York: Pantheon, 1997.

Morrow, Bradford. "Chinua Achebe, An Interview, Part II." *Conjunctions* 17 (1991). www.conjunctions.com/archives/c17-cal.htm. September 14, 2015.

Moses, Wilson Jeremiah. *The Golden Age of Black Nationalism, 1850–1925*. New York: Oxford UP, 1978.

———. "The Lost World of the Negro, 1895–1919: Black Literary and Intellectual Life before the Renaissance." *Black American Literature Forum* 21.1/2 (Spring–Summer 1987): 61–84.

Mudimbe, V. Y. *The Idea of Africa*. Bloomington: Indiana UP, 1994.

———. *The Invention of Africa: Gnosis, Philosophy, and the Order of Knowledge*. Bloomington: Indiana UP, 1988.

Mũgo, Mĩcere Gĩthae, and Hebert G. Ruffin II, eds. *Illuminations on Chinua Achebe: The Art of Resistance*. Trenton, NJ: Africa World, 2017.

Mulrine, Anna. Rev. of "This Side of Paradise." *U.S. News & World Report* 124.2 (1998): 71.

Munton, Alan. "Misreading Morrison, Mishearing Jazz: A Response to Toni Morrison's Jazz Critics." *Journal of American Studies* 31.2 (1997): 235–51.

Murphy, Laura T. "Into the Bush of Ghosts: Specters of the Slave Trade in West African Fiction." *Research in African Literatures* 38.4 (2007): 141–52.

———. *Metaphor and the Slave Trade in West African Literature*. Columbus: Ohio UP, 2012.

Mwangi, Evan Maina. *Africa Writes Back to Self: Metafiction, Gender, Sexuality*. Albany: State U of New York P, 2009.

Nagel, James. "General Editor's Note." *Critical Essays on Toni Morrison's Beloved*. Ed. Barbara H. Solomon. Boston: G. K. Hall, 1998. xi.

Nagel, Mechthild. "The Case for Penal Abolition and Ludic Ubuntu in *Arrow of God*." *Illuminations on Chinua Achebe: The Art of Resistance*. Ed. Mĩcere Gĩthae Mũgo and Hebert G. Ruffin II. Trenton, NJ: Africa World, 2017. 135–46.

Naylor, Gloria. "A Conversation: Gloria Naylor and Toni Morrison." *Conversations with Toni Morrison*. Ed. Danille Taylor-Guthrie. Jackson: UP of Mississippi, 1994. 188–217.

———. *Mama Day*. Vintage Contemporaries, 1989.

Ndibe, Okey. *Foreign Gods, Inc.* New York: Soho, 2014.

———. "Learning Stories from a Master: Encounters with Chinua Achebe." *Illuminations on Chinua Achebe: The Art of Resistance*. Ed. Mĩcere Gĩthae Mũgo and Hebert G. Ruffin II. Trenton, NJ: Africa World, 2017. 77–96.

Neal, Larry. "The Black Arts Movement." *Within the Circle: An Anthology of African American Literary Criticism from the Harlem Renaissance to the Present*. Ed. Angelyn Mitchell. Durham, NC: Duke UP, 1994. 184–98.

Nelson, William E. "Criminality and Sexual Morality in New York, 1920–1980." *Yale Journal of Law & the Humanities* 5.2 (2013): 265–341.

Neustadt, Kathy. "The Visit of the Writers Toni Morrison and Eudora Welty." *Conversations with Toni Morrison*. Ed. Danille Taylor-Guthrie. Jackson: UP of Mississippi, 1994. 84–92.

Newell, Stephanie. *Histories of Dirt: Media and Urban Life in Colonial and Postcolonial Lagos*. Ebook. Durham, NC: Duke UP, 2020.

Newkirk, Vann R., II. "The Great Land Robbery: The Shameful Story of How 1 Million Black Families Have Been Ripped from Their Farms." *Atlantic*

September 2019. www.theatlantic.com/magazine/archive/2019/09/this-land -was-our-land/594742/.

Ngũgĩ wa Thiong'o. *Decolonising the Mind: The Politics of Language in African Literature*. Woodbridge, Suffolk, UK: James Currey, 1986.

———. "Imperialism of Language: English, a Language of the World?" *Moving the Centre: The Struggle for Cultural Freedoms*. By Ngũgĩ. Woodbridge, Suffolk, UK: James Currey, 1992. 30–41.

———. *Moving the Centre: The Struggle for Cultural Freedoms*. Woodbridge, Suffolk, UK: James Currey, 1992.

———. "The Universality of Local Knowledge." *Moving the Centre: The Struggle for Cultural Freedoms*. By Ngũgĩ. Woodbridge, Suffolk, UK: James Currey, 1992. 25–29.

———. *Weep Not, Child*. London: Heinemann Educational, 1964.

Niven, Alastair. "Another Look at *Arrow of God*." *Literary Half Yearly* 16.2 (1975): 53–68.

Njoku, Raphael Chijioke. "The Making of Igbo Ethnicity in the Nigerian Setting: Colonialism, Identity, and Politics of Difference." *Igbo in the Atlantic World: African Origins and Diasporic Destinations*. Ed. Toyin Falola and Njoku. Bloomington: Indiana UP, 2016. 265–84.

Nkosi, Lewis. "Chinua Achebe." *Conversations with Chinua Achebe*. Ed. Bernth Lindfors. Jackson: UP of Mississippi, 1997. 3–6.

Nkosi, Lewis, and Wole Soyinka. "Conversation with Chinua Achebe." *Conversations with Chinua Achebe*. Ed. Bernth Lindfors. Jackson: UP of Mississippi, 1997. 11–17.

Nnolim, Charles. "A Source for 'Arrow of God.'" *Research in African Literatures* 8.1 (1977): 1–26.

———. "Technique and Meaning in *Arrow of God*." *Remembering a Legend: Chinua Achebe*. Ed. Ernest N. Emenyonu and Charles E. Nnolim. New York: African Heritage, 2014. 97–118.

Nwankwo, Chimalum. "'I is': Toni Morrison, the Past, and Africa." *Of Dreams Deferred, Dead or Alive: African Perspectives on African-American Writers*. Ed. Femi Ojo-Ade. Westport, CT: Greenwood, 1996. 171–80.

Nwankwo, Ifeoma Kiddoe. *Black Cosmopolitanism: Racial Consciousness and the Transnational Identity in the Nineteenth-Century Americas*. Philadelphia: U of Pennsylvania P, 2005.

Nwaubani, Adaobi Tricia. *I Do Not Come to You by Chance: A Novel*. Westport, CT: Hyperion, 2009.

Nwokeji, G. Ugo. *The Slave Trade and Culture in the Bight of Biafra: An African Society in the Atlantic World*. Cambridge: Cambridge UP, 2010.

Nyamndi, George. *The West African Village Novel with Particular Reference to Elechi Amadi's "The Concubine."* Frankfurt: Peter Lang, 1982.

Obiechina, Emmanuel. *Culture, Tradition and Society in the West African Novel.* Cambridge: Cambridge UP, 1975.

——. Introduction. *Onitsha Market Literature.* Ed. Obiechina. New York: Africana P, 1972. 1–30.

——. *Language and Theme: Essays on African Literature.* Washington, DC: Howard UP, 1990.

Obioma, Chigozie. *The Fishermen: A Novel.* New York: Back Bay Books, 2015.

——. "Toni Morrison: Farewell to America's Greatest Writer—We All Owe Her So Much." *The Guardian.com.* 7 August 2019. www.theguardian.com/books /2019/aug/07/toni-morrison-farewell-to-americas-greatest-writer-we-all -owe-her-so-much.

Obiwu. "The Pan-African Brotherhood of Langston Hughes and Nnamdi Azikiwe." *Dialectical Anthropology* 31.1 (2007): 143–65.

Ochiagha, Terri. *Achebe and Friends at Umuahia: The Making of a Literary Elite.* Woodbridge, Suffolk, UK: James Currey, 2015.

——. "Decolonizing the Mind Onitsha-Style: Reexamining Ogali A. Ogali's Cultural Nationalism in *The Juju Priest.*" *Research in African Literatures* 46.1 (2015): 90–106.

——. *A Short History of Chinua Achebe's Things Fall Apart.* Columbus: Ohio UP, 2018.

Oforlea, Aaron Ngozi. *James Baldwin, Toni Morrison, and the Rhetorics of Black Male Subjectivity.* Columbus: Ohio State UP, 2017.

Ogbaa, Kalu. *Gods, Oracles and Divination: Folkways in Chinua Achebe's Novels.* Trenton, NJ: Africa World, 1992.

——. "An Interview with Chinua Achebe." *Conversations with Chinua Achebe.* Ed. Bernth Lindfors. Jackson: UP of Mississippi, 1997. 64–75.

——. *The Life and Times of Chinua Achebe.* London: Penguin, 2021.

Ogude, S. E. "Slavery and the African Imagination: A Critical Perspective." *World Literature Today* 55.1 (1981): 21–25.

Ogwude, Sophie. "Achebe on the Woman Question." *Emerging Perspectives on Chinua Achebe.* Vol. 2: *ISINKA: The Artistic Purpose; Chinua Achebe and the Theory of African Literature.* Ed. Ernest N. Emenyonu and Iniobong I. Uko. Trenton, NJ: Africa World, 2004. 331–37.

Ojike, Mbonu. *I Have Two Countries.* New York: John Day, 1947.

——. *My Africa.* New York: John Day, 1946.

Ojo-Ade, Femi. "Africa and America: A Question of Continuities, Cleavage, and Dreams Deferred." *Of Dreams Deferred, Dead or Alive: African Perspectives on African-American Writers.* Ed. Ojo-Ade. Westport, CT: Greenwood, 1996. 1–27.

Okafor, Chinyere G. *Gender, Performance and Communication: African Ikeji Mask Festivals of Aro and Diaspora.* Trenton, NJ: Africa World, 2017.

Okafor, Clem Abiaziem. "The Inscrutability of the Gods: Motivation of Behaviour in Chinua Achebe's *Arrow of God.*" *Présence Africaine* 63.3 (1967): 207–14.

Okechukwu, Chinwe Christina. *Achebe the Orator: The Art of Persuasion in Chinua Achebe's Novels.* Westport, CT: Greenwood, 2001.

———. "Oratory and Social Responsibility: Chinua Achebe's *Arrow of God.*" *Callaloo* 25.2 (2002): 567–83.

Okeke-Agulu, Chika. "Drawing and the Poetic Imagination." *Obiora Udechukwu: Line, Image, Text.* Milan, Italy: Skira, 2016. 13–23.

———. Introduction: "The Persistence of Memory." *Maske.* By Phyllis Galembo. London: Chris Boot, 2010. 4–9.

Okome, Onookome. "Nollywood, Lagos, and the Good-Time Woman." *Research in African Literatures* 43.4 (2012): 166–86.

Okonkwo, Chidi. *Decolonization Agonistics in Postcolonial Fiction.* New York: St. Martin's, 1999.

Okonkwo, Christopher. "Chinua Achebe's Blue Notes: Toward a Critical Recording of *Things Fall Apart*'s Blues and Jazz Sensibility." *Research in African Literatures* 47.1 (2016): 109–27.

———. "A Critical Divination: Reading Sula as Ogbanje-Abiku." *African American Review* 38.4 (2004): 651–68.

———. *A Spirit of Dialogue: Incarnations of Ogbanje, the Born-to-Die, in African American Literature.* Knoxville: U of Tennessee P, 2008.

Okoye, Emmanuel Meziemadu. *The Traditional Religion and Its Encounter with Christianity in Achebe's Novels.* Bern, Switzerland: Peter Lang, 1987.

Okpewho, Isidore, and Nkiru Nzegwu. *Call Me by My Rightful Name.* Trenton, NJ: Africa World, 2004.

———. *The New African Diaspora.* Bloomington: Indiana UP, 2009.

Okpewho, Isidore, Carole Boyce Davies, and Ali A. Mazrui, eds. *The African Diaspora: African Origins and New World Identities.* Bloomington: Indiana UP, 2001.

Olaogun, Modupe. "Slavery and Etiological Discourse in the Writing of Ama Ata Aidoo, Bessie, and Buchi Emecheta." *Research in African Literatures* 33.2 (2002): 171–93.

O'Reilly, Andrea. *Toni Morrison and Motherhood: A Politics of the Heart.* Albany: State U of New York P, 2004.

Oriji, John N. "Igboland, Slavery, and the Drums of War." *Fighting the Slave Trade: West African Strategies.* Ed. Sylvianne A. Diouf. Columbus: Ohio UP. 121–31.

Osei-Nyame, Kwadwo, Jr. "The Politics of 'Translation' in African Postcolonial Literature: Olaudah Equiano, Ayi Kwei Armah, Toni Morrison, Ama Ata Aidoo,

Tayeb Salih and Leila Aboulea." *Journal of African Cultural Studies* 21.1 (2009): 91–103.

Osinubi, Taiwo Adetunji. "The African Atlantic: West African Literatures and Slavery Studies." *Research in African Literatures* 47.1 (2016): 149–59.

——. "Chinua Achebe and the Uptakes of African Slaveries." *Research in African Literatures* 40.4 (2009): 25–44.

——. "Slavery, Death, and the Village: Localizing Imperatives of Nigerian Writing." *University of Toronto Quarterly* 84.4 (2015): 131–52.

Osofsky, Gilbert. *Harlem: The Making of a Ghetto; Negro New York, 1890–1930*. New York: Harper and Row, 1967.

Oti, Sonny. *Highlife Music in West Africa: Down Memory Lane*. Lagos, Nigeria: Malthouse, 2009.

Ottenberg, Simon. "Ibo Receptivity to Change." *Continuity and Change in African Cultures* Ed. William R. Bascom and Melville Herskovits. Chicago: U of Chicago P, 1959. 130–43.

Page, Philip. "Circularity in Toni Morrison's *Beloved*." *African American Review* 26.15 (1992): 31–39.

——. *Dangerous Freedom: Fusion and Fragmentation in Toni Morrison's Novels*. Jackson: UP of Mississippi, 1995.

——. "Furrowing All the Brows: Interpretation and the Transcendent in Toni Morrison's *Paradise*." *African American Review* 35.4 (2001): 637–49.

——. *Reclaiming Community in Contemporary African American Fiction*. Jackson: UP of Mississippi, 1999.

Patterson, Orlando. *Rituals of Blood: Consequences of Slavery in Two American Centuries*. Washington, DC: Civitas/Counterpoint, 1998.

——. *Slavery and Social Death: A Comparative Study*. Cambridge, MA: Harvard UP, 1982.

Patton, Venetria K. *The Grasp That Reaches beyond the Grave: The Ancestral Call in Black Women's Texts*. Albany: State U of New York P, 2013.

Pérez-Torres, Rafael. "Knitting and Knotting the Narrative Threat: *Beloved* as Postmodern Novel." *Toni Morrison: Critical and Theoretical Approaches*. Ed. Nancy J. Peterson. Johns Hopkins UP, 1997. 91–109.

Peterson, Nancy J. "Introduction: Canonizing Toni Morrison." *Modern Fiction Studies* 39.3&4 (1993): 461–79.

——. *Toni Morrison: Critical and Theoretical Approaches*. Baltimore: Johns Hopkins UP, 1993.

Phelan, James. "Toward a Rhetorical Reader-Response Criticism: The Difficult, The Stubborn, and the Ending of *Beloved*." *Toni Morrison: Critical and Theoretical Approaches*. Ed. Nancy J. Peterson. Baltimore: Johns Hopkins UP, 1997. 225–44.

Phillips, Patrick. *Blood at the Root: A Racial Cleansing in America*. New York: Norton, 2017.

Phiri, Aretha. "Expanding Black Subjectivities in Toni Morrison's *Song of Solomon* and Chimamanda Ngozi Adichie's *Americanah*. *Cultural Studies* 31.1 (2017): 121–42.

Pieterse, Cosmo, and Dennis Duerden, eds. *African Writers Talking: A Collection of Radio Interviews*. London: Heinemann, 1972.

Plageman, Nate. *Highlife Saturday Night: Popular Music and Social Change in Urban Ghana*. Bloomington: Indiana UP, 2013.

Plasa, Carl. *Textual Politics from Slavery to Postcolonialism: Race and Identification*. New York: St. Martins, 2000.

Posnock, Ross. *Color and Culture; Black Writers and the Making of the Modern Intellectual*. Cambridge, MA: Harvard UP, 1998.

Quayson, Ato. "Self-Writing and Existential Alienation in African Literature: Achebe's *Arrow of God*." *Research in African Literatures* 42.2 (2011): 30–45.

Raban, Jonathan. *Soft City*. London: Hamish Hamilton, 1974.

Raboteau, Albert J. *Slave Religion: The "Invisible Institution" in the Antebellum South*. Oxford: Oxford UP, 1978.

Rampersad, Arnold, and David Ruessel, eds. *The Collected Poems of Langston Hughes*. New York: Knopf, 1997.

Raphavacharyulu, D.V.K., et al. "Achebe Interviewed." *Conversations with Chinua Achebe*. Ed. Bernth Lindfors. Jackson: UP of Mississippi, 1997. 88–93.

Rawley, James A. *London, Metropolis of the Slave Trade*. Columbia: U of Missouri P, 2003.

Rehm, Diane. "The Diane Rehm Show May 21, 1999, 11 A.M.–12 Noon: A Discussion of Chinua Achebe's *Things Fall Apart*." *Callaloo* 25.2 (2002): 597–611.

Reid-Pharr, Robert F. *Conjugal Union: The Body, the House, and the Black American*. Oxford: Oxford UP, 1999.

Rigley, Barbara Hill. *The Voices of Toni Morrison*. Columbus: Ohio State UP, 1991.

Rogers, Philip. "*No Longer at Ease*: Chinua Achebe's 'Heart of Darkness.'" *Modern African Fiction*. Spec. issue of *Research in African Literatures* 14.2 (1983): 165–83.

Röschenthaler, Ute. "The Blood Men of Old Calabar—a Slave Revolt of the Nineteenth Century?" *African Vices on Slavery and the Slave Trade*. Ed. Alice Bellagamba et al. Cambridge: Cambridge UP, 2013. 445–65.

Roynon, Tessa. "Aeschylus, Euripides, and Toni Morrison: Miasma, Revenge, and Atonement." *Toni Morrison: Memory and Meaning*. Ed. Adrienne Lanier Seward and Justin Tally. Jackson: UP of Mississippi, 2014. 172–84.

———. *The Cambridge Introduction to Toni Morrison*. Cambridge: Cambridge UP, 2013.

————. *Toni Morrison and the Classical Tradition: Transforming American Culture.* Oxford: Oxford UP, 2013.

Ruas, Charles. "Toni Morrison." *Conversations with Toni Morrison.* Ed. Danille Taylor-Guthrie. Jackson: UP of Mississippi, 1994. 93–118.

Rushdie, Salman. "An Interview with Toni Morrison." *Toni Morrison: Conversations.* Ed. Carolyn C. Denard. Jackson: UP of Mississippi, 2008. 51–61.

Russell, Danielle. *Between the Angle and the Curve: Mapping Gender, Race, Space, and Identity in Willa Carter and Toni Morrison.* London: Routledge, 2006.

Ryan, Judylyn S. "Language and Narrative Technique in Toni Morrison's Novels." *The Cambridge Companion to Toni Morrison.* Ed. Justine Tally. Cambridge: Cambridge UP, 2007. 151–61.

Sáez, Elena Machado. *Market Aesthetics: The Purchase of the Past in Caribbean Fiction.* Charlottesville: U of Virginia P, 2015.

Sahlins, Marshall. *What Kinship Is—And Is Not.* Chicago: U of Chicago P, 2012.

Said, Edward W. *Orientalism.* New York: Pantheon, 1978.

Salafia, Matthew. *Slavery's Borderland: Freedom and Bondage along the Ohio River.* Philadelphia: U of Pennsylvania P, 2013.

Samatar, Sofia. "Charting the Constellation: Past and Present in *Things Fall Apart.*" *Achebe's World: African Literature at Fifty.* Spec. issue of *Research in African Literatures* 42.2 (2011): 60–71.

Samuels, Robert. *Writing Prejudices: The Psychoanalysis and Pedagogy of Discrimination from Shakespeare to Toni Morrison.* Albany: State U of New York P, 2001.

Samuels, Wilfred D., and Clenora Hudson-Weems. *Toni Morrison.* Woodbridge, CT: Twayne, 1990.

Sanneh, Lamin. *Abolitionists Abroad: American Blacks and the Making of Modern West Africa.* Cambridge, MA: Harvard UP, 1999.

Sartre, Jean-Paul. "Black Orpheus." *Race.* Ed. Robert Bernasconi. Malden, MA: Blackwell, 2001.

Schappell, Elissa. "Toni Morrison: The Art of Fiction." *Toni Morrison: Conversations.* Ed. Carolyn C. Denard. Jackson: UP of Mississippi, 2008. 62–90.

Schreiber, Evelyn Jaffe. *Subversive Voices: Eroticizing the Other in William Faulkner and Toni Morrison.* Knoxville: U of Tennessee P, 2001.

Schuyler, George S. *Black No More.* Boston: Northeastern UP, 1989.

————. "The Negro-Art Hokum." *Within the Circle: An Anthology of African American Literary Criticism from the Harlem Renaissance to the Present.* Ed. Angelyn Mitchell. Durham, NC: Duke UP, 1994. 51–59.

Searle, Chris. "Achebe and the Bruised Heart of Africa." *Conversations with Chinua Achebe.* Ed. Bernth Lindfors. Jackson: UP of Mississippi, 1997. 155–64.

Setka, Stella. "Phantasmic Reincarnation: Igbo Cosmology in Octavia Butler's *Kindred.*" *MELUS* 41.1 (2016): 93–124.

Sibley, Francis M. "Tragedy in the Novels of Chinua Achebe." *Southern Humanities Review* 9.4 (1975): 359–73.

Silverblatt, Michael. "Michael Silverblatt Talks with Toni Morrison about *Love*." *Toni Morrison: Conversations.* Ed. Carolyn C. Denard. Jackson: UP of Mississippi, 2008. 216–23.

Smith, Dinitia. "Toni Morrison's Mix of Tragedy, Domesticity, and Folklore." *New York Times* 8 January 1998.

Smith, Robert S. *The Lagos Consulate 1851–1861.* Berkeley: U of California P, 1979.

Smith, Valerie. *Toni Morrison: Writing the Moral Imagination.* Hoboken, NJ: Wiley-Blackwell, 2012.

Smith, Zadie. Foreword. *The Measure of Our Lives: A Gathering of Wisdom.* By Toni Morrison. New York: Knopf, 2019. v–viii.

Sougu, Omar. "Didactic Aesthetics: Achebe, the Griot and Mbari Artist." *Emerging Perspectives on Chinua Achebe.* Vol. 2: *ISINKA, the Artistic Purpose: Chinua Achebe and the Theory of African Literature.* Ed. Ernest N. Emenyonu and Iniobong I. Uko. Trenton, NJ: Africa World, 2004. 33–47.

Soyinka, Wole. *Art, Dialogue, and Outrage: Essays on Literature and Culture.* New York: Pantheon, 1988.

——. "From a Common Backcloth: A Reassessment of the African Literary Image." *Art, Dialogue, and Outrage.* By Soyinka. New York: Pantheon, 1988. 7–14.

——. "Language as Boundary." *Art, Dialogue, and Outrage.* By Soyinka. New York: Pantheon, 1988. 82–94.

——. "The Writer in a Modern African State." *Art, Dialogue, and Outrage.* By Soyinka. New York: Pantheon, 1988. 15–20.

Stave, Shirley A. "From Eden to Paradise: A Pilgrimage through Toni Morrison's Trilogy." *Toni Morrison: Memory and Meaning.* Ed. Adrienne Lanier Seward and Justine Tally. Jackson: UP of Mississippi, 2014. 107–18.

——, ed. *Toni Morrison and the Bible: Contested Intertextualities.* New York: Peter Lang, 2006.

Stepto, Robert. "Intimate Things in Place: A Conversation with Toni Morrison." *Conversations with Toni Morrison.* Ed. Danille Taylor-Guthrie. Jackson: UP of Mississippi, 1994. 10–29.

Stewart, Alexander. "Make It Funky: Fela Kuti, James Brown and the Invention of Afrobeat." *American Studies* 52.4 (2013): 99–118.

Story, Ralph D. "Sacrifice and Surrender: Sethe in Toni Morrison's *Beloved*." *CLA Journal* 46.1 (2002): 21–29.

Suggs, Donald. "Interview with Toni Morrison." *Toni Morrison: Conversations.* Ed. Carolyn C. Denard. Jackson: UP of Mississippi, 2008. 32–37.

Sundquist, Eric J. Introduction. *Cultural Contexts for Ralph Ellison's Invisible Man.* Ed. Sundquist. Boston: Bedford Books, 1995. 1–28.

Swain, Susan. "In Depth: Toni Morrison." C-SPAN.org, 4 February 2001. www.c
-span.org/video/?162375–1/toni-morrison-nobel-laureate-dies-88.

Tabone, Mark A. "Rethinking Paradise: Toni Morrison and Utopia at the Millen-
nium." *African American Review* 49.2 (2016): 129–44.

Talbot, Percy Amaury. *The Peoples of Southern Nigeria: A Sketch of Their History, Ethnology and Culture with an Abstract of the 1921 Census.* London: Oxford UP, 1926.

Tally, Justine. "The Nobel Prize in Literature 1993." *Nobelprize.org.* Nobel Media AB
2014. 23 August 2017. www.nobelprize.org/nobel_prizes/literature/laureates
/1993/.

———. *"Paradise" Reconsidered: Toni Morrison's (Hi)stories and Truths.* Piscataway,
NJ: Transaction, 1999.

———. *The Story of Jazz: Toni Morrison's Dialogic Imagination.* Piscataway, NJ:
Transaction, 2001.

———. *Toni Morrison's "Beloved": Origins.* London: Routledge, 2009.

Thorp, Ellen. *Ladder of Bones.* London: Jonathan Cape, 1956.

Tibbles, Anthony. *Liverpool and the Slave Trade.* Liverpool, UK: Liverpool UP, 2018.

Tillet, Salamishah. "In the Shadow of the Castle: (Trans)Nationalism, African
American Tourism, and Goree Island." *Writing Slavery in(to) the African Diaspora.* Spec. issue of *Research in African Literatures* 40.4 (2009): 122–41.

Tompkins, Jane. *Sensational Designs: The Cultural Work of American Fiction, 1790–
1860.* New York: Oxford UP, 1985.

Troupe, Quincy, ed. *James Baldwin: The Legacy.* New York: Simon and Schuster,
1989.

Troupe, Quincy, and Rainer Schulte, eds. *Giant Talk: An Anthology of Third World
Writings.* New York: Random House, 1975.

Tsuruta, Dorothy Randall. "James Baldwin and Chinua Achebe." *Black Scholar:
Journal of Black Studies and Research* 2.2 (1981): 72–79.

Uchendu, Victor. *The Igbo of Southeast Nigeria.* New York: Holt, Rinehart and Winston, 1965.

Verdelle, A. J. "Loose Magic: A. J. Verdelle Interviews Toni Morrison." *Toni Morrison:
Conversations.* Ed. Carolyn C. Denard. Jackson: UP of Mississippi, 2008. 159–70.

Von Eschen, Penny M. *Satchmo Blows up the World: Jazz Ambassadors Play the Cold
War.* Cambridge, MA: Harvard UP, 2004.

Wagner-Martin, Linda. *Toni Morrison: A Literary Life.* London: Palgrave, 2015.

———. *Toni Morrison and the Maternal: From "The Bluest Eye" to "Home."* New York:
Peter Lang, 2015.

Walker, Melissa. *Black Women's Novels in the Wake of the Civil Rights Movement,
1966–1989.* New Haven, CT: Yale UP, 1991.

Wall, Cheryl A. *Worrying the Line: Black Women Writers, Lineage, and Literary Tradition.* Chapel Hill: U of North Carolina P, 2005.

Wallace, Thurman. *The Blacker the Berry . . . A Novel of Negro Life.* New York: Collier, 1970.

———. *Infants of the Spring.* Boston: Northeastern UP, 1992.

Ward, Jesmyn, ed. *The Fire This Time: A New Generation Speaks about Race.* New York: Scribner, 2016.

———. *Sing, Unburied, Sing.* New York: Scribner, 2017.

Wardi, Anissa Jadine. *Water and African American Memory: An Ecocritical Perspective.* Gainesville: U of Florida P, 2011.

Weisenburger, Steven. *Modern Medea: A Family Story of Slavery and Child-Murder from the Old South.* New York: Hill and Wang, 1998.

West, Elizabeth. *African Spirituality in Black Women's Fiction: Threaded Visions of Memory, Community, Nature, and Being.* Lanham, MD: Lexington, 2011.

West, Emily, and R. J. Knight. "Mothers' Milk: Slavery, Wet-Nursing, and Black and White Women in the Antebellum South." *Journal of Southern History* 83.1 (2017): 37–68.

White, Hayden. *The Content of the Form: Narrative Discourse and Historical Representation.* Baltimore: Johns Hopkins UP, 1987.

Whitehead, Colson. *The Underground Railroad.* New York: Doubleday, 2016.

Wilder, Craig Steven. *Ebony & Ivy: Race, Slavery, and the Troubled History of America's Universities.* London: Bloomsbury, 2013.

Wilentz, Gay. *Binding Cultures: Black Women Writers in Africa and the Diaspora.* Bloomington: Indiana UP, 1993.

Wilkerson, Isabel. *Caste: The Origins of Our Discontents.* New York: Random House, 2020.

———. *The Warmth of Other Suns: The Epic Story of America's Great Black Migration.* New York: Vintage, 2010.

Wilkinson, Jane. "Chinua Achebe." *Talking with African Writers: Interviews with African Poets, Playwrights and Novelists.* Woodbridge, Suffolk, UK: James Currey, 1992. 47–57.

Williams, Dana A. "To Make a Humanist Black: Toni Wofford's Howard Years." *Toni Morrison: Memory and Meaning.* Ed. Adrienne Lanier Seward and Justine Tally. Jackson: UP of Mississippi, 2014. 42–50.

Williams, Lisa. *The Artist as Outsider in the Novels of Toni Morrison and Virginia Woolf.* Westport, CT: Greenwood, 2000.

Williams, Philip G. "Comparative Approach to Afro-American and Neo-African Novels: Ellison and Achebe." *Studies in Black Literature* 7.1 (1976): 15–18.

Wilson, Judith. "A Conversation with Toni Morrison." *Conversations with Toni Morrison.* Ed. Danille Taylor-Guthrie. Jackson: UP of Mississippi, 1994. 129–37.

Wilson, Roderick. "Eliot and Achebe: An Analysis of Some Formal and Philosophical Qualities of *No Longer at Ease.*" *Critical Perspectives on Chinua Achebe.*

Ed. C. L. Innes and Bernth Lindfors. Washington, DC: Three Continents, 1978. 160–68.

Winks, Christopher. "Into the Heart of the Great Wilderness: Understanding Baldwin's Quarrel with *Négritude*." *African American Review* 46.4 (2013): 605–14.

Wisker, Gina. *Post-Colonial and African American Women's Writing: A Critical Introduction*. New York: St. Martin's, 2000.

Wittenberg, Judith Bryant. "Faulkner and Women Writers." *Faulkner and Women: Faulkner and Yoknapatawpha, 1985*. Ed. Doreen Fowler and Ann J. Abadie. Jackson: U of Mississippi P, 1985. 270–94.

Woodard, Helena. Rev. of *Metaphor and the Slave Trade in West Africa*, by Laura Murphy. *Writing Africa in the Short Story*. Spec. issue of *African Literature Today* 31 (2013): 174–76.

Wren, Robert M. "Achebe's Revisions of *Arrow of God*." *Research in African Literature* 7.1 (1976): 53–58.

———. *Achebe's World: The Historical and Cultural Context of the Novels of Chinua Achebe*. London: Longman, 1980.

———. "From Ulu to Christ: The Transfer of Faith in Chinua Achebe's *Arrow of God*." *Christianity and Literature* 27.2 (1978): 28–40.

———. "Those Magical Years." *Conversations with Chinua Achebe*. Ed. Bernth Lindfors. Jackson: UP of Mississippi, 1997. 99–109.

———. *Those Magical Years: The Making of Nigerian Literature at Ibadan: 1948–1966*. Washington, DC: Three Continents, 1991.

Wright, Richard. "Blueprint for Negro Writing." *Within the Circle: An Anthology of African American Literary Criticism from the Harlem Renaissance to the Present*. Ed. Angelyn Mitchell. Durham, NC: Duke UP, 1994. 97–106.

Wyatt, Jean. *Love and Narrative Form in Toni Morrison's Later Novels*. Athens: U of Georgia P, 2017.

Wynter, Sylvia. "History, Ideology, and the Reinvention of the Past in Achebe's *Things Fall Apart* and Laye's *The Dark Child*." *Minority Voices* 2.1 (1978): 43–61.

Yancy, George. *Black Bodies, White Gazes: The Continuing Significance of Race*. Lanham, MD: Rowman and Littlefield. 2008.

Yemitan, Oladipo. *Madame Tinubu: Merchant and King-Maker*. Ibadan, Nigeria: Ibadan UP, 1987.

Young, Robert. *White Mythologies: Writing History and the West*. London: Routledge, 1990.

Zauditu-Selassie, Kokahvah. *African Spiritual Traditions in the Novels of Toni Morrison*. Gainesville: UP of Florida, 2009.

INDEX

Printed in the USA
CPSIA information can be obtained
at www.ICGtesting.com
LVHW061226071023
760363LV00002B/185